# MORECAMBE & WISE

Graham McCann writes regularly on politics and culture for a wide range of publications. His previous book was *Cary Grant: A Class Apart* (Fourth Estate, 1996).

# Morecambe
## &
# Wise

## Graham McCann

FOURTH ESTATE · *London*

This paperback edition published in 1999
First published in Great Britain in 1998 by
Fourth Estate Limited
6 Salem Road
London W2 4BU

1 3 5 7 9 10 8 6 4 2

A catalogue record for this book is available from the British
Library.

ISBN 1-85702-760-4

Typeset by Rowland Phototypesetting Ltd,
Bury St Edmunds, Suffolk
Printed in Great Britain by
Clays Ltd, St Ives plc

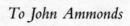

*To John Ammonds*

# Contents

# *List of Photographs*

# Acknowledgements

I must begin by recording a very special debt of gratitude to the following people: John Ammonds, Eddie Braben, Bill Cotton, Ann Hamilton, Ernest Maxin, Gary Morecambe and Joan Morecambe. Not only did each one of them respond to all of my various intrusions with unfailing kindness and good humour, but they also afforded me invaluable advice, information and encouragement throughout the book's creation without ever seeking to influence its conclusions. They will always have both my deepest admiration and warmest affection.

I am also pleased to acknowledge the generous contributions of all of those who were kind enough to share with me their own memories of, or insights into, Morecambe and Wise: Michael Aspel, Max Bygraves, Mike Craig, Ken Dodd, Bruce Forsyth, William Franklyn, Baron Grade of Elstree, Michael Grade, Baron Healey of Riddlesden, Edmund Hockridge, Jonathan James-Moore, Sir Paul McCartney, Francis Matthews, Patrick Moore, Frank Muir, Denis Norden, Barry Norman, André Previn, Sir Cliff Richard, Dame Diana Rigg, Angela Rippon, Graham Stark, Tommy Steele, Wendy Toye and Edward Woodward.

For their help with specific queries I would like to thank the following: Emma Baddeley, Catharine Bassindale, Jeremy Beadle, Nicholas Bethell, Clare Braben, the staffs of the British Film Institute's Library and Stills Archive, the staff of the British Library's Newspaper Library, the staff of Cambridge University Library, Lisa Cardy at the National Sound Archive, James Hanning, Jane Harding at Pinewood Studios, Wyn Howard-Thomas, Norman Hudis, John Junkin, Jacqueline Kavanagh at the BBC's Written Archives Centre, Jan Kennedy at the Billy Marsh Agency, Jennifer Maffini, Debbie Martin, Irene Melling, Alex Mitchison at Polygram Spoken Word, Deanna

Okun at BBC Worldwide, Veronica Taylor at the BFI and Max Tyler at the British Music Hall Society. I feel particularly grateful to John Davis at the BBC's Written Archives Centre, Dave Miles at the Morecambe and Wise Fan Club and Bobbie Mitchell at the BBC Photographic Library for their excellent advice and assistance on innumerable occasions.

For varied courtesies, encouragements and insights I am also indebted to Reg Arnold, Alan Belgrove, Tom Brass, Bill Burton, Tony Clayton, Charles Drazin, Paul Gallagher, Angie Matthews and Gail Stuart. My parents were, as always, an inspiration.

At Fourth Estate I must thank my editor, Christopher Potter, and his assistant, Leo Hollis, for their wise counsel and reassuring enthusiasm, as well as Nell Cooke-Hurle, Sarah White and Susie Dunlop for their many efforts on my, and my book's, behalf. I am also very grateful to my agent, Mic Cheetham, for her patience, faith and expertise. Finally, I must express my gratitude to Silvana Dean, without whose encouragement, assistance and thoughtfulness this book would not have been completed.

*Great comedy, great wit, makes the ceiling fly off, and suddenly liberates us again as we were when we were much younger and saw no reason not to believe that we could fly, or become someone else, or bound on a trampoline and not come down.*
PENELOPE GILLIAT

# PROLOGUE

ERIC       *Let's face it: he's half a star, isn't he?*
ERNIE      *Yes: I'm half a star.*

*Television has shaped us – you can blame it for 'abbreviated attention span' and a failure to believe in realities; or you can notice how it promotes a low-level passive surrealism in expectations, and an uncatalogued memory bank for our minds. We may be more like crazed movie editors trying to splice our lives together because of TV. There is a resistance it has bred, as well as a chaos: you can't have one without the other. And in the end, there is no point in being gloomy or cheerful about it. It's there, here, without moratorium or chance of reversal.*

DAVID THOMSON

*Among those whom I like or admire, I can find no common denominator, but among those whom I love, I can: all of them make me laugh.*

W. H. AUDEN

It happened one night. It happened, to be precise, at 8.55 p.m. on the night of 25 December 1977, when an estimated 28,835,000 people[1] – more than half of the total population of the United Kingdom – tuned their television sets to BBC1 and spent the next hour and ten minutes in the company of a rather tall man called Eric and a rather short man called Ernie.

It was an extraordinary night for British television in general and for the BBC in particular: 28,835,000 viewers for a single show. It was – at least as far as that catholic and capacious category known, somewhat apologetically, as 'light entertainment' was concerned – as close as British television had ever come, in some forty-one years of trying,[2] to being a genuine *mass* medium. None of the usual rigid divisions and omissions were apparent in the broad audience of that remarkable night: no stark class bias, no pronounced gender

3

imbalance, no obvious age asymmetry, no generalised demographic obliquities.[3] The show had found its way into dense council estates, lofty tower blocks, smart suburban squares and leafily discreet country retreats — it was even watched with uncommon avidity at Windsor Castle, where assembled members of the Royal Family delayed their Christmas dinner until they had seen the show through to its proper conclusion.[4]

It was also, of course, an extraordinary night for the two stars of that show: Eric Morecambe and Ernie Wise — by far the most illustrious, and the best-loved, double-act that Britain has ever produced. Exceptionally professional yet endearingly personable, they were wonderful together as partners, as friends, as almost a distinct entity: not 'Morecambe and Wise' but 'Morecambewise' — one never could see the join. There was Eric and there was Ernie: one of them an idiot, the other a bigger idiot, each of them half a star, together a whole star, forever hopeful of that 'brand new, bright tomorrow' that they sang about at the end of each show. True, Eric would often slap Ernie smartly on the cheeks, but that was just a welling-up of applause that had been brought to a head: they clearly thought the world of each other, and the world thought a great deal of them, too.

Their show succeeded in attracting such a massive following on that memorable night because it had, over the course of the previous nine years or so, established, and then enhanced, an enviable reputation for consistency, inventiveness, unparalleled professional polish and, last but by no means least, a strong and sincere respect for its audience. *The Morecambe & Wise Show* stood for something greater, something far more precious, than mere first-rate but evanescent entertainment; it had come to stand — just as persuasively and as proudly as any earnest documentary or any epic drama — for excellence in broadcasting, the result not just of two gifted performers (great talent, alas, does not of itself guarantee great television) but also of a richly proficient and supremely committed production team. Together they combined to realise the basic ideal of public service broadcasting: that admirable old Reithian ambition to make excellence accessible, 'to carry into the greatest possible number of homes *everything* that is best in *every* department of human knowledge, endeavour, and achievement'.[5]

The show, culminating in the record-breaking triumph of that 1977 special, represented an achievement in high-quality popular programme-making that is now fast assuming the aura of a fairy tale – destined, one fears, to be passed on with bemused fascination from one doubtful generation to its even more disbelieving successor as the seemingly endless proliferation of new channels and novel forms of distraction continue to divide and disperse the old mass audience in the name of that remorseless (and self-fulfilling) quest for 'quality demographics' and 'niche audiences'. *The Morecambe & Wise Show* appeared at a time before home video, before satellite dishes and cable technology, before the dawning of the digital revolution, a time when it was still considered desirable, as well as practicable, to make a television programme that might – just *might* – excite most of the people most of the time. Not every programme-maker and performer from this time was particularly well equipped or strongly inclined to pursue such a possibility, but Morecambe and Wise, working in close collaboration with the BBC, most certainly were.

*The Morecambe & Wise Show* had an identity: it was not just some show that just happened to be transmitted by the BBC[6] – it was a bona fide *BBC* show, the kind of show that the BBC, when it has a mind to, can and does do best. Judicious, well crafted and characterful, *The Morecambe & Wise Show* made viewers feel pampered rather than patronised. Whether it was the sight of the set for the *Singin' in the Rain* routine that mirrored the MGM original down to the last detail (except, of course, for the rain), or the full orchestra that sat patiently in silence while 'Mr Preview' tried in vain to extend the introduction to Grieg's Piano Concerto by 'about a yard', or the exquisite timing of Eric's laconic reaction to the fleeting sound of a passing police car's siren ('He's not going to sell much ice-cream going at that speed'), one always knew that every single element had been tried and triple-tested before being allowed on to the screen. This was a show, in short, that worked hard to please its public; this was a show that *cared*.

Neither Morecambe nor Wise ever looked down on, or up at, anyone (except, of course, each other); both of them looked straight back at their audience on level terms. No celebrated guest was ever allowed to challenge this comic democracy: within the confines of the show, the rich and the famous went unrecognised and frequently unpaid (a running gag in that 1977 Christmas special had Elton John wander awkwardly and anonymously along the begrimed and labyrinthine corridors of Television Centre in search of the right studio – ELTON: 'I've been all over the place.' ERIC: 'In that suit?'); venerable actors with grand theatrical reputations were greeted routinely by Eric's *sotto voce* alert to Ernie: 'Don't look now. A drunk's just come on. To your right. A drunk. I'll get rid of him'; a stray patrician mien was mocked (as, indeed, was any word like 'mien') by a pointedly plebian comeuppance (the very posh Penelope Keith was obliged to cut short her near-regal entrance, hitch up her dress, clamber down from an unfinished staircase and hobble angrily off the stage); the starchy sobriety of the professionally serious was spirited swiftly away by elaborately pixillated concoctions (an unlikely troupe of newsreaders, sports presenters and critics, all dressed up in crisp white sailor suits, were pictured performing some joyously improbable somersaults, handsprings and cartwheels while singing 'There's Nothing Like a Dame' from *South Pacific*); and two resolutely down-to-earth working-class comedians from the North of England gleefully reaffirmed the remarkably deep, warm and sure relationship that existed between themselves and the British public.

'It was', reminisced Ernie Wise, 'a sort of great big office party for the whole country, a bit of fun people could understand.'[7] From the first few seconds of their opening comic routine to the final few notes and motions of their closing song and dance, Morecambe and Wise did their very best to draw people together rather than drive them apart. Instead of pandering submissively to the smug exclusivity of the *cognoscenti* (they were flattered when a well-regarded critic praised the sly '*oeillade*' that accompanied Eric's sarcastic asides, but they still mocked him mercilessly for the literary conceit[8]), and instead of settling – as so many of their supposed successors would do with such unseemly haste – for the easy security of a 'cult following' ('Can we say "cult"?' Eric would have inquired anxiously of someone lurking in the wings), Morecambe and Wise always aimed to entertain the whole nation.

It happened one night, but it had taken years to realise. The seventies were the great years of Morecambe and Wise, the 'golden years' when they came to be regarded as national treasures – admired in the quality press as 'the most accomplished performing artists at present active in this country',[9] applauded in the tabloids as 'the people's choice',[10] and asked by the Queen Mother to teach her their trusty 'paper bag trick'[11] – but this exalted status had only been won after some thirty years of hard work in front of hard audiences, making mistakes, trying out new tricks, mastering old ones, refining their technique, sharpening their wits and, slowly but surely, evolving a style that was entirely their own. By the start of the seventies, therefore, Morecambe and Wise were more than ready for their close-up, and, when it came, they made sure that they made the most of it.

When viewers watched that final show at the end of 1977, they witnessed a rare and rich compendium of the very best in popular culture: the happy summation of a joint career that had traversed all of the key developments associated with the rise of mass entertainment in Britain, encompassing the faint but still discernible traces of Victorian music-hall, the crowded animation of Edwardian Variety, the wordy populism of the wireless, the spectacular impact of the movies and, finally, the more intimate pervasiveness of television. When it was all over, it was sorely missed.

Eric Morecambe died in 1984 and Ernie Wise in 1999,[12] and on each of these sad occasions it felt to many as if they had lost an old and precious friend rather than merely a vividly endearing entertainer. The shows, however, remain, and the shows continue to matter. In November 1996, at the ceremony that marked the sixtieth anniversary of BBC TV, it was announced to no one's great surprise that viewers had voted Morecambe and Wise the all-time Best Light Entertainment Performers, and *The Morecambe & Wise Show* the all-time Best Light Entertainment Series, and, in September 1998, the readers of the *Radio Times* voted the programme the all-time Best Comedy Show. Excellence never dates: even now, so many years after that last great night, millions of viewers still settle down to watch the old repeats, and to be entertained all over again by a rather tall man called Eric and a rather short man called Ernie. They were simply irreplaceable.

# MUSIC-HALL

*We are two people with one background between us.*
ERNIE WISE

## CHAPTER I

# Northern Songs and Dances

*We've always considered ourselves sophisticated Northerners.*
ERIC MORECAMBE

*Music-hall . . . was professional, and our early ambition was always to become professional.*
ERNIE WISE

Morecambe and Wise[1] were made in the North of England. Their North of England, as far as their television conversations were concerned, was squeezed into a surreal and nameless little town that somehow managed to straddle the Pennines, a timeless place where clog dancing and cloth caps were forever to be found in fashion, and where all events of any real significance took place at one or other of five peculiar locations: the very modest working-class home of the Morecambe family, the rather grander working-class home of the Wise family, the somewhat insalubrious Milverton Street School, the long, dense and exotic Tarryassan Street or the compact but endlessly fascinating strip of land over which Ada Bailey would hang out her knickers to dry. Their North of England, in reality, was the materially impoverished but culturally rich North of England of the twenties and thirties, an area that stretched more freely over Lancashire, Yorkshire and a small but significant portion of Northumberland.

Eric Morecambe was a Lancastrian. One only had to hear his memorable voice utter a phrase like, 'I'll tell you for why . . .', or invite a distinguished politician to 'sit down and take the weight off your manifestoes', or respond to a sudden show of affection from a male friend by shouting, '*Geddoff!* Smash your face in!', or greet the inexplicable with an exclamation that slipped out from under a sigh, 'Hhahh-there's no answer to that!', to appreciate the effectiveness of that warmly authoritative Lancastrian accent. It was J. B. Priestley who, during his *English Journey* of the early thirties, remarked on the fact that the 'rather flat but broad-vowelled speech' of the Lancastrian had come to be regarded as 'almost the official accent of music-hall humour'[2] – and that, coming from a Yorkshireman, was quite an admission.

It is certainly hard not to be struck by the fact that so many of the most memorable and original performers associated with a comic tradition running from the earliest days of music-hall through Variety and the BBC's old North of England Home Service to the era of television have come from this solitary county: Billy Bennett, Harry Weldon, Robb Wilton, Fred Yule, Arthur Askey, Tommy Handley and Ken Dodd (all from Liverpool); George Formby Senior (from Ashton-under-Lyne); George Formby Junior, Frank Randle and Ted Ray (all from Wigan); Hylda Baker (Farnworth); Ted Lune (Bolton); Tubby Turner (Preston); Wilkie Bard and Les Dawson (Manchester); Al Read (Salford); and Gracie Fields, Tommy Fields and 'Lancashire's Ambassador of Mirth', Norman Evans (Rochdale). What all of these otherwise disparate performers had in common was an accent that proved itself, as Priestley put it, 'admirable for comic effect, being able to suggest either shrewdness or simplicity, or, what is more likely than not, a humorous mixture of both',[3] lending itself both to ironical under-statement (such as the exceptionally serviceable 'Fancy!' – used to register surprise at anything from run-of-the-mill gossip to declarations of war) and ingeniously sly put-downs (such as, "Ave you 'ad your tea? We've 'ad ours!' or, 'I'd offer you a slice of pie, love, but there's none cut into').[4] Priestley, attempting to define the distinctive character of the sound, listed 'shrewdness, homely simplicity, irony, fierce independence, an impish delight in mocking whatever is thought to be affected and pretentious. That is Lancashire'.[5] It was also, of course, unmistakably Eric Morecambe.

Ernie Wise, on the other hand, was a Yorkshireman. He was more than happy on stage and screen to play up to all of the old stereotypical character traits associated with the flat-capped tyke: arrogance ('Welcome to the show,' he would say to the audience. 'What a pleasure it must be for you to be seeing me once again!'), conceit (the much-mocked wig), bluntness (when roused he would not hesitate to itemise all of his partner's inadequacies) and stinginess (he would always be ashen-faced whenever a guest was brave enough to inquire about the possibility of a fee). There was also, of course, the Yorkshire accent – 'quieter, less sociable and less given to pleasure', according to the Bradford-born Priestley, 'more self-sufficient and more conceited, I think, than the people at the other and softer side of the Pennines'[6] – capable itself of conveying varying degrees of warmth, vulnerability and wit (witness the delivery of such gifted and popular comics as Albert Modley, Dave Morris, Harry Worth or Sandy Powell[7]), but ideally suited to the special technical skills of the straight-man.

Placed side by side, like their respective counties, Morecambe and Wise were able to play out their own private War of the Roses. Eric was hot, Ernie was cold. Eric was supple, Ernie was stiff. Eric was droll, Ernie was dour. Eric was playful with language, Ernie was respectful of it. Eric had the quick wit, Ernie the slow burn (ERNIE: 'How do you spell incompetent?' ERIC: 'E-R-N-I-E.' ERNIE: 'E-R- . . . Doh!'). Eric knew all about the *double entendre*, Ernie still had much to learn about the *single entendre* (ERNIE: 'I've always said there are no people like show people.' ERIC: 'Ask any prison warden.'). Eric liked to dress down (string vest, oversized khaki shorts, black suspenders, black socks and black shoes), Ernie loved to dress up (ill-advised 'fashionable' garments, odd 'writerly' outfits or white tie and tails). Eric was happy to appear less intelligent and cultured than he really was ('I saw a play on TV last night: there was this woman – you could see her bum!'), Ernie yearned to appear less stupid and gauche than he really was ('I've got 23 A levels, you know – 17 in Mathematics, and another 2, making 23'). While Eric had his feet planted firmly on the ground, Ernie's head would sometimes float high up into the clouds (ERNIE: 'You're ruining everything! You're making us look like a cheap music-hall act!' ERIC: 'But we *are* a cheap music-hall act!').

Morecambe and Wise never were, strictly speaking, a music-hall act (the music-hall, as a distinct form of entertainment, had given way to the more structured commercial appeal of Variety long before either of them was born[8]), nor were they, except in the very early days, 'cheap', but the allusion, in spite of this, made sense. Both Morecambe and Wise grew up in poor communities rich in music-hall traditions: 'We're working-class comics,' said Wise. 'We didn't go to college.'[9] They went, instead, to the halls, where they studied every facet of Northern humour. 'There used to be a big difference between North and South in humour,' observed Wise, 'and there used to be a definite dividing line between "Oop fert cup" and all that.'[10]

Many of the old theatres were still standing and most of them were still in use – such as the huge Winter Gardens in Morecambe and the small but very popular City Varieties in Leeds – although some had been transformed into cinemas by the twenties and thirties. These halls, situated as they often were in the poorer areas of the industrial towns, could seem to young people with dreams of better futures like strange, exotic and magical places of escape and adventure. The look of them alone was extraordinary – such as the Moorish Palace Theatre in Hull, with its glass-roofed conservatory, sumptuous crush-room and Indian-style entrance festooned with palms and ferns; or the shoe-box-small Argyle in Birkenhead, a self-consciously nostalgic construction with long narrow galleries and a uniquely warm and intimate atmosphere; or the medium-sized Bradford Alhambra, designed in the English Renaissance style and accommodating an exceptionally wide stage for all kinds of odd and ambitious productions.

Once inside these unworldly places the curious encountered novel sights and sounds of even deeper resonance: acrobats, unicyclists, tight-rope walkers, jugglers, paper-tearers, illusionists, dancers and singers. There were novelty acts such as the man who dressed up in a red wig and the uniform of the Ruritanian Navy, balanced himself on the top rung of a swaying ladder and then sang a song about his mother, or the contortionist who would leap out from within a little box and throw himself into fearsome postures, or Herr Gross and his Educated Baboons and John Higgins, 'The Human Kangaroo'. Centre-stage, up and down the bill, were the comics – some brash and flashy, some shy and reserved, some piebald and pinguid – full of jokes about the mother-in-law, the lodger, the wife, the neighbours, the coal-mines and the cotton mills, showing off their red wigs and redder noses, check trousers and big boots, never stopping, never serious, never giving up. A splendid time was guaranteed for all.

'It's a fantastic thing,' said Ernie Wise, reflecting on the success of his partnership with Eric Morecambe, 'because all we have done is adapt music-hall on to the television and make it acceptable.'[11] It was, as an explanation, a simplification of a complex process, but it was, none the less, a revealing observation. Much of what came to be associated with Morecambe and Wise, in terms of gestures, phrases, attitudes and even routines, had its roots firmly in the music-hall experiences of their youth. The sand dance performed by Morecambe and Wise and Glenda Jackson in their celebrated 'Cleopatra' sketch was a homage to the great eccentric dancers Wilson, Keppel and Betty. The cod-vent act, performed by Eric Morecambe with dummies of varying shapes and sizes, owed much to Sandy Powell's earlier version (POWELL: 'How are you?' DUMMY: 'Aying gerry yell chrankchyew!' POWELL: 'He says he's very well.'). Eric's impromptu monologues ('They were married at Hoo-Flung-Wotnot/But they had no children sweet/He was fifty and fat/She was fatter than that/So n'ere the twain will meet – boom boom!') were borrowed from Billy Bennett. The regular bits of comic business involving the plush golden 'tabs' – tableaux curtains – such as Eric's 'mad throttler' mime, had been inherited from innumerable half-forgotten old comics who once worked the halls. The direct address to the audience – 'What do you think of the show so far?' – harked back to a bygone era of a more intimate brand of popular entertainment.

The world of Morecambe and Wise – even after the former had decamped to Harpenden and the latter to Peterborough – remained the comic world of the traditional Northern humorist. This world was peopled by sad-faced, snail-paced, put-upon pedants like Robb Wilton's fire chief ('Oh, yes, oh aye, it's a pretty big fire . . . should be, by now . . . oh, and I say, Arnold – Arnold – take the dog with you, it'll be a run for him. He hasn't been out lately . . . Oh, good gracious me, what's the *matter* with the engine?'[12]), tactless busybodies like Norman Evans' Auntie Doleful ('You what? You're feeling a lot better? Ah, well, you never know – I mean, there was Mrs White – it were nobbut last Thursday, you know – she was doin' nicely, just like you are, you know – and all of a sudden she started off with spasms round the heart – she went off like a flash of lightning on

Friday. They're burying her today.'[13]), inveterate gossips like Evans' Fanny Fairbottom ('That woman at number seven? Is she? Gerraway! Well, I'm not surprised. Not really. She's asked for it . . . I knew what she was as soon as I saw her . . . And that coalman. I wouldn't put it past him, either . . . Not since he shouted "Whoa" to his horse from her bedroom window . . .'[14]) and spiky geriatrics like Frank Randle's permanently louche octogenarian ('I'm as full of vim as a butcher's dog – I'm as lively as a cricket. Why I'll take anybody on of me age and weight, dead or alive.'[15]).

This was a world where harsh reality intruded rudely into the most rhapsodic of disquisitions, forever dragging idle dreamers like Les Dawson's Walter Mittyish ex-Hoover salesman back down to earth:

> Last evening, I was sitting at the bottom of my garden, smoking a reflective cheroot, when I chanced to look up at the night sky. As I gazed, I marvelled at the myriad of stars glistening like pieces of quicksilver cast carelessly on to black velvet. In awe, I watched the waxen moon ride like an amber chariot across the zenith of the heavens, towards the ebony void of infinite space, wherein the tethered bulks of Jupiter and Mars hung forever festooned in their orbital majesty. And as I stared in wonderment, I thought to myself . . . I must put a roof on this outside lavatory.[16]

This was a world in which marriage was regarded as two becoming one with forty years to determine which one it was. Al Read's many vivid scenes featuring the desperately active wife and the deviously slothful husband captured the struggle memorably:

| | |
|---|---|
| WIFE | Are you going to cut that grass or are you waiting till it comes in the hall? |
| HUSBAND | Er, what d'you mean, love? |
| WIFE | That garden's a disgrace! You don't seem to have any interest in it at all. First time the neighbours see you with a pair of shears in your hand they'll swear you're out for bother! And shift your feet – I've asked you to fill |

|  | that coal bucket twice and you've cracked on you've not heard me! What we weren't going to have in that garden – hanging baskets, a lily pond and goodness knows what! And what *have* we got? An air-raid shelter full of water and a tin hat with a daisy in it! |
| HUSBAND | Now, what time have I – |
| WIFE | Finds time next door! *He's* made some beautiful shapes out of his privets – love birds and all sorts. I wouldn't care, but he always does our hedge up to the gate. The only time I got you to do his, you went and cut the tail off his peacock! |
| HUSBAND | Well, I gave it 'im back!¹⁷ |

The Northern music-hall favoured the comedy of recognition, inclusive rather than exclusive in its attitude. 'The traditional northern comic gets great sympathy,' remarked James Casey (a writer and producer of radio comedy for the BBC's North Region). 'The southern comics didn't get sympathy – they were smart, they would basically tell you how they topped somebody ... The northern comedian [in contrast] would tell you how he was made a fool of.'¹⁸

At the centre of this world stood – a little unsurely at times – the great comic from Stockton-on-Tees, Jimmy James, a lugubrious and vaguely melancholic figure with gimlet eyes and protruding, cushiony lips. He usually found himself sandwiched between two prize idiots – Hutton Conyers on one side, Bretton Woods on the other. 'Are you puttin' it around that I'm barmy?' one of them would ask him. 'Why?' James would reply. 'Did you want to keep it a secret?' Playfully indulgent, he would listen politely to his companions as they talked their way deeper into the depths of illogicality, rambling on about keeping man-eating lions in shoe-boxes and receiving sentimental gifts from South African trips. Sometimes he would interpose the odd supportive observation ('Oh, well ... they're nice people, the Nyasas. I'll bet *they* gave you something.'), or register a mild sense of surprise ('*Pardon?*'), while pursuing a policy of divide and rule by encouraging the idiot on one side to think that the *real* idiot was on the other side ('Dial 999 – *somebody* must be looking for him! . . . Go and get two coffees – I'll try and keep him talking.'[19]).

These triangular conversations would be revived on television in the seventies whenever a special guest would wander on to the stage to join Morecambe and Wise, with the guest on one side, Ernie on the other, and Eric, always running things, in the middle:

| ERIC | (*looking up at Vanessa Redgrave*) Good lord! Are you on a box or (*glancing down at Ernie*) is he standing in a hole? |
| ERNIE | Eric – Miss Redgrave . . . |
| ERIC | (*kissing her hand*) Vanilla, how are you? |
| REDGRAVE | Vanessa. |
| ERIC | Oh? (*kisses hand again*) Tastes like vanilla. We had your dad on one of our shows, you know. |
| REDGRAVE | He's never forgotten it. |
| ERNIE | They never do. |
| ERIC | Very talented man, your dad. The way he played those spoons up and down his legs! Fantastic! Dessert spoons as well – they can be painful if you miss . . . |

'Whenever you hear me using any of your dad's material,' Eric Morecambe told Jimmy James's son, 'there are two reasons. One is because it's a kind of tribute, and the other is because it's very funny. But mostly', he added, 'it's because it's very funny.'[20] All of the other old routines were drawn on for very much the same reason: they still seemed very funny.

'Look at that,' Robb Wilton is reputed to have said, watching from the wings as an acrobatic troupe clambered up on to each other's shoulders, balanced themselves on chairs that were in turn balanced on tall poles and then spun themselves around at a dizzying speed. 'All that', muttered Wilton, shaking his head incredulously, 'just because the buggers are too lazy to learn a comic song.'[21] The same sly irreverence, the same effortless timing, the same sharp response to someone else's airs and graces, could be found, all those years later, in Eric Morecambe's remorseless teasing of Ernie Wise's pretensions to being part of something altogether grander than a mere cheap music-hall act.

Early on in their shared career, when their prospects seemed bleak, Ernie Wise was heard to complain: 'We're Northern . . . You can't win if you're Northern.'[22] He could not, as far as the future of Morecambe and Wise was concerned, have been more wrong.

## CHAPTER II

# Morecambe before Wise

*I'm an enigma, a one-off.*
ERIC MORECAMBE

Eric Morecambe was fond of informing people that he had taken his name from the place of his birth: Eric. His real name, in fact, was John Eric Bartholomew, and the actual place of his birth was the small North Lancashire seaside town of Morecambe.[1]

He came, as he often said, from an ordinary working-class family.[2] His father, George Bartholomew, had worked as a labourer for the Morecambe and Heysham Corporation since leaving school at the age of fourteen. His mother, Sarah ('Sadie') Elizabeth Bartholomew (née Robinson), had worked as a cotton weaver and later as a waitress, but she was often obliged to take on a variety of part-time jobs in order to supplement a very modest family income.

They had, in terms of background, much in common with each other. Both came from large families: George had seven brothers and three sisters, Sadie three sisters and two brothers. George had grown up in Morecambe, Sadie in nearby Lancaster. Both had known considerable hardship, and both – each in their own distinctive ways – harboured hopes of a less onerous future.

As personalities, however, they were stark opposites. George, a tall, thin man with a long, narrow face, slightly protruding ears, sharp, attentive eyes and a hairstyle topped off by a Stan Laurel tuft, was by all accounts an even-tempered, warm, happy-go-lucky character who always gave the impression of being more concerned with enjoying what he had than with yearning for what he continued to lack. Sadie, a short, somewhat thick-set woman with dark curly hair, faintly quizzical grey eyes, full cheeks, a sharp wit and, if anything, an even sharper tongue, was a naturally intelligent, imaginative, doughty woman who, had she been born in more propitious times and more fortunate circumstances, might well have pursued an interesting and rewarding career of her own.

They had met at a dance at the Winter Gardens in Morecambe, but their respective reactions to the occasion said much, in retrospect, about their subsequent relationship: whereas George had been sufficiently impressed by Sadie to consider the possibility of an open-ended series of dates, Sadie had decided, there and then, that George Bartholomew was the man she would marry. Sadie got her way. A relatively short time after, on 26 February 1921, they were married in nearby Accrington. Their first and only child, John Eric, was born – somewhat unexpectedly – at 12.30 p.m. on 14 May 1926 ('If my father hadn't been so shy I would have been two years older.'[3]) in the front living-room of a neighbour's house at 42 Buxton Street, Morecambe.[4] The Bartholomew family's own house, at 48 Buxton Street, would be the house that Eric would come to think of as his first home, but he and his parents could not have stayed there for more than a few short months, because the building was by then in a state of terminal disrepair.

His first vivid memory, he would always say, was of the ceiling having fallen in: 'I remember being lifted on to the kitchen table by my mother and having my coat pulled on and my scarf tied round my neck, and being taken out of the house.'[5] He would have been no more than ten months old at the time.[6] The unwelcome and unexpected period of disruption turned out, however, to have been something of a blessing in disguise, because the local Corporation relocated the family into a relatively new and reassuringly sturdy council house – 'with three bedrooms and an outside loo'[7] – at 43 Christie Avenue. A measure of stability and security for the Bartholomews had, at last, been achieved.

The next few years were, Eric would admit, 'hazy'[8] in his memory, but his mother likened her infant son to 'a little doll with a head of blond curls'.[9] He was, it seems, a rather precocious baby, beginning to walk at around nine or ten months old, and learning to speak soon after that. Sadie would always insist, sometimes over the top of her adult son's meek objections, that he was a born performer:

We had a gramophone and he knew every record we possessed. It's clear in my memory . . . He would come in and say, 'What do you want playing?' 'Play me so and so,' I'd say. He would go through the records, and though he couldn't read, he would find the very one I had named, put it on, and start dancing to it.

Whenever we took him out to relatives, all he wanted to do was perform . . . 'I want to do my party piece. I want to sing and dance.'

'Wait a minute, love,' he would be told.

I remember one particular night when the pianist told him to wait, and he said, 'All right, I'll wait under the table.' He must have been about three. From time to time he would announce, 'I'm here, and I'm still waiting.'[10]

Eric could, Sadie recalled, be 'quite a handful.'[11] Both she and her husband had to remember never to leave their front door ajar; they knew that little Eric, had he ever glimpsed a chink of light through the narrowest of gaps, would have pushed the door wide open and wandered off down the street in search of adventure. Whenever Sadie needed to take him shopping with her she found that the only thing she could do to keep him still while she prepared for the trip was to tie him by his scarf to the door-knob and let him sit outside on the step. Even this, however, was sometimes not enough to hold him: on one occasion he managed to convince a passerby that he had tied himself – as part of some obscure prank – too tightly to the door, and needed the assistance of a kind-hearted individual to help him get free. An anxious Sadie tracked him down, eventually, to a damp and dirty building site some distance away at the bottom of Lancaster Road. She found him entertaining the workers by reciting nursery rhymes and performing such songs as 'Blue Moon' and 'I'm Dancing with Tears in My Eyes', and encouraging them to reward him by tossing coins into his strategically positioned tam-o'-shanter:

When I got there his little white suit was spattered with mud, his shoes and socks were caked where he had squelched through a really sticky patch, and his face was filthy. He saw me and announced to his audience, 'I'd better go now, there's me Mam.'

One of the builders said, 'That little lad's a wonderful entertainer.'

'I'll *entertain* him when I get him home,' I said.

'Oh,' said Eric, 'that means I will have to have my bottom slapped, won't I, Mum?'

'You've never spoken a truer word.'

'Well, folks,' said Eric to his audience, 'I'll have to be going. Goodbye everybody. See you tomorrow.'[12]

It was, in spite of the usual kind of deprivations and occasional crises experienced by all working-class families of the period, a happy childhood. 'I have wonderful memories of both my mother and father,' Eric would later remark, 'absolutely fantastic memories, and I think of them a lot and with great happiness.'[13] The gentle, easy-going George, his family always said, would start whistling contentedly to himself 'from the moment his feet touched the ground each morning'.[14] He took great pleasure in spending time with his son watching football matches (often at the modest little ground of Morecambe FC; sometimes, as an occasional treat, thirty miles away at Deepdale, the altogether more impressive stadium of Preston North End). George would also take Eric fishing, or picking mushrooms in the fields around their home, and sometimes for long and rambling walks around the town reminiscing about his own childhood days and telling elaborate, funny stories that frequently concealed unexpected twists in their tail. Sadie, Eric remembered, had less time to spare – understandably – for casual outings, but whenever her work brought her into contact with any aspect of the entertainment world she would make a point of bringing him along for a tantalising glimpse behind the scenes. When an opportunity did present itself for a family excursion of some kind or another it was always made the most of. A photograph dating from 1932, for example, pictures what appears to be the end of a very enjoyable afternoon out in the sun, with George, Sadie and Eric sitting down close together on the grass, their makeshift tent standing behind them, all smiling broadly and each with a ukulele in their hands.

Although Eric was an only child he did not want for the companionship of friends of his own age. He was well liked by most of the other children in the area. He joined in all the chaotic games of football with the other boys in the park at the back of Christie Avenue, and accompanied several of his friends on their regular visits to Halfway House – the local sweet shop. On most weekends, he queued with his cousin 'Sonny' Threlfall outside the Palladium cinema – known affectionately as 'The Ranch' – to see the latest movies (Westerns were his favourite) and, during relatively uneventful moments, fire peashooters at bald-headed men in the rows below.

Morecambe – like most English seaside resorts – was a place of stark, seasonal contrasts: cold, dull and quiet in the winter months; warm, bright and noisy in the summer months. Eric, looking back on his childhood, would describe his memories of his home town as 'serene and ageless. They emerge vivid and sharp. Happy and bright, not dull and ugly.'[15] One of the clearest images was of seeing his parents share the 'supreme joy' of sitting together and 'watching the Turneresque sunset over Morecambe Bay'.[16]

The town, in those days, was often referred to formally as part of a broader area – 'Morecambe and Heysham'. Morecambe, as Eric would take pleasure in pointing out, 'was a double act long before I met Ernie'.[17] Spring, as far as Eric was concerned, was the season that marked the town's sudden re-awakening, and summer the enchanting time when the town 'became a different place'.[18] As the temperature began to rise and the sun started to shine, the town moved rapidly from being a rather insular and unobtrusive Lancashire town to become a lively centre for recreation, a welcoming place that boasted all kinds of entertainment.

Morecambe – the 'Naples of the North', a 'smaller Blackpool'[19] – was at this time in the process of creeping gentrification. The process culminated in the early thirties with the establishment of the art deco Midland Hotel, an ambitiously lavish new high-style building on the seaward side of the promenade that soon attracted the likes of David Niven, Mrs Wallis Simpson and Noël Coward. In the summer, as the holiday season began and strangers flocked to the town from all directions, it was, said Eric, 'like being brought up to date; finding out what was going on in the world. You never saw many cars in those days, yet August brought a veritable motorcade of Austin Sevens and Morris Eights driven by the "well-to-do" paying their £3 a week, full board at the town's desirable residences.'[20]

On the sands, littered with sleepy bodies slouched deep in deckchairs and mazy formations of energetic boys and girls, the regular daily entertainment was provided by 'the Nigger Minstrels' – 'then undeterred', Eric would later note, 'by the racial overtones of their titles'.[21] They would sometimes hold talent contests, and Eric, whenever possible, would enter them – winning on at least three occasions (after his last success, he recalled, 'They found out I was a local boy and stopped me from entering.'[22]). Summer also brought with it the prospect of a chance sighting of a visiting celebrity, and Eric was particularly excited one year to see 'the magnificent' portly British movie star Sydney Howard[23] – fresh from appearing in *Shipyard Sally* (1939) alongside Gracie Fields – strolling sedately along the pier. The season always ended with the relatively modest but rather beautiful illuminations, a final few visits to the 'fairyland' of Happy Mount Park and the first chill winds that accompanied the holidaymakers' 'final glimpse of annual escape'.[24]

'I was proud', Eric would say, 'to know that people came to my town for a holiday. It always seemed a pity that they couldn't stop the whole year round [because] in those golden growing up years, there was a sort of magic about Morecambe. It had a lot to offer and I took it.'[25] The one place in town, however, where it seems that he usually took rather less than was being offered him was the classroom: 'I wasn't just hopeless in class,' he said. 'I was terrible.'[26] This was, typically, something of an exaggeration – he was far from being a slow-witted young boy, and there is some evidence to suggest that he showed a reasonable aptitude for certain subjects,[27] but, nevertheless, school was never a place that would ever be able to command his full attention.

He attended two schools in Morecambe: Lancaster Road Junior and then, with markedly less frequency and enthusiasm, Euston Road Senior. He was, to begin with, happy enough to set off there each morning – particularly because Sadie allowed him to take with him a bag of his favourite confection – 'cocoa dip', a mixture of cocoa powder and sugar: 'The idea was to have the bag open in my coat pocket and keep dipping a wet finger into the mixture . . . at regular intervals on the way to school. It was like nectar.'[28]

In time, however, a combination of boredom and, increasingly, absenteeism ensured that the standard of his work declined alarmingly: 'I spent most of my time', he later confessed, 'in the school lavatory smoking anything I could ignite.'[29] Sadie, who had hoped that her son would do well enough to go to a grammar school, was too attentive a mother to have remained unaware of the problem for very long, but, when the school reports started to underline just how poorly he was faring, she felt shocked and angry.

One report in particular, which arrived at the Bartholomew house early in April 1936, announced curtly that the nine-year-old Eric was forty-fifth out of forty-nine pupils (although, judging from his marks, it is not at all clear how he managed to come ahead of the other four). A teacher's scribbled addendum – 'He was absent most of the exams' – pointed out an obvious contributory factor.[30] Sadie (it appears that George left such responsibilities to her) wrote back to the school immediately, declaring on the back of the same sheet: 'I am disgusted with this report, and I would be obliged if you would make him do more homework,' adding, menacingly as far as Eric was concerned, 'I would see he did it here.'[31] She, typically, was determined that her son should arrest his dizzying decline as speedily as possible and then – she hoped – start to improve. After visiting his school and talking to several of his teachers, however, Sadie was, eventually, forced to accept the fact that he was never going to achieve the academic success she had dreamed of. 'Mrs Bartholomew,' said the headmaster, 'I've been teaching boys for thirty years. Take my advice. It would be a complete waste of time [to expect any improvement].' She had offered to pay for further tuition but was told, 'It would be money down the drain.'[32]

This rejection only seemed to spur Sadie on in her search for a suitable career for Eric. It surprised no one who knew her that she reacted to the undeniably deep disappointment of this setback in such a remarkably spirited and positive manner. Her most passionate wish was for her son to grow up to live a better and more rewarding life than either she or her husband had known, and, even if that wish did not seem likely to be realised through academic achievement, she was not prepared to abandon it. Eric's widow, Joan – who would in later years come to know Sadie extremely well – stressed how committed she was to her son's betterment:

She really was a good woman. She was hard, yes, in some

ways, but she *had* to be a hard woman in that kind of harsh environment. She wasn't the sort of pushy 'stage mother' that some people have portrayed her as being. She didn't keep pushing Eric because she wanted fame and fortune through her child. She was much too fair and too intelligent for that to be her motive. Everything she did, she did for Eric's sake. Just after Eric was born, George had had a terrible accident playing football, he'd broken his leg, and they'd wanted to amputate it, the breaks were so severe. He'd refused, and luckily his leg was OK, but it was something like two years before he was able to work again – and all through that time Sadie went out to work while George stayed at home with Eric, and she really had to work to keep them all going. That was the great strength these people had, and Sadie was not just strong but also, in so many ways, so shrewd and far-seeing.[33]

'It's up to me', Sadie said to her son, 'to see that you are never tied to a whistle like your dad.'[34] Her problem now was to find an alternative means to achieve that dream.

The solution, when she thought about it, seemed obvious if also fraught with serious risks and the threat of future hazards. If Eric was too distracted to succeed at school, she reasoned, then she would have to make the source of his distraction into his principal vocation. He was not only a natural performer, she felt, but he also had, like many of his contemporaries, a growing fascination for the world of entertainment. Entertaining people, thrilling them, making them laugh and applaud, seemed a marvellous job, whether it involved racing up and down the wings of a football pitch or standing on the stage of a music-hall. Eric, while unsure of how suited he really was to such a world, would certainly have known that, for a working-class youth, it represented a possible escape from a future of endless toil in humble circumstances.

He would, he said, 'have liked to have been a professional footballer. Purely and simply because it meant £5 a week. That was a lot of money. My father was getting 30 bob. Five pounds a week for playing a game of football I thought was easy. But I was never ever big or strong enough.'[35] Such physical limitations would not, however, preclude a career on the stage, or, indeed, the screen, as other youthful British-born performers from working-class backgrounds – such as Charlie Chaplin (from South London) and Stan Laurel (from Ulverston, just the other side of Morecambe Bay) – had already demonstrated. This was also, of course, a period when the precocious child star – such as Shirley Temple, Mickey Rooney, Judy Garland and the London-born boy with the very familiar surname, Freddie Bartholomew – was firmly in fashion. This was, as Joan Morecambe put it, 'all dream stuff',[36] and Sadie allowed herself, just a little, to dream.

Eric had become an avid movie-goer, showing particular enthusiasm for – besides the ubiquitous Westerns – comedians such as Will Hay, Laurel and Hardy (it was the era of *Our Relations*, *Way Out West* and *Block-Heads*), Harold Lloyd and Buster Keaton (both of whom were long past their best but whose classic shows were still in circulation) and – hugely popular at the time – Abbott and Costello (in such box-office successes as *Who Done It?* and *Pardon My Sarong*). His admiration for Variety performers such as Arthur Askey grew through listening to him regularly on the wireless (the BBC started broadcasting *Band Waggon* in 1938); and he could hardly have failed to have been impressed by the extraordinary national celebrity of George Formby Junior.

Formby – guided by his formidable wife, Beryl – had gone from the difficult early days of playing the Northern music-halls in the shadow of his then famous father to first stage and then screen stardom. He held the enviable position of top British box-office attraction from 1937 to 1943 with the help of such movies as *I See Ice* and *Trouble Brewing* and such popular songs as 'When I'm Cleaning Windows' and 'Chinese Laundry Blues'. Eric was by no means an unequivocal fan, even in those days, of everything Formby was famous for – the songs, he thought, were wonderful, but 'as a comic he was about as funny as a cry for help'[37] – but he did, none the less, come to think of him as something of a personal hero. It is not difficult to imagine why.

Formby, with his flattened vowels and thickened twang, the general air of under-nourishment about him and that spectacularly unfortunate face that seemed forever pressed tight against the outside of a fish-and-chip shop window, must have appeared triumphantly, perhaps even deliriously, 'ordinary'. A popular anecdote from that time – probably apocryphal but quite believable none the less – had a young boy point to a poster outside a theatre and ask his father, 'Dad, is that George Formby?' His father is said to have nodded and replied, 'Yes, and if you keep playing with yourself *you'll* end up looking like that!'[38] Although he was not, in reality, from the conventional working-class background that his image suggested, he was, like Eric, a Lancastrian, and, with his humorous songs that poked unpretentious fun at the back-street lives, humdrum experiences and minor embarrassments of his public, he was a professional performer who never seemed to let down those who identified with him. At a time when more than two million people found themselves face to face with what George Orwell called 'the frightful doom of a decent working man suddenly thrown on the streets after a lifetime of steady work',[39] and thousands more than that were contemplating a probable future of bleak immobility and deadly deprivation, George Formby, however implausibly, seemed an inspirational figure.

Sadie was convinced that Eric, if only he applied himself to the task, had the ability to become, like Formby, a professional performer. She made every effort to encourage him to explore his latent talents. It would not, she appreciated, be easy: she had a name for him – 'Jifflearse'[40] – that had been inspired by the strange, nervy restlessness that characterised so much of his behaviour, and it would be heard often, and at high decibels, during the months that followed. She did succeed in persuading him to learn how to play the piano, the clarinet, the guitar, the trumpet, the euphonium, the accordion and the mandolin. 'But', she would complain, 'when he'd got it, he dropped it.'[41] At the same time, she also decided – on what seems to have been not much more than a whim – that he should go to dance lessons. One day, when Eric was ten years old, his cousin Peggy – a near-neighbour – called at the house: 'Aunt Sadie,' she is reputed to have said, 'I'm going to dancing class on Saturday.' 'Where's that?' Sadie replied. 'Miss Hunter's, above the Plaza,' Peggy said. 'A shilling a lesson.' 'Do me a favour,' asked Sadie, sensing a chance for a brief break from the antics of her increasingly boisterous son, 'take Eric with you.'[42]

Eric, it appears, was rather impressed when he discovered that his first dancing partner was to be a girl – slightly older than him –

named Molly Bunting. Miss Hunter, it appears, was rather impressed as well when she discovered that her new pupil could dance. Eric remembered:

> Miss Hunter, after I'd been there about six weeks, came and saw my mother and said, 'I think this boy's got something, Mrs Bartholomew, he's got a *rhythm*, you know!' and me mother said, 'Oh!' So Miss Hunter said, 'Yes, I think he ought to have private lessons' – private lessons with her in her front room in Rosebury Avenue, at half a crown a time! So me mother said, 'Oh, yes, all right then, give him private lessons if you think he's got talent.'[43]

Sadie, in order to pay for those lessons, had to take on work – in addition to her existing job as an usherette at the Central Pier Theatre – as a daily help, cleaning at three or four houses every week, but she did so, more or less, without complaint, because she now felt a sense of vindication: Eric was, at long last, succeeding at something.

She found a plank of wood for him to tap-dance on at home, and made him a cut-down Fred Astaire-style outfit of top hat, white tie and tails for his lessons. She worked with him over time on a series of mini-routines that included borrowings from the likes of Flanagan and Allen and the latest Hollywood musicals.[44] She also had a calling-card made – 'Master Eric Bartholomew. Vocal Comedy & Dancing' – and started to find him opportunities to perform in front of an audience: low-key social events known locally as 'pies and peas' (because young amateur performers entertained elderly people – usually in a church hall – and, in return, were given a hot meal of meat pies and mushy peas). On at least a couple of occasions Eric also appeared at benefits at the Central Pier, where he would black-up and imitate G. H. Elliott, 'The Chocolate-Coloured Coon' – a very popular musical act of the time – singing 'Lily of Leguna'.[45] Offers of further work started to arrive. When George and Sadie took Eric to the Silver Jubilee Club – a working men's club – in nearby Torrisholme, the concert secretary asked George if Eric would perform for them at dinner time on the following Saturday. Eric recalled: 'My dad said, "Oh, yes, he'll do it." So the feller said, "How much will he want?" My dad said, "He'll do it for nothing." *He* didn't want anything for it! And me mother hit him.'[46] After Sadie's swift intervention a fee of five shillings was agreed – the first sum of money Eric had ever earned for a performance. He arrived on time, put on his pumps ('they wouldn't let me put my taps on'), clambered up on to the billiard table that had been commandeered as a make-shift stage, and, there and then, did his act ('There were balls flying everywhere!').[47] So popular was the performance that Eric found himself booked again for the following week.

His parents applied for a special licence from the local Education Committee that enabled him to perform in the local clubs, and the bookings began to accumulate: 'For a Saturday dinner time and Saturday evening we used to get, I think, fifteen shillings to a pound, which was quite an addition to the family budget.'[48] Sadie soon realised that the act would need more material to hold the attention of the often noisy and easily distracted audiences. She came across the sheet music for an old song made famous by Ella Shields – a male impersonator – entitled 'I'm Not All There' which, she felt, would be perfect – once shorn of its saucy connotations – for 'Our Eric': 'I'm not all there, there's something missing,/I'm not all there, so the folks declare./They call me looby,/Looby as a great big booby . . .' Eric, who thought the song was 'ghastly',[49] was also unimpressed by the costume Sadie designed to accompany it: from the top down, he wore a flat black beret, a kiss curl, round turtleshell spectacles, black bootlace-tie over a white shirt, a very tight waiter's jacket 'with a great big pin where the button should be', very short pin-stripe 'business trousers', suspenders (which he would use to such comic effect thirty years later), red socks and black shoes, and he held in his hand an enormous lollipop – 'as big as a plate' – with a child-size bite taken out of it.[50] From club to club, week after week, in front of audiences swelled by the combined presence of Sadie, George and all of George's brothers, Eric would stand, dressed in this outfit, sporting a suitably gormless expression on his pasty-white face, and sing the song he grew to hate.

'In those days', he recalled somewhat ruefully, 'it was a Northern trait that a comic had to be dressed "funny" – to tell everyone, "look, folks, I'm the comic!"'[51] Although the 'I'm Not All There' routine worked extremely well, thus confirming Sadie's shrewdness as his unofficial manager, he always resented having to perform it.

The warm reception his act usually received may well have been welcome, but the succession of cramped and dingy clubs, each one smelling of stale ale and cigarette ash, harboured no hint of glamour for a young boy uneasy in his 'gormless' attire. 'It was a thing I never *really* wanted to do,' he would later protest. 'I never really wanted to be a performer.'[52] There was, it seems, no burning ambition, no sharp sense of urgency, no irresistible will to succeed, no discernible drive: 'I had no bright ambitions. To me my future was clear. At fifteen I would get myself a paper round. At seventeen I would learn to read it. And at eighteen I would get a job on the Corporation like my dad.'[53]

If it had not been for his mother's forcefulness, it seems doubtful that Eric would ever have become a professional entertainer. In later years he would certainly appear eager to seize any opportunity to express the opinion that Sadie had been a hard taskmistress – sometimes too hard – and a few of the jokes he would make at her expense seemed to carry just a hint of bitterness beneath the surface playfulness:

ERIC      Ah, that's me mother's favourite song, that. If she
          was out there in the audience tonight there'd be
          tears in her eyes.
ERNIE     Why?
ERIC      She can't stand me.

Deep down, however, there were genuine feelings of respect and, in time, gratitude. As much as he adored his father, Eric knew that 'the reason no one ever had a bad thing to say about him is because he never put himself in a position where he had to rock the boat, where he had to be judged',[54] whereas Sadie would sometimes be prepared to come into conflict with her son – and, for that matter, anyone else – if she believed that she had his best interests at heart.

'The truth', reflected Gary Morecambe, his son, 'was that he would have achieved much less in his life without her constant support. Since this was perfectly well understood between them, the gibes were a ritualistic repartee of their relationship.'[55] Joan, Morecambe's widow, agreed: 'They'd always row. Always. Never in a vicious sense, not like that, but they would never see eye to eye, so you always used to know that they were going to clash over something or other. You'd know it was ticking away somewhere in between them, ready to explode at any minute.'[56]

Eric may well have found performing a 'chore', and he may well have felt 'a right Charlie' in his comical costumes, but he knew that his 'mother's motives were the highest'. As he watched her cut out every reference to him in the local newspapers and paste them carefully into her album, he came to appreciate the fact that, for all their occasional disagreements, she clearly was devoted to him.[57] It is also unlikely, said Gary Morecambe, that Sadie, had she known just how uncomfortable performing was making her son feel, would have persisted with her plans: 'She genuinely believed he adored performing, and was unaware of his real feelings . . . Had Eric displayed abject misery, then she would not have pushed at all.'[58]

As it was, Sadie continued to push and to push. She entered her son in a swift succession of local talent competitions, and he did well enough to win several of them, attracting as a consequence his first reviews in the local press:

### MORECAMBE BOY FIRST

A show within a show was staged at the Arcadian Theatre on Saturday night when the final of the talent-spotting competition took place.

The standard of local talent was surprisingly high and the audience enjoyed it immensely. It was only after considerable difficulty that Peter Bernard, one of the artistes in the Variety show, was able to select the three winners, who were chosen by the applause the audience gave them.

First prize was won by the Morecambe boy, Eric Bartholomew, whose singing of 'I'm Not All There' really got the crowd going.[59]

One day early in 1939, after a number of minor successes, a relatively major opportunity presented itself. Sadie came across an advertisement for a talent contest to be held at the Kingsway Cinema down in Hoylake, near Birkenhead. 'In those days', Eric would recall, 'to me, going to Hoylake was like going to Australia.'[60] This, however, was no ordinary contest: organised by a music weekly,

*Melody Maker*, this was the Lancashire and Cheshire area heat of a national 'search-for-talent' competition, and the prize for whoever came first was an audition before the important impresario Jack Hylton. Sadie travelled with Eric, and *Melody Maker* carried a report on the final in its next issue:

> There were a hundred competitors in the area and the ten finalists appeared at the Kingsway Cinema, Hoylake, a week ago. Eric Bartholomew put over a brilliant comedy act which caused the audience to roar with laughter. In an interview, he said, 'My ambition is to become a comedian. My hero is George Formby.'[61]

Eric was less than thrilled, to say the least, to discover that his prize amounted to nothing more than yet another audition. He found auditions nerve-wracking affairs at the best of times, and this one, in the presence of the well-known band leader and showman Jack Hylton, struck him as more of a punishment than a prize. Sadie, of course, was delighted. They were instructed to travel to Manchester, where Hylton's latest touring show was next due to visit. This, Sadie reminded her apprehensive son, would be the opportunity that they had both been working so hard for. It would also be, unbeknownst to either of them, the first, fleeting, opportunity for Eric Bartholomew to set eyes upon the boy who would eventually become his partner, one Ernest Wiseman.

## CHAPTER III

# Wise before Morecambe

*Good evening ladies and gentlemen and welcome to the show.*
ERNIE WISE

The past would never die for Ernie Wise. It would thrive in his mind throughout all the years of arduous struggle and subsequent success, and, even deep into advanced middle-age, his reference points would remain the same: 'Hollywood', for him, would always be the Hollywood of the 'Golden Age' of the thirties and forties, and 'Yorkshire' would always be the Yorkshire of cloth caps, coal, parkin and pies, and 'celebrity' would always be a relative state to be measured against the extraordinary renown of the luminous idols of youth.

The memories, far from fading, seemed to grow more vivid with each passing year, with every cherished moment, retrieved in the mind, appearing more detailed and less doubtful than before, gleaming sharply with the over-polished clarity of a rare and precious piece of crystal. The following, for example, is his adult recollection of a weekly routine from some forty or so years before:

Breakfast was usually bread and dripping, and that went for tea when, occasionally, there might also be a boiled egg. The big meal was dinner, at midday, for which my mother usually made a stew in a saucepan as large as a wash-basin with perhaps fifteen or sixteen large dumplings. We ate a lot of rice pudding – she would put a pint of milk into a pudding and bake it in the oven with a grating of nutmeg and a flavouring of vanilla. Does that make your mouth water? It does mine.

Sunday dinner was the meal of the week. It began with a

huge, hot Yorkshire pudding which you ate with steaming gravy. Then came the meat, veg and potatoes, and finally probably a caramel custard.

Monday was washday. Mother rose at six and went to the outhouse where she lit a fire under her copper boiler and in it she boiled the clothes in soapy water. The wash would be done by eight o'clock. It was pegged out to dry, then ironed with a heavy flat iron that had to be heated from time to time on the range.[1]

Whereas Eric Morecambe, looking back on his childhood, might have thought it sufficient to mention in passing that his mother cooked her stew in a large saucepan, Ernie Wise was always the more likely one of the two to pause and recall more precisely the dimensions of the container and the number of the dumplings; and whereas Morecambe, when reminiscing, tended to jump impatiently from one powerful idea to the next (which is, in a way, how a comic thinks), Wise tended to proceed methodically, showing a very disciplined attention to detail (which is, in a way, how a straight-man thinks).

There is something rather poignant about the way in which Wise recounted events with such jealous exactitude, sounding at times as if his readiness to savour every lost sound, smell, taste and touch was more for his own benefit than it was for that of his audience – a private, belated reward, perhaps, for a hard-working man who had missed more than he cared to admit of a childhood compressed and consumed by the demands of a life lived solely in showbusiness.

The fact of the matter was that Ernie Wise – or, to call him by his real name, Ernest Wiseman – was singled out for stardom long before anyone – outside of Sadie's initially small but enthusiastic coterie – had even heard of a performer called Eric Bartholomew. Unlike his future partner, he had, from a very early age, worked deliberately and impatiently in pursuit of such recognition. 'I've been ambitious all my life,' he acknowledged. 'I was a pusher from the beginning. It's always been push, push, push.'[2] There was to be nothing remotely labyrinthine about *his* route to fame: it would stretch out before him straight and laser-sharp, unimpeded by childish distractions of any kind.

He was born in Leeds on 27 November 1925 at the local maternity hospital. His father, Harry, was a railway signal and lamp man. His mother, Connie, had worked originally as a box-loom weaver in Pudsey. Their marriage was – like that of the Bartholomews – an alliance of contrasting personalities. Harry – a thin, wiry, warm-hearted and outgoing man – came from a very poor family. His father had died when he was just fourteen years of age, and his mother was blind. At the age of sixteen he had pretended to be older than he actually was in order to join the Army, and he went on to win the Military Medal during the 1914–18 war for saving his ser-geant's life. He was a generally optimistic, gregarious kind of charac-ter, hopelessly impractical when it came to financial matters but always prepared to lift the mood of any social gathering with an impromptu song and dance. Connie, in contrast, was a rather shy and somewhat religious young woman[3] who came from a relatively 'well-to-do' working-class family, and, as far as the abstruse yet important intra-class distinctions of the time were concerned, was considered to be 'a highly respectable young lady'.[4]

Harry Wiseman met Connie Wright on a tram, when Harry, as he was making his way to the front of the carriage, tripped over Connie's umbrella. It was, according to Ernie, love at first sight. The relationship, as it blossomed, did not, however, unite their respective families. Although Harry's family was, it seems, enthusiastic about the prospect of marriage, Connie's, in contrast, was most certainly not. Her father was, according to Ernie, 'a dour man . . . hard, of the sort only Yorkshire breeds',[5] and Harry was far removed from the kind of future son-in-law he had envisaged. It was bad enough, reasoned Connie's father, that Harry came from such a 'common' family, but his carefree attitude to money, he concluded, made him a disastrous choice as a husband.

Connie was eventually handed an ultimatum: marry Harry Wise-man, said her formidable father, and she would be ostracised by her own family. 'I'll make sure no worthless husband of yours gets a penny of my money,' he announced. 'You're my favourite daughter, but you'll get nowt from me.'[6] She chose to go ahead and marry Harry, and, sure enough, she was shunned by her family. All that she was allowed to leave home with were her clothes and the upright piano she had bought from out of her savings.

Harry and Connie, once they had married, moved into a single room in lodgings at 6 Atlanta Street, Bramley in Leeds – the place where Ernie would spend the first few months of his life. As soon as they could afford to they left to rent a modest one-up, one-down house in Warder Street – also in Leeds. This was followed shortly after by another house in Kingsley, near Hemsworth, and then, at last, they settled in the end-of-terrace house that Ernie would come to look back on as being his first real home: 12 Station Terrace, a small but relatively pleasant railway cottage in East Ardsley, midway between Wakefield and Leeds. Ernie was their first child; he was followed by a brother, Gordon, and two sisters, Ann and Constance (another brother, Arthur, died of peritonitis at the age of two).

'We were a happy family,' Ernie would recall. 'We always had shoes.'[7] It was never, however, the most secure of upbringings. Harry was earning barely enough to sustain the whole family, and, although he handed over the majority of his salary at the end of each week to Connie, he still managed to fritter away what little he had left on alcohol and tobacco. Connie – doubtless with her estranged father's words ringing loudly in her ears – was often exasperated by her husband's inability to save what little money he had, and, as Ernie would recall, the house reverberated with the sound of all the endless rows about financial matters.

Connie did her best to keep things on an even keel. She had seven mouths to feed on a basic income of £2 per week, and, as a consequence, she was noted for her thriftiness. ' "Save a little, spend a little and remember that your bank book is your best friend" was', said Ernie, 'one of the constant refrains of my childhood,' leaving him with a lifelong 'horror of debt and a steely determination to pay my own way'.[8] In spite of such sobering moral lessons, Harry still somehow managed to contrive on countless occasions to stun Connie with his capriciousness. On one such occasion he decided – without informing Connie – that he urgently needed a 'home cinematograph' he had seen advertised in the local newspaper. It arrived with one film, which, in the absence of a screen, he proceeded to project, over and over again, on to the pantry wall. He never quite got round to buying a proper screen, nor did he ever quite get round to purchasing any more films, either.

One reason why Connie was prepared to tolerate such behaviour was the fact that, deep down, she had always valued his unforced charm and his ebullient sense of showmanship. Although she was never happier than when she had the time to sit at the piano and sing her favourite songs, she was, Ernie recalled, 'temperamentally reluctant to perform in public'.[9] The quixotic Harry, in contrast, was an instinctive performer, and talented enough (like his father before him) to take his amateur song and dance routines on to the local club circuit. Full of amusing stories, tried-and-tested jokes and familiar crowd-pleasing songs, Harry 'would have made the perfect Butlin's Redcoat',[10] and Connie, for all of her well-founded fears about their future, loved and admired – and perhaps even gently envied – that untamed and indomitable sense of fun.

She was not the only one who did. Ernie, from a very early age, was entranced by 'this warm, immensely attractive man with a sunny personality and an optimistic disposition'.[11] If there is one word that appears more often than any other in the autobiography of Ernie Wise, then that word is 'devoted'.[12] Beneath the bustling ambitiousness there was always a rare generosity of spirit about Ernie Wise, a genuine admiration of other performers. This uncommon yet thoroughly decent quality first became evident in the obvious enthusiasm that he showed for his father's burgeoning stage career. He wanted to follow in his father's footsteps – not to compete with him but rather to join him – help him – and share in his joyful escapism.

When he reached the age of six or seven Ernie began to ask his mother to teach him some popular songs, such as 'The Sheikh of Araby', which he would then dutifully memorise and proceed to rehearse interminably. One evening, after Harry had finished his tea, Connie instructed him to get up from the table and go into the other room. 'Ernest', she said conspiratorially, 'has something to show you.'[13] When he opened the door to the living-room he was confronted by the unexpected sight of his diminutive son, complete with an old towel tied around the top of his head, rocking purposefully from side to side in a well-rehearsed way while singing of strange and exotic foreign climes. 'I will never forget the reaction I got,' Ernie would recall. 'He was so bowled over, so excited and thrilled that his eldest son had taken after him and had a spark of talent that there were tears in his eyes.'[14]

Harry, from that point on, determined to teach his son everything he knew about performing. Tap-dancing lessons came first: Connie would play something on the piano while Harry watched their son practise three basic steps on the cold and hard kitchen floor. Songs and short comic routines followed on in the same methodical fashion. It is not entirely clear whether Harry, to begin with, saw in Ernie another potential child star in the making or merely a brief but charming effusion of juvenescent exuberance, but we do know that he wasted little time in drafting his son into his own act. Ernie, at the tender age of seven, joined Harry as part of a novelty double-act called, initially, Carson and Kid.

There is something quite remarkable, perhaps even Proustian, about Ernie's typically detailed recollection of those first days on the stage, something almost reverential about the slow and precise route he charted through the rich minutiae hidden within the prosaic experience of playing the working men's clubs:

[There would be] a big room with usually a long bar running along one side and a stage, the room filled with marble-topped, cast-iron tables, chairs and against the wall, benches. There'd be a snooker room and a place where you played darts. There'd be fruit machines. There'd be beer and sandwiches, pies, potato crisps, pickles and bottles of tomato sauce, the whole place crowded for the concert with working-class people dressed in their Sunday best. The men wore blue serge suits, white shirts with detachable, boned collars and patterned ties fastened to the shirt front by a clip, pocket handkerchiefs to match, black shoes and short hair slicked down. The women and girls wore home-made dresses, their hair in tight curls still smelling faintly of heated tongs, and the bolder, unmarried ones wore make-up. There'd be a scattering of children running about, getting in the way of waiters in white coats and long white aprons carrying trays laden with drinks, mainly beer; if they were paid with a note, you'd see them holding it in their teeth till they had produced the correct change. In the middle of it all there'd be the concert secretary at a table near the stage ringing his official bell and saying, 'Now give order for the next act on the bill which is going to be, ladies and gentlemen – CARSON AND KID!'[15]

Ernie's principal stage outfit in those days consisted of a black bowler hat with the brim cut off, a cut-down dinner jacket with a white carnation pinned to the left lapel, a white wing-collar shirt, a black bow tie, thin black-and-grey-striped trousers and little red clogs. His other occasional, more flamboyant, costumes included what might best be described as a kind of plaid Charlie Chaplin – complete with false moustache – and, made out of what looked suspiciously like the very same material, a most eye-catching little number that flared out wildly at the shoulders and thighs to form an elaborate butterfly shape. The songs that father and son sang together included 'It Happened on the Beach at Bali Bali' and 'Walking in a Winter Wonderland', while Ernie's solo repertoire included 'I'm Knee Deep in Daisies' and 'Let's Have a Tiddly at the Milk Bar':

> Let's have a tiddly at the Milk Bar.
> Let's make a night of it tonight.
> Let's have a tiddly at the Milk Bar.
> Let's paint the town a lovely white.
> You buy a half pint, I'll buy a half pint.
> We'll try to drink a pint somehow.
> Let's have a tiddly at the Milk Bar.
> And drink to the dear old cow.[16]

The act was usually broken up into two single spots and a double: Harry would come on first and perform an abbreviated version of his old routine, then Ernie would appear and perform his own solo routine (lasting five or six minutes) and then, for the second half of the show, father would join son for a double-act.

One reason for the distinctive appeal of Carson and Kid (or, as they were sometimes billed, 'Bert Carson and his Little Wonder' or, in honour of the local distillery, 'The Two Tetleys') was the incongruity of a boy of seven or eight taking part in cross-talk of an 'adult' nature. One joke, for example, had Ernie announce, 'There were two fellahs passing by a pub, and one said to the other as he saw a trickle of water coming from under the door, "What's that? White Horse?" "No," said the man bending down to taste it. "Fox terrier." '[17] A second reason for their popularity may have been their

readiness to mix light comedy with the occasional detour into maud-
lin music-hall territory. One successful routine, 'Little Pal', had Harry
blacked-up to resemble Al Jolson and Ernie sitting on his knee;
Harry would sing:

> Little pal, if daddy goes away.
> If some day you should be
> On a new daddy's knee
> Don't forget about me, little pal.

Ernie, looking up plaintively at his father, replied:

> If some day I should be
> On a new daddy's knee
> Don't forget about me, little pal.[18]

To audiences with relatively fresh memories of the loss and disruption that accompanied, and followed, the 1914–18 war, such an
unashamedly manipulative exercise in sentimentality went down very
well indeed.

Carson and Kid usually had at least three engagements every week
– once on a Saturday evening, once at Sunday lunchtime and once
on Sunday evening – which amounted to fees totalling £3 10s.,
doubling the family income at a stroke. If, as Ernie later claimed,[19]
his parents expected him to grow up to join his father on the railways
– first as a fireman, later as a driver – the success of his sudden entry
into showbusiness, even if it was only at the humble level of the
local working men's club circuit, appears to have prompted them
to start having second thoughts. The extra income, of course, was
extremely welcome, but there was more to it than that: Ernie was
clearly enjoying the experience, and, as Harry could testify, he was
getting to be very good at it. 'I loved it,' he would remember. 'I
had found my purpose in life.'[20] There was none of the ambivalence
exhibited by Eric Bartholomew in Ernie Wiseman's attitude to
showbusiness: 'There is this incredible need to perform in front of
people and I've had it since I was six years of age. This isn't a job
– it's a way of life.'[21]

What the young Ernie Wiseman *did* have in common –

unwittingly – with the young Eric Bartholomew, however, was an increasingly undistinguished school record. His nascent performing career was beginning to take its toll. The exciting but energy-sapping routine of Sunday evening shows followed by an often frenzied rush to catch the last bus home and then, a few hours later, the demoralising struggle to shake off the sleep and set off for school (two miles away in Thorpe) on Monday morning proved a punishing schedule. Ernie, predictably, started falling asleep during lessons. This resulted in a stern letter being sent to the Wisemans by the Leeds education authority, pointing out that exploiting juveniles was against the law and would have to stop immediately. Although the Wisemans were genuinely concerned about their son's schoolwork, they knew that they could not do without the money he was helping to bring in, and they also appreciated the fact that he was by now in no mood to abandon the act. A not entirely satisfactory short-term solution was found: 'We played a game of cat and mouse: if the authorities spotted us in Leeds we moved our activities to Wakefield and if, after a while, they rumbled us in Wakefield we slipped quietly back to Leeds and Bradford. I'm sure in the end they turned a blind eye.'[22]

The reputation of Bert Carson and His Little Wonder – as they had come to style themselves – continued to spread across the West Riding region, and the bookings began to multiply. In 1936, at the age of eleven, Ernie had the chance of securing what he would later describe as his 'first real launch into mainstream performing'.[23] The local paper, the *Bradford Telegraph and Argus*, organised an annual week-long charity event at the Alhambra Theatre that went under what now seems the improbable name of the 'Nignog Revue'. During the year, children who had joined the club could take part in a variety of Nignog activities, such as talent competitions and the local 'pies and peas'. Ernie soon became a 'devoted' – that word again – member, and he found in the Revue's organiser, a certain Mr Timperley, a man 'absolutely devoted' to producing first-rate children's entertainment.[24] During the next two years Ernie played an important part in all of the Revues, and his self-confidence – which had never, in truth, seemed egregiously undernourished – grew immeasurably as a consequence of appearing on the stage of a great music-hall in front of two thousand people.

Not everyone, however, was impressed by his success. His school, by this time, was East Ardsley Secondary School, a large, dark, Victorian building which Ernie had come to hate the sight of. He was never, he admitted, a model pupil – describing himself as 'just plain dumb'.[25] He also found that his considerable reputation as a local performer only served to provoke some of his more mean-spirited teachers – and, indeed, some of his fellow pupils – to further acts of cruelty as he was routinely punished and humiliated for allowing his schoolwork to suffer. 'Come up here, tap-dancer,' one particularly malicious teacher would shout regularly at Ernie, his darkly sarcastic tone making the word 'tap-dancer' sound like quite the worst thing that a young Yorkshire boy could possibly be associated with, and then, on some pretext or other, the teacher would either smack him in front of the class or send him off to be caned. 'Whatever he hoped to achieve by such public ridicule I do not know,' Ernie would write, 'but its effect was to turn me against the school and all it stood for and to alienate me from my classmates.'[26]

Such treatment, understandably, only served to strengthen his resolve to pursue a career of some kind in showbusiness. On the stage, dressed up in a costume, Ernie Wiseman felt different, more important, more sure of who he was and what he was capable of: 'Entertaining was a sort of personality prop which helped me to cover up a deep-rooted shyness and sense of inadequacy. Entertaining brought me out of myself . . . I was able to step out of my very private little world and be an entirely different person, a cheeky chappie.'[27]

His stage persona was certainly bright and brash. There was something of the crowd-pleasing ebullience and somewhat dandified appearance of another Yorkshire comic singer of the time, Whit Cunliffe, in his carefree and cocksure performances. It helped him stand out from most of his contemporaries as a strong and seemingly nerveless entertainer with an unusually promising future ahead of him. That was certainly the impression he made on the impresario Bryan Michie when, in the autumn of 1938, he toured all over the North in search of new juvenile talent to showcase in a revue. Harry Wiseman had heard that Michie was holding auditions at the Leeds Empire, so he made sure that Ernie went along. Michie sat close to the front of the stalls, watching impassively as Ernie strode on to the stage, told a few jokes, sang one of his usual songs – 'Knee-Deep in Daisies' – and finished with his by now extremely competent quick-tempo clog dance. He left without hearing of any response – positive or negative – from Michie. Several months of silence passed, and Ernie, a little disheartened perhaps, returned to the old round of club dates and local talent competitions. Two things happened to lift his spirits again: first, he managed to make a brief appearance on a talent show in Leeds that was being broadcast by the BBC – an achievement that won him considerable respect among his friends and also, just as importantly, a fee of two guineas; and second, a letter finally arrived from London – not from Michie himself, but from his fellow impresario Jack Hylton. Hylton invited Ernie down to London for an audition. 'There was,' Ernie would recall, 'great excitement in the house.'[28]

The subsequent events followed each other at a breathless pace. Harry travelled with Ernie down to London by train on 6 January 1939.[29] On their arrival they went straight to the office of Jack Hylton, and the audition was held there and then. 'He must have liked me,' said Ernie, 'because that same evening he put me in the show.'[30] The show in question was a West End revue called *Band Waggon* – adapted from the hugely successful BBC radio programme of the same name – and, in spite of Arthur Askey's presence at the top of the bill, it was not doing anything like as well as had been expected. Hylton's impetuous decision may have been prompted more by an urgent need to improve his ailing production than it was by the precocious talents of the young stranger in his office, but, whatever the reasons, it was a decision that later that night proved itself to be inspired: Ernie was the talking-point in all of the reviews. The following morning the *Daily Express*, for example, reported:

At 6.40 last night Ernest Wiseman, fair, perky-faced, quiffy-haired thirteen-year-old son of a parcels porter at Leeds Central Station, made his first professional appearance on the stage in Jack Hylton's *Band Waggon* at Princes Theatre [now the Shaftesbury]. The moment he went on he became Ernie Wise. That in future will be his name. I believe you are going to hear it often . . .

Ernie, one-quarter Max Miller, one-quarter Sydney Howard, and the other half a mixture of all the comics who have ever amused you, wears a squashed-in billycock hat, striped black and grey City trousers (too small for him), a black frock coat with a pink carnation in the buttonhole, grey spats, and brown clogs.

His timing and confidence are remarkable. At thirteen he is an old-time performer.[31]

Arthur Askey, interviewed almost forty years later, recalled his reaction to this new addition to the cast: '[He was a] fresh-faced, delightful kid, totally stage-struck. He had a good face, a good singing voice, and he was a very fair little dancer. He had a neat little evening dress with brown clogs on his feet – which didn't quite go together – but he did a good clog dance.'[32]

It seemed as though Ernie, all of a sudden, was actually living the kind of Hollywood fantasy that he had always found so irresistible. Sitting in the unfamiliar splendour of the large room in the Shaftesbury Hotel ('it boasted a courtesy light in the loo'[33]), Harry read through all of the newspaper reports of his son's extraordinary achievement. Quickly, he came to the realisation that he would no longer be needed as either a co-performer or mentor. He had cried with pride the previous evening as he sat through the show, but now, in spite of receiving an offer from Jack Hylton to stay on as a kind of personal assistant to Ernie, he made up his mind to go back home to Yorkshire at the end of the following week.

Jack Hylton, in his absence, became, in effect, a surrogate father to Ernie, taking control of his career, his image and, for a time, his financial concerns. Ernest Wiseman became, on Hylton's advice, Ernie Wise (easier to remember, he reasoned), and he was awarded a five-year contract that started at £6 per week (twice as much as Harry was earning at the time). Hylton moved him into a flat above the Fifty-Fifty, an Italian restaurant in St Martin's Lane, and found him a chaperone in the form of a Mrs Rodway, a woman who had considerable experience in looking after juvenile performers.

Harry and Connie did begin to benefit financially from their son's dramatic success – Mrs Rodway, on Ernie's insistence, sent at least £3 home each week before banking the rest (Ernie kept the bank book) – but, in his absence, it was a bitter-sweet experience. Years later, after Harry had died, Connie confided to her son that going back home alone had been 'the breaking of him'.[34] He had tried, for a while, to keep the act going with other young performers, but his heart was not in it and he gave up performing altogether. His health began to decline, and, with all of the extra money coming in each week from London, he virtually stopped working altogether.

Ernie, busy settling into a new routine and novel surroundings down South, was, it seems, entirely unaware of his father's feelings. Everything was new and exciting and glamorous to the newly named Ernie Wise, West End star, and he threw himself into his new life 'with all the ignorance and insouciance of the thirteen-year-old that I was'.[35] Although he was never quite the stolid and adamantine character that the public persona sometimes would suggest, the self-assured manner in which he coped with his sudden change of fortune was undeniably striking for one so young. One journalist who interviewed him immediately after his début in the show was understandably taken aback when Ernie, responding to a question concerning who would be looking after him during his time in London, answered coolly: 'Nobody. Why should they?'[36]

'Ernie', commented Arthur Askey, 'was rather like a young Hylton then and I think that is one reason Jack liked him so much. He looked on him almost as a son.'[37] Hylton, a down-to-earth Lancastrian, made every effort to see that Ernie's progress was not overly hindered by feelings of homesickness. After noting, for example, that the Italian food from the restaurant was not agreeing with Ernie's East Ardsley appetite, Hylton invited him into his office to share meals of pork pie (made specially for him in Bolton) or cold tripe. Ernie respected him greatly, and was particularly impressed by his habit of keeping several thick rolls of banknotes stuffed inside his bulging pockets. Here, he thought, was a man worth listening to.

'It was Jack Hylton who shaped my stage persona,' he would say. 'He knocked the raw edges off my act.'[38] The brown clogs were replaced with smart black tap shoes; the battered bowler hat was abandoned in favour of a new straw boater; and the odd, ill-fitting coat and striped trousers gave way to a sophisticated-looking bespoke white dinner jacket and black trousers. It represented a very deliberate and radical change of image: he now resembled more a cosmopolitan song-and-dance man than a parochial Northern comic, 'more Maurice Chevalier than Max Miller'.[39] Hylton planned to promote

Ernie Wise as 'an altogether slicker product' than before, a 'boule-vardier' who performed like 'an adult before his time' (even if, as a consequence, that meant, as Wise would later reflect, that he remained 'a child without a childhood').[40]

It was a sobering contradiction: while on stage Ernie Wise seemed to mature at a rapid rate, off stage and deep down there was something oddly immature about him. He noticed the difference himself when, after *Band Waggon* had finally bowed to public indifference and folded, he joined Jack Hylton and his band on a tour of the halls. The law required Wise to continue attending school while he trav-elled, and it was during his brief – sometimes just single-day – visits to the schools at each venue that he was struck by how much more worldly-wise other boys of his age appeared to be: 'Their knowledge of sex, of smoking, of swearing and so on left me completely puzzled and made me feel like a very much younger brother learning the facts of life from his elders.'[41] Although he was delighted to have the opportunity to perform professionally, there was, perhaps, some lingering sense of regret at the life he had been forced to overlook: 'I led a very confined life, sheltered from ordinary boyhood influences and rigorously shielded by adults themselves from the raw adult world outside the theatre.'[42]

He also found himself feeling just a little unsettled when, in the spring of 1939, he came across another juvenile performer, even younger than himself, whose ability to make people laugh caused him to wonder to himself if he might soon have a serious rival to contend with. When Eric Bartholomew went with his mother to the Manchester cinema for his audition before Jack Hylton, he was oblivious to the fact that among the audience, casting an 'experi-enced' eye over the new acts, was Hylton's thirteen-year-old protégé, Ernie Wise. Wise, however, was extremely impressed by this unknown comic – as, indeed, was everyone else among Hylton's entourage: 'So much so that the boys in the band turned round to me and said (only half-joking!), "Bye, then, Ernie. Things won't be the same with this new lad around, but I dare say we'll soon get used to him. What are you going to do now?"'[43] Eric and Sadie, after receiving the not entirely reassuring news from Hylton that he would 'let you know', returned home to Morecambe without discovering just how popular the act had been, but Ernie, now sitting a little less comfortably than before in the darkness of the auditorium, knew exactly what had happened: 'I had a lot of push in those days . . . but I have to admit my self-esteem took a bit of a knock from Eric even though we never said a word to each other.'[44]

For the moment, however, Ernie Wise remained, without much doubt, the country's pre-eminent child star. He continued to tour with Jack Hylton, and, when war broke out in September and the theatres closed down, he was invited to stay with Hylton and his wife and two daughters at Villa Daheim, the impresario's country house in Angmering-on-Sea in Sussex. Hylton and his wife had a chauffeur, a German cook, a German maid and a nanny. Arthur Askey was a near-neighbour, as was George Black – another powerful West End impresario. Wise was given pocket money, substantial meals, a generous supply of sweets and was generally treated like one of the family. Surrounded by the self-conscious grandeur of a self-made man, as well as the bright appeal of an upmarket holiday resort that nestled snugly between Bognor Regis and Worthing, Ernie Wise would have been forgiven for wanting to stay as long as possible: 'For a young lad from East Ardsley', he recalled, 'it could have been Hawaii.'[45] After a while, however, he became homesick, and so, with Hylton's blessing, he made his way back North to his parents' new home in Leeds.[46]

His return only served, in a cruel way, to help him to sever most of the remaining emotional ties that had pulled him back there in the first place. He was shocked to see his father, now showing the physical effects of rheumatoid arthritis, looking so much older, and he was profoundly saddened by the greeting he received from him: 'Why did you come home?' his father asked him. 'You had it made.'[47] It suddenly seemed a mistake to have left Villa Daheim. Without the prospect of resurrecting the old father–son act, and without any enthusiasm for the odd solo spot in venues he had long since grown out of, he felt, at the age of fourteen, a burden: 'I was, after all, just another mouth to feed, and hadn't Mum said often enough to Dad, "When there's no money in the house, love flies out the window"?'[48]

After working for a few difficult months as a coalman's labourer, he was very relieved to receive a telegram from Bryan Michie, inviting him down to the Swansea Empire to join the touring version of

*Youth Takes a Bow*. It was the opportunity – and the excuse – that he had been waiting for. He left immediately, desperate to resume his career in entertainment. He would never go home again.

## CHAPTER IV

# Double Act, Single Vision

*It was fate – I happened to pull the Christmas cracker and
Ernie was in it.*
ERIC MORECAMBE

*We're a real Hollywood film, us – all the drama, the comedy.*
ERNIE WISE

When Eric met Ernie, it was the former who found himself nursing
feelings of envy towards the latter. Watching from the shadowy
wings of the Swansea Empire, Eric was left in no doubt as to who
was now the star of the show: Ernie. It was Ernie, the newcomer,
Ernie, whose reputation as 'The Jack Buchanan of Tomorrow', 'The
Young Max Miller' and 'Britain's own Mickey Rooney' had preceded
him,[1] Ernie, taller – at that stage – than Eric and, indeed, better paid
than Eric, who was now the real star of *Youth Takes a Bow*. As this
supremely self-assured young man glided through his polished act,
his immaculate made-to-measure suit accentuating each crisply competent step and gesture, Eric, standing silently to one side with arms
tightly folded, could only think to himself: 'Bighead.'[2]

Just two short months ago it had all been very different. After the
worryingly long silence that had followed his audition for Jack Hylton
in Manchester, Eric – in the company of Sadie, his chaperone – had
been invited to join the cast of *Youth Takes a Bow* as one of Bryan
Michie's Discoveries. He made his debut at the Nottingham Empire,
and, on a salary of £5 per week plus travelling expenses, the future
seemed bright. He grew rapidly in confidence, attracted a fair number
of complimentary notices and won the respect of the other members
of the cast. Then, however, the rumours began: Ernie Wise, it was

whispered, was about to join the show. Ernie Wise overshadowed them all. They had all heard him on the wireless exchanging comic repartee with the likes of Arthur Askey and Richard Murdoch; they had all read about his triumphant performances on the West End stage; and they all knew that he was regarded in the business as Jack Hylton's 'golden boy'. When, therefore, he bounded on to the train at Crewe, his thick, shiny hair flopping over his forehead, his expensive-looking overcoat flapping loosely as he moved, he became – without any discernible effort on his part – instantly the centre of attention, and Eric, like many of the other boys in the carriage, was more than a little jealous.

It did not help, of course, that Ernie, almost as soon as he arrived, had taken to calling Eric 'sonny'; nor did it help that Ernie, at the age of fifteen, was no longer required to go to school; and it certainly did not help that the combination of his greater height, more adult-looking clothes (long trousers, in contrast to Eric's baggy shorts), superior wage (£2 per week more than Eric's), fame and freedom from parental interference in his affairs caused him to appear, in Eric's anxious eyes, a far more attractive proposition to the girls in the company. It must have seemed to Eric as though everything that he had begun to achieve over the past few weeks was now set to be eclipsed in an instant by the presence of this noisy bundle of energy and dreams.

Eric's mother, however, knew better. Sadie saw straight through Ernie's bravado and understood that, underneath, he was actually an insecure and forlorn little boy, far younger emotionally than he seemed, still struggling to repress the sadness he felt over his father's broken spirit and only just beginning to settle into a peripatetic existence on the road. She observed him, to start with, from a distance, watching admiringly as he took complete responsibility for all of his travel and accommodation arrangements, sent the usual proportion of his weekly wage back home to his parents and, of course, banked the majority of the remainder. For all of his private problems, he never seemed, to the casual spectator, anything less than the very model of a self-reliant young professional, solid and sure-footed, but in reality he craved – perhaps more strongly than even Sadie had suspected – the very kind of support and security from which the vast majority of his contemporaries in the company were contriving to escape.

The only place where he felt genuinely sure of his worth was up on a stage in front of an audience. He knew that when he was up there he was good; he knew that audiences liked him. The rest of the company – adults and juveniles alike – admired him, too. *Youth Takes a Bow* was the second half of a two-part Variety show. The first half – usually billed as *Secrets of the BBC* – featured adult professional acts (such as Alice and Rosie Lloyd, sisters of the well-known music-hall star Marie Lloyd, and comedians Archie Glen, Dicky 'large lumps' Hassett and the double-act George Moon and Dick Bentley), while the second half was devoted to such young performers as Eric and Ernie, the singer Mary Naylor, the acrobat Jean Bamforth and the harmonica player Arthur Tolcher (who, thirty years later, would make regular, but comically curtailed, appearances on *The Morecambe & Wise Show*). Ernie Wise brought a certain amount of precious West End glamour to the latter part of the bill.

Although Eric, as the tour went on, grew to like Ernie as a person as well as to respect him as a performer, there was no obvious suggestion that their fast-blossoming friendship was likely to lead in the near future to the formation of an on-stage partnership. Eric was a comic, whereas Ernie was more of a song-and-dance man. Eric was appearing as the gormless little boy in the home-made comedy outfit, Ernie was playing the sharp-suited boulevardier – they seemed set on separate courses, pursuing different goals. Six months would go by until a combination of wartime exigencies and unexpected good fortune conspired to draw Ernie closer to Eric, and both of them nearer to the invention of a double-act.

At some point early in 1940, the cast arrived in Oxford for a show at the New Theatre, and, as usual, all of the individual performers dispersed to check in at their temporary accommodation. Ernie, however, had, for the first time, failed to book ahead, and, in a town that was packed full of troops, he had no choice but to trudge through the streets in search of a vacancy. Time and again he knocked on a door only to be informed that all rooms were occupied. Darkness fell, the temperature dropped, and Ernie was still wandering the streets on his own. It was well after ten o'clock at night that a cold and desolate Ernie Wise was found by a fellow member of the cast, a singer called Doreen Stevens.

Taking pity on him, she decided – even though her own room was waiting for her in another part of the town – to accompany him until they found somewhere for him to rest. After numerous disappointments, they reached yet another guest house and knocked on the door. 'This is little Ernie Wise,' said Doreen to the landlady. 'Have you got any room in your house?' Before the landlady could finish telling her that the house was fully booked for the whole week, Sadie Bartholomew's distinctive voice could be heard from the top of the stairs: 'Is it our Ernie?'[3] Hurrying down to the door, with Eric following on behind her at a rather more leisurely pace, she announced that Ernie must come inside immediately and that he would be welcome to sleep with Eric in *his* bed. The next morning, as the three of them had their breakfast, Sadie suggested that Ernie – in order to avoid something similar to the traumatic experience of the previous evening ever happening again – might like to travel with them in future and leave all of the accommodation arrangements to her. He agreed, without the slightest hesitation, and, from that moment on, the three of them were virtually inseparable.

Ernie Wise did not just come to be treated by the Bartholomews as one of the family; he also came to rival Eric in Sadie's affections. They clearly saw in each other a kindred spirit. 'Ernie,' Sadie would recall, 'was gentle and shy, and sincere':

Eric used to call him Lilywhite. 'Look at Lilywhite, he never puts a foot wrong,' he would say. He was right. Ernie never did wrong. Not that he was prim or prissy, or goody-goody, which is a person who just acts good but is really not good inside. Ernie was just naturally good, naturally truthful, fair and honest. We toured and lived together for years. I *know* Ernie.[4]

Ernie, in turn, saw in Sadie the same kind of enthusiasm and drive that he had once associated with his father. He felt that she, like him, possessed 'a tungsten carbide core of solid ambition',[5] and he came to trust her implicitly.

According to Joan Morecambe, Sadie became a kind of second mother to Ernie:

I think she loved Ernie as much as she loved Eric. I really do. She'd never do something for one of them unless she could also do it for the other. That's the way she felt about it.

I'm sure that she thought that Ernie was a positive influence on Eric. *He'd* push him in the same way that *she'd* always pushed him. Eric wasn't like Sadie, he was more like his dad. Ernie was very much like Sadie – they were both very businesslike, very determined characters.[6]

So attached, in fact, did Ernie become to his surrogate family that, whenever he had the chance to relax for a few days, he chose to do so with the Bartholomews in Morecambe rather than the Wisemans in Leeds.

It was, perhaps, inevitable that Eric and Ernie, now that they spent most of every day together, living almost like brothers, should develop an unusually deep kind of mutual understanding. Each would finish the other's sentences, seeming to know what he was thinking and feeling, and each would try his best to make the other laugh. They never tired of telling jokes, singing songs and imitating all of the other acts. Sadie, at first, was amused by all of this, but after enduring a succession of increasingly loud, long and boisterous sessions on the way to and from each performance her patience was wearing thin. When, late in November 1940, the show reached the recently blitzed city of Coventry, she was at her wit's end.

They had to commute each day from Birmingham – the site of their previous engagement – because the digs that Sadie had booked for them in Coventry had been destroyed by one of the bombs. If this was not bad enough, an additional problem was that the twenty-one-mile train ride each day was frequently disrupted and delayed by the damage that had been caused by the Blitz. Sadie, trapped in a stationary carriage with two hyperactive teenagers endlessly repeating comic routines to each other, could stand it no longer: why, she asked them, did they not channel their energy and talent more constructively by working together on a double-act that might actually help their careers as well as provide her with just a little peace and quiet? Both Eric and Ernie, it appears, thought this to be an inspired idea.

It started out, according to Ernie, as merely 'a hobby, a sideline which we would work on in addition to the solo spots we each had'.[7] Within days of Sadie's suggestion, however, they had already worked out a basic routine, comprising of a few gags ('adapted' from Moon and Bentley's repertoire) and a soft-shoe shuffle to the tune of 'By the Light of the Silvery Moon'. They had also, with the speed and the ease that they would later come to be noted for, shaken hands on the ground rules for their professional association: everything was to be split down the middle, fifty-fifty, and it was never, ever, to matter who got the laughs (the only thing that mattered, they agreed, was that *someone* should get the laughs). Even Sadie was a little taken aback by the extent to which her suggestion, which had only been semi-serious in the first place, had captured their imaginations, but, once she saw how well they worked together, she became, as always, totally committed to their cause.

Ernie Wise would say that Sadie was 'the key element' in the development of their act.[8] While they continued to concentrate primarily on their solo acts – which, as Ernie reminded Eric, were still the things that earned them their wages – Sadie studied the other performers, scoured old joke books for suitable material, thought about possible props and bits of comic business, and watched and listened attentively as they rehearsed tirelessly in front of her. The great quality she felt that both of them possessed was that of professionalism: 'They always worked very hard. It was perfection or nothing.'[9]

Ernie became the straight-man, said Sadie, because 'he was the good-looking personality boy', and Eric became the comic, 'because he could look like a vacant American college dude in glasses and a big fedora hat'.[10] They based their style, to begin with, on the rapid and rather soulless cross-talk associated at the time with Abbott and Costello, and their homage went as far as assuming American accents. Their early material would inevitably have a patchwork quality about it, incorporating the radio-oriented puns of Askey and Murdoch:

| ERNIE | (*points to a coat hanger*) What's that? |
| ERIC | A hanger. |
| ERNIE | What's it for? |
| ERIC | An aeroplane. |

and the considerably more louche humour of the music-hall:

ERNIE      What are you supposed to be?
ERIC        I'm a businessman.
ERNIE      A businessman doesn't walk like that.
ERIC        You don't know my business.[11]

After several months of sustained effort ('we lived, ate and slept the double-act'[12]) they – and Sadie – felt that they were ready. They approached Bryan Michie in the hope that he might consider allowing them to perform the act within the existing show. Although he seemed to like what they could do, he remained non-committal: Jack Hylton, he said, would have to see it first, and he was next due to visit the show when it reached Liverpool in the summer of 1941. 'Leave it to me,' announced Ernie. 'I'll tackle Mr Hylton.'[13] He did, and Hylton, after suggesting a few changes – the most significant of which involved using another song, 'Only a Bird in a Gilded Cage', to complement their soft-shoe shuffle[14] – instructed Michie to remove one of the acts from the bill so that Eric and Ernie could have their chance.

The double-act of Bartholomew and Wise duly made its début on the night of Friday 28 August 1941[15] at the Liverpool Empire. Sadie, standing next to Jack Hylton, watched proudly from the wings. Even though their material was blatantly unoriginal (their later exchange – ERNIE: That's an Old Vic type joke./ERIC: I was there when old Vic told it – would have served as an apt evaluation of the antiquated nature of the affair), the audience, according to Sadie's account, was sufficiently impressed to award her two 'ardent and hard-working little troupers' a 'marvellous reception'.[16] The show was due to move on to a week-long engagement in Edinburgh,[17] and Hylton decreed that the double-act, in addition to Eric and Ernie's existing solo acts, was, for the time being, to remain on the bill.

It took a while, none the less, for the partnership to find a regular spot in the show. Bryan Michie, fearful of incurring the wrath of the other mothers – some of whom could make formidable opponents – by appearing to indulge the whims of Sadie's two boys, was hesitant at first. He only slipped the double-act on to the bill when he felt that he had a good enough reason to do so. There is no doubt, however, that Michie believed that it was worth persevering with – although not, he felt, with the names 'Bartholomew and Wise'. He suggested either 'Barlow and Wise' or 'Bartlett and Wise',[18] but neither sounded right to Eric and Ernie.

The matter was settled, eventually, when the tour reached the Midlands – Eric would remember the venue as being in Nottingham,[19] Ernie in Coventry.[20] According to most sources, the American singer Adelaide Hall and her husband Bert Hicks were appearing on the same bill as Eric and Ernie when Sadie encountered them backstage. 'We're trying to think of a name for Eric,'[21] she explained. Hicks is reputed to have suggested that Eric should follow the example of an old friend of his who, in a similar situation, had assumed the name of his home town of Rochester in Minnesota. According to Michael Freedland,[22] who ghostwrote Morecambe and Wise's 1981 autobiography *There's No Answer to That!*, Hicks was referring to Eddie Anderson, the song-and-dance man who found international fame in the role of Jack Benny's gravel-voiced butler, Rochester. The only answer one can give to this assertion is a non-committal 'yes and no': Anderson *was* an old friend of Hicks, and he *did* come to be thought of as originating from Rochester, but, in reality, he had been born in Oakland, California, and one of Jack Benny's writers had created the character called 'Rochester' long before Eddie Anderson ever came to audition for the role.[23] What we *can* be sure of is that Sadie and Eric acted on Hicks' basic advice and decided to change his name to Eric Morecambe. Ernie, perhaps overwhelmed momentarily by the spirit of adventure that was in the air, came close to changing *his* name to that of 'Eddie Leeds',[24] but, in a cool hour, he realised that 'Morecambe and Leeds' sounded too much like a railway return ticket, and he thought better of it.

They would later discover that even this new combination was not without its own little drawbacks – Morecambe was frequently misspelt as 'Morecombe'[25] and, on at least one miserable afternoon during summer season, a compère shouting out to the audience, 'Who goes with Morecambe?' received the sarcastic reply, 'Heysham!'[26] Both Eric and Ernie agreed, however, that it had the same kind of auspiciously euphonious feel to it as 'Laurel and Hardy', and so, in the autumn of 1941, a new double-act called 'Morecambe and Wise' was born.

One advantage that they had over most of the famous double-acts they hoped one day to emulate was that their partnership had been formed at such an early stage in their careers. Unlike, say, Laurel and Hardy, who had come together when Laurel was aged thirty-seven and Hardy thirty-five, or Abbott and Costello, who had met when Abbott was thirty-six and Costello twenty-five, Morecambe and Wise formed their professional partnership when Morecambe was only fifteen and Wise not quite sixteen, before either had acquired a fixed identity or style, and they could grow together unencumbered by the baggage of earlier associations. Whereas many of their heroes had been obliged to work against their individual pasts, Morecambe and Wise would have the luxury of being able, from the very start, to work for their long-term collective future.

'There's no such thing as an original to start with,' Eric Morecambe once remarked. 'You start by copying and once you've built up confidence and worked hard enough, the real person begins to come out.'[27] Morecambe and Wise had plenty of good double-acts to copy; the early forties were auspicious years for the format. Britain, for example, could offer Flanagan and Allen, Clapham and Dwyer, Murray and Mooney, Elsie and Doris Waters, Naughton and Gold, the Western Brothers and the increasingly popular Jewel and Warriss. America offered Burns and Allen, Olsen and Johnson, Hope and Crosby (intermittently), Laurel and Hardy and, then at their commercial peak, Abbott and Costello. Although Morecambe and Wise studied all of the British acts carefully (and, indeed, they would retain such a strong sense of affection for Flanagan and Allen that in the early seventies they would record a tribute album of their songs[28]), they drew most of their inspiration from the American double-acts that they watched on the movie screen.

Abbott and Costello, they always said, started them off: 'They were *the* double-act of the time.'[29] Eric and Ernie would go together to see each of their movies as soon as they were released: *One Night in the Tropics, Buck Privates*,[30] *In the Navy* (1940); *Hold That Ghost, Keep 'Em Flying* (1941); *Ride 'Em Cowboy, Rio Rita, Pardon My Sarong* and *Who Done It?* (1942). They were viewed and reviewed, their accents copied and best routines memorised and not so subtly revised.

For the next two or three years, Morecambe and Wise *were*, in their own minds at least, Abbott and Costello. Eric was Lou, slow-witted and submissive, and Ernie was Bud, dapper and domineering. They had the same hats turned up at the front, the same catchphrases ('I'm a *ba-a-a-d* boy!') and they tried their best to employ the same kind of breathlessly aggressive style of delivery. Years later they would revive one of these old routines for their television show:

| | |
|---|---|
| ERIC | Lend me two pounds. One'll do – now you owe me one. |
| ERNIE | I don't understand. |
| ERIC | Lend me two pounds. One'll do – now you owe me one. |
| ERNIE | I don't understand. |
| ERIC | Well, I'll show you. Ask me for two pounds. |
| ERNIE | Lend me two pounds. |
| ERIC | There's two pounds. How much have you asked for? |
| ERNIE | Two pounds. |
| ERIC | How much have I given you? |
| ERNIE | Two pounds. |
| ERIC | How much do you owe me? |
| ERNIE | Two pounds. |
| ERIC | Thank you.[31] |

The lightning pace of such routines did not just provide Morecambe and Wise with a fashionably dynamic act; it also prevented potential hecklers in the audience from ever getting a word in edgeways. Later on, as their confidence grew, they would look more to the character-based humour of Laurel and Hardy, a far warmer and more nuanced style of comedy, with the cheerfully diffident Laurel's dazed-looking double-takes, the courteously pompous Hardy's quietly despairing stares at the camera, and a shared attitude to bachelorhood that was coexistent with their nature as perpetual schoolboys. It would be an important change of direction for Morecambe and Wise, because at the heart of Laurel and Hardy was an immutable friendship, whereas at the heart of Abbott and Costello was a simmering hatred, and Morecambe and Wise, like Laurel and

Hardy, were able to make people *care* about them rather than – as was the case with Abbott and Costello – merely respect them.

Morecambe, according to Wise's account, was somewhat reluctant initially to play the dopey comic to Ernie's sophisticated straight-man: 'There was a part of Eric that longed to be a sort of Cary Grant figure, and part of him that resented being the comic while the straight man had the style.'[32] If Morecambe did have any reservations about his role then they soon faded away – perhaps because of the laughs that he was getting – and the act settled down along the conventional lines of comic and feed. Sometimes, as the tour started to wind down and several members of the cast drifted away, they teamed up with Jean Bamforth as 'Morecambe, Bamforth and Wise', and sometimes they reverted to the double-act. Whatever the situation warranted, they worked and they reflected and they learned. By the end of 1941 they had built up the act to last seven minutes – or ten if they chose to work slowly. Their confidence was high, which was just as well, because early in 1942, as a result of a precipitous decline in fortune at the box-office, Jack Hylton decided to close the show: in future, they would have to fend for themselves.

Although Morecambe and Wise, full of youthful optimism, expected London agents to be queuing up for their signature, Sadie Bartholomew knew better. They were still known as 'child discoveries', and there were currently no shows that were in need of such performers. They would have to learn to be patient. Eric returned very reluctantly to Morecambe, where he found a job working a ten-hour day in the local razor-blade factory. Ernie, unwilling to go home to Leeds and convinced, in spite of the redoubtable Sadie's judgement to the contrary, that someone just *must* be ready to find him a slot in another show, tried his luck in London. He lodged with a Japanese family of acrobats while he searched through the showbusiness papers in the hope of spotting an opening. Variety in the capital, however, was now virtually at a standstill on account of all the bombings, and eventually Ernie was left with no alternative but to return to Yorkshire and find work on a local coal round.

Throughout the three months during which they were apart, however, Morecambe and Wise kept in touch with each other, and, at the end of that period, Ernie, unable to stand the situation any longer, went to stay with Eric in Morecambe. Reunited, they tried seaside concert parties, working men's clubs and all the agents in the area, but there were no engagements to be had. They were saved, yet again, by Sadie. Seeing how no adversity seemed to shake their resolve to resume a career in showbusiness, she decided to accompany them to London and get them their chance. It was an extraordinary act of faith on her part, not to mention a serious financial sacrifice at an uncertain time, but it was certainly appreciated by both Eric and Ernie.

With Sadie at their side they felt that something positive was always likely to happen. She was disciplined, imaginative and, when she needed to be, cunning, and she was certainly tireless in the pursuit of her goals. After finding the three of them a flat – in Mornington Crescent – she took them to see an agent[33] she had heard of in Charing Cross Road. The agent did not offer to sign them up, but he did make the suggestion that they might go round to the Hippodrome[34] in Cranbourne Street on the following Monday and attend the auditions that were being held for a new show, *Strike a New Note*.

George Black, the show's producer, knew Ernie Wise from the days when they used to meet at Angmering-on-Sea. He had heard a few favourable reports about Morecambe and Wise in recent months, but, when they auditioned before him, he seemed less than enthusiastic. 'How much are you earning these days, boys?' he asked. Wise, belying his growing reputation as a shrewd negotiator, answered honestly, 'Oh, about £20 between the two of us.' Black smiled and said, 'Right. I'll give you that!'[35] The failure to follow the bargaining ritual of naming an exaggerated sum before accepting, with mock reluctance, a lower but still very satisfactory offer was, at such an early stage in their careers, understandable. This was not, however, the last of their disappointments: Black did not want the double-act at all, he revealed, but just the two of them as individuals 'doing bits and pieces'.[36]

They were crestfallen. Ernie, with the daring stubbornness for which he would later become famous, responded: 'Mr Black, if you don't want our act, I don't think we are really interested.'[37] Black – not to mention Morecambe – was somewhat taken aback by the sheer impudence of this, but, quickly regaining his composure, he made a minor concession: if the second comic in the show, Alec

'Mr Funny Face' Pleon, was ever indisposed, the double-act could take his place. At that, they shook hands with Black and went off with Sadie to celebrate their first engagement in over three months.

*Strike a New Note* opened at the Prince of Wales Theatre on 18 March 1943. The programme heralded 'George Black and the Rising Generation', and, inside, an insert read: 'HERE IS YOUTH. These boys and girls have been gathered from every part of the country. All are players of experience, needing but the opportunity to make themselves known. They have worked, they have learned; this then is their chance to show what they are worth.'[38] The cast included the comedian and singer Derek Roy, the South African musical comedy performer Zoe Gail, Bernard Hunter, Betty and Billy Dainty and the dancer Johnny Brandon, but, without any doubt, the stars of the show very quickly became the brilliant comedian from Birmingham Sid Field and his excellent straight-man Jerry Desmonde.

Field was hardly a representative of 'Youth'. He had been touring the provinces for years, largely unknown to Southern audiences and critics, and now, suddenly, at the age of thirty-nine, he found himself being hailed as the proverbial 'overnight success'. He was a comic with a gift for dialects ('I'm not drinking that *sterf*!') and his own personal repertory of characters: the spiv 'Slasher Green', the camp photographer, the would-be snooker player, the unteachable golfer, the music professor and the quick-change artiste. 'No more naturalistic clown walked the land,' wrote Kenneth Tynan of him, adding that now, with the assistance of the admirably disciplined and unselfish Jerry Desmonde, he appeared beyond comparison: 'Nobody has done such things before on our stages'.[39] Another, very experienced, critic said of that first night:

> Never before have I heard such gales of laughter and applause whirling through a theatre . . . The man in front of me laughed so helplessly that he had to be carried out, and given first aid. I, myself, felt weak with mirth. I was sure that every man and woman was longing to shout to the comedian on that stage: 'For mercy's sake, stop! You'll kill us with laughter.'[40]

It was a good show to be a part of. Although neither Morecambe nor Wise had much to do, and Alec Pleon's health – in spite of daily prayers to the contrary from Eric and Ernie – remained depressingly hardy, both of them realised that there was a priceless education to be had from watching two inspired performers like Field and Desmonde, and they also appreciated the fact that the sight of such a successful show on any performer's *curriculum vitae* – regardless of how minor a role they may actually have played in its popularity – was guaranteed to impress prospective employers. They relished the opportunity to bask vicariously in Fields' newly won celebrity: any star who happened to be visiting London at the time seemed to make a point of seeing the show, and among the visitors backstage whom Eric Morecambe and Ernie Wise encountered were Clark Gable, Jimmy Stewart, Deborah Kerr, Alfred Hitchcock and George Raft. On one memorable occasion, Adolphe Menjou complimented Wise on his typically spirited impression of Jimmy Cagney singing 'Yankee Doodle Dandy' (which proved, of course, sufficient encouragement for him to reprise the performance at regular intervals during the next thirty years). They also met innumerable West End stars at drinks parties hosted by Wendy Toye, the show's choreographer.

Throughout all of the seductive hubbub of this brightly unfamiliar showbusiness world, Morecambe and Wise continued to work diligently to promote their critically neglected double-act: 'At least *we* loved our act,' said Wise; 'we thought it wonderful and were prepared to do it anywhere, anytime, at the drop of a hat.'[41] They played several dates at the American officers' club in Hans Crescent, off the Brompton Road. They stood in at short notice for indisposed acts on local Variety bills. They even played in people's front rooms – anything to keep in practise and keep being noticed. They also managed during this period to make their very first radio appearances together when the BBC broadcast a special version of *Strike a New Note* on 16 April 1943, followed in May and June by a 'spin-off' series, *Youth Must Have Its Swing*, on the Home Service.[42] In spite of their persistence, however, not everyone was convinced that the double-act had a future. Wendy Toye, for example – who had watched them perform both in the theatre and, slightly less willingly perhaps, in the middle of one of her soirées – continued to regard their partnership with a certain amount of scepticism. 'I was very fond of both of them,' she would recall, 'but I did all I could to separate them':

I remember saying to Eric, 'You know, Eric, you're such a wonderful comedian, you ought to be your own stand-up comedian,' and I remember taking Ernie to one side and saying to him, 'That lad's holding you back – you ought to be a solo song-and-dance man. You'd go straight into musicals and do very, very well.' They stuck together, thank goodness, but just think: I nearly put a stop to that great double-act![43]

Ernie Wise, by this time, was quite impervious to such advice. His often overlooked yet invaluable capacity for loyalty was very evident here – as, indeed, it would be at several crucial points later on in the act's development – and even Sadie was surprised by how utterly devoted he had become to his partner. Although Wise was, strictly speaking, the one with the more distinguished past and still, some were saying, the more obviously promising future, he seemed perfectly content to let Morecambe berate him at regular intervals for his supposed inadequacies. 'You're not a bit of good,' Morecambe would shout at him after he had forgotten or mistimed a tag line. 'You're supposed to have learnt this.'[44] On one occasion, Sadie, feeling that things had gone too far, intervened by ordering Eric to leave the room. Ernie's reaction, she would recall, was entirely unexpected:

> Ernie turned to me. 'You know, you shouldn't have interfered.'
> 'But I'm sticking up for you,' I said.
> 'Don't you see? Eric is only trying to make me the best feed in the country, like Jerry Desmonde is to Sid Field,' Ernie said.
> 'Make *you* the feed!'
> 'Yes, and shall I tell you something? He's going to be the best comic in the British Isles.'
> Later I told Eric this, and there was no more temperament from my son, never another cross word, never any more argument.[45]

Their progress, however, was interrupted abruptly on 27 November 1943 with the arrival of Ernie Wise's call-up papers. He had the option of joining the Army, the Merchant Navy or going down the mines; he decided to join the Merchant Navy, anticipating an exotic life at sea but ending up ferrying coal from Newcastle and South Shields down to Battersea Power Station in London for the Gas Light and Coke Company. Eric Morecambe, who was not due to be called up before May of the following year, stayed on in *Strike a New Note* until it finally broke up. He then found a job in ENSA (Entertainments National Service Association[46]) as a straight-man to a Blackpool comic called Gus Morris (brother of the more talented Dave Morris). When his papers did eventually arrive, he opted to become a Bevin Boy,[47] volunteering to work down the mines in Accrington for Hargreaves Collieries. Eleven months later, however, he was classified C3 with what was referred to at the time as a touch of heart trouble and was sent home to Morecambe – first to rest and regain his good health, and then to work once again at the local razor-blade factory.

Sadie Bartholomew, scanning the 'wanted' columns in *The Stage*, came across the news that a touring show was looking for a straight-man for its principal comic, Billy Revell. Morecambe got the job, earning £12 per week, and the show ran for six months. Wise was also doing his best to keep himself involved in showbusiness during this period. He had been made part of a permanent reserve of seamen available for placement anywhere in the world at short notice, but, as there were often long breaks between postings, he took the opportunity to keep in touch with a circle of agents and producers who provided him with a steady supply of short-term engagements around the country (billing him as a 'boy from the brave merchant navy'[48]). When at last he was discharged in April 1945 he returned to a civilian life still committed to the world of entertainment but now, it seemed, as a solo performer. During his prolonged separation from Morecambe the idea of being part of a double-act had lost some of its appeal – perhaps because of a belief that, at eighteen, it was time to redeem a once promising but recently stalled career, and a solo act might prove more adaptable than a double-act in an increasingly competitive market-place.

Morecambe and Wise might never have reformed their partnership had not, yet again, another happy accident intervened. Sadie had taken Eric to London in order to assist him, once again, in his search for work.[49] After finding a suitable base in theatrical digs owned and presided over by a Mrs Nell Duer at 13 Clifton Gardens, in Chiswick, they had started the onerous task of scouring all of the showbusiness papers and visiting innumerable agents in the hope of chancing upon an opening. One day, as they walked purposefully along Regent Street, Eric glanced across to see the familiar figure of Ernie Wise waving frantically from the other side of the street.[50] When Sadie discovered that Ernie was staying in a rather insalubrious form of accommodation in Brixton, she invited him to move in with her and Eric: 'You two might as well be out of work together as separately,' she remarked.[51]

As it happened, Sadie soon found work for both of them in a peculiar hybrid of a show that went under the grandiose title of *Lord John Sanger's Circus & Variety*. This particular combination of Circus and Variety had been popularised in the Victorian era by a colourful showman called 'Lord' George Sanger.[52] George Sanger's involvement had ended abruptly back in 1911 when his manservant – in an egregious fit of pique – battered him to death with a hatchet, but the tradition stretched on into the post-war years under the watchful eye of the similarly self-ennobled 'Lord' John. The reasoning behind the project was that provincial audiences, starved of top-class professional entertainment and lacking the grand music-halls of the big cities, would welcome the opportunity to sample the respective delights of Circus and Variety within the same makeshift arena. It seemed, as both Morecambe and Wise would later remark, a good idea at the time.

Sanger's brother, Edward – who had known Morecambe and Wise since the days when he assisted Bryan Michie on *Youth Takes a Bow* – booked each of them separately for the tour. Wise was selected first – as a comic – on a wage of £12 per week. Morecambe, much to his and Sadie's surprise, was selected as Wise's 'Wellma boy' – the straight-man who starts with the self-assured line 'Well, my boy, and what are *you* going to do tonight?' only to be insulted by the irreverent comic – on a wage of £10 per week.[53] It was, at least as far as Eric and Sadie were concerned, a less than satisfactory arrangement, but, as no alternative engagements were available and no money was coming in, there was nothing to do but to accept it.

The show travelled from place to place in a slow procession of converted RAF trailers, putting up the big top on village greens or in conveniently situated fields. On arrival, the performers themselves were obliged to set out seats for up to seven hundred people, put down the sawdust, set up the stage and help sell the tickets. Included on the bill were Speedy Yelding, 'Britain's Greatest Clown'; the singer Mollie Seddon, 'A Thrill to Your Eyes, Ears & Heart'; Peter, 'The Equine Marvel'; Evelyn's Dogs & Pigeons; a quartet of dancers, 'The Four Flashes'; Eric Morecambe and 'England's Mickey Rooney', Ernie Wise. Each prospective member of the audience, as he or she pondered the 3s. 6d. that was the price of admission, was urged not to 'fail to visit the pets corner after the performance'.[54]

It did not go to plan. Audiences – when there were any – arrived expecting an event of Barnum and Bailey proportions, and were not at all pleased to discover that, far from a fierce menagerie of lions, tigers and elephants, the best that Sanger could offer them was one tired-looking donkey, a silent parrot, two chubby hamsters, a team of performing dogs, a shivering wallaby and a ring-tailed lemur. In between these so-called Circus acts the Variety performers, such as Morecambe and Wise, filled-in with, in their own words, 'unfunny sketches and unfunny jokes'.[55]

Sanger himself lived and travelled in comfort, but his employees were not so fortunate. Each battered old trailer contained a canvas bucket as a make-shift sink and the artistes' bathroom at each site consisted of a hole in the ground surrounded by a malodorous canvas screen. Meals were cooked over campfires and served on dented tin plates to be consumed under a nearby tree. Although both More-cambe and Wise came from relatively humble backgrounds, they enjoyed their creature comforts none the less and loathed this sharp taste of life on the road. Their lowest point came when they were obliged to perform in front of an audience made up of just six young boys, all of whom were seated right at the very back of the cavernous marquee in the cheapest of the seven hundred seats.

Things went from bad to worse. First, everyone was obliged to take a cut in their wages: Morecambe's went down to £5 per week, Wise's to £7. They were then forced into taking part in an increas-ingly embarrassing and exhausting succession of gimmicks, the last of which involved the marquee being converted into a booth through which the audience wandered while the company somehow managed to perform no fewer than seventy-three shows in three days. Finally, to the disappointment of no one except, perhaps, Sanger himself, the show came to a premature end in October 1947 at Nottingham's Goose Fair. Morecambe and Wise, tired-eyed and chap-fallen, dragged themselves back to their old digs at Mrs Duer's in Chiswick and pondered their immediate future.

It was, without doubt, a bleak time for both of them, but perhaps especially so for Ernie Wise, whose career had begun almost a decade before in such propitious circumstances. Mickey Rooney, by the tender age of twenty-two, had made over a hundred two-reel Hollywood comedies, been handed a special Academy Award and had married the very beautiful Ava Gardner, whereas Wise – supposedly Britain's answer to America's indefatigably spirited child star – was at the same age stuck in cramped digs in Chiswick, single, unemployed and in very grave danger, it seemed, of being forgotten. Sadie Bartholomew, by this time, had returned home to Morecambe, which left the two of them feeling even more insecure and uncertain. Sadie's endless stream of sobering proverbs – such as 'Marry a girl and your fourpenny pie will cost you eight pence'[56] – continued to echo in their heads. Neither of them yet drank alcohol, nor did either of them have any time for any of the other recreational pursuits associated with their profession, and each tried as best he could (Wise with greater success than Morecambe) to save what money he possessed, but it was still a period of considerable anxiety.

Out-of-work Variety acts, they soon discovered, tended to converge on an unprepossessing Express Dairy café that was situated, in those days, near the Leicester Square tube station. Every morning the place would be packed with the usual mixture of young, old, ex- and would-be performers, each cupping their hands gratefully around hot mugs of tea and announcing loudly but unconvincingly that they had, or would soon have, or would definitely have for certain in a month or two, a marvellous job lined up for themselves. Overhearing these fanciful monologues, Morecambe and Wise noticed that agents seemed to be crucial figures in this profession, and, as a consequence, they made up their minds to find one for themselves as soon as possible.

One way to attract an agent, they were told, was to get oneself on to the bill of certain key Variety theatres – such as the Metropolitan on the Edgware Road, the Brixton Empress or the East Ham

Palace – which functioned as shop windows for new talent, but, paradoxically, Morecambe and Wise found it hard to secure a booking at such places without the assistance of an agent: it was a vicious circle. Determined somehow to get noticed, and to improve their act in the process, they lowered their sights and started accepting anything: one-off club and pub nights, masonic dances, a very rough week at a rowdy venue near Barry Docks in Cardiff, the odd date with ENSA, the occasional day's work at the Nuffield Centre (a club just off Piccadilly where ex- and current servicemen could perform), a short tour of the American army camps in Germany and even the occasional private party. The only bona fide Variety engagement they attracted during this depressingly barren period was for a week at the Palace, Walthamstow in March 1948, but even this modest success was diminished by the fact that because one of the other, more established acts was called Vic Wise and Nita Lane, Morecambe and Wise – to avoid causing any confusion – were billed as 'Morecambe and Wisdom'.[57]

The one bright spot amidst all of this gloom was the kindness of their landlady, Nell Duer. Although there were stretches of fourteen to eighteen weeks at a time when Morecambe and Wise were unable to pay their rent she remained remarkably sympathetic to their plight, telling them just to pay her when they could afford to. When things became intolerable they would take an overnight bus to Morecambe and stay with Eric's parents for a week – sometimes a fortnight – before returning, well-fed and with a couple more pounds in their pockets, to mount yet another attempt at finding long-term employment. Oddly enough, however, neither Morecambe nor Wise was ever tempted during this time to seek a job outside of showbusiness: 'The matter was never broached between us,' said Wise. 'We were Variety artists; we were pros. To consider anything else would have been heresy.'[58]

The post-war years were not easy times for any young entertainer to find employment. London was besieged by returning ex-servicemen nursing hopes of establishing (or, in a few cases, re-establishing) themselves in showbusiness: comics such as Peter Sellers, Spike Milligan, Harry Secombe, Michael Bentine, Eric Sykes, Graham Stark, Jimmy Edwards, Tommy Cooper, Benny Hill, Dick Emery, Eric Barker, Harry Worth, Frankie Howerd, Tony Hancock,

Max Bygraves, Bruce Forsyth, Norman Wisdom, Alfred Marks and Arthur English were all back in the capital and all clamouring for an opportunity to show an agent or impresario or a BBC producer just what they could do. It was, to say the least, a fiercely competitive time. Morecambe and Wise, in the course of their long-running search for work, gravitated – like most other comics – to the one place in London where they felt they might be given the chance to perform: the Windmill Theatre in Great Windmill Street, Soho. The Windmill, since 1932, had been permitted by the Lord Chamberlain to present – as one element of the Variety revues known as *Revudeville* – nude tableaux on condition that all of the young women remained perfectly still for the duration of each presentation, the stage lighting was always 'subdued' and no 'artificial aids to vision' were permitted in the auditorium.

Its owner, Vivian Van Damm (known to everyone as 'VD'), was involved in every aspect of the running of the theatre, from opening the office mail to hiring and firing the artistes. He was sufficiently proud of the fact that the Windmill had remained open throughout the war to coin the slogan, 'We Never Closed', and he was sufficiently astute not to object when this was perverted into 'We Never Clothed' by the habitués of the shows for which his stage was famous. Ann Hamilton, who in 1959 became the five hundredth Windmill Girl and would later become the regular female presence in *The Morecambe & Wise Show*, recalled: 'He would always say that we were in showbusiness – with the accent on show. Because of censorship he never told the girls to show everything, but, as far as the Fan Dance was concerned, he certainly wasn't averse to the fans being lowered to reveal the breasts, which could always be explained away as an unfortunate slip.'[59]

Van Damm preferred to employ women as young as fourteen and a half, but he would often continue to employ them until it was deemed that they required the support of a bra. He was part benevolent father figure, part seedy voyeur: on the one hand, he would see that all of his young women were groomed in elocution, make-up, deportment, dress sense and singing and dancing skills, and also that each of them received free medical and dental treatment; on the other hand, as Ann Hamilton recalled:

He would never knock when he entered the dressing-room. It was so hot in there, deep in the bowels of the earth where the girls had to change, that people would sit around with nothing on – because it was all girls together. He knew that, and he always walked straight in, but we'd know when he was on his way because you could hear his little shuffling footsteps and smell the smoke from his cigar.[60]

Although Van Damm took great delight in erecting a mahogany plaque outside on the corner of his theatre that listed all of those 'Stars of Today Who Started Their Careers in This Theatre', most if not all of the performers whom he claimed to have either 'discovered' or 'nurtured' were, in reality, regarded merely as tolerable distractions during the brief intervals that separated one nude tableau from the next. His policy was to audition almost anyone who applied to him, but he was by no means as easy to please as has sometimes been implied (his daughter, Sheila, estimated that around 75 per cent of all applicants were rejected[61]). Harry Secombe, who worked there during 1946, remembered the sad fate suffered by a Chinese illusionist who was auditioned by Van Damm: after spending most of the previous night sweating over his routine and preparing all of his elaborate props and painting on his intricate make-up, he shuffled on to the stage, bowed slowly with Chinese precision, and was just about to open his mouth when Van Damm shouted 'Thank you', thus forcing him to shuffle all the way back off again in silence.[62] In his time, Van Damm also dismissed, with a similarly curt 'Thank you', Spike Milligan, Roy Castle, Charlie Drake, Norman Wisdom, Benny Hill and Kenneth Tynan. It was, however, as Morecambe and Wise discovered, one of the least worst places to attract the attention of a relatively good London agent. Peter Prichard, a regular visitor in those days, remarked:

It became the nursery for comedians in this country. We used to go, as agents, to spot the talent. We could hardly ever get a seat, because there was the famous 'Windmill Jump' – these guys would sit in the audience for two or three shows and, eventually, if one in the front got up to leave, all the others would jump over the seats to try and get the front seat.[63]

Michael Bentine played there as part of a novelty double-act called Sherwood and Forrest:

> An *extraordinary* place. *Very* small theatre. *Very* small stage. And statuesque and *beautiful* girls. And, of course, the mackintosh brigade came in, as you can imagine, with a copy of *The Times*, and, shall we say, 'engaged' with other interests, and suddenly one of the girls would come off after a scene and say, 'Row 3, seat 26: *dirty bastard!*' The guy would be picked up by the muscle men and thrown out the door.[64]

It seems likely that Morecambe and Wise knew at least a little about this when one Sunday morning they went up to Van Damm's tiny, dark and smoke-filled office near the top of the theatre, but they were determined to find somewhere that allowed them to perform. Van Damm sat at his desk (behind which the observation 'There are No Pockets in Shrouds' was spelled out in large Gothic type) and puffed on his cigar as they went through all ten minutes of their current act. He nodded his approval – a slow nod to register only mild approval – and informed them that he was prepared to engage them for one week (six shows a day, from 12.15 p.m. until 10.30 p.m.) with an option for a further five weeks. Their wage, between them, was to be £25.[65] Their rehearsal – the 'undress rehearsal' as some called it – went rather well, and they both looked forward to the first week of what they hoped would be a long run in the show.

They were swiftly disabused of such dreams. On the Monday they found themselves having to follow an act which involved bare-chested male dancers squeezed into tights, cracking whips and adopting vaguely Wagnerian poses, female dancers performing their various jetés with the assistance of 'artistic' lighting effects, and, of course, several stationary nudes. They had seen nothing like this at the Bradford Alhambra. When the curtain came down they walked out on the stage to complete silence, and started their act in what they hoped would soon be familiar as their 'usual way' – 'Hello, music lovers!' They continued for seven painfully elongated minutes, facing an impersonal mass of crumpled broadsheet newspapers, before walking back slowly and disconsolately to the shelter of the wings. The same thing happened throughout the rest of the day – at the second house, and the third, fourth, fifth and sixth – each appearance eliciting complete indifference. Tuesday, if anything, was worse still, and after the last of their appearances on the Wednesday they were met at their dressing-room by a grim-faced Ben Fuller, the burly stage-door keeper who was often called upon to act as the harbinger of bad news.

Fuller, ominously silent, escorted the two of them up to Van Damm's office. 'I'm sorry,' said Van Damm with a wan smile. 'My patrons seem to prefer the other double-act, Hank and Scott.'[66] 'Hank' was a young Tony Hancock, and 'Scott' was the pianist Derek Scott. 'I'm not taking the option up, boys,' Wise recalled Van Damm informing them 'with all the charm of a surgeon telling you the worst',[67] and they were instructed to leave at the end of their first and only week. Although both of them knew that their act had failed to capture the imagination of the Windmill audience, they also knew that most of the other acts had failed to capture the imagination of the Windmill audience, and so they were, therefore, 'devastated' by this news;[68] not only was it a cruel blow to their self-esteem, but it was also, more seriously still, a major setback to their hopes of finding an agent. Fortunately, Wise – with typically sound business sense – recovered enough of his composure before leaving to ask Van Damm if he would object if they sought to limit the damage to their professional reputation by placing a notice in *The Stage* to the effect that Morecambe and Wise were leaving the Windmill purely because of certain prior commitments. Van Damm smiled and acceded to the request and they parted company on as amicable terms as the sorry circumstances would allow.[69]

They played out the remaining days of that week and hoped that someone might see them and show some interest before they returned once again to obscurity. One agent did just that: Gordon Norval. Norval agreed to help them out, and he arranged for them to perform two spots the following Monday evening in yet another nude revue – this one entitled *Fig Leaves and Apple Sauce* – at the Clapham Grand. Unbeknown to Norval, however, there was a problem: they had agreed to perform two spots rather than one because the fee was £2 10s. more, but they were well aware of the fact that they had only twelve minutes of material rehearsed and there was no possibility that any number of Jack Benny-style pauses and silent stares could stretch this out for the duration of two whole spots. Panic, remembered Wise, was, in the absence of Sadie, 'the mother of our invention':[70] locking themselves away in their digs and forcing themselves to come up with new ideas, they managed, just in time, to have a second act ready.

Arriving at the Grand on Monday evening, they had a plan fixed firmly in their minds: they would use their 'proper', well-rehearsed act for the first spot, win over the audience and then rely to some extent on that residual warmth to waft the remainder of their wafer-thin material through to the end of their second spot. The plan, however, had to be aborted after their first, disastrous appearance saw them walk off to the arctic chill that was known locally as the 'Clapham silence'. Now all they had to rely on for their second spot was the residual indifference of the audience. They began with a barely concealed feeling of terror. What saved them was the unlikely success of a routine they had recently devised that featured Ernie teaching Eric how to sing 'The Woody Woodpecker's Song'; Eric, assured that he had the most important part, was eventually reduced to the famous five-note pay-off ('Huh-huh-huh-*huh*-hah!') at the end of each verse. It was a routine that they would return to later on in their career (with such songs as 'Boom Oo Yatta-Ta-Ta'[71]) and it certainly proved popular with the audience that night – so much so, in fact, that not one but several theatre managers rushed backstage after the performance with offers of work. It was a turning-point in the development of the partnership. Suddenly, after the bleakest of times, they were in demand.

Nat Tennens, who ran the Kilburn Empire, booked them 'act as seen' for the following week. This time they reversed the order, starting with their new material. It was again so successful that it even seemed to breathe new life into the old act, and their confidence started to soar. They went on to make another appearance at the Clapham Grand, and the week after that they returned to the Kilburn Empire – only this time at the top of the bill. They were now earning £40 per week, and Gordon Norval, the man who had been in the right place at the right time to help them, became their first agent.

Their next stroke of good fortune, however, was prompted not by Norval but by a young dancer, Doreen Blythe, who had worked with Morecambe and Wise in Lord John Sanger's touring show as one of 'The Four Flashes'. She had grown sufficiently close to Wise to have carried on a correspondence with him once that unfortunate enterprise had ended. She was now appearing in another touring show, this one run by an impresario named Reggie Dennis, and – knowing of Morecambe and Wise's recent success, and keen to find a way to spend more time with Ernie – she urged Dennis to go to see the double-act with a view to booking it for the next leg of the tour. He did so, and, liking what he saw, offered them the chance of almost a year's continuous work in the revue he was calling *Front Page Personalities*. They accepted, and, on tour for the next eleven months, they polished their technique, improved their material and, for the first time, began to really relax in front of an audience.

It was towards the end of this tour, in the autumn of 1950, that Morecambe and Wise came to the attention of an extremely influential London-based agent called Frank Pope.[72] Pope seemed to have a hand in most of the important theatre circuits in Variety. He was responsible, for example, for booking all of the acts for one of the key circuits associated with post-war Variety: the so-called 'FJB' circuit, set up by an enterprising man by the name of Freddy J. Butterworth after purchasing a dozen ailing cinemas and turning them back into music-halls.[73] Pope also supplied acts to the far mightier Moss Empires circuit, which at that time owned around twenty-four large and well-run theatres (including the prestigious London Palladium). There could, therefore, have been few more suitable agents for Morecambe and Wise at this particular point in their career, because, as Morecambe noted: 'In the early days our ambition [had been] to be second top of the bill at Moss Empires. Not top. At second top it was not your responsibility to fill the theatres,'[74] and now, as Wise would recall, they were feeling so optimistic that they were ready to think of making the top of the bill at the Palladium 'the apex of our ambition'.[75] After coming to an amicable agreement with Gordon Norval, Pope signed Morecambe and Wise to what was a sole agency agreement (guaranteeing them a minimum of £10 per week but obliging them to give him at least six months' notice if they ever wanted to opt out). They now, at long last, had the kind of backing that would provide them with a reasonably full diary of top-flight Variety dates, a rewarding annual pantomime season as well as the chance to become recognised as fully fledged stars.

'Eric always said to me', Wise would recall, 'that the reason we were so successful was that we stayed together. A simple enough statement,' he added, 'but also very profound. We were together from 1943, and from that moment on we sweated at it.'[76] By the early 1950s the tremendous amount of effort that they had invested in their act was finally starting to pay dividends, but with these rewards came a new set of challenges: as Wise observed, in the old days of the 'youth discovery' shows, 'the audiences are on your side. They say, "Oh, aren't they good for amateurs!" But it's when you turn professional – *that's* when it becomes *hard*,'[77] and not all of the audiences they now performed to were particularly easy to please. Southern audiences could sometimes be a problem, treating Northern comics with a certain amount of suspicion until they were satisfied that they could understand the accent and identify with the humour. Northern audiences, though obviously more suited in those days to an act like Morecambe and Wise (who by that time had abandoned their Abbott and Costello-style mannerisms and looked instead to Northern comics like Jimmy James and Dave Morris for inspiration[78]), could still be hard work (indeed, the old story about the two grim-faced Northerners watching a comic perform his act – 'He's not too bad, is he?' says one of them. 'He's all right if you like laughing,' mutters the other – was made real for Harry Secombe when a member of the audience in Blackpool 'congratulated' him by remarking, 'You nearly had me laughing when you were on, you know'[79]). Clubs – even the relatively plush ones that were starting to emerge – were never among the favourite venues of Morecambe and Wise, in part because of the added burden of having to compete with the bar for the audience's attention (one inexperienced comic, struggling in vain to win over an unresponsive crowd, was interrupted by a very loud and entirely unexpected roar of approval: 'Don't worry,' the chairman told him. 'It's just that the hot pies have come . . .'[80]).

By far the most intimidating venue on the circuit, at least as far as English comics were concerned, was the notorious Glasgow Empire. When Cissie Williams – the formidable woman in charge of all bookings for Moss Empires – sent Morecambe and Wise up there

for a week-long engagement, she paid them an extra £10 – not just
to cover the rail fare and any other expenses but also to compensate
them for the trauma of playing to such an aggressive audience. Everyone felt the same: whenever Jimmy James arrived at Glasgow station
he would step out slowly on to the platform, sniff the air suspiciously,
pause for a moment and say, 'By 'eck, it's been a long week!'[81]
Glaswegians loved American singers, but had serious reservations
about most other performers and had a special aversion to acts from
south of the border. 'They always opened the show with kilts –
McKenzie Reid and Dorothy and their accordions, or a cripple,'
Wise recalled. 'There's nothing more guaranteed to get sympathy
than a crippled man playing an accordion, especially if it's a bit too
heavy for him,' added Morecambe knowingly.[82] It was actually the
sudden and premature death of McKenzie – he was run over by a tram
– that led to the famously harrowing experience of Des O'Connor ('It
was the time', Morecambe observed, 'when Des really stood for
desperate'[83]). McKenzie's widow, Dorothy, insisted that the show
must go on, and, with the assistance of a young nephew, she duly
appeared, night after night, singing such songs as 'Will Ye No' Come
Back Again?' to uncharacteristically emotional audiences. O'Connor,
unfortunately, was obliged to follow this act, night after night, with
his amusing gags and humorous anecdotes about life down in Step-
ney. Each night proved worse than the previous one, until Dorothy,
overcome with grief, cut short her act and thus forced O'Connor,
coiled up in fear in a corner of his dressing-room, to hurry out
and attempt to entertain a full-house of three thousand choked-up
Glaswegians. He panicked, telling one story twice, then telling the
end of the next joke before its beginning, all to an increasingly
threatening kind of silence. With his mouth now bone-dry and his
forehead dripping with sweat, he started to sway slowly from side
to side and then, according to a gleeful Eric Morecambe, passed out:
'He said, "Ladies and gentlemen, I-I-I-" *Bumph!* He fainted! Actually
fainted! From nerves, you know. And he was lifted up under the
backcloth, and he was carried slowly off. His legs disappeared and
he had "Goodbye" written on the soles of his shoes . . . I think that's
the best he's ever gone!'[84]

When Morecambe and Wise came to make their début in Glasgow, they, like the vast majority of English comics who preceded

A new double act: Morecambe at sixteen, Wise at seventeen, in 1942.

With pantomime and a summer
season each year, they said, 'We knew
we were unlikely to starve.'

Blackpool, 1953: it was during their summer here that the BBC's Ronnie Waldman offered them their first TV series.

A brand-new bright tomorrow? A post Running Wild appearance in 1957 on the BBC's Double Six.

The Fab Four
meet the fab
two: The Beatles
on The More-
cambe and Wise
Show in 1964.

Morecambe and
Wise, watched
by Joan and
Doreen, sign a
three movie deal
with the Rank
Organisation in
1964.

The Intelligence Men (1965): Francis Matthews, William Franklyn and Terence Alexander provided admirable support.

'Run down that corridor and fall down . . .' director Robert Asher shares his idea with a doubtful-looking cast.

Cannes, 1965: with Lionel Jeffries, Tony Curtis and Suzanne Lloyd.

A triumphant return: outside Television Centre in 1968.

Bill Cotton Jr.: the man who brought Morecambe and Wise back to the BBC.

The first BBC2 series in 1968: not only Eric and Ern, but also Sid and Dick.

The poet of Tarryassan Street: scriptwriter Eddie Braben
at home in Liverpool.

Morecambe and Wise with producer/director John Ammonds in the BBC rehearsal room.

The multi-talented Ernest Maxin: producer/director, choreographer and creator of musical comedy.

them, walked off, shoulders slumped, to the terrible, flat sound of their own footsteps. As they passed the sad-faced fireman who always stood in the wings, he fixed them with a knowing look, flicked what little was left of his cigarette into a sandbucket and muttered, 'They're beginning to like you.'[85] Occasions such as these, though hard to take at the time, helped them to continue to improve: 'We needed to have experienced the knocks, working in Variety,' Wise reflected. 'It chipped the rough edges off us.'[86] What that arduous process allowed was the emergence of something original from within the merely banal, taking the old music-hall cross-talk routine, technically elaborate but remorselessly anonymous, and adapting it to suit their own very special relationship. 'I think there's a simple revolution in what they did,' Michael Grade remarked:

> If you ever saw the double-acts of the thirties, forties or fifties, they never really talked *to* each other – they would only com-municate to each other through the *audience*, and they would 'work out', as I call it. Whereas Eric and Ernie were the first double-act to develop an intimate style, they were the first to talk *to* one another, to *listen* to one another. The old acts had this big yawning distance that separated them from each other. Eric and Ernie were the first ones to really have a proper relationship on the stage.[87]

Their partnership had already lasted longer than most before they had even worked their way to the brink of stardom, and both of them appreciated the elective affinity that had drawn them so closely together. 'There was a kind of lightning thing that went between us,'[88] said Wise. 'We were, I suppose, like brothers who rarely, if ever, quarrelled and could cope with what was an intense partnership without any fear of its overheating.'[89]

It was the sort of relationship that was well suited to the special demands of the next medium that they intended to master: radio. They understood the importance of radio to their future because Variety was on the decline and the mass audience could now only be reached, it seemed, through the wireless. They also recognised the remarkable power of the medium and its potential for transforming regional stars into national celebrities. This had been underlined in

1949 by the extraordinary public reaction to the death of the comedian Tommy Handley ('a national calamity' according to the *Spectator*), when thousands lined the streets of London to watch his funeral cortège and hundreds more went on to St Paul's Cathedral for the national memorial service.[90] Getting on to the wireless – and then staying on it – was the goal of any ambitious performer at this time.

Succeeding in radio, however, was something that was easier said than done. Eric Morecambe would look back on it as 'the hardest medium of all',[91] and not without reason. The BBC was still uneasy about Variety's lively unpredictability, and no performer was acceptable unless he or she could prove themselves to be adaptable. The infamous *Green Book*, devised in 1949 by the then Director of Variety Michael Standing as a guide for producers, writers and artistes, sought to preclude the slightest hint of a nudge or a wink from broadcast Variety. 'Music-hall, stage, and to a lesser degree, screen standards', the guide announced, 'are not suitable to broadcasting,' and all producers and performers were warned that any 'crudities, coarseness and innuendo' that might pass as entertainment on the Variety circuits were most certainly not acceptable on the wireless. There was, for example, an 'absolute ban' on trade names and 'Americanisms', as well as jokes about lavatories, effeminacy in men and 'immorality of any kind', suggestive references to honeymoon couples, chambermaids, fig leaves, prostitution, 'ladies' underwear, e.g. winter draws on', 'animal habits, e.g. rabbits', lodgers, commercial travellers, prenatal influences, 'e.g. "His mother was frightened by a donkey"', and marital infidelity. If one had to err, the *Green Book* advised, it was best to err on the side of caution: '"When in doubt, take it out" is the wisest maxim.'[92]

Such draconian rules left many popular comics with barely any material fit for broadcasting, and led to a few, such as Max Miller, being banned on several occasions (one of them prompted by his notorious optician joke: 'That's funny – every time I see F, you see K!'). Writers, too, were often driven to despair by the multiple objections to perfectly inoffensive scripts (Frank Muir, for example, remembered being ordered by Charles Maxwell, his producer, 'to remove any mention of the word "towel" from a script Denis Norden and I had written for *Take It From Here* because it had "connotations"'[93]), causing them either to devise increasingly devious ways of outwitting the censors (an example being the regular appearance of a character named 'Hugh Jampton' – from the rhyming slang 'Hampton Wick' meaning dick – in *The Goon Show*) or else to focus more on comic situations than on comic lines.

Morecambe and Wise took some time to find a way into this imposing and unfamiliar medium. Since contributing to *Youth Must Have Its Swing* they had found further radio work hard to come by – just a couple of editions of the talent show *Beginners, Please!* (one in 1947, the other in 1948) and a single edition of *Show Time* in 1948. It was only in 1949, after writing a hopeful letter to Bowker Andrews, a BBC producer based in Manchester, asking him to consider using them in his Northern Variety broadcasts and reassuring him that 'we are also both North Country',[94] that they started participating on a more regular basis. In 1952,[95] after taking part in an edition of *Workers' Playtime*, they were invited to be guests on one of the best Variety shows transmitted by the BBC's North of England Home Service:[96] *Variety Fanfare*, produced by Ronnie Taylor. Taylor (who was also responsible, as a writer as well as a producer, for such popular programmes as *The Al Read Show* and Jimmy Clitheroe's *Call Boy*) was one of the BBC's great nurturers of young talent on both sides of the microphone. His support for Morecambe and Wise over the next few years would prove to be invaluable. His initial enthusiasm for them, however, was only translated into a firm offer of further appearances after they had planted an entirely spurious story – via a third party – which suggested that the producers of the show's more prestigious Southern equivalent, *Variety Bandbox*, were on the verge of offering them a residency. Anxious not to let one of his discoveries be poached by his colleagues in London, he proceeded to book Morecambe and Wise for a succession of *Variety Fanfares*.[97]

'That was the big break for us,' Eric Morecambe would say of this run of appearances, 'even if it was only Northern Home Service in those days.'[98] It served, said Ernie Wise, a dual purpose: on the one hand acting as 'a useful safety net to cushion us when we fell on relatively lean times',[99] and, on the other, as a showcase that might attract the attention of other producers. 'We had to get *in* on something,' Morecambe recalled. 'We had to get *in* somewhere and make this niche for ourselves.'[100] In fact, in spite of their later claims to the contrary, they would have much preferred to have established this niche in London, on *Variety Bandbox*, rather than in Manchester, on *Variety Fanfare*.

*Variety Bandbox*, a weekly show that ran from the early forties through to the early fifties, was for many years the high-spot of the BBC's Variety output and, as Morecambe and Wise well understood, the ideal programme for up-and-coming performers. It billed itself as the show that presented 'the people of Variety to a variety of people', and it had an excellent reputation for discovering and promoting new talent (such as Derek Roy, Frankie Howerd, Beryl Reid, Dick Emery, Max Bygraves, Tony Hancock, Reg Dixon and Bill Kerr). The failure of Morecambe and Wise to impress the show's producer, Joy Russell-Smith, is a topic that is passed over in somewhat perfunctory fashion in their autobiography,[101] and Eric Morecambe once claimed – erroneously – that they never did manage to appear on the show,[102] but in fact – as the many letters preserved in the BBC's archives reveal – they bombarded Russell-Smith and her colleagues for just over four years with their requests for a chance to take part.

The first letter (signed, like all subsequent ones, 'Morecambe and Wise' – as if the two of them were one person) was sent on 2 April 1948, and several more followed in quick succession until Joy Russell-Smith wrote back on 3 June inviting them for a private audition at Studio 2 of the BBC's lofty Aeolian Hall in Bond Street on the afternoon of 10 June. No record of how they fared has been preserved in the archives, but, according to Eric Morecambe,[103] Russell-Smith told them that they sounded 'too much like Jewel and Warriss' and advised them to try again 'in five years' once they had developed a more distinctive style. Far from resigning themselves to being pigeonholed as 'Northern comics', however, they persisted in writing both to Russell-Smith and to anyone else whom they felt might offer them an opportunity to take part in such a prestigious show. On 28 November 1950, writing from the Palace Theatre, Plymouth, they contacted Bryan Sears, another *Bandbox* producer:

Dear Sir,

We shall be at Finsbury Park Empire next month followed by Empire Shepherd's Bush. We shall then be at the Hippodrome

Golders Green for Pantomime which means we shall be in London for the next 12 weeks.

We know you are a very busy man and may not be able to get along to see us. So do you think you could arrange to give us an audition with a view to booking us on Variety Bandbox?

We know you are always looking for comedians, so how about giving us a chance to show our ability?

Thanking you,

Sincerely,

Morecambe and Wise[104]

Frank Pope, once he became their agent, added his weight to this long-running campaign, writing on 16 July 1951 to the then Deputy Head of Variety Pat Hillyard and urging him and his producers to at least go to see his clients perform. Someone *did* act on this request, because the following note, scribbled in pencil, was sent by a producer to Patrick Newman, the bookings manager, shortly after:

I saw this act last night and came to the conclusion that the act is, of necessity, too visual, and certainly with too much slap-stick for Sound.

Television might well be interested in them, but there is nothing I could say is outstanding. Some of their patter struck *me* as being rather aged.[105]

It seems likely that Morecambe and Wise – and Frank Pope – remained ignorant of this negative verdict, because their campaign continued unchecked, and culminated in the decision of May 1952 by John Foreman, one of the last producers of *Variety Bandbox*, to include them in one of the programmes. It proved to be something of a pyrrhic victory – the show closed down for good in September that year – but it served as a testimony to the extraordinary tenacity exhibited by Morecambe and Wise in their pursuit of what seemed to them a worthwhile goal.[106]

Throughout this period their broadcasts from Manchester were winning them some influential admirers, and Ronnie Taylor, in particular, was coming rapidly to the conclusion that they might well be worth the gamble of a show of their own. It was the very thing that they had been hoping for: a chance to grow, to develop a lasting relationship with a large radio audience, to amass a substantial body of work and negotiate a pay-rise – 20 guineas per show – into the bargain. The first series of *You're Only Young Once* (*YoYo* as it became known) started on 9 November 1953[107] with Ronnie Taylor as producer, Frank Roscoe as writer and a cast that included Pearl Carr and Deryck Guyler. The shows consisted of short sketches, a musical interlude and a guest star, and were based – very loosely – around the framework of a detective agency run by Morecambe and Wise. When the second series began the following year, Taylor – now Head of Light Entertainment at BBC North – handed over the production duties to one of his most talented young protégés, John Ammonds. Ammonds had joined the BBC in 1941, acquiring invaluable experience during the following thirteen years working in the BBC's Variety department at London, Bristol and Bangor before moving to Manchester and working closely with Taylor on a number of radio projects. Programmes were made at a very rapid pace in those days, and producers were often called upon to rewrite material – and sometimes, indeed, to conjure up material which had simply failed to arrive – shortly before a recording. Ammonds, in particular, had shown a real talent for this, and, as a consequence, he proved to be an enormously reassuring presence as Morecambe and Wise worked hard to improve on the basic format of the show.

'Frank Roscoe was a pretty good writer,'[108] Ammonds recalled, 'but he was always working on about three scripts at once – he was doing a script for Ken Platt and other stand-up comics, and one for us. There'd always be parts of the script we'd have to work on once we got it. I'd change this and that, add the odd line here and there, and, of course, the boys – Eric and Ernie – would turn up with all these big old joke books they carried everywhere with them and attempt to fill up the script with gags from those.'[109] Ammonds struck up a friendship with them that would last for the rest of their careers:

> We got on well from the start. They weren't just good performers, they were nice people, too. Easy to work with – very keen, quick learners and very, very hard workers, even way back then.

Of course, they were much more 'Northern' in those days. Eric was playing this gormless type of character, and his accent was fairly strong, whereas Ernie sounded pretty much then as he did years later on the TV shows.[110]

*YoYo*'s style of comedy was, even in 1954, slightly dated – owing more than a little to the kind of fast, pun-packed cross-talk (itself influenced by American radio shows) popularised in Britain by the writing team of Bob Monkhouse and Denis Goodwin – but it retained an engaging spirit:

ERIC      Men: when you go to a dance, are you a wall-flower? When you get up to leave at the end, is the seat you've been sitting on warmer than you are? Instead of dancing like Astaire, do you dance like you've just tripped over one?

ERNIE     Well, then, what you need is the Swanee Dancing Course. It comes to you by post in six easy lessons, and here are some of the useful hints: '*How to improve your chasse*' –

ERIC      Eat less.

ERNIE     '*How to make women fall for you on the ballroom floor*' –

ERIC      Trip 'em up.

ERNIE     '*What to do when a lady says "Excuse me"*' –

ERIC      Offer her a mint.

ERNIE     Yes, men, the Swanee Dancing Course is what you need. So why not enrol today? Just send us five pounds in notes to Morecambe and Wise. And those of you who have already sent us the money, don't forget our slogan –

ERIC      Up the Swanee!

The relative success of this series, and the financial remuneration (by now 30 guineas per show) that went with it, was a great source of comfort to Morecambe and Wise at a time when they were not only still working hard on the Moss circuit but had also both recently married – Wise, at long last, to Doreen Blythe, and Morecambe, as soon as he possibly could, to a young soubrette called Joan Bartlett.[111] 'The first sighting', Joan recalled, 'was at a bandcall on a Monday morning at the Empire in Edinburgh, because Eric always used to say they should put a plaque there saying, "Eric Morecambe Fell Here".'[112] 'I saw this tall girl,' he said, 'who was very beautiful with wonderful eyes, and who had a wonderful kind of sweetness which made your knees buckle ... I knew at once that she was the one for me for life. It was as sudden as that.'[113] Although Joan, once she had sensed something of his ardour, was not exactly encouraging – 'I thought, "Not a hope – nope, fat chance he's got!" '[114] – he remained undeterred. In Joan he saw not just a very attractive woman but also someone who would be a calming influence on him, some- one who – as a talented performer herself – would understand his anxieties and offer him encouragement as well as constructive criti- cism. 'How on earth anyone could possibly have worked all *that* out in a single glance is beyond me,' she laughed, 'but that's the kind of man he was, and the pursuit was on.'[115] Morecambe – as decisive and as determined about some things as he was indecisive and irreso- lute about others – persisted, and on 11 December 1952, a mere six months after that first meeting, they were married. Ernie Wise, who was best man, spent the day in a kind of daze: 'I think it was the fact that it had all happened so quickly,' Joan recalled. 'He was like somebody is after an accident, in a state of complete shock!'[116] Doreen, who had already chided Wise for his lack of a sense of romance,[117] was probably quick to help him recover sufficiently to see the obvious moral to be drawn from this episode, and, after five years of courtship, they too were married on 18 January 1953.

These were brightly propitious times for Morecambe and Wise. Settled and secure in their personal lives, increasingly successful in their professional lives, they must have taken special pleasure in responding to an offer of more work at the end of 1953 from the once-unapproachable BBC by sending back a telegram that read: 'VERY SORRY UNABLE TO ACCEPT = MORECAMBE AND WISE.'[118] The tables had, at long last, been turned. Now producers had to pursue Morecambe and Wise. They were starting to be billed as 'stars of radio', and, after just one brief appearance on a televised Variety show, they were even being touted in some quarters as 'the white hopes of television humour'.[119].

Such talk did nothing to unnerve them. 'There is nobody making a mark on television now,' Eric was reported as having said. 'We would like to try.'[120] They did not, in fact, have long to wait. They were appearing at the Winter Gardens in Blackpool when Ronnie Waldman, the man responsible for BBC TV's light entertainment output, arrived backstage at their dressing-room with the offer of a television series of their own. 'Ernie and I looked at each other,' recalled Morecambe, 'and we said, "We'll do it!"'[121]

# TELEVISION

*We are privileged if we can work in this, the most entrancing of all the many palaces of varieties. Switch on, tune in and grow.*
DENNIS POTTER

WOMAN     *Have you noticed?*
MAN         *What?*
WOMAN     *There's no TV in this room.*
MAN         *Then why does it exist?*

THIRD ROCK FROM THE SUN

## CHAPTER V

# A Box in the Corner

*I've been in the theatre, in cabaret, in films and television – and this is
undoubtedly the toughest job of them all.*
RONNIE WALDMAN

*'Light Entertainment.' What is it meant to be the* opposite *of? Heavy
Entertainment? or Dark Entertainment?*
ERIC MASCHWITZ

'When we start analysing our good fortune,' reflected Ernie Wise
from the vantage point of the late 1970s, 'a great deal of it comes
from the fact that we came in at the tail-end of the music-hall era,
and we were young enough to start again in a new medium, television.'[1] Eric Morecambe agreed: 'If we hadn't gone through the
transition, we would have ended up as unknowns doing the whole
of the North in the clubs.'[2] Neither man was joking: surviving that
transition had been the greatest challenge of their entire career. Morecambe and Wise took a long time to discover how to make the most
of television, and television took an even longer time to discover
how to make the most of Morecambe and Wise.

Television, in fact, took quite a long time to discover how to
make the most of television. The fitful nature of its early evolution
(launched in 1936, suspended in 1939, relaunched in 1946) did nothing to help matters, and neither did its exorbitant cost (the price of
a post-war 'budget-model' set was in the region of £50, while the
average weekly industrial wage was just under £7) and its limited
reach (full, nationwide coverage would not be achieved for several
more years because tight Government control of capital expenditure
restricted the construction of new transmitters).[3] Even by the early

fifties, when the 'television public' was estimated to be around 22 per cent of the UK population[4] and the number of people with television licences was beginning to increase significantly,[5] the BBC continued to exhibit a certain ambivalence in its attitude to the fledgling medium, slipping its television schedule at the back of the *Radio Times* as a four-page afterthought. This unhappy situation owed more than a little to the intransigence of Sir William Haley, Director-General of the BBC between 1944 and 1952. Television, noted Grace Wyndham Goldie (a producer at the time), was Haley's 'blind spot. He appeared to distrust and dislike it and his attitudes ... seemed to be rooted in a moral disapproval of the medium itself.'[6]

Hours of viewing, like hours of public drinking, were limited in the interests of temperance: transmitters were turned on at three o'clock in the afternoon during weekdays and five o'clock on Sundays; the screen was blank between six and seven o'clock each evening in order to ensure that parents were not distracted from the task of putting their children to bed; and transmission ended at around half past ten on most nights or, on very special occasions, at quarter to eleven. Even in between programmes there were often soothing 'interludes' featuring windmills turning, horse ploughs ploughing, waves breaking and potters' wheels revolving. For long stretches of the day there was nothing on offer other than a blank screen or the sound of something from one of Mozart's less sensational compositions.

The situation changed dramatically in 1953 with the televised coverage of the coronation of Queen Elizabeth II. Until that moment, remarked Peter Dimmock (the man responsible for producing the historic broadcast), the Establishment, and a fair proportion of the general public, had looked upon television 'as a bit of a peep-show'.[7] Then, with a near-flawless production involving the use of 5 cameras inside Westminster Abbey and 21 cameras situated at 5 separate sites outside, the visual power and immediacy of the medium was, at last, underlined. More than 19 million people – 53 per cent of the adult population of Great Britain – saw the television coverage, with 7,800,000 viewing in their own homes, 10,400,000 in the homes of friends and a further 1,500,000 in cinemas, halls and public houses.[8] It was the first time that a television audience had exceeded a radio audience. The critics reacted positively – the *Star* declaring that 'television had cornered the right to put its name first over the BBC door', and Philip Hope-Wallace announcing, 'This was television's Coronation'[9] – and so, judging from the BBC's own research, did the public at large – 98 per cent of television viewers (as opposed to 84 per cent of radio listeners) declaring themselves to be 'completely satisfied' with the coverage.[10]

The BBC now had in Sir Ian Jacob, its Director-General between 1952 and 1959, a man who appreciated both the potential of television to capture the public imagination and also the duty of programme-makers to realise that potential. 'A public service broadcasting service,' he wrote, 'must set as its aim the best available in every field . . . [This] means that in covering the whole range of broadcasting the opportunity should be given to each individual to choose freely between the best of the one kind of programme with which he is familiar, and the best of another kind which may be less familiar.'[11] By the early fifties, a fair proportion of the BBC's output had begun to live up to that high ideal, with its dramatic productions in particular succeeding in bringing classic literature to an increasingly broad audience ('We are only a working-class family,' wrote one group of grateful viewers after seeing a performance of *King John*. 'You showed our England to us. Please give us more Shakespeare'[12]). When it came to Variety, however, the results were, to say the least, unsatisfactory.

The BBC's inaugural *Variety Party* of 7 June 1946 was merely the first in a long line of embarrassingly ham-fisted attempts at forcing the bright, brash exuberance of the halls to fit the gently flickering intimacy of the small screen. Peter Waring, looking more like a slightly shifty butler than the insouciant comic that he was, set the tone when he stood stock-still in his over-starched white tie and tails and welcomed viewers with the confession: 'I must say, I feel a trifle self-conscious going into the lens of this thing.'[13] The problem was that television did not know what to *do* with Variety. The BBC had been quick enough to devise ways of adapting theatrical plays for the small screen, but it seemed at a loss when confronted with the task of taking a form as bold and as boisterous as music-hall – which thrived on its interaction with a lively audience – and distilling it into a medium intended to be experienced in the privacy of the family living-room. The BBC, without any doubt, *meant* well, but for a long time its attitude to Variety seemed akin to that of Mr Gladstone's attitude to fallen women – more a case of pity than passion.

The newspaper critics, though unimpressed by the standard of many of the programmes being transmitted, were at least prepared to persevere with the enterprise. The *Observer*'s J. P. W. Mallalieu, with his distinctive brand of hopeful ambivalence, urged his fellow viewers not to give up:

We select, and what we select more often than not stimulates rather than depresses. I do not mean that what we select is always good. It is often terrible. But even in what is probably the most terrible BBC effort of all – the portrayal of Variety – when I have seen a performer on my screen I am more interested than I would otherwise have been to see him on the stage, if only to find out whether he is quite as bad as all that.[14]

It was a different story in America, where Variety was the least of commercial television's worries. Unencumbered by any public service ethic, and urged on by sponsors eager for it to embrace all of the most glittering prizes thrown up by the more demotic of pursuits, American television was busy raiding vaudeville, radio and Hollywood in search of available talent. By the early fifties it could boast such hugely popular shows as *The Honeymooners, I Love Lucy, The Burns and Allen Show, The Jack Benny Show, The Milton Berle Show, Your Show of Shows*, Groucho Marx's *You Bet Your Life, The Abbott and Costello Show, The Colgate Comedy Hour* and Ed Sullivan's increasingly influential *The Toast of the Town*. It was estimated during this period that television stations in New York were devoting as much as 53.3 per cent of their time to light entertainment – in stark contrast to the BBC in London, which was devoting as little as 15.7 per cent to the same kind of material.[15] This yawning disparity was underlined by the BBC's use of several US imports in its schedules. When, for example, *Amos 'n' Andy* was shown for the first time on the BBC in 1954, the *Daily Mirror*'s Clifford Davis greeted it with the warmest of praise, pointing out that such a 'slick, professional effort' served to make the Corporation's home-grown comedy shows seem 'puny by comparison'.[16]

It was, in some ways, an unfair comparison to make. For all the brilliance of the very best of American television's Variety output, it was still the case that the sheer crassness of the rest was closer to the norm, and even if the BBC had somehow found a way to raise the vast sums of money it would have needed to lure stars of comparable stature to its own studios it seems unlikely that many of them would have risen to the bait. Variety agents and managers – echoing their earlier reaction to the advent of radio – eyed television with considerable suspicion, believing initially that it represented little more than a particularly devious way of exhausting an entire career's worth of material in a single evening, and, as a consequence, hastening the decline of an already precarious business.

Undeterred by such predictable resistance, the BBC struggled on, but for some time yet Variety on television would continue to take the form of *televised* Variety rather than *television* Variety. The best examples of this – such as Barney Colehan's self-consciously antiquated *The Good Old Days* (which ran from 1953 to 1983), and Bill Cotton Senior's band shows – had their own unpretentious charm, and the BBC would learn to produce them far more impressively than any of its future competitors ever would, but the worst – such as the half-hearted *Café Continental* (a cabaret-style show based at the Chiswick Empire) – seemed merely superfluous. It was not obvious, however, how the situation might best be remedied. One problem was that Variety performers tended to fail on television because they would over-project, forgetting the fact that now, instead of reaching out above all the hubbub to the back of the cavernous halls, they were supposed to be reaching directly into someone's cosy front room. Jimmy Grafton, one of the producers obliged to deal with this issue, recalled a typical example: 'Ethel Revnell, who was a very strong cockney character comedienne in Variety, was in an early [television show]; we brought her in to play a character in a situation comedy, and she played it like a Variety sketch, expecting she was going to get a laugh when she came on, and grimacing at the audience. She was so much larger than life that we had to scrap the show.'[17]

The performers who survived the transition were those who had been both willing and able to adapt. Terry-Thomas, for example, was handed his own comedy series, *How Do You View?*, in 1951, and others, such as Frankie Howerd, Max Wall, Arthur Askey, Jimmy Edwards and Bob Monkhouse started to appear on a regular basis soon after. Terry-Thomas commanded £100 for each fortnightly show – and by 1953 this had risen to 140 guineas[18] – but most of those who were signed up at this time were placed on salaries that, compared both to radio and the most prestigious Variety circuits, were relatively modest. Ronnie Waldman – the BBC's Head of Television Light Entertainment – certainly did believe in the viability of television Variety, but he was subject to the same degree of financial limitations as his opposite number in radio, even though his expenses, of necessity, were far greater (as average programme costs for television in 1954 were £892 per hour[19]). As a consequence, promising radio stars, such as Bernard Braden, or up-and-coming screen stars, such as Norman Wisdom, tended to be too expensive to hire more than occasionally. 'Personality programmes', such as the very popular *What's My Line?*, proved to be far easier and cheaper to broadcast than Variety, as they had no need of well-written scripts or elaborate stage sets, and they also created their own television-bred celebrities, such as the notoriously brusque Gilbert Harding.

Waldman, however, was a determined man. Writing in the *Radio Times* shortly after assuming control of his department in 1951, he declared that he and his team of producers were committed to the creation of 'something that had never existed before the invention of television – something that we call Television Light Entertainment . . . Our aim', he continued, 'is now to try and bring the entertainment profession as a whole to believe, with us, that television does not mean the mere photographing of something that could be entertaining in a theatre or a cinema. Television demands a very high standard of performance and an immense degree of polish from its artists. Inexperience and lack of "authority" . . . are things with which the television camera has no mercy. Only the best is good enough for television.'[20] *His* department, he insisted, was going to be dedicated to the ideal of making 'as many people as possible as happy as possible'.[21] Eager to find new and exciting ideas with which he might invigorate his department, he set off on a fact-finding tour of the United States of America – 'to see how the other chap does it'[22] – taking in 114 different television programmes during a tour that took in New York, Connecticut, Illinois, California, Arizona and Nevada. What impressed him most was not the commercial aspect of American television, but rather its lack of embarrassment about the idea of *popular* television. On his return to Britain, Waldman was in a bullish mood: his ambition, he announced, was 'to give viewers what they want – but better than they expect it'.[23] By the beginning of 1954, he took great pleasure in drawing his colleagues' attention to the fact that the Light Entertainment department was now producing around 400 shows per year – 'a vastly greater output than that of any theatrical or film organisation'.[24] This was in spite of the fact that its full-time staff numbered no more than thirty seriously over-worked people. In the future, he concluded, there would be no excuse for a lack of variety in television Variety.

Morecambe and Wise were regarded within the BBC at this time as two of Waldman's protégés, but the irony was that their television career – like their radio career – began only after years of unanswered letters, abortive engagements and innumerable false dawns. They had actually been trying to appear on television since 1948 – the year in which Ernie Wise first resolved to subject the BBC's television producers and bookings managers to the same kind of remorseless letter-writing campaign that he had already begun to inflict on their radio counterparts.[25] On 21 April of that year, in fact, they were invited to an audition at Star Sound Studios near Baker Street in London; the report card has been preserved in the BBC's archives[26]:

MORECAMBE & WISE (Comedy duo)

| | |
|---|---|
| DESCRIPTION | 2 young men in 'Healthy Hank' & 'Lingering Death' make-up. |
| DATE OF AUDITION | 21 April, 1948. |
| PERFORMANCE | Cross talk, Inkspots impe[rsonation], Vocal finish with 'dance' movements. |
| TIME | 8 mins. |
| EXPERIENCE | Equity. Panto. B[roa]dcast. |
| REMARKS | Parts of this act might be suitable. Suggestive material & dancing together should be omitted. |
| [SCORE] | 8. |

Although this was judged to have been good enough to warrant a further invitation for a test 'under normal Television studio conditions, at Alexandra Palace, as soon as possible',[27] nothing came of it as far as actual television appearances were concerned. They did manage a brief appearance on *Youth Parade* in the autumn of 1951,[28] but it was not until *Stars at Blackpool*, in 1953, and their subsequent encounter with Waldman himself, that their luck really changed for the better.

Had Ronnie Waldman been a less understanding patron, Morecambe and Wise could easily have found themselves ostracised before their television career had really begun. While Waldman, from a discreet distance, was monitoring their development and making tentative plans to sign them up for a series of their own, Frank Pope, their agent, and George Campey, a journalist friend from the London *Evening Standard*, were allowing themselves to get carried away by their various efforts at publicising the act. Things came to a head when, due to some kind of failure of communication between Pope and Campey, an aggressively pro-Morecambe and Wise article by Campey[29] (which practically ordered Waldman to sign them up immediately, and even suggested what their salary should be) appeared several days *after* Waldman had assured them that he was very close to confirming the series for the 1954 spring schedules. Pope, fearing the worst, wrote to Waldman on 9 November 1953[30] – the same day as the appearance of the offending article – explaining that it had all been a most unfortunate mistake and apologising profusely for any embarrassment that might have been caused. Waldman, however, was more amused than angered by the unsolicited advice, and he continued as before with his plans for the series.

Morecambe and Wise had regarded Waldman's initial offer to them as representing 'a delirious moment',[31] and they had been young enough and ambitious enough to refuse to be unnerved by the various warnings they received from older performers once the news began to circulate. Ernie Wise recalled:

You will hear old pros tell you that the twenties were the heyday of music-hall, or Variety, as it became known, and that by 1939 it was already dying, that the cinema was killing it. Yet, when we started in 1939, Variety was booming. We believe that if anything killed Variety it was the war when a lot of brilliant acts disappeared and the Palladium embarked on a policy of using only American tops of the bill . . . [O]n top of that TV was in the ascendancy despite the pundits who scoffed at the new medium. 'TV will never kill Variety,' we heard so many say. 'Who'll bother to watch a screen when you can see acts live in the theatre?'[32]

The answer, Morecambe and Wise believed, was 'an increasingly significant number', and they were determined to make the most of the opportunity they had been handed to be in at the start of an exciting new era. They certainly *felt* as though they were malleable enough to adapt: they had done so once before, for radio, and saw no reason why they could not now do so again. They appreciated the fact that there was much that needed changing. Morecambe acknowledged that the act they 'had in music–hall had 15 to 20 minutes of material in it', which could have been used continuously for years on the circuit (because 'if a boy saw you doing a sketch when he was 15 he'd usually have completely forgotten it by the time he was 19'[33]). They needed a new one – several new ones, in fact – to satisfy the voracious appetite of television. Between them, they soon came up with a number of ideas – some drawn from personal experience, some from writer friends, and some from the trusted old joke books they carried everywhere with them – and so, when Bryan Sears, their new producer/director,[34] arranged to visit them in Sheffield, where they were playing, to commence prelimi-nary discussions, they looked forward to the meeting with more than a little confidence. It proved, however, to have been confidence misplaced.

Ronnie Waldman may well have been in charge of the BBC's Light Entertainment division, and he may well have believed fer-vently in breaking down the old cultural barriers that divided the North from the South, but not all of the producers underneath him were inclined to act entirely in accordance with his admirable ideals. Bryan Sears, for one, did not share his superior's optimism as far as Morecambe and Wise's future on television was concerned. The first thing that he did after having listened politely to all of their ideas was to tell them that none of them would work 'down South'. They should be aware, he informed them, that they had a serious problem, and the problem was that they came from the 'wrong' part of the country. Both Morecambe and Wise sat open-mouthed as Sears explained that they were unfortunate to be '"Northern" comics, [and] that a barrier of prejudice existed separating the North from the South and from Wales, Scotland and Ireland as well'.[35] This must have sounded somewhat surprising to performers who only recently had played to large and very appreciative audiences in various parts of London, and whose London-based agent was at that very moment busy responding to numerous requests for return engagements in such places as Bedford, Brighton, Oxford and Norwich. It would have seemed equally fanciful to those in the radio division of the BBCs Variety department who were more eager than ever to offer Morecambe and Wise further opportunities to appear on shows that were broadcast nationally. This, however, was television, and Sears was a television producer, and a good one at that, so they assumed that he must know what was best for them now.

Although one can question his reasoning, one can hardly doubt that Bryan Sears was committed to doing what he felt was most likely to make Morecambe and Wise's first television series a success. His primary goal, of course, was to produce a good show – rather than to ensure that Morecambe and Wise became stars – but it seemed logical to presume that by doing the former he would probably also be doing the latter. He informed them that they would require a great deal of help if they were to overcome all of the obstacles that were facing them, and that they would therefore need to be ready to make a number of compromises in order to benefit from the support that he and the rest of his production team were willing to offer. Morecambe and Wise agreed, although privately they were now considerably more apprehensive than before.

The pace of the preparations began to quicken. A list of possible titles for the series was drawn up and discussed:

*Hi There!*
*Hey There!*
*Side by Side!*
*Running Riot*
*Running Wild*

*Stand Well Back*
*Look Who's Here*
*Easy Does It*
*These Foolish Things*[36]

*Running Wild* emerged, eventually, as the unanimous choice. Sears, who possessed a bone-dry wit, also started sending Morecambe and Wise a series of well-intentioned but not always well-received 'tips' regarding their performance style, such as:

> With regard to the act itself, there is one very small point over which I am slightly concerned. Ernie's habit, admirable on the stage, of taking the audience into his confidence and laughing with them about Eric. On TV, this being a much more intimate medium, this could create quite the wrong impression, i.e., over-confidence – which certainly none of us would be feeling.[37]

As far as possible scriptwriters were concerned, Morecambe and Wise – or Bryan Sears – first contacted the in-demand – and reassuringly Southern – writing team of Denis Goodwin and Bob Monkhouse, but, for one reason or another, an agreement failed to materialise.[38] There was very little time, however, to search for other reliable sources of comic material; in the middle of February Sears asked Morecambe and Wise: 'Will you have a word with your other Script-writers . . . all contributions will be gratefully received. Time is pressing, as you know, and we must see something on paper within the next fortnight – and the first full script . . . in the next three weeks.'[39]

Sears arranged eventually for no fewer than six writers to be used on the shows, although the BBC's file on the series contains evidence of further contributions from several other sources.[40] A supporting cast was assembled: Alma Cogan – a great friend of both Morecambe and Wise – was installed as the show's resident singer. Other 'regulars' would include Ray Buckingham, another singer; Hermione Harvey, a dancer; and the Four in A Crowd, a close-harmony quartet. The up-and-coming cockney comedy actor Bernard Bresslaw was hired to appear in the first few sketches, and a number of other 'Southern' performers were sounded out as to their willingness to appear on subsequent shows as guest stars. Sears also did what he could to reassure Morecambe and Wise that, with this team behind them and after working hard at rehearsal, they could still look forward to an exciting and rewarding experience. Morecambe and Wise did their best, in return, to believe him.

As soon as they could complete their other engagements they made their way to London in order to prepare for the first show. Ernie Wise had bought a house in Peterborough, Doreen's home town, while Eric and Joan Morecambe, who were not yet in a position to purchase a home of their own, rented a house in Acton.[41] Exploring the unfamiliar interiors of the BBC studio at the old Shepherd's Bush Empire, observing other shows being made and introducing themselves to the various technicians and administrators with whom they would soon be working, their enthusiasm started to return. This, they reasoned, was, without any doubt, going to be an unforgettable adventure.

Ronnie Waldman – as positive now as he had been when he came to see them in Blackpool a few months previously – was a welcome presence, and several favourable newspaper previews, such as the following example, provided them with some positive publicity:

> The series will start in April and will comprise six shows, which will be presented once a fortnight until the end of June.
>
> Not only are Morecambe and Wise among the first northern comedians to get a regular series but they are also among the youngest – Eric Morecambe is 27, Ernie Wise 28. Their new contract comes immediately after the prediction of many TV critics that the pair will be the outstanding television discovery of 1954. Commenting on their opportunity today, Ernie Wise said: 'It's easily our biggest break so far, but it's also rather frightening.'[42]

It would take just one of these shows for Morecambe and Wise to discover just how frightening, and fickle, and cruel, television sometimes could be.

CHAPTER VI

# Running Wild

*In art the important thing is not that one takes eggs and fat, but that one has a fire and a pan.*
KARL KRAUS

*What do you think of the show so far?*
ERIC MORECAMBE

The first show of the series was set to go out 'live' on Wednesday 21 April 1954 at 9.40 p.m. It simply *had* to succeed: not just, or even primarily, for the sake of Morecambe and Wise, but also for the sake of the rest of that evening's schedule. Unlike the following year, when a second channel was made available,[1] in the spring of 1954 there were just two choices open to the viewer: to watch the BBC or to switch off the set. There was no obscure slot in the schedules to gamble on new talent, nowhere for novices to make their mistakes – either one sank or one swam. It was a terrible responsibility for any untried television performer, but, then again, it was also an extraordinary opportunity for a relatively unknown figure to become, overnight, a national celebrity.

The schedule for the evening of 21 April was as follows:

| | |
|---|---|
| 7.30 | *Newsreel* |
| 7.50 | *Coracle Carnival* |
| 8.20 | *Association Football: Aldershot vs. The Army* |
| 9.10 | *Gravelhanger* |
| 9.40 | *Running Wild* |
| 10.10 | *Indo-China: A Discussion* |

10.40   *News* (sound only)

10.45   *Closedown*

It was hardly – even by those conventions peculiar to mid-fifties programming – a particularly enticing bill of fare: *Coracle Carnival*, for example, pitted a team from Carmarthenshire against a team from Cardiganshire in a decidedly quaint sporting contest that consisted of fishing for salmon and paddling up and down a river in Roman-style boats; *Gravelhanger* was a dreary drama serial that had already incurred the wrath of several critics as a result of its pedestrian plot and leaden acting. The smug sobriety of the Indo-China dialogue was not designed to ingratiate itself with those viewers for whom the halls of revelry held far more appeal than did the halls of academe. Bryan Sears did his best, however, to turn the dullness of the surroundings to his own show's advantage: the current edition of the *Radio Times* quoted him as saying that he was looking forward to making the show in front of a 'real lusty-laughing audience' at the Television Theatre ('We could have had a Lime Grove studio, but you can't wake the echoes there'[2]) – the implication being that he could not guarantee that the viewers at home would *like* the show, but he could at least make sure that they would know when it was on.

At 9.39 p.m. on the day itself, it seemed as if everyone who knew of and liked Eric Morecambe and Ernie Wise was sitting expectantly in front of a television set and waiting to see two familiar figures appear in black-and-white within the ten-inch screen. George and Sadie Bartholomew sat together in Morecambe, Harry and Connie Wiseman in Leeds, Ronnie Taylor in Manchester, Ronnie Waldman in Wood Lane, Frank Pope in South London, Joan on her own in Acton and Doreen in Peterborough. Doors were shut, curtains drawn, telephones unhooked and fingers crossed: this was to be their special moment. At 9.40 p.m. precisely the title of the new show was announced and its stars introduced: 'Morecambe and Wise are "Running Wild"!' What followed – judging from the accounts of some of those who saw it[3] – was neither unmissable nor unwatchable: much of the material, certainly, was patently unoriginal, and the performances, perhaps, relatively uninspired, but at least there were none of the fluffed lines, mistimed entrances and embarrassing instances of complicated camera arrangements coming adrift that had plagued many other live shows of the period.

When the half-hour was up, the initial mood – at least among Morecambe and Wise's most loyal followers and friends – was one of cautious optimism: the first, nerve-racking challenge had been surmounted, and they would now be able to go on in future weeks to relax a little, regain some self-confidence and begin to develop a rapport with a regular audience. Just how Morecambe and Wise themselves were feeling at that moment is not entirely clear: exhausted, certainly, somewhat disappointed, perhaps, but by no means despondent – they knew that they could have done better, but they also knew that they could have done far, far worse.

It had, none the less, been a strange night. For the first time in their lives they could not be sure of what their audience – the audience at home – had really thought of them. They missed the immediacy of the authentic theatrical experience. There was no curtain call on television, no way of peering out at all the faces and listening to all the noise and applause. Even after the worst of times on stage – at the Clapham Grand, or the Windmill, or the Glasgow Empire – there had never been a feeling quite like this: a kind of gnawing bewilderment, as if one was somehow unsure as to whether one had just been present at a wedding or a wake. As they departed from their dressing-rooms, there was only the silence of the darkened studio and the emptiness of the over-bright corridors to accompany them on their way home. How many people had been watching the show? How many had laughed? How many had stared stoney-faced at the screen? How many had walked out or switched off? All that they had that night were questions.

Some unwelcome answers arrived early the following day along with the morning papers. Peter Black, the *Daily Mail*'s influential critic, had clearly been disappointed by what he had watched:

> *Running Wild*, a new comedy series starring Morecambe and Wise, began in favourable circumstances. It followed *Gravel-hanger*.
>
> On me, the mood of relief was shortlived. Still, so long as TV has only one programme we must be philosophical about light entertainment, and remember that *Running Wild* was designed for the guffaw rather than the chuckle.

What was alarming from the point of view of the comedians was that guffaws, even from an invited audience within the television theatre, were by no means reverberating freely.

When people who have got in for nothing do not bray their heads off, the sombre moral needs no underlining from me.[4]

There was worse – far worse – to come. Mark Johns of the *Daily Sketch* complained that *Running Wild*, coming after 'the misery of another instalment of *Gravelhanger*', should have cheered viewers up instead of adding to their depression. Expanding on what he believed to be wrong with Morecambe and Wise 'and their flop of a show', he claimed that 'their gags were weak, their sketches corny' and he concluded by noting mournfully that after 'last night's attempt I sank back gloomily to a chat about Indo-China'.[5] Emery Pearce, writing in the *Daily Herald*, was equally dismissive: 'Why on earth millions of viewers had to be given this stuff I just don't know. I rate it as TV's worst effort for months.'[6] Each critic seemed to hold the two stars – not the producer, or the writers, or any of the supporting cast – solely responsible for the poor quality of the show. The *Daily Mirror*'s Clifford Davis, for example, paused to observe that Alma Cogan was 'much too good to be mixed up with such stuff' before proceeding to launch a vitriolic attack on Morecambe and Wise that concluded with the painful Pirandellian pun, '"Running Wild" is about right. *Just sick characters in search of an author, in fact.*'[7] Ernie sat with Doreen, and Eric sat with Joan, both couples surveying the pile of papers in front of them with stunned expressions. 'I do not remember, before or since, such a barrage of ugly criticism,' Joan would write. 'It was almost as if there was a conspiracy to knock Morecambe and Wise on the head before they had even started.'[8]

Each damning review, Eric remarked, 'felt like a slap in the face with a wet fish'.[9] Things might not have seemed quite so bleak had the critical onslaught shown signs of abating after that first dark day, but, on the contrary, it grew even worse. That weekend witnessed another set of excoriating reviews, the most memorable of which – a model of spiteful concision – appeared in the *People*:

### NO FLOWERS

Definition of the week:– TV set: the box in which they buried
Morecambe and Wise.[10]

Eric Morecambe, in particular, never forgot that smart little conceit,
and, indeed, he would carry the yellowing clipping around with him
in his wallet for the rest of his life.

It was, without the slightest doubt, the very lowest point in their
career. 'We were both knocked sideways,' Ernie Wise would recall.
'Initial shock gave way to depression and a serious reconsideration
of our future.'[11] Eric Morecambe, who was already looking almost
unbearably morose, was made to feel even more unhappy by a particularly ill-timed and ill-considered telephone call from his mother:
'What the devil are you two playing at?' Sadie shouted down the
line. 'I daren't show my face outside the house. We'll have to move.
We'll have to change our name.'[12] Ernie Wise, for once, seemed
similarly demoralised: much of his face and neck was now covered
in ointment and lint after he had suddenly broken out in a rash of
nervous boils. 'Those critics,' Morecambe would lament, 'they broke
my heart, they broke my wife's heart, they broke my partner's
heart.'[13]

The mood was barely any better back at Television Centre. Both
Ronnie Waldman and Bryan Sears arrived at their respective offices
on Friday 23 April to find a copy of the following memorandum from
Huw Wheldon, the BBC's Television Publicity Officer, waiting for
them on their desk:

Among the notices of 'RUNNING WILD' on 22nd April,
1954, in the daily and/or Sunday National Press, the following
may be of some interest to you. This has been gathered from
what has come on to my desk so far:

EVENING STANDARD: '. . . Among the gags and situations
that shrivelled and died, there were enough high spots to forecast
an hilarious run for the show.'
THE STAR: 'Improvement needed for Running Wild to make
the grade.'

The papers can be seen in the Press Office, Room C2, Lime Grove. Miss Gilbert will turn them up for you if you so wish.'[14]

Wheldon, a young man with an immense amount of sympathy for embattled performers and programme-makers (indeed, he would go on not just to make and appear in programmes himself but also to be an inspiration to successive generations of BBC producers during a long and illustrious career), had clearly made a point of passing on the two least distressing notices that he could find, but it was to no avail – far worse news was still to come.

The BBC's Audience Research Department, charged with the task of assessing the reception of a wide range of programmes, was about to deliver a thoroughly depressing internal report on the first edition of *Running Wild*. Only 48 per cent of the viewing public (equivalent to 12.5 per cent of the adult population of the United Kingdom), the report revealed, had watched the show – well below the average of 61 per cent for recent mid-week light entertainment programmes. As is standard practice for these reports,[15] a 'viewing panel' – which approximated to being a representative sample of the viewing public – had been asked a number of questions in order to determine the relative success or failure of certain aspects of the show. A 'fair number' of this panel, it was noted, remarked that Morecambe and Wise did not seem to be 'on form', while others thought their material very weak and 'corny in the extreme'. Most of the panel 'thought the show lacked "pep" and "punch" and complained that, what with "hackneyed situations" and "corny" dialogue, the whole programme seemed tame and distressingly unoriginal'. The so-called 'Reaction Index'[16] – a figure, based on the results of completed questionnaires, which was intended to serve as a sign of the overall reaction of the audience to a particular show – was 43: 'a very poor figure', the report underlined, 'well below the average (63) for television Light Entertainment programmes'.[17]

Something needed to be done – and done quickly. Ronnie Waldman wrote immediately to Cecil McGivern – the somewhat prickly Controller of Programmes – in order to assure him that he and his team would 'do all we can to improve [the show]', adding that he was confident that 'it *will* improve'.[18] He then proceeded to discuss a variety of possible changes with both the producer/director and the two stars. It seems fair to assume that Waldman was feeling slightly defensive about his association with the series. He had hailed Morecambe and Wise as two of his most promising new stars – and yet now they were under attack for appearing to be out of their depth. He had styled himself, not entirely without internal opposition, as a modernist in television terms, and yet now he found himself being held (at least in part) accountable for a show which, 'with its irrelevant crooners and flouncing dancers', was being widely mocked by the critics for following 'an ancient routine which is no earthly use to television and should be resolutely scrapped'.[19]

Changes were duly made: an additional writer – the experienced Ronnie Hanbury – was brought in to improve the quality of the scripts. Bryan Sears resolved to take a closer interest in the music and dance routines;[20] and Ronnie Waldman arranged several informal meetings with Morecambe and Wise with a view to raising their morale. The second show in the series, broadcast on 5 May, was something of an improvement on the first, but it did nothing to turn the tide of critical opinion: no significant new reviews appeared, and the newspapers soon slipped into the habit of contrasting the failure of *Running Wild* with the success of Bob Monkhouse's new show, *Fast and Loose*. As far as the press was concerned, there was no hope of redemption.

Morecambe and Wise, perhaps sensing this, went to see Ronnie Waldman after the third show had been transmitted and suggested that it might be in everyone's interests if the remaining shows were cancelled. Waldman, somewhat to their surprise, appeared to be as positive as ever: 'I liked the first show,' he told them. 'It had a few rough passages here and there, but', he assured them, 'we can iron those out.'[21] In ordinary circumstances, of course, Morecambe and Wise would have been grateful to have received this vote of confidence, and perhaps, in a way, they were grateful then, but the barrage of critical abuse had brought them perilously close to a state of abject despair, and they urged Waldman to think again: 'We're scared to death,' Wise confessed. 'If it's all the same to you we'd like to pull out.'[22] Waldman stood firm: 'I'm going to hold you to that contract, not because I'm being bloody-minded or because I can't find anybody else to do me a half-hour comedy series every fortnight – most young comics in Britain would give their right arms for a chance like this. No, I'm doing it because you are first-rate TV comedy material.'[23] As they left his office, he called out to them: 'Stick it out. I have faith in you.'[24]

That faith might in private have faltered a little after that opening show – when Waldman had complained to Cecil McGivern that the task of improving the current television comedy format 'with only second-rate artists and fourth-rate writers at our disposal is pretty heartbreaking!'[25] – but now, midway through the series, it drew strength from the fact that the show was beginning to claw back some support. The latest Audience Research Report, for example, announced a modest upturn in its fortunes: the majority of viewers, it revealed, had found the third show of the series to have been 'a little better', while a 'small group of enthusiasts' had judged the show to have been 'a good laugh'. The Reaction Index, which was always taken seriously by BBC executives, had risen from the embarrassing low of 43 for the opening show to 47 for the second and 50 for the third.[26] Another mildly encouraging sign was the appearance on 20 May of a newspaper review – written by the Canadian critic Bob Kesten for the London *Evening Standard* – that actually took the trouble to attempt a genuinely *constructive* analysis of the show's shortcomings:

> I once commended Morecambe and Wise as young comedians who had something to offer light entertainment on television.
>
> After watching their *Running Wild* show last night I was relieved – and disappointed. *Relieved* because in their way they are amusing. *Disappointed* because they are not more so. Theirs is the humour of the music-hall sketch – a sketch we have seen a thousand times. But they are a droll pair, good for a few smiles, if not hearty laughter.
>
> Can they develop beyond this? They might if they had a script. Last night there was little sign of one. And experience has shown that a talking comedian without a good script makes no headway on TV.[27]

Such responses, while doing nothing seriously to challenge the general view of the show as an unmitigated disaster,[28] did at least lend some support to Waldman's professed belief that had Morecambe and Wise been given more of a chance by the press they could have overcome their understandably shaky start and might even have gone on to provide viewers with more than a glimpse of their true potential.

Morale on the show, however, only failed to fall any lower because it had already reached rock-bottom. On the morning of 17 June, the day after the fifth show in the series had been broadcast, Morecambe and Wise went to see Frank Pope. They simply could not bear to go back in front of the cameras; they had suffered enough. Pope wrote immediately to Ronnie Waldman in order to inform him that he was refusing to allow Morecambe and Wise to see out their contract: the previous evening's show, he declared, had featured 'the worst performance I have ever witnessed my clients giving, not because of their inability, but plainly and simply because the material etc. supplied for them to appear in was most unsuitable and inadequate'. He was absolutely determined, he said, that they should not be forced to 'jeopardize any further their reputation', and, as a consequence, he demanded that the final show in the series be cancelled.[29] Waldman replied by return of post:

Dear Mr Pope,

Thank you for your letter of today's date concerning Morecambe and Wise.

I must admit that I am at a complete loss to understand this letter since the reaction figures from our Audience Research Department have been rising consistently during the whole of the 'Running Wild' series and the only National morning newspaper to carry a review of last night's programme mentioned that it continued to improve.

We have, as you know, provided Ronnie Hanbury to strengthen the writing on this series. Ronnie Hanbury has proved himself with both Jewel and Warriss and 'Life With The Lyons' to be a very good comedy scriptwriter; it would be difficult to uphold your statement, therefore, that the Corporation have provided your clients with poor material.

There is also, of course, the question of the contract which remains in existence for the sixth and last programme of this series in thirteen days' time. From all points of view I think the decision you seem to have taken is a hasty and unwise one and I would most earnestly ask you to reconsider it.

> Yours sincerely,
>
> Ronald Waldman[30]

Pope backed down: Morecambe and Wise were trapped.

The final show, predictably, was a dismal affair: there was no Alma Cogan – she had been allowed to move on to more attractive engagements[31] – no improved script and precious few laughs. The following dialogue – from a *Frankenstein* spoof – was sadly typical of the standard of the material as a whole:

| GIRL | What brings you to our humble village of Vasaria? |
| ERNIE | We're from BBC Television. |
| ERIC | Yes – Eurovision. |
| GIRL | Eurovision? |
| ERIC | You're – a – vision yourself![32] |

The final Audience Research Report – while not quite as negative as had been expected – made for sobering reading; after the fourth show in the series had managed to attract a Reaction Index of 53 – still below average, but at least an improvement on the three previous scores – the audience response to the fifth show had slipped back down to 43, and the sixth and final edition had managed no higher than 51. This last show, it was reported, had actually been rated by 'a fair number of viewers' as being 'a distinct improvement on any previous edition', although only a few had 'found it more than moderately entertaining'. A 'small group of enthusiasts', once again, volunteered the information that they had 'got a good laugh' from the show, but, the report concluded gravely, 'the majority were obviously no more impressed than a Wages Cashier who wrote: "A little better but it is still a very mediocre show. Very weak material, not very funny and altogether a bit third rate." '[33]

Once the series had ended, a somewhat shell-shocked Bryan Sears sent out a memorandum to all of the various heads of departments connected with the show, thanking them for their help: 'This was particularly appreciated,' he added, 'remembering that it was not the most successful television programme of all time, and [therefore your support] did much to help us all through a very difficult period.'[34] Morecambe and Wise cleared out their dressing-rooms, said their goodbyes and slipped quietly away. There was little that anyone could have said that would have made any sense: it had been an utterly unpleasant ordeal for all of those involved, and now there was just a deep sense of relief that it was finally over.

The post-mortem did not take long. As far as the BBC in London was concerned, *Running Wild* had failed in part because its two stars had been too 'Northern' (Sears) and in part because they had not quite been 'ready' (Waldman). While the first part of this explanation had never been particularly convincing – it was not, after all, as though Morecambe and Wise had wandered into Television Centre with a bag of barm cakes and a tale of woe from Coketown – the second, admittedly, had some truth in it. Morecambe and Wise had not been 'ready' for television, but probably only in the sense that any performer new to television is never anything other than not 'ready' for television, since one can hardly be expected to have mastered a medium prior to working in it. What the BBC executives in London seemed disinclined to consider was the possibility that they themselves might have been culpable, at least in part, for the poor performance of *Running Wild*. Morecambe and Wise may well have been guilty, initially, of having acted more out of passion than prudence, but they had certainly not been helped, subsequently, by the fact that they were saddled with a producer/director who did not appear to believe in them and a team of writers who did not appear to understand them.

Such mismanagement did not go unnoticed by the BBC's Northern contingent. 'Those of us who'd been grooming Eric and Ernie up in Manchester', John Ammonds recalled, 'were, shall we say, "displeased", because they'd been ruined down in London.'[35] Morecambe and Wise had not quite been 'ready' for a radio series of their own back in 1953, but, with the support and advice of talented, practical and sensitive producers like Ammonds and Ronnie Taylor, they had grown immeasurably both in confidence and expertise over a relatively short period of time. They had not quite been 'ready' for a television series of their own in 1954, and, without anything approaching the same kind of support, they had floundered.

Those six shows, Joan Morecambe would reflect, had been 'a

shattering experience'.[36] In the space of three short months More-cambe and Wise had gone from being television's future to tele-vision's past, with their supposed 'big break' breaking nothing other than their own spirits. 'When Eric and Ernie did what they believed to be right for them,' said Joan, 'they seldom put a foot wrong. The only times they went astray were when they did what other people told them.'[37] If they had learned anything at all, therefore, from the débâcle of *Running Wild*, then it was probably the virtue of self-reliance.

## CHAPTER VII

# A Brand New Bright Tomorrow?

*Showbusiness is dog eat dog. It's worse than dog eat dog. It's dog doesn't return dog's phone calls.*
WOODY ALLEN

| | |
|---|---|
| *STRANGER* | *Are you Eric Morecambe?* |
| *ERIC* | *Have you a television set?* |
| *STRANGER* | *No.* |
| *ERIC* | *Well, then yes. I'm Eric Morecambe.* |

YOU'RE ONLY YOUNG ONCE

By far the most frustrating time to find oneself excluded from a medium is when that medium is in the process of gaining ascendancy over its rivals, and Morecambe and Wise suffered the misfortune of being dismissed by television at the very moment that television was on the ascent. Theatrical impresarios such as Jack Hylton and Val Parnell were busy doing their best to exert some influence over the new commercial channel due on air by September 1955, and the BBC, having been ambivalent for so long, was finally starting to regard television rather than radio as its first priority (a change in attitude that was reflected in the decision to adapt some of its most popular radio shows – such as *Hancock's Half Hour* and *Life with the Lyons*[1] – for the small screen). While many of their contemporaries were looking forward to exploiting this trend, Morecambe and Wise could only look back and feel exploited.

It must have been a profoundly disorientating experience to have gone from being marketed as the next stars of television to being mocked as the ex-stars of television in such a short space of time; it was as if one had retired one night with the talent of Groucho Marx and awoken the following morning with the talent of Zeppo. Neither Morecambe nor Wise found it easy to comprehend, and Morecambe, in particular, had fallen into a deep depression. Whenever Wise visited him in those empty days and weeks that followed the end of *Running Wild*, he found him 'terribly morose' and convinced that they had no future in television: 'Dejection hung over him like an actual, physical presence.'[2] It was on occasions such as these that Wise, who had the thicker skin, would take it upon himself to do what he could to cheer his partner up: 'I took the view that we had to keep going rather than allow this setback to get us down.'[3] Although in public Wise continued to play the role of the doughty campaigner, in private even he was struggling to shake off the air of defeatism that seemed to have enveloped them both. Particularly worrying was the way in which he appeared to have internalised Bryan Sears' view of Morecambe and Wise's supposedly limited appeal: we are Northerners, he kept complaining, and everyone knows that Northerners can never succeed in the South: 'Look at Dave Morris, a Northern comic – brilliant. He never made it in the South. Sid Field. He was forty-five before he got past the barrier.'[4] Such successes as Arthur Askey, Ted Ray, Tommy Handley, Al Read and Jewel and Warriss had been forgotten temporarily. This was not, it seemed, a time when bright fact was able to impinge on gloomy fiction.

It was a period in which each man withdrew into the privacy of a family life which, because both had been working so hard, neither had previously had the time fully to appreciate. Both men were fortunate to have married women who were willing to provide them with constant and invaluable support. Joan Morecambe had given up a promising career of her own as a solo performer under the aegis of Lew and Leslie Grade in order to marry Eric. She had known right from the start that he was a man who craved the warmth and stability of a good, loving relationship: 'Eric said to me from the very beginning that he had to have a woman in his life.'[5] She also knew that she was marrying a man for whom the vicissitudes of everyday life could sometimes seem inscrutable: 'I don't know what she sees in our Eric,' Sadie Bartholomew would joke. 'It certainly can't be his money!"[6] He was, Joan would admit, a person who needed a great deal of cosseting, as well as practical advice – he was, for example, a considerably less conscientious keeper of accounts than was Ernie – but she did not resent her multiple roles:

> It was just how things worked out. We both made sacrifices. I suppose, in a way, I *might* have liked to have gone on performing – I'd always been stage-struck, I was smitten – but straight after we married we had one big 'accident' – Gail, our first child! I became pregnant *instantly* – it just goes to show that all pre-cautions don't necessarily work! We idolised her, of course, we absolutely loved our baby, but, in retrospect, it was a shame I became pregnant *so* quickly because we hadn't had a real court-ship, any time to really get to know each other, and in this day and age the marriage wouldn't have lasted five minutes.
>
> It was a difficult time. We had to grow up quickly. More-cambe and Wise were touring all the time, and in order to allow Eric to do his work and really concentrate on that, I had to be very supportive. The marriage just wouldn't have worked unless you'd been prepared to do that, and I did it quite happily, really.[7]

She certainly helped him recover from the trauma of *Running Wild*, as, indeed, she would help him overcome numerous other real and imagined setbacks in subsequent years. 'Joan was special – she was a tower of strength,' said John Ammonds. 'I can't imagine that Eric was always the easiest person in the world to live with – there must have been times when he'd worry himself into a terrible state – but Joan was always there. Everyone who knew Eric knew how impor-tant Joan was to him.'[8] There was no doubting the depth of Eric's affection for his wife: in 1953, on the morning of the day after Joan had given birth to their first child, he celebrated by going outside, mixing some cement and inscribing a message that read, 'Joan, thank you and I love you, Eric.'[9] It was but one of many typically impulsive romantic gestures. 'He put me on a pedestal for thirty-two years,' she would say. 'To him, I was in a class of my own and he never wanted anyone else. He never ceased to tell me how much he loved me, even if he shouted at me now and again!'[10]

Ernie Wise benefited similarly from the staunch support he received from his own wife, Doreen. Having been immersed in the peculiar reality of the entertainment world from such an early age, there was something endearingly unworldly about him, as well as a certain naïvety which sometimes meant that his trust was easily abused, and Doreen helped shield him from the less than benign figures and forces that lurked within the prosaic world of everyday life. Her own performing career had ended before she married Ernie, but she – like him – continued to relish all aspects of the lifestyle and settled very easily into the role of the supportive – and, when necessary, fiercely protective – showbusiness wife. Unlike Eric and Joan, Ernie and Doreen had made 'a conscious decision not to have any children, so that the two of us would not have to spend time apart', and they devoted themselves to a life of hectic touring, 'sharing every aspect of each other's lives', interspersed with the occasional evening spent relaxing in the company of their showbusiness friends.[11] 'My mother warned me off women,' he once revealed. 'She said they were either after your body or your money. Doreen has been my only one. I've never strayed.'[12] In spite of his readiness in public to play up to a stereotypical image of himself as, in his words, 'an unfeeling Yorkshireman'[13] – affecting, for example, a self-conscious little sniff whenever he wished to advertise the supposed coolness of any particular observation – Doreen knew that, in private, he could be deeply wounded by some of the more personalised forms of attack. She also appreciated how important it was to highlight the significance of her husband's contribution to the double-act. If ever there was any suggestion, therefore, that Morecambe and Wise were merely Morecambe and one other, the redoubtable Doreen could always be relied on to correct the misapprehension.

In the late summer of 1954, both couples realised how vital it was for the act to be resurrected as soon as possible, but neither of them was really sure of the kind of reception the first post-*Running Wild* appearance would elicit. Morecambe and Wise found themselves placed fourth on the bill at Manchester's Ardwick Hippodrome. It was quite an humiliating come-down for an act that only a few months before had been considered a major box-office attraction in the area – and it was clear that something out of the ordinary was required to confound the audience's most likely expectations. 'We need a new act with new material,' said Morecambe, 'we've been too static up to this [point]. Not only that, let's start putting our own personalities across.'[14] As they had done years before, they shut themselves away and, with their customary intensity, devised, debated and rehearsed a number of new routines. 'To our surprise and joy', recalled Wise, 'we clicked.'[15] When they walked out on stage in Manchester and started to perform again, it felt good – the confidence came surging back – and when they walked back off at the end it was to the very welcome sound of a standing ovation. The sense of elation back in the dressing-room was mixed with more than a little relief: the failure of their highly prized first series – though it had undoubtedly administered a sharp blow to their *amour propre* – had clearly caused no lasting damage to their most basic self-belief.

Both of them left the theatre that night in a kind of daze. After weeks of deep depression, rereading in their minds each embittering review, they were back in front of a real audience, a visible, audible, tangible group of enthusiastic theatregoers, and they felt *liked* again. 'That did wonders for their confidence,' said Joan Morecambe of the performance. 'And I always remember a write-up they got for that show which said: "These can't be the same two I saw on television the other night because these guys are brilliant and are going places."'[16] In the weeks and months that followed, not only did they discover that Variety audiences were either unaware of or unconcerned by the critical onslaught that *Running Wild* had incurred (in fact they soon found themselves being billed, without conscious irony, as 'fresh from their brilliantly successful TV series', or as 'those inimitable TV comedians'[17]), but they also came to realise just how well-liked they were by their fellow professionals. 'A lot of people who knew them well understood what a setback it was,' Harry Secombe said of their series, 'but every comic needs a disaster. It makes you more streetwise.'[18] He, like many other performers who had worked or socialised with Morecambe and Wise, was quick to reassure them that because of 'the great chemistry of their relationship, and the innate pathos in Eric that made you want to reach out and hug him',[19] it would not be long before they succeeded in re-establishing themselves in the public consciousness.

He would be proved right. Morecambe and Wise began to fight

back. They had at last reached that point where they were able to admit – to themselves as much as to anyone else – that they had not been solely responsible for the mediocrity of their television début. Not all of the bitterness had gone – 'You never forget something like that in spite of anything that happens afterwards,'[20] they both would say, and Eric Morecambe, even though he had taken to declaring that the 'hardest thing to find is yesterday's newspaper!',[21] continued to carry cuttings of the worst reviews around with him wherever he went – but at the end of 1954 the general mood was one of unabashed affirmation. Morecambe and Wise were ready not just to resurrect their career but also, for the first time, to take control of it. From now on, they resolved, they would place their trust in their own judgement as far as their material was concerned, and, if they were ever again to be invited to work for someone who wanted them to be anything other than 'Morecambe and Wise', then More-cambe and Wise would, politely but firmly, decline.

They also agreed that never again would they allow themselves to be placed in a situation where their livelihood depended on the whim of another person. They would work as hard and as often as they possibly could, resist ever being seduced into risking everything on a single project and never, ever, allow sentiment to intrude on judgement when their professional future was at stake. 'Showbusiness is show-*business* and it's very tough,' Ernie Wise would argue. 'The fact is that in our business it is wrong to talk in terms of loyalty. It simply isn't like that. If you produce the goods everybody wants you, and the minute you don't no one wants to know. It was inconceivable that managers would have been "loyal" to us if we had ceased to deliver first-rate shows. And the same would have held true for every other performer.'[22] Both men remembered the advice that Max Miller had given them back in 1948 – 'Don't forget, boys, in this business when one door shuts, they all bloody shut!'[23] – and, even if the uncompromising attitude that it demanded probably came somewhat more easily to Wise than it ever would to Morecambe, both of them agreed that, in the light of recent experiences, it was the only kind that made sense.

The nature of their relationship with the press changed in more subtle ways. Although they would continue to cultivate and maintain the friendship of a number of journalists, they would never again be quite as open or as trusting as before. The charm was still there – 'We must be the friendliest people the press have ever known,' they once reflected. 'We're not rude to them and they can always contact us'[24] – but in future there would be steel behind their smiles. Morecambe and Wise began to use the press just as much – if not more so – than the press used them. With the assistance of their first – and, as it would turn out, their only – publicist, George Bartram, Morecambe and Wise spent the remainder of the decade devising innumerable – and sometimes quite ingenious – methods for keeping themselves in the public eye. Enduring relationships were cultivated with influential newspaper columnists; a web of useful contacts were established all over the country with a wide range of local reporters; 'photo-opportunities' during the summer season and pantomime runs were always invited; and a regular supply of news, rumours and anecdotes was fed to hungry and up-and-coming writers eager to build up their bylines.

Such diligence was by no means unnecessary. With newspapers and their 'showbusiness correspondents' starting to turn away from Variety and radio in favour of television, movies and popular music, Morecambe and Wise needed to work hard to preserve, let alone add to, what press contacts they had, and the occasional minor error – such as a casual reference in the *Daily Sketch* early in 1957 to an 'Eddie Wise'[25] – assumed an exaggeratedly ominous look if one happened to be battling against the threat of obscurity. One long-running but unorthodox strategy designed to stave off such fears involved the planting of brief observations by Morecambe and Wise on the minutiae of everyday life – each one containing a crafty little reference, *en passant*, to their current professional activities – in the 'Letters' columns of the most widely read daily newspapers. These curious missives started appearing in the mid-fifties and would continue well into the next decade. The following example, dating from 1960, is typical of the form:

Now that the dark, winter nights are with us and children are on holiday, we will no doubt be receiving the usual exhortations to take special care when driving.

The other night we were on the road at about four o'clock. It was misty and dark. Suddenly, out of the gloom came one of the white-coated children's traffic wardens carrying the usual 'Stop, Children Crossing' sign.

It was all we could do in the time we had to jam on our brakes and an accident was prevented only by inches and seconds.

Surely, during the winter mists and fogs, these wardens should be provided with illuminated signs – white coats are just not adequate.

MORECAMBE & WISE
Birmingham[26]

Some of these letters were almost certainly concocted on Morecambe and Wise's behalf – and not always with their knowledge – by the irrepressible George Bartram. Although they appreciated his dedication to their cause, there were occasions when they had reason to feel somewhat embarrassed by his efforts. One letter, for example – even though its sole purpose was to remind the public of Morecambe and Wise's latest itinerary – provoked an unexpectedly passionate response:

We do much road travelling and fog makes us shudder at the prospect of driving. On the open road we are aided by the cat's eyes.

Mr Marples [the Minister of Transport] may like to consider installing these along the kerbs of roads within town or city boundaries. This would greatly alleviate traffic chaos caused by fog in peak periods.

MORECAMBE & WISE
Liverpool[27]

A. J. Whitton, of Sevenoaks in Kent, was but one of several readers who wrote in to point out somewhat tetchily that the effectiveness of cat's eyes on roads 'depends on their being kept clean by the pressure of traffic passing over them. Cat's eyes on the edge of kerbs, suggested by Morecambe and Wise, would become mud-coated.'[28] Another long-running campaign to highlight the appeal of 'tegestology' on behalf of the British Beer Mat Collectors' Society would prove similarly ineffective.[29] 'I think that dear old George used to drive them mad sometimes,' Joan Morecambe recalled. 'He was always *doing* things. He even got me involved sometimes. He'd send off these recipes to the papers and magazines – in *my* name! – and then people would write to me and say, "You need your brains testing! What a *terrible* recipe!" And I'd think, "Well, I didn't send anyone any recipe. What on earth's going on?" And it would turn out to have been good old George.'[30]

A more conventional source of publicity was their stage work – which was much in demand and widely admired. 'I always used to say to people', Joan recalled, 'that you always knew where Morecambe and Wise were because of the laughter that was coming out of that dressing-room. They attracted people like magnets, because the humour used to just flow from those two young guys and anybody in the neighbourhood used to be in there all the time.'[31] By the spring of 1956, Morecambe and Wise, encouraged by their return to popularity on the Variety circuit, informed Frank Pope that they were ready to make another attempt at achieving television success.[32] They were in luck: Dickie Leeman, a producer at ATV (Associated Television), invited them to perform a regular spot in a forthcoming series of shows starring the popular honky-tonk pianist Winifred Atwell; they did not hesitate to accept.

Two factors contributed to their sudden feeling of optimism. One was the fact that they were not, on this occasion, to be the stars of the series, and therefore would not be burdened by the weight of expectation that had marred the making of *Running Wild*. The other was the fact that the material, which was to be written by Johnny Speight, would be shaped to suit their established style. Speight – a former milkman from the East End of London – was, at the age of thirty-five, on the verge of becoming one of the most significant comedy writers in television. He would go on to write the very popular *Arthur Haynes Show*, Frankie Howerd's 'comeback' appearances in the early sixties and, most notoriously, create the loud-mouthed working-class bigot Alf Garnett in the BBC's *Till Death Do Us Part*, but in 1956 he was just as hungry for success as Morecambe and Wise were.

They would work well together: Speight was the first writer who saw Morecambe and Wise as 'Eric and Ernie', two *personalities* who were, he believed, 'natural for television',[33] while Morecambe and Wise, in turn, were the very kind of industrious and inventive performers that Speight had long been seeking to write for. As the date of their début appearance drew near – Saturday, 21 April, two years to the day after the first edition of *Running Wild* – the old anxieties started to surface; they knew that they could ill-afford another poorly received performance on prime-time national television. Morecambe, again, was the more outwardly concerned of the two, and, on this occasion, he had good reason to be: not only was he facing a key challenge in his professional career, but he was also expecting Joan, his wife, to give birth to their second child at some point during that very same day. Although Dickie Leeman had done his best during rehearsal to assuage Morecambe's nerves – 'Look, Eric, relax. This is only a TV comedy series.'[34] – the day itself would prove to be just as emotionally draining as he had expected it to be. Joan gave birth to a son – Gary – several hours early in a nursing home in Enfield, which meant that Eric had just enough time to visit them before going on to the studio at the Wood Green Empire and joining Ernie for the live broadcast at 8.15 p.m. The show itself went rather well. Johnny Speight was highly impressed by Morecambe's comic appeal – 'You just laughed at him as he walked in the room . . . His expressions just came naturally. He was a good dancer and mover and he could do a wonderful fall – the best of any comic I have ever seen.'[35] Dickie Leeman was delighted with the seemingly nerveless manner whereby both of them had ad-libbed their way out of trouble after various props had malfunctioned. Subsequent appearances were, if anything, even more successful, and the positive reviews that their contributions attracted did much to lay the ghost of *Running Wild*.

During the following year or so Morecambe and Wise would make several more guest appearances on a variety of television shows – including, for the BBC, five editions of the popular *Double Six* – and, as a consequence, they started to feel more comfortable in front of the cameras. In the early autumn of 1958, however, they disappeared from the screen in order to join the cast of *The Winifred Atwell Show* on a six-month tour of Australia; the prospect of refreshing both themselves and their (by now somewhat over-exposed) act in an unfamiliar but reassuringly friendly environment – Australian audiences were considered in those days to be considerably less demanding than their British counterparts – had proven to be too attractive for them to resist. It was, as expected, an enjoyable experience. They spent three months in Melbourne and a further three in Sydney, playing the best theatres, trying out new material, relaxing with Joan and Doreen on the beach and attending the Test matches between England and Australia. Six months was, however, a long time for them to be out of the public eye back home in Britain, and it is clear from the following letter that they sent to John Ammonds that, as the tour began to wind down, they were starting to feel mildly anxious about the prospect of having to find work on their return:

> Tivoli Theatre,
> Sydney
> 10th of February 1959

Dear Johnny,

It seems a long time since we saw everybody in Manchester but we often think about you all and wonder how you are all getting on.

We have done very well in Australia, having had two good seasons in Melbourne and Sydney, also appeared on T.V. and radio.

. . . Can now tell you our plans. We are leaving on the 22nd of February and coming home through America – we shall spend some time [there] and should be back in England about March 7th, so after that date we will be okay for radio or T.V. bookings.

. . . Please give our regards to everybody and we are looking forward to seeing you in the near future.

> Cheerio
> Morecambe and Wise[36]

When they did return home they were shocked by the changes that had occurred during their prolonged absence: many good Variety theatres (along with many more mediocre ones) had been forced to close down, and there was fierce competition among their fellow performers for the fewer bookings that remained. Although their immediate future was relatively secure – a lucrative summer season in Blackpool had already been arranged – their long-term future suddenly seemed uncertain. Frank Pope, their agent, no longer had the old Butterworth circuit to rely on, and, as a consequence, all that he would now be in a position to offer his best clients were engagements at second- and third-rate theatres which had hardly been acceptable to them several years before. Morecambe and Wise knew that a sensible long-term solution had to be found, and, after a period of soul-searching, both of them arrived at the same conclusion: they had no choice but to commit themselves in future to television.

What made this decision harder to take than it might otherwise have been was the fact that, once it was made, it would necessitate a change of agent, and both Morecambe and Wise had come to think of Frank Pope as a friend of the family. Pope, however, lacked both the contacts and the expertise to present them effectively in the fiercely competitive and rapidly changing world of television, and so, reluctantly, Morecambe and Wise placed an advertisement in *The Stage* to the effect that they had parted company with their agent of nine years' standing and would welcome offers of representation. Several first-rate theatrical agents replied, but Morecambe and Wise were determined that they should sign with someone who had a proven track record in the field of television. The man whom they found – Billy Marsh – was the perfect choice.

Marsh was a remarkable figure. He had joined Bernard Delfont's agency back in 1942, previously having been a manager of touring revues, and it had not taken him long to convince Delfont that he could be trusted to run the business single-handed. Unlike many theatrical agents, Marsh was, at least as far as his specialist area of interest was concerned, a well-read man. His walls were lined with hundreds of books on all aspects of showbusiness, and there was little that he did not know about either the rules or the exceptions to the rules when it came to stories of how an act could, or should, acquire both popularity and power. Not only was he an outstanding judge of new talent, but he was also a diligent and thoroughly reassuring manager of established stars. If any performer ever felt anxious about an appearance, or just eager for sound advice, they would call on Billy Marsh. 'Your job', he once said of his role, 'is to get them bookings when they're unknown . . . and look after their affairs when they get to the top.'[37] He kept things simple and neat, and encouraged his clients to follow his example. 'He was a great judge of talent,' said Michael Grade, who would eventually become his partner. 'A great judge of talent, a great judge of temperament and a very shrewd negotiator – he always knew when to strike a deal and when not to. But he wasn't just a great judge of talent, he was a great *respecter* of talent, too. He understood the mentality of performers very well, what each one of them needed. He worked out the psychology of each situation so well.'[38]

When Morecambe and Wise went to see him in his Jermyn Street office, they could not have been anything other than impressed: Billy Marsh *looked* like an agent. The room was filled with cigar smoke, the large desk decorated with a line of important-looking, colour-coded telephones, and, leaning back in a large leather chair, sat the slight but very smart figure of Billy Marsh, smoking incessantly, flicking ash over his left shoulder and squinting through the grey light at his two new prospective clients. Addressing them – as was his custom with both stars and strangers alike – as 'Sir', he was, from the very start, encouraging: Morecambe and Wise, he announced, were an excellent act that should never, in the future, be satisfied with anything other than the top of the bill. Television was the only way forward, he declared, but there was no reason why Morecambe and Wise should not become genuine stars of that particular medium. 'I'm sure I can get you TV,'[39] he told them in an impressively matter-of-fact tone of voice, and, without hesitating, he proceeded to pick up one of his colour-coded telephones and called up Alec Fine, a booker for ATV; Fine agreed to give them a spot on the hugely popular Variety show, *Sunday Night at the Prince of Wales*. Marsh put down the telephone and said, 'That's it then, but remember television is not like touring . . . It's a totally different medium that few stage people really appreciate. But if you can keep coming up with good, fresh stuff, I can get you all the television you want.'[40] They shook hands on the agreement, and Billy Marsh became Morecambe and Wise's agent.

He would be as good as his word: in 1960 – his first full year with them – he secured a summer season in Weymouth and, on television, twelve appearances on *Val Parnell's Sunday Night at the London Palladium*, six spots on *Saturday Spectacular* and four on *Star Time*. Suddenly, Morecambe and Wise appeared to be everywhere. 'By now,' Morecambe would recall, 'we had come to love doing television,'[41] and with good reason. With the backing of Billy Marsh behind them, Morecambe and Wise felt capable of conquering the medium that had formerly been the source of so much bitter frustration.

## CHAPTER VIII

# Two of a Kind

| ERN | *I'm a group.* |
|---|---|
| ERIC | *By yourself?* |
| ERN | *No, no. There's a group of us.* |
| ERIC | *Is there?* |
| ERN | *Yes. There's Sid and Dick.* |

THE MORECAMBE AND WISE SHOW

Morecambe and Wise became stars in the sixties without ever becoming stars *of* the sixties. True, they *were* Northern and working-class, and being Northern and working-class proved to be as great an advantage in the sixties as it had been a disadvantage in the fifties. In most other respects, however, Morecambe and Wise were hardly what anyone at the time would have called *à la mode*. Both of them, after all, were bordering on middle age; both were happily married; both preferred short hair and smart suits to long hair and kaftans; both had far more in common with Ted Ray than they did with Timothy Leary; and, if either of them had ever been tempted to go somewhere else, it would have been to Hollywood, not Haight-Ashbury. The sixties, however, in spite of all of this, was still *their* decade – the decade that saw them establish themselves, after twenty years of false starts and bitter endings, as the nation's favourite double-act.

If their success owed relatively little to the warp and weft of any supposed *Zeitgeist*, it certainly owed a great deal to their prodigious work-rate throughout this memorable period. Morecambe and Wise, quite simply, never stopped working. In addition to appearing in their own television series, they somehow found the time to star in their own radio series;[1] release several singles and long-playing records;[2] launch their own comic strip;[3] make several guest appearances on US television;[4] star in three feature-length movies;[5] play to packed houses every year in pantomime and summer season; and, as if that was not more than sufficient, they also continued to tour the old theatres and the new night-clubs, give countless interviews, judge a fair number of talent contests, deliver the occasional after-dinner speech and open innumerable shops, sales and garden fêtes. It made little sense as a schedule – it made little sense as a life – but this was their time, their moment, and they neither wanted nor dared to catch themselves wasting a single second of it.

There was one thing that certainly was propitious about the sixties as far as Morecambe and Wise were concerned, and that was television. '[We] caught the television wave at just the right moment,' Ernie Wise recalled, 'and [were] carried by it, intact, to arrive on the long-promised shores of personal and professional fulfilment.'[6] It was not the quality of television during the decade that was so significant, but rather its impact as a popular medium. Whether it was the opportunistic ramblings of an academic such as Marshall McLuhan, wafting his windy rhetoric about the global village into every dusty recess of the quality press,[7] or the strident invective of self-appointed moral crusaders such as Mary Whitehouse,[8] alarmed by the bovine stupidity of everyone except themselves, or the all-purpose ululations of the new brand of box-bred talking-head, such as David Frost, it seemed as though expressing an opinion about television – preferably *on* television – was *de rigueur* in the sixties. The journalist Keith Waterhouse, commenting in 1966 on this peculiar phenomenon, expressed his surprise at just how much people talked about television:

The novelty value, for something so patently un-novel, is amazing. Are schoolmasters' conferences *still* complaining about the undesirable effects of television? Yes, they are. Are doctors *still* inventing boring new complaints: TV neck and TV shoulder and all the rest of it? Yes, by the casebook. If television hadn't killed vaudeville stone dead there'd be music hall songs about it: 'I saw you on the Telly, Nelly' or 'All the nice girls love a Dalek.'[9]

Morecambe and Wise – like so many of their contemporaries – wanted to be a part of this experience. They wanted to be watched by millions of viewers each week, to be talked about each day in factories, schools, pubs and clubs, to be sought after, to be admired, to be imitated, to be, in short, television stars. In Billy Marsh, they had an agent who would not rest until that dream came true. He had already succeeded in bringing them back on to the small screen and securing them several high-profile guest spots on popular peak-time programmes, but now, at the start of 1961, he felt that they were ready – and, in a way, British television was ready – for another series of their own.

Marsh, like any good agent, set his sights high: he called Lew Grade, managing director of ATV – the most powerful of the independent television companies – and the man who was on the verge of becoming the single most influential voice in the whole of British commercial television.[10] There was little that Marsh did not know about any of the Grades – aside from his many dealings with Lew, he had worked for both of his brothers, Bernard Delfont and Leslie Grade, and he would later act as a mentor to Leslie's son, Michael – but, when it came to business, he knew that no favours would be granted him by any of them. When, therefore, he proposed that Morecambe and Wise should be signed up by ATV for a series of their own, the response, though disappointing, was hardly unexpected: 'You must be joking!' exclaimed Lew Grade. 'I wouldn't give *them* a series.'[11] Marsh did not give up without a fight, but Grade, on this occasion, proved implacable: yes, he said, he was well aware that they had improved considerably since the unmitigated disaster that was *Running Wild*, and yes, he had indeed seen them deliver some fairly effective performances in such shows as *Sunday Night at the London Palladium*, but nothing that he had seen so far had convinced him that this was now an act worth gambling an entire series on. There would, he concluded, be no deal as far as Morecambe and Wise were concerned.

Marsh, reluctantly, lowered his sights a little and started calling a number of other television executives. A few days after that initial conversation, however, one of Marsh's many colour-coded telephones rang again: it was Lew Grade. Not even Billy Marsh, who was accustomed to the nervy capriciousness of commercial television bosses, had, it seemed, expected such a call. Grade wanted to know if Morecambe and Wise were members of either of the two current theatrical unions – Equity or the Variety Artists' Federation (VAF);[12] Marsh informed him that they were currently with the VAF. 'Okay then,' drawled Grade, 'you've got yourself a series.'[13] Just what had prompted this dramatic about-turn was never made entirely clear by Grade – it might, perhaps, have had more than a little to do with his anticipation of the imminent industrial action being discussed by Equity's activists at that time – but Marsh, though curious about the cause, was more than happy with the effect.

The same, however, could not have been said of the two men – Eric Maschwitz, Head of Light Entertainment at BBC TV, and Tom Sloan, his deputy – who for the past year or so had been harbouring hopes of bringing Morecambe and Wise back to the BBC.[14] A brand-new comedy series, called *Four Aces and a King*, had been developed as a starring vehicle for Morecambe and Wise, under the close supervision of the BBC's two recently appointed 'Advisors and Consultants on comedy shows and scripts',[15] Frank Muir and Denis Norden. This was a serious project: a great deal of time and effort – as the correspondence preserved in the BBC archives makes abundantly clear – had been invested in each stage of its development. By the autumn of 1960, six complete scripts had been written (by whom remains unclear[16]) and forwarded to Morecambe and Wise for approval. On 6 October, Muir and Norden sent the following memorandum to Eric Maschwitz:

> We have now heard from Morecambe and Wise themselves that they like the scripts and are keen to do the series. However, they are committed till March next. Can we therefore moot this for the April/June offers. Taking into account the preliminary objections that have been made, we still think this adds up to a worthwhile programme. We don't think of it as a situation-comedy. What we see possible here is a flat-out fast broad-comedy laugh show which still has some new ideas in presentation and construction.[17]

Just what happened next, however, remains something of a mystery.[18] Although both Maschwitz and Sloan, having accepted Muir and

Norden's advice, made several attempts over the following three months to secure the services of Morecambe and Wise, any response from either the artistes or their agent is conspicuous by its absence from the archives. On 23 January 1961, Tom Sloan – who by this time was growing increasingly exasperated by the inexplicable delay – wrote the following letter to Billy Marsh:

Dear Billy,

I have tried to contact you several times on the telephone without success. Can you please give me an immediate answer as to whether Morecambe and Wise are available to BBC Television to perform in a series of scripts which we have available either in the period June to mid-July, or perhaps in the October/December Quarter?

The matter is now urgent and, of course, such an offer is conditional of them not appearing in a similar series on I.T.A. this year.

Yours sincerely,
Tom Sloan[19]

On 8 February Marsh finally responded, but with bad news for Maschwitz and Sloan: not only, he claimed, had he been 'completely unaware' that the BBC had been interested in signing his clients, but he had also just secured a contract for them with ATV.[20]

This is all very puzzling. Although Lew Grade, when asked about this matter, confessed that he simply could not remember 'the exact timing of [the] move to ATV',[21] Morecambe and Wise themselves always said that they did not even *hear* about the ATV offer before June 1961, when they started a summer season – *Show Time* – at the Princess Theatre in Torquay,[22] and Billy Marsh – whenever he was interviewed on the subject – always agreed.[23] It seems unlikely that so shrewd (and responsible) an agent as Marsh would have turned the BBC offer down without first ensuring that an alternative deal was already signed and sealed, but one can only guess at the real reason why the offer of *Four Aces and a King* – and a return to the BBC – was not only passed up on at the time but also never – until now – acknowledged as ever having existed. What *is* clear, however, is that Billy Marsh, at some point in 1961, united with Lew Grade to ensure that Morecambe and Wise's immediate future would be with ATV.

Neither Morecambe nor Wise was quite sure as to how to react when Marsh called them with the news. On the one hand, they were very ambitious, and the prospect of their own series of thirteen half-hour shows, to be transmitted live all over the country, was something they relished. On the other hand, however, the old doubts, in spite of their frequent claims to the contrary, continued to lurk deep inside their minds, and they feared that television, once it had fixed them with its unforgiving gaze, would, once again, find them wanting. Unsettled and confused, they sought out some shrewd advice from the more experienced of their fellow performers in Torquay. Jewel and Warriss – another double-act – were starring near by at the Pavilion in *Laughing Room Only*, and they were certainly well worth listening to; not only had they been the stars of one of the first comedy series to be broadcast on British television – 1951's *Turn It Up* – but they had also continued to attract large television audiences with further popular series of their own, so their views on the subject deserved to be taken very seriously indeed. Warriss stressed the fact that thirteen weeks was a long time, and that it could easily seem like thirteen months unless Morecambe and Wise were able to start with three essential ingredients in place: an abundance of good ideas; a team of talented and sympathetic writers; and an experienced producer. Warriss noted that he and his partner had been fortunate in their last series to have had two excellent writers – Dick Hills and Sid Green – and a tolerant, knowledgeable and very supportive producer – Colin Clews. If Morecambe and Wise could secure the services of these people, or others like them, they stood a fair chance, said Warriss, of being extremely successful in a television series of their own.

The following day, Ernie Wise – with Eric Morecambe's full agreement – called Billy Marsh and said that they would very much like to accept Lew Grade's offer – so long as they could have Hills and Green as their writers and Colin Clews as their producer. Marsh, more amused than angered by such impudence, explained that none of these people were available. Morecambe and Wise, more out of anxiety than arrogance, held firm, and, after various calls, negotiations and fortuitous strokes of luck, the team was duly assembled. Late in

September, Hills and Green visited Morecambe and Wise in Torquay; they brought with them a record – Johnny Mercer's 'Two of a Kind' – which they felt would be an ideal theme song for the show.

It was a typically clever Hills and Green suggestion – sharply perceptive yet knowingly populist – although, as Eric Morecambe years later observed,[24] it was actually a song that suited Hills and Green almost as well as it did Morecambe and Wise. Hills – the short, pudgy, puckish one – and Green – the tall, thin, slightly queasy-looking one – had been writing together, on and off, since their days as pupils at the same well-to-do London public school (Haberdashers' Aske's in Elstree); both had worked for a time as teachers before deciding, over a post-match beer at the Old Askean Rugby Club, to team up again to write professionally for such performers as Dave King, Jewel and Warriss, Harry Secombe, Charlie Drake, Jon Pertwee, Arthur Askey, Anthony Newley, Roy Castle and Bruce Forsyth; and both men were very talented, very ambitious and very, very, confident. By the start of the sixties they had established themselves as one of the most sought-after writing partnerships in British television, and it was a mark of the high regard in which they had come to be held that when Ray Galton and Alan Simpson opted out of writing a second series of the Sid James vehicle *Citizen James* (in order to concentrate on *Steptoe and Son*), the BBC chose Hills and Green as their replacements.

The Galton and Simpson connection seems, in retrospect, somewhat ironic, for Hills and Green would not, as characters, have looked out of place in a typical Galton and Simpson situation-comedy (the lugubrious Sid Green, in particular, would have made a suitably combative next-door neighbour for Anthony Aloysius St John Hancock). As writers, however, there was little similarity between the two partnerships: Hills and Green lacked Galton and Simpson's compassion, their ability to invent believable, complicated characters and then – as in *Steptoe and Son* – place them in situations that, deep down, were as much tragic as they were comic. Hills and Green, in contrast, were at their best writing lively, unorthodox and often very witty sketches; they could take a single idea, image or gesture and construct the most fantastic environment in which it could flourish. What, perhaps, was most significant about Hills and Green was the fact that they were genuine *television* writers: their style echoed the strange, staccato rhythms of the medium itself; their tastes, when it was deemed necessary, could seem almost as fickle; and their frame of reference stretched all the way from one side of the small screen to the other, with any and every show, format and famous figure representing one further opportunity for a timely pastiche or parody. Hills and Green, in short, were not trying to write a radio show with pictures or a stage show for the studio; rather than merely working *in* the medium, they were doing their best to work *with* the medium to create something that stood out as novel, animated and contemporary – a bona fide television show. As a consequence of doing so, Hills and Green – while not always serving to complement the more traditional elements that helped make up Morecambe and Wise's act – certainly accentuated their youthful appeal without alienating their old Variety audience.

It was not, however, a working relationship that brought instant success. When they first started work on the series, Morecambe and Wise were probably guilty of treating their illustrious writers with too much respect, while Hills and Green, in turn, were probably guilty of treating their would-be stars with rather too little. The first script, when it appeared, proved to be something of a disappointment to Morecambe and Wise: sketch after sketch, they complained, featured such densely populated scenes that they – the stars – might as well not have been present, and one sketch in particular – a spy movie spoof – was so crowded with extras, said Morecambe, that 'I couldn't even find Ernie'.[25] Hills and Green sat back, reminded Morecambe and Wise that *they*, the writers – not them, the performers – were the double-act with the proven track record in television and insisted that they follow the script to the letter. Morecambe and Wise were somewhat intimidated by their writers' air of self-confidence: 'Sid and Dick were very talented guys,' Wise recalled, 'better educated than the pair of us and a bit older, too,'[26] and it seemed a little perverse, after risking so much to secure their services, to start questioning their judgement, so the performers relented and the writers won.

The first show went out from the old Wood Green Empire at 8 o'clock on Thursday, 12 October 1961. Though far from being reminiscent of the first edition of *Running Wild*, it was still a messy, disjointed affair which met, Morecambe recalled, with a reception that was 'lukewarm to say the least'.[27] Undeterred by this setback, Hills and Green withdrew, paused, and then returned with an outline for the second show that, if anything, appeared to compound the errors of the first. Morecambe and Wise, gazing at page after page of the same 'epic' sketches, were aghast at the arrogance of their two 'dogmatic writers': 'The jokes were there. We had some very funny lines, but again we were sure it was *wrong* for us.'[28] Enraged, the stars declared war on the writers: if Morecambe and Wise were going to fail on television for a second time, they declared, then it would be as Morecambe and Wise, and not, under any circumstances, as the on-screen *alter egos* of Hills and Green.

What brought this potentially unseemly squabble to a premature end was, of all things, a strike: Equity, the principal actors' union, called out all of its members, and thus left the autumn television schedules in tatters. 'You're done for,' said Sid Green. 'Not at all,' replied Morecambe and Wise, 'we belong to VAF.'[29] The tables had been turned. In the absence of the usual small army of extras (all of whom had been Equity members), out went the crowded sketches and in came more modest situations featuring Eric and Ernie and, sometimes, 'Sid and Dick' – Morecambe and Wise's new all-purpose stooges. It was sweet revenge. Hills and Green now had no choice but to write the very kind of short, simple, funny sketches that Morecambe and Wise had been asking for from the very beginning, and, just to add insult to injury, they then had to appear in these same sketches and regularly bear the brunt of Eric Morecambe's often caustic ad-libs.

Out of chaos came order. For what remained of the series, Morecambe and Wise were free to be more like themselves: they ceased, as far as television viewers were concerned, to be 'Morecambe and Wise' and became 'Eric and Ern' – the one with the glasses and the one with the short, fat, hairy legs; the big fool and his friend the bigger fool – two instantly recognisable, and very likeable, comic characters. It turned out to have been an astute transformation, for, as J. B. Priestley once observed, such figures 'have always been the idols of the English people, who prefer a droll chunk of personality to comic acting. They do not like a comedian to be always different, but to be for ever himself, or, if you will, to be more himself each time they see him.'[30] 'Eric and Ern' were, as characters, by no means as finely drawn as the 'Eric and Ernie' of the later BBC shows would be, but they functioned very well in terms of the traditional double-act dynamic. Speaking in the late seventies, Eric Morecambe recalled:

> There have been two formulas for us on television. The first was basically the idea that Hills and Green took to ATV. Ernie was the basic straight-man . . . [or] more of a straight-man than he is now. And I was the comic, who never got the girl, never even kissed one. If I saw a girl with a big bust, my hat used to rise – and that wasn't the only thing.[31]

Unlike their later, more mature, screen relationship – which John Mortimer would liken to 'an English marriage, missing out the sex as many English marriages do'[32] – their ATV relationship was more like that between a slow-witted parent (Ern) and his mischievous son (Eric). In one particularly well-constructed sketch, for example, Eric and Ern prepare to spend the night in an hotel room: Ern asks Eric to turn the light out, but Eric confesses that he is afraid of the dark; Ern, desperate to get some sleep, asks what it will take to calm him down, and Eric suggests that Ern sing him a lullaby 'like me mam used to do'; Ern duly sings him to sleep, but he wakes straight back up again as soon as Ern tiptoes towards the light-switch; Ern tries again, but this time Eric joins in – sending Ern to sleep; Eric wakes Ern up again, they shout at each other, and the noise wakes up a young woman in the next room; when she calls to complain, Eric persuades *her* to sing him to sleep – ''cos you look more like me mam than he does – not a *lot* more, but . . .' – and then tells a baffled Ern to turn the light out.

Eric and Ern were joined in some of the sketches by Sid and Dick – or rather, to be more accurate, by Hills and Green doing their very best, but failing miserably, to play 'Sid and Dick'. It made for a bizarre sight, somewhat akin to that of Salieri bounding on to the stage during a performance of *Die Zauberflöte* and attempting to play the spoons, but, for want of an alternative, they persevered. Their chronic incompetence, in fact, only added to the comedy; there was something strangely appealing about the manner in which, week after week, they would either stand stiffly through an entire sketch like two teak totem poles, or else stagger around like two naughty schoolboys, giggling silently to themselves. In one particularly memorable scene, Eric and Ern were supposed to be sitting at a canteen table eating a plate of chips each, and Sid and Dick were meant to join them and then, quite nonchalantly, start stealing chips, one by one, from Eric's plate; unfortunately, Sid Green, after filling his mouth full of chips, started laughing, thus rendering the sketch useless but also setting off a delightful sequence of ad-libbed lines from Eric. The scrappiness of such scenes – Eric Morecambe always took a great delight in shouting out, 'He made a right mess of that, didn't he?' whenever either Hills or Green fluffed a line – contributed to the distinctive charm of the show as a whole, and Morecambe and Wise, by now, were so good at improvising their way to the end of such sequences that they seemed to relish the prospect of each unexpected detour.

The Equity strike lasted twelve more weeks – matching the run of the series – and, by its conclusion, even Hills and Green were forced to admit that they had ended up with a winning formula. ATV was delighted with the overall performance of the show, and moved quickly to commission another series (there would be five more between 1961 and 1968). *The Morecambe and Wise Show* had – with more than a little luck – made itself into one of the most consistently watchable light entertainment shows on television. Every aspect of it helped to promote its burgeoning popularity: the catchphrases ('Get out of that!'; 'I'll smash your face in!'; 'That's not nice!'; 'Pardon?'; and, of course, the evergreen 'Tea, Ern?'); the familiar bits of comic business (most notably, of course, Eric Morecambe's paper bag trick); the memorable way of opening the show (short, sharp parodies of other shows, such as *The Man From UNCLE*, *Dixon of Dock Green* and *Take Your Pick*) and closing it (running gags – usually unfinished – such as, 'There were two old men sitting in deck chairs . . .'); and the catholic taste in special guests (who ranged from 'mature' Variety-style acts, such as Pearl Carr and Teddy Johnson, to youthful pop stars of the moment, such as the Beatles[33]).

There was something about the way in which Morecambe and Wise treated stars like the Beatles – and, indeed, there was something about the way in which stars like the Beatles responded to such treatment – that helped make the show, and them, stand out as something exceptional. Gone was the ungainly genuflection so beloved by many shows of the period: Morecambe and Wise greeted each guest with a playful irreverence that put them swiftly at ease. Paul McCartney, for example, said that *The Morecambe and Wise Show* was his favourite of all the television shows that the Beatles appeared on, and that what distinguished it from the rest was the memory of 'what great *fun* it was'.[34] What was certainly evident throughout the sketch was the strong sense of mutual respect, and admiration,[35] as well as the obvious pleasure that each took in the other's attempted ab-libs:

ERIC     Hey! It's the Kaye Sisters!

PAUL    (*shaking Eric's hand*) I remember you – you're the one with the short, fat, hairy legs.

ERIC     No, no! (*points at Ern*) *He's* the one with the short, fat, hairy legs.

GEORGE  We're the ones with the big, fat, hairy heads! (*he puts his hand under Eric's chin*) Get out of *that!*

ERIC     What's it like being famous?

JOHN    Well, it's not like in *your* day, you know.

ERIC     *What?* No, that's an insult that, isn't it? (*looks at Ern*) *You* didn't expect that, did you? (*turns back to face John*) What do you mean, 'not like in my day'?

JOHN    Well, me dad used to tell me about *you*, you know. (*he lowers a hand, belatedly, to signify himself as a small child*)

ERIC     (*looking at the hand*) Have you only got a little dad then?

There were two men in the sixties who could have been forgiven for envying Morecambe and Wise their extraordinary critical and commercial success, and they were the two men who were supposed to be Morecambe and Wise's great rivals: Mike and Bernie Winters. Like Morecambe and Wise, they had served a long and arduous apprenticeship in Variety before graduating to television. Unlike Morecambe and Wise, they had always seemed to lack the imagination – as well as, perhaps, the courage – to progress beyond the static combination of gormless grotesque and pompous know-all with which they had started. Mike – the oleaginous straight-man – would always open the act by playing a clarinet solo, at the conclusion of which Bernie – the goofy clown – would signal his first appearance by poking his bowler-hatted head through the centre curtains and emitting his slobbering catchphrase: *'Eeeeeeh!'* Much to Mike and Bernie's chagrin, everyone in showbusiness seemed to know – and relish retelling – the story of how the failure of this routine one night at the Glasgow Empire had inspired their most apposite notice. After Mike's clarinet solo had met with a particularly hostile kind of silence, Bernie, as usual, had poked his bowler-hatted head through the centre curtains and emitted his trademark *'Eeeeeeh!'* 'Christ,' groaned an old man from the gallery, 'there's *two* of 'em!'[36] They persevered, however, and, by the early sixties, their television show was sufficiently popular – with audiences if not with critics – to prompt some of the more mischievous members of the press to plant stories that suggested an increasingly bitter rivalry between Mike and Bernie and Eric and Ernie. It was quite untrue[37] – Morecambe and Wise had no real reason to feel threatened, either in terms of ratings or critical approbation, by an act like Mike and Bernie Winters, and, if there *was* any rivalry at the time, then it was confined to the sibling variety that was sometimes evident between Mike and Bernie themselves. It did not help matters, however, when Eric, asked what he and Ernie would probably have been had they not been comedians, replied, 'Mike and Bernie Winters'.[38]

'Eric and Ernie were always very generous about Mike and Bernie,' recalled Michael Grade, who worked closely with both double-acts during the mid-sixties. 'They were extremely generous about most performers, in fact. They *adored* Harry Worth, for example, and Tommy Cooper, and Bruce Forsyth, but they were very, very confident in their own ability at that point and they didn't feel threatened by, and they weren't jealous of, any other act.'[39] The majority of the critics, however, were not so discreet, and, after pausing momentarily to itemise what they considered to be Mike and Bernie's many inadequacies, did their best to dispatch them swiftly into obscurity by burdening them with the legend, 'the poor man's Morecambe and Wise'.[40] It was not, implied Michael Grade, a put-down that was entirely undeserved:

Let's put it this way: they were both classic double-acts, but if you watched Eric and Ernie work, and then you watched Mike and Bernie work – and I saw them both – you'd know why Morecambe and Wise were Morecambe and Wise and why Mike and Bernie Winters were Mike and Bernie Winters. I think the big difference between them was to do with industry and intelligence. Eric and Ernie would rehearse and rehearse until they had something that they could build on. And they also had much more range in imagination and confidence. Mike and Bernie weren't such good judges of material. Eric and Ernie were *brilliant* judges of material.[41]

If there *was* any rivalry during the sixties between Morecambe and Wise and another double-act, then it was not with Mike and Bernie Winters, but with Hills and Green. Although, after that shaky start, the two teams had established an excellent rapport, the working relationship continued to be unsettled, on certain occasions, by mutual suspicion and resentment. 'The relationship between writer and performer is a complex one,' commented Ernie Wise tactfully, 'since both bring complementary skills to the final product and both are egotistical enough to want to claim the credit.'[42] The problem was that Hills and Green, as time went on, became rather *too* egoistical for Morecambe and Wise's taste. Knowing how much they, as performers, had contributed to each script during the read-throughs and rehearsals, neither Eric nor Ernie was particularly pleased when their writers took to boasting to interviewers, 'We can devise a Morecambe and Wise script as we pass in opposite directions on a Tube escalator.'[43] This conceit would prove to be remarkably resilient: more than twenty years after their association with Morecambe and Wise had ended, Dick Hills was still boasting unashamedly about how 'inexhaustibly inventive' he and Sid Green had been.[44]

'You have to be very careful with writers,' Joan Morecambe observed, 'because writers do, in the end, feel that they are totally responsible for the success of something, and they forget that you actually worked with them every single day and helped to produce this work and then went on and actually performed it.'[45] There can certainly be no doubt about the fact that each and every edition of

*The Morecambe and Wise Show* was the result of four – not two – people's creative input. Preparation for each show began not with the 'inexhaustibly inventive' Hills and Green marching purposefully into the rehearsal rooms with a complete, neatly typed script for Morecambe and Wise to peruse, but rather with Dick Hills arriving on his own at ten o'clock in the morning – Sid Green was invariably half an hour or so late with what Morecambe and Wise referred to as 'a touch of the domestics'[46] – clutching a single piece of paper that bore the title 'Our Ideas for the Week'. The actual script, recalled Morecambe, was then produced by all four of them 'collectively ad-libbing around [the basic ideas] while a girl took the gags down, the draft was rushed out, polished and finally rehearsed'.[47] These sessions, according to Ernie Wise, were 'full of laughs and good humour but not without [their] tensions'.[48] Tempers would sometimes flare when proceedings were interrupted by the late arrival of a morose-looking Sid Green, who would shamble in clutching a cup of tea, slump into a chair and launch immediately into a swingeing critique of what the other three had managed to come up with in his absence. Eric Morecambe, in particular, would respond to this affront with a few sarcastic remarks of his own. 'I think it was inevitable', admitted Joan Morecambe, 'that a few sparks would fly between Eric and Sid now and again, given their personalities, but I don't think it was ever anything *serious*.'[49] Ernie Wise would normally be the one to act as peace-maker, calming each of them down in turn, and such sessions would then, more often than not, continue without further incident.

Even the normally placid Ernie Wise, however, could sometimes be provoked into arguing with Hills and Green. There was a marked tendency, he said, for the writers to claim the credit for the jokes that went well while blaming the performers for those that fell flat:

Sid and Dick might say, 'Look, we wrote a perfectly funny gag which got lots of laughs in rehearsal but you ruined it by doing such and such a thing.' We would counter that by saying, 'It was only thanks to us that the gag managed to raise a smile. It was a weak idea in the first place which we managed to rescue by delivering it in such and such a way.'[50]

This was – and would remain[51] – something of a sore point as far as Morecambe and Wise were concerned, because their contribution to the success of any script – though uncredited – was crucial. 'The makers of Morecambe and Wise were Eric and I,' Ernie Wise insisted. 'We were indebted to our writers . . . But in the final analysis, we had to shape the scripts to our own personalities.'[52] It was Hills and Green's insensitivity to this fact, said Michael Grade, that was at the root of the tension between them:

That was the thing that was always going to fracture the relationship eventually. I mean, I can remember going into Eric and Ernie's dressing-room after they'd recorded a show and finding Eric *seething* because Hills and Green had already been round to criticise them. They just never gave Eric and Ernie enough credit for what they achieved with their material – and they deserved a huge amount of credit. I'll give you an example. There was a Spanish dancing sketch that Sid and Dick had written for them: Eric was supposed to be playing a flamenco guitar, and Ernie was supposed to do the heel-tapping. And apparently in rehearsals it was going well, it was okay, but it wasn't catching fire. Eric, halfway through working the sketch up, said, 'We're playing the wrong parts.' He said, '*I* should be doing the heel-tapping and Ernie should be doing the singing and playing the guitar.' And it just *made* the sketch. They were just brilliant. Little things like that – working out how to take a piece of material and work it till it was, you know, just right. It might be 100 per cent when it arrived and 300 per cent by the time they finished with it. They took their work *very* seriously.[53]

While wholehearted praise for their achievements may seldom have been forthcoming from their writers, it seemed to arrive from most other quarters during the sixties with disarming regularity. In 1963, for example, they were congratulated by ATV for the fact that the third series of *The Morecambe and Wise Show*[54] had come second only to the then fresh soap opera, *Coronation Street*, in the Television Audience Measurement (TAM)[55] top twenty ratings; an outstandingly successful twenty-week-long summer season in

Blackpool attracted further excellent publicity; several newspapers carried articles relating to their new status as the highest paid double-act in the country;[56] they received their first BAFTA award,[57] and the Guild of TV Producers and Directors voted them Britain's top TV Light Entertainment Personalities of the Year. The year 1964 began with more of the same: a pantomime appearance at the Bristol Hippodrome that broke all previous box-office records for that theatre (as well as the bonus of a visit backstage from a warmly appreciative Cary Grant[58]); Wally Ridley, an EMI producer, took them into Abbey Road studios and recorded their first album of comic songs and sketches, *Mr Morecambe Meets Mr Wise*;[59] they were signed up by the Rank Organisation to make their first movie;[60] their fourth series attracted even larger audiences than its predecessors; the Variety Club of Great Britain awarded them Silver Hearts to mark their being declared showbusiness personalities of the year; and they were even summoned to Windsor Castle to perform in front of the Royal Family.[61] 'It seemed', Ernie Wise recalled, 'that we could do no wrong.'[62] Each year brought some new award, some novel tribute – such as Eric Morecambe, on more than one occasion, being handed the title (whether he wanted it or not) of the 'Most Distinctively Bespectacled Man in Great Britain'.[63]

Even among their peers there was a feeling that Morecambe and Wise had, by the mid-sixties, become something rather special. Bruce Forsyth, for example, had not been slow to note the change when he appeared on stage with them at the Palladium in 1964:

We'd worked on the same bill together several times before – when we were both nobodies, you know, or less nobodies than we finished up to be, shall we say – and I'd always liked them. They were the kind of act that you'd always like to stand on the side of the stage and watch, because of the way they played off each other. There were always these little extra bits that would creep into the show, you know, so they were always worth watching from the side, even if you couldn't be in the audience because you were working on the same bill.

When I was top of the bill at the Palladium, however, in 1964, that was the period when they were really starting to hit it *big*. Their TV series was really clicking, and during the summer they'd become very big names, and you could tell, as soon as they came out at the beginning of the show, that something was happening. You could see from the greeting they were given by the audience – it wasn't the kind of greeting they'd give to a couple of people who were just one of the acts on the bill. You could tell that their popularity was growing – and growing very, very quickly.[64]

'We are at our peak,' Eric Morecambe declared at the end of 1964. 'Now. Not last year. Maybe not next year. But now.'[65] It was, they would recall, a 'wonderful' yet 'bewildering' time in which the very success they had courted over so many years now seemed not just to have arrived but also to have 'overtaken us in spite of ourselves'.[66] Eric Morecambe was able to move his wife and two children into a beautiful house next to a golf course in Harpenden, but during their first year he spent a total of no more than twenty days there (Gary Morecambe likened his father at this time to 'an affectionate stranger'[67]). Ernie Wise – even though his wife, Doreen, travelled everywhere with him – was similarly frustrated by the fact that an increase in means had not been accompanied by any discernible increase in leisure. 'People were making demands on us constantly,'[68] he would complain, but neither he nor his partner felt sufficiently secure in their standing to put up more than token resistance. What, they wondered, would count now as 'progress': taking one more step forward, or not taking one step back? The strain was particularly evident in Eric Morecambe's demeanour: ever the 'Jifflearse', he was not only smoking anything between sixty and one hundred cigarettes each day, but he was also, recalled his wife, 'so unrelaxed at times that you couldn't even get him to sit still long enough to have a meal. He'd be up and down like a jack-in-the-box.'[69]

Neither Morecambe nor Wise dared to believe that their good fortune might continue indefinitely. 'I wake up every morning and ask how long the success is going to last,' Morecambe confessed. 'I keep imagining one day the phone is going to ring and a distant voice at the other end is going to say, "Can we have it all back, please?"'[70] They continued to work, by their own admission, 'compulsively': 'We came off stage exhausted and dripping with perspiration, collapsed in chairs in the dressing-room sometimes too tired to stand, and had no time in between bookings to replenish our reserves of energy.'[71]

It was not fear, however, so much as undiminished ambition that spurred them on. Both of them realised that, for all their notable achievements on British television, they still had something to prove. 'If you want to be big, really big,' Ernie Wise insisted, 'you've got to do it in America.'[72] By the mid-sixties, Morecambe and Wise felt ready for the challenge.

# MOVIES

| | |
|---|---|
| ERIC | *Sit down. Now, I know you're all excited and every-thing, but I don't want you to get upset when I tell you something about Hollywood.* |
| ERNIE | *What?* |
| ERIC | *Shirley Temple is almost forty-seven.* |
| ERNIE | *Really?* |
| ERIC | *Yes. She's Lee Marvin's mother. And Donald Duck's a cartoon!* |
| ERNIE | *That's a terrible disillusionment for me.* |

THE MORECAMBE & WISE SHOW

## CHAPTER IX

# American Visions

*The fundamental temper of America tends towards an existential ideal
which can probably never be reached, but can never be discarded: equal
rights to variety, to construct your life as you see fit, to choose your
travelling companions . . . America is a construction of mind, not of race or
inherited class or ancestral territory.*
ROBERT HUGHES

*I am ready to die out of nature, and be born again into this new, yet
unapproachable America I have found in the West.*
RALPH WALDO EMERSON

It only used to cost a few pence each for Eric Bartholomew and
Ernest Wiseman to transport themselves to America once or twice
a week. This was not America the physical continent – neither of
them would set foot on *that* until 1959[1] – but rather 'America' the
imaginary realm of promise, expectation and unbounded hope that
came to life in the dark on every local movie screen. Simply by
entering any cinema, Bartholomew and Wise could go anywhere
and see anything: Frank Capra's Washington, Busby Berkeley's
Broadway, John Ford's Monument Valley, the night-life at Chasen's
and Ciro's and the Coconut Grove, the high life at Bel-Air and San
Simeon – a vast, variegated, magical place where names were
changed, identities transformed, fortunes amassed and ideals made
real.

'It was Shangri-La to us,' recalled Ernie Wise. 'And we idolised
everything about it – open cars, chewing-gum, hot dogs. The films
were spectacular, the music and the dancing were spectacular.'[2] They
were drawn to the glamour, not the grit: 'What we saw then was

upper-class middle-America . . . In the films Mickey Rooney's dad always lent him a beautiful car to take out his girls in. The girls were always beautiful – Lana Turner, Judy Garland. Love meant smooching.'[3] This was the egalitarian America whose golden door was forever open, whose world-wide welcome to the tired, the poor, the huddled masses was never anything but thrillingly real. 'In those days', recalled Eric, 'we all believed in the Shirley Temple, Mickey Rooney, Freddie Bartholomew fantasy.'[4] Even years later, long after Bartholomew had become Morecambe and Wiseman Wise, both of them remained enthralled by those powerful images: 'We lived an American fantasy, sang American songs, used American expressions, spoke with American accents.'[5] *This* was *their* America, and, in a way, it always would be.

Long after they had established themselves in Britain as television stars, they continued to crave the very special approbation that only American audiences and critics could bestow on them. 'What we would dearly like', said Eric Morecambe, 'is to be able to put ourselves across in America. All the great American comics – Laurel and Hardy, Abbott and Costello, Hope, Kaye, Skelton – were launched around the world from Hollywood.'[6] Most of the great British comics, he might have added ruefully, were spurned around the world by Hollywood. Neither the prolific George Formby nor the more gifted Will Hay – Britain's two pre-eminent box-office attractions of the thirties and early forties – made any impression on American audiences,[7] and few of their successors would fare any better. Sid Field, for example, was invited over to Hollywood in 1948 and feted by Danny Kaye, Bob Hope, Cary Grant, Charlie Chaplin and Jack Benny, but he was never given a chance to make a movie there,[8] while neither Norman Wisdom nor Tony Hancock were able to convince American audiences that their appeal was anything other than 'inscrutable'.[9] Morecambe and Wise were well aware of this sad record of rejection, but they took heart from their own history of dogged self-belief: 'Ernie and I, as an act, always fought back,' said Eric. 'Before we were stars we were often hammered down, and we would have to say, "Well, we will prove to you we *are* good." '[10] As far as America was concerned, therefore, they were prepared to fight back.

In the summer of 1964,[11] Morecambe and Wise were handed an opportunity to begin their campaign. They were appearing at the London Palladium with Bruce Forsyth, and Ed Sullivan – the host of the most important Variety show on American television at that time – was sitting in the stalls on a night when their act was particularly well received ('We paralysed the audience that night,'[12] Eric Morecambe recalled). Sullivan was, it seems, greatly impressed, and, as soon as the show was over, he sought out Billy Marsh – who, rather conveniently, was also in the audience that night – and expressed a firm interest in booking them for three appearances at £5,000 per show. Marsh accepted the offer on his clients' behalf,[13] and then wandered backstage to inform them that they would soon be appearing on the other side of the Atlantic, in the centre of Manhattan, on prime-time national television, before an estimated audience of 53 million viewers. 'We were', said Ernie Wise, 'thrilled to bits.'[14]

There was no other show quite like *The Ed Sullivan Show*. It had been – in one form or another[15] – a fixture on US television since 1948. Every Sunday night at 8 o'clock Eastern Standard Time, millions of Americans tuned in to CBS for another hour-long edition of a show that was sometimes shambolic, frequently uneven but always, without fail, eye-catchingly, audaciously, unapologetically eclectic.[16] One never quite knew what to expect: 'We got a really big she*ow* for you tonight,' Sullivan would say – more or less – and then sometimes there would be a plate-spinner, a soft-shoe shuffler, a noisy comic and a numerate shih-tzu; sometimes there would be a patriotic recitation, an eccentric dancer and seventeen minutes of Maria Callas singing arias from *Tosca*; and sometimes – over a dozen times, in fact – there would be another spirited routine from the inimitable Peg Leg Bates, Sullivan's all-time favourite one-legged dancer. The range of star guests was, by any standard, extraordinary: Fred Astaire, Irving Berlin, Albert Schweitzer, Humphrey Bogart, Norman Evans, Bill 'Bojangles' Robinson, Bing Crosby, Montgomery Clift, Bo Diddley, Marlon Brando, Itzhak Perlman, Brigitte Bardot, Sid Caesar, Yehudi Menuhin, Jack Benny, Judy Garland, Fidel Castro, Topo Gigio, Cole Porter, Phil Silvers, Rudolf Nureyev, Frank Sinatra, Sophie Tucker, Orson Welles, Willie Mays and Elvis Presley had all appeared on the show at some point during its sixteen-year existence.[17]

Ed Sullivan presided over each show with the twitchy, distracted demeanour of a man who expected to be arrested at any moment. Flat-lipped and full-browed, he resembled Richard Nixon's older, slower, brother (the comic Joe E. Lewis said of Sullivan that he 'could brighten a room simply by leaving it'[18]). His malapropisms (he once introduced Robert Merrill with the words, 'I'd like to prevent Robert Merrill . . .', and welcomed Dolores Gray as 'one of the fine singing stars of Broadway now starving at the Alvin Theatre'), his maladroit interjections ('Let's hear it for the Samoans from Samoa!') and his embarrassing *faux pas* (introducing clarinetist Benny Goodman as a 'trumpeter', describing a group of native New Zealanders as 'the fierce Maori tribe from New England', calling Terry-Thomas 'England's top television star, Tommy Tucker', and urging a paraplegic in the audience to 'please stand up and take a bow') were legion.[19] *The Ed Sullivan Show*, his critics complained, was 'the only live show with a dead host',[20] but not even they could deny its remarkable – and burgeoning – popularity: on 9 February 1964, when the Beatles made their first appearance on the show, Sullivan scored a Nielsen rating[21] of 23,240,000 viewing homes, which meant that approximately 73,000,000 people had been watching the show – the largest viewing audience yet in television history.[22] Morecambe and Wise, arriving soon after *that*, could not have made a more high-profile American début.

Sullivan, said Ernie Wise, was 'charm itself'.[23] 'Charming' was not the first word that sprang to most people's mind when they met 'Mr Sunday Night', but there was, in fact, something vaguely endearing about his awkwardness, and he genuinely did know – and appreciate – talent when he saw it. He made Morecambe and Wise feel like authentic international stars, and he was a generally encouraging presence during the all-important afternoon rehearsals. 'He really did like them,' Michael Grade recalled. 'They made him laugh at the afternoon show, which was the key thing. He'd always have a run-through of the show in the afternoon, in front of a studio audience, and if he didn't like you *then*, he'd probably just pay you off. Morecambe and Wise always went down well in the afternoons.'[24]

Sullivan, however, was an habitual worrier, and it was not unusual for him to change his mind about the 'appropriateness' of certain lines, gestures or even whole routines that had received his blessing just an hour or so earlier. 'Off the show', said one regular guest, 'he was the nicest, classiest man. On the show itself, he became very intense . . . He became very nervous before each show. He was just trying to make the show as perfect as possible, and he was very insecure.'[25] Sullivan once summed up the 'philosophy' of his show as: 'Open big, have a good comedy act, put in something for the children, keep the show clean.'[26] His great, abiding fear, therefore, was that one day he would grow careless and overlook that single spot of smut or innuendo that would bring shame upon his show (and his sponsors), and therefore he tended to take offence at even the most innocuous of material. In Morecambe and Wise's case, a number of lines (e.g. ERNIE: 'I never knew you were a ventriloquist! I didn't think you were interested in it.' ERIC: 'I'm not any more. I'm too old. That's why I took *this* up!') were cut immediately because of their 'raciness'; a little later on, a line from their musical routine – 'Rum-titty-tum-tum' – was changed to 'Dum-diddy-dum-dum' in order to avert the slightest possibility of causing offence to the Midwestern 'Bible Belt' audience.[27]

The show itself – in spite of these unwelcome and unsettling last-minute revisions at rehearsals – went reasonably well. Ed Sullivan was his usual astatic self, introducing Morecambe and Wise as 'Morrey, Camby and Wise' (in subsequent shows he would experiment with 'Morton and White' before settling on 'Bartholomew and Wisdom')[28] and then rashly joining them for a fairly confusing rendition of the Hills and Green comic song 'Boom Oo Yatta-Ta-Ta' ('His part in the song was just to sing "Boom",' remembered Eric. 'Even that he couldn't remember'[29]), but there were no serious mishaps and the performance – though ill-paced and a little edgy, understandably, by their usual standards – was never less than briskly professional. After the show, however, the disagreements began: Ernie Wise was upbeat and cautiously optimistic, believing that the worst was now over, but Eric Morecambe, in contrast, was not remotely sanguine about their long-term future in America. 'He was unhappy with the reception we got,' remembered Wise, 'unhappy that the applause wasn't overwhelming, unhappy, I think, because he didn't *feel* he was funny enough.'[30] It was a rare – but significant – difference of opinion between the two of them that would never really be resolved.

Ed Sullivan remained a firm admirer of the pair – both as performers and as people – and they made around sixteen further appearances on the show during the next four years, but lasting, nationwide, success in North America continued to elude them.[31] 'They just never had enough time,' said Michael Grade of these occasional guest spots. 'They always did well, but, you know, they never got more than three, four, maybe five minutes at the most, and that was no time at all to really register.'[32] Grade did what he could to rectify the situation: early in May 1968, for example, he set up an audacious project (dubbed 'Operation Madcap' by the press after he had joked that 'everyone who has heard about it thinks we are mad'[33]) that involved transferring the entire company of a London Palladium show – starring Morecambe and Wise and Millicent Martin[34] – to the O'Keefe Centre in Toronto. 'That was *fun*,' he recalled:

We'd had this offer to take a London Palladium show over to Canada, and it was a good offer, because all the expenses were paid and the box-office receipts were guaranteed at a certain level, so we knew that if it did well, we'd get some money, and if it was a disaster, we wouldn't lose money. We talked to Eric and Ernie to see if they wanted to go, and they were happy to do an adventure – something different for two weeks in Toronto.[35]

To coincide with their arrival, they co-wrote a brief article for the *Toronto Telegram* which they hoped would help sell them, and the show, to the Canadian public:

They say Englishmen are at their best at a time of crisis and it's certainly true in our case. The audience love it because they are never sure if something has gone wrong or whether it was planned to happen. We can tell them this much; if things look wrong, then they're right.

... The rivalry we have when we are working together is one of county and home ... It's the Wars of the Roses all over again. Which county wins? Lancashire, of course, according to Morecambe, and Yorkshire, according to Wise.

The advantages of this type of humour is that it never reaches saturation point; mutual gossip and mockery is self-perpetuating. Our act remains unaffected by great events and mutations, and in this sense it is timeless. Wars can break out, and new islands can be discovered, but we're still at it – taking the rise out of each other.[36]

They were not, in fact, entirely unfamiliar to Canadian audiences at this time: the previous year, ATV had sold *Piccadilly Palace* – a special thirteen-part Variety series starring Morecambe and Wise and Millicent Martin and made with the North American market very much in mind – to the ABC network in the US.[37] It had performed particularly well in Canada,[38] so they had good reason to look forward to their two-week-long season (beginning on 13 May) with a fair degree of optimism. When they arrived, however, some of the old anxieties began, according to Michael Grade, to resurface:

It was only when we got there that Eric started with his, '*God!* These people don't *know* me!' and 'They've never *heard* of us – how are we going . . .' He started to get quite nervous. But on opening night they were an absolute sensation. Absolute sensation. It was really great *fun*.

I particularly remember the 'Over the wall' sketch they did with Millie. They'd done that before – the three of them – on one of their ATV shows. Ernie sat on a brick wall and sang 'Moonlight Becomes You' in a duet with Millicent Martin, and Eric was lurking behind the wall. He pulled Ernie off and climbed up next to Millie, then Ernie would pull *him* off, and they'd keep pulling each other off until they'd get confused and pull *her* off, and then finally she'd climb back and pull both of *them* off. It was one of those mad, mad things, and on stage it worked very, very well. The audience loved it.[39]

It was, however, an isolated success, and the critical response to their final appearance on *The Ed Sullivan Show* – also in May 1968 – was damning: 'There was one curiously out of place vaudeville team called Morecambe and Wise which should remain England's problem, not ours.'[40] When the time came to apportion blame for their abortive American adventure, Eric Morecambe chose to single out their strategy – they had attempted to do a full-time job on a part-time basis. Ernie Wise chose to single out Eric Morecambe: for his ambivalence, his nervousness, his parochialism – for his failure, in short, to be less like Eric Morecambe and more like Ernie Wise.

To be fair, there was some truth in both of these accounts. Morecambe and Wise did not spend enough time in America for American audiences to get to know them. The unparalleled exposure that *The Ed Sullivan Show* afforded a performer was only of any lasting value if that performer was prepared to tour the country almost incessantly, keeping their name firmly in the public eye, and getting to know what material works best in which parts of a huge, ethnically and culturally diverse nation like the United States of America. Morecambe and Wise, however, used to make an appearance and then disappear straight back to England, thus ensuring that whatever impact they might have made would soon have faded away. One consequence of this, it seems, is that American audiences never had the opportunity to familiarise themselves with Morecambe and Wise's Northern accents: 'I didn't think the audiences quite understood Eric and I,' said Ernie Wise. 'We spoke too quickly – particularly Eric. They used to say it was rather difficult to understand Eric, with his accent, and of course the difficulty was that *he* had most of the funny lines.'[41] Lew Grade told them on more than one occasion 'to slow down their pace a little', but, he would claim, they 'refused to do this'; the result, he said, was 'that although they were well received in America, they didn't get high ratings'.[42] Several years later, when Bill Cotton Junior – Head of Light Entertainment at the BBC at the time – tried to interest American networks in *The Morecambe & Wise Show*, he discovered that this particular theory still had some influential supporters:

I talked about this to quite a few people. I spoke to Bob Hope, for example. I asked him, 'You know about this as much as anybody – why don't Morecambe and Wise go so well in America?' And he replied, 'Because Eric Morecambe talks too quickly.' I said, 'Too quickly?' He said, 'Yeah. I'm known as a quick-fire comedian, but I've been brought up in a country that has whole towns and streets where American is second language to German or French, and you have to actually speak LIKE-THIS-All-THE-TIME in those places so that they can understand exactly what you're saying, and Eric's just too quick.'

And then I must admit I started listening more carefully to American comedians and I saw exactly what he meant – they *do* speak slower than you think. I mean, Max Miller would have been *completely* incomprehensible to the Americans, I should think.[43]

The *pace* of Morecambe's delivery, however, was surely not the principal cause of any supposed confusion on the part of the audience. When Bob Hope toured the country in vaudeville during the 1910s and 1920s, the annual rate of immigration was at its peak,[44] and the US then was, undeniably, 'a teeming of nations',[45] but the subsequent homogenising effects of radio, movies and television helped to flatten out many of these cultural differences, and by the sixties most audiences were perfectly capable of following such fast-talking comics as Phil Silvers, Jackie Mason, Charlie Callas, Mort Sahl, Henny Youngman, Jonathan Winters and Shecky Green (all of whose pace outstripped that of Eric Morecambe). What some sections of the audience may still have found difficult to understand, however, was the unfamiliar Northern accent, but it seems likely that even this problem could, in time, have been overcome.

What irritated Ernie Wise was his partner's apparent reluctance to come to terms with such problems. 'I was willing to give it a try,' he said. 'I was willing to work at it.'[46] Eric Morecambe, however, seemed disinclined to adapt. He was not, he complained, 'a born traveller anyway. I'm not keen on seeing far-away places like Ernie is.'[47] He also hated flying: 'I used to try to anaesthetise him before take-off with a good slug of whisky,' said Wise. 'But you'd see him gripping the arms of his seat like a condemned man in an electric chair, and he'd stay like that until we landed in New York.'[48] After each appearance, according to his partner, he was so unhappy that he insisted on catching the next available flight home.[49] To Ernie Wise, who believed – passionately – that 'you haven't made it to the top unless you've made it in America',[50] it was inexplicable behaviour. The more he tried to push forward, the more his partner seemed to pull back. 'It was probably', he would say, 'the only time I became impatient with Eric.'[51] This difference of opinion would, eventually, be turned into a source of comedy for their act, with Eric's essential Englishness being contrasted with Ernie's bedazzlement by all things American. In one sketch, for example, Ernie has convinced himself that Bob Hope wants him to emigrate to the US and become his head writer:

| ERIC | Bob Hope? He lives in America, doesn't he? |
|------|--------------------------------------------|
| ERNIE | Of course he lives in America! I will have to leave you and this country, and go and live in Hollywood in a big house. With lots of shirts. And a car with a button that you press that makes the roof go up! |
| ERIC | A car with a button that you press that makes the roof go up? |
| ERNIE | Yes! |
| ERIC | You're joking! |
| ERNIE | I'm not joking! I've never been more serious in all my life! |

An exchange recorded in their 1981 book *There's No Answer to That!*, however, underlined the extent to which this difference in attitude persisted in real life:

| WISE | That's what dreams are made of. |
|------|--------------------------------|
| MORECAMBE | But we've made a dream. The dream came true. It's here. What you're going for is the meringue on the pie. |
| WISE | What I'm saying is, I was going to be another Mickey Rooney . . . |
| MORECAMBE | But you became Ernie Wise. Isn't being the first Ernie Wise better than being another Mickey Rooney? |
| WISE | Yes, now. But I'm talking about when I was twelve. |
| MORECAMBE | But you're *still* talking about 'when I get to Hollywood' as if Hollywood was the big answer. But it isn't, is it? Look what it did for Bruce Forsyth. Nothing! |
| WISE | It's just travelling and having somewhere to go, that's all.[52] |

'Eric and Ernie *could* have made it in America,' insisted Michael Grade. 'They would have adapted, because they were very smart at adapting to all kinds of situations, but it would have meant living there. You can't conquer America from here.'[53] Joan Morecambe agreed:

I feel sure that, had they settled in America, Eric and Ernie would have become enormously successful. But Eric just didn't have any interest in becoming Americanised. He simply would not change. He always said, 'If we go over to the States and try to make the act a success, we'll have to live there – tear up our roots, throw away all that we've achieved in this country, which has taken us all our lives, and start again.' He felt that it was *this* country that had made them stars, and they'd be throwing that away if they'd concentrated on America. And he didn't think it was worth it.[54]

Ernie Wise, however, would never stop thinking back to what he called 'the break that never was',[55] nor would he ever stop believing that 'we could have made it in America':[56] 'The American episode ended without bitterness but with the lurking feeling, on my part at least, that this was unfinished business.'[57]

The one thing that neither of them was ever prepared to abandon hope of was the opportunity to make a genuinely good movie. They first signalled their intention in the early sixties with an audacious bid to buy their own studio. On 19 February 1964, the *Financial Times* carried the following report:

## ANOTHER BID FOR BRITISH LION?

Mr Eric Morecambe and Mr Ernie Wise, the comedians, are interested in the future of British Lion Films. They have written to Mr Edward Heath at the Board of Trade asking for financial details. If these are favourable they plan to approach other entertainers to join them in a combined bid for the company.

Mr Wise stated yesterday that they had not yet had a reply from Mr Heath. An obvious outlet for British Lion would be the production of television films, particularly for export, he said.

A spokesman for the National Film Finance Corporation, which is selling British Lion, said that a communication had been received by the Board of Trade from Mr Morecambe and Mr Wise. But it is regarded as doubtful if a bid would be considered, in view of the decision of the corporation to make January 31 the deadline for offers from prospective purchasers.[58]

On the same day, the *Daily Telegraph* reported Ernie Wise as saying: 'The pattern so far is for bidders to form a production unit and then hire the stars. We would like to reverse the process: the stars would hire the production unit.'[59] Just how serious the bid actually was is something that remains unclear: not only were they up against some extremely powerful opponents (including Sir Michael Balcon, Sam Spiegel, Leslie Grade, Jack Hylton, Brian Epstein and Sidney Box), but they and their associates would have needed to have raised £1,600,000 in order to stand any chance at all of winning the contest. Although Ernie Wise – who appears to have been masterminding the entire operation from the inside of a cramped dressing-room at the Bristol Hippodrome – assured reporters that he 'thought they could get the backing',[60] the lateness of the attempt suggests that this was probably not much more than an imaginative exercise in self-promotion.

'I can't remember *what* motivated it, actually,' Joan Morecambe remarked. 'Something did set it off, obviously, but I *suspect* – I'm not absolutely sure – it was probably a little bit tongue-in-cheek.'[61] News of the bid certainly vanished just as suddenly and as mysteriously as it had appeared,[62] and no mention would be made of it in either one of their autobiographies, but, at the very least, it succeeded in alerting people of influence within the British film industry to the fact that Morecambe and Wise were nursing ambitions that stretched some distance beyond mere television stardom.

At least one movie producer had, as it happened, been hoping to work with Morecambe and Wise since 1960. Hugh Stewart – a former editor for Victor Saville, Alfred Hitchcock and Michael Powell – had seen them one evening when they were appearing in summer season in Weymouth,[63] where he and his director, Robert Asher, were shooting the Norman Wisdom movie *The Bulldog Breed*. He had been sufficiently impressed by what he saw to make a note of them as an act whose progress was well worth monitoring. Four years later, with Morecambe and Wise established as the stars of their own television show, he made his move. The Rank Organisation, acting on his advice, approached them with the offer of a contract to star in three movies in three years. They signed up with barely any hesitation: it might have been Pinewood, England rather than Hollywood, America, but, they reasoned, it was still a chance to make a movie, still a chance to reach beyond a British audience and still a chance, perhaps, to find their Shangri-La.

## CHAPTER X

# The Intelligence Men

*Comedians are stuck like postage stamps on to British Films.*
ALBERTO CAVALCANTI

*Run down that corridor and fall down, that always gets a laugh.*
ROBERT ASHER

That first day, they would say, was wonderful. Everything about Pinewood, it seemed to them, was in keeping with the vision they had long held of how a movie studio should be: a grandiose exterior ('unfocused English Baroque', according to one observer[1]); the fabulously protean interiors (the opulent relics from *Cleopatra*, recycled for *Carry On Cleo*, were in the process of being replaced by the austere metropolitan sets of *The Ipcress File*); the feverish, vaguely choreographed flurries of activity (cameras rolling along the stages, plasterers and carpenters rushing from job to job, gofers zigzagging anxiously on multiple last-minute errands); and the eye-catching array of portraits (Lean, Reed, Hitchcock, Guinness, Olivier, Monroe) in commemoration of illustrious visitors. Ernie Wise would come to look back on that day as 'the greatest moment I remember in showbusiness'.[2] Wandering wide-eyed from one set to the next, this hopeful man – whose own suggestion for his epitaph had been, 'I was still on my way to Hollywood'[3] – could not contain his feelings of sheer excitement: 'I was certain I was now going to become that international film star.'[4]

It did not take long for harsh reality to intrude on this reverie. Shooting his first scene on location, Wise's initial delight in finding that he had been accorded the honour of his own personal trailer ('That was status, to start with') turned abruptly to dismay when he looked inside: 'I walked into the van and discovered there was neither heating nor running water. I stayed there while my stand-in pushed my dinner through the window on a paper plate.'[5] Eric Morecambe, sitting in the bar at Pinewood later that same day, was similarly disillusioned. Expecting it to be like the Hollywood of the thirties, 'when all the stars sat around and were buddy-buddy with each other',[6] he was surprised to discover that most of his new colleagues had departed just as soon as filming had finished. 'I had to sit in the bar on my own, waiting for the traffic to ease off before I could go home. We never did use all that booze.'[7]

Such disappointments are all too common for newcomers on movie sets as the bright novelty of the first few days gives way to the dull monotony of the average shooting schedule, but Morecambe and Wise soon had other, far more serious reasons for feeling anxious about the fate of their initial starring vehicle. Before they arrived at Pinewood, they had announced their intention 'to bring to the films the same originality we've brought to television. We don't want them', they added, 'to be just typical British comedies with all the usual ingredients.'[8] It was soon made clear to them, however, that while they may have been expecting to emulate such heroes as Laurel and Hardy and the Marx Brothers by creating their own distinctive brand of screen comedy, the Rank Organisation was expecting them to emulate none other than its current British box-office success, Norman Wisdom. The arrival of each member of the production team served to draw attention to this connection: first came Norman Wisdom's regular producer, Hugh Stewart; then his regular director, Robert Asher; then his cameraman, Jack Asher; then his composer, Philip Green; and then one of his writers, Peter Blackmore. Once this group of Rank stalwarts was installed, another one of those 'typical British movies with all the usual ingredients' looked to be by far the most likely outcome of Morecambe and Wise's first movie venture.[9]

This lack of imagination on the part of the Rank Organisation was hardly surprising. Although the British film industry was reputed to be enjoying something of a renascence at that time, it was, in reality, in a precarious condition: cinema admissions were in precipitous decline,[10] cinemas were closing at a rate of around 240 each year and American money was behind the vast majority of the major productions of the period.[11] Rank itself, after failing at the end of the previous decade to open up the US market through its own distribution set-up, was in the process of diversifying into other areas, such as Rank-Xerox.[12] As far as film production was concerned, it was looking for industrial efficiency rather than artistic ingenuity. Its Norman Wisdom series exemplified this attitude: ever since the remarkable success of *Trouble in Store* (1953), Rank had been churning out Wisdom movies at the rate of around one a year. The formula bred contentment: each variation on the theme of the little man versus the big, bullying authority figure blended effortlessly into an endless black-and-white blur. The critics, by the early sixties, had started expressing their regret at the misuse of a very talented performer ('Every Norman Wisdom film', lamented one reviewer, 'is dispiriting for the flashes which from time to time suggest that, used with taste and discipline, he might have been a good comic'[13]), and the long-suffering Wisdom had himself begun to complain that Rank 'don't seem to realise that I have grown up and can get laughs without falling downstairs',[14] but his faithful fans still flocked to the box-office for each new instalment. What the conservative Rank regime expected from Morecambe and Wise, therefore, was more of the same.

If there was one aspect of Rank's preparation that could not be faulted, however, it was the quality of the supporting cast, which was full of such experienced and accomplished British actors as William Franklyn, Francis Matthews, Terence Alexander, Warren Mitchell and Richard Vernon. The presence of both Franklyn[15] and Matthews[16] must have been particularly reassuring as far as Morecambe and Wise were concerned, not only because of their considerable expertise in playing light comedy but also because of their undisguised admiration of, and affection for, Eric Morecambe and Ernie Wise. William Franklyn, for example, had been one of their first and most vocal supporters since seeing them perform on stage in the early fifties:

> The first time I saw them was in pantomime, a matinee, at Golders Green Hippodrome – it must have been about 1953. My father [Leo Franklyn] was playing the Dame, and just before I went round to get my seat he told me: 'Oh, by the way, the

two robbers are off. We've got this other double-act who are covering. I'd be interested to see what you think of them.' Well, within about fifteen seconds of them coming on I was beginning to get *hysterical* with laughter. It wasn't the gags, it was the characterisation – particularly of the one who wore glasses – and I just laughed and laughed.

I went round to Dad afterwards and said: 'Those two men have got a future, Dad! They're wonderful! Since Sid Field I've seen nobody to compare with them. I've had the greatest afternoon of my life!' And this was Eric Morecambe and Ernie Wise, who hadn't even been billed! They used to go out to the theatre every day in case anybody was off and then they'd go in. And they were just *wonderful*.[17]

Francis Matthews was similarly enthusiastic:

I'd always been a great fan – one of their first, I should think! I remember seeing them in *Running Wild*. Everybody was saying, '*That* couple? They're terrible!', but I was *riveted*. I used to say to people, 'You've got to see these two characters, they are so *funny*!' I can even remember some of the routines; some of the things they did back then, and got slaughtered for, they did again ten years later, and then everybody adored them!

When I first met Angie [Angela Browne], my wife, I used to tell her: 'If you want to see really high-class comedy, you've got to watch a man called Eric Morecambe with his partner Ernie Wise. They're music-hall comedians, but they're much more than music-hall comedians, particularly Eric – he works like an actor, he times things just like a great actor does.' Oh, I just *loved* them, I really did.

I met them for the first time in the mid-fifties at a party in Notting Hill Gate. They actually came up to me and Eric said: 'I know you – I've seen you on the telly. I love your stuff!' And I said, 'Well, it's mutual – yours is my favourite comedy show.' He said: 'Ah, it's rubbish! Nobody likes it. We'll never do television again; they don't want us on television.' But I was from the North, like them, and we enjoyed the same kind of humour, loved the same comedians, so we got on very well right from the start. I was full of admiration for them, I really was.'[18]

Both Morecambe and Wise, Matthews recalled, were visibly excited by the prospect of appearing in their first movie:

I remember Bill [Franklyn] and I were having lunch in the restaurant on the first day of the film, and Eric came in and joined us. He'd never been in a film studio before, and he was glancing round at a few of the other actors and saying to us, 'Oh, this is *great!*' Then Ernie came in and joined us, and he said: 'Where are all the stars, then? Where are they? Where?' I said: '*You're* the stars here.' And Ernie said: 'No, no. I'm talking about *film stars*, you know, real *film* stars.' I said: '*You're* making a film. *You're* film stars now – and you're better known than most of the other people in this room!' And, you know, all of the actors really *did* want to meet them, because they *were* big stars by then in this country. The TV show was huge. But they were such modest men. It was always, 'Come on, Fran! Introduce us to some *stars!*'[19]

*The Intelligence Men* was set to be a spy spoof. The success of the first James Bond movie, *Dr No*, in 1962, followed by *From Russia with Love* in 1963 and then *Goldfinger* (which had recently been released), coupled with the fact that Hugh Stewart felt that Hills and Green were at their best when writing parodies of popular shows and familiar formats ('Their whole technique', he said, 'was based on really codding other things like *The Count of Monte Cristo*'[20]), convinced Rank that such a 'timely' spoof would appeal to the widest domestic audience as well as stand a reasonable chance of succeeding in the US (where it would be retitled *Spylarks*). Unfortunately, as far as the movie's novelty value was concerned, another spy spoof, *Carry on Spying*, appeared a short time before shooting on *The Intelligence Men* commenced, and neither Peter Blackmore – who came up with the basic storyline – nor Hills and Green – who wrote the screenplay – appear to have had a particularly sharp sense of just what form a spoof should take of a genre that already had its tongue tucked firmly inside its cheek.

What they ended up with was a cross between Bob Hope's *My Favorite Spy* (1951) and Alfred Hitchcock's *The Lady Vanishes* (1938) – which sounds considerably more intriguing than it actually was. Morecambe played the imaginatively named 'Eric Morecambe', the ebullient proprietor of a poky Soho coffee bar, and Wise played 'Ernie Sage', the most ambitious tea-boy at MI5. The plot concerns an attempt by SCHLECT, a shady international crime organisation, to sabotage Anglo-Soviet relations by assassinating Madame Petrovna – Russia's great prima ballerina – when she next appears in a production of *Swan Lake* at Covent Garden. The problem facing MI5's Colonel Grant (William Franklyn) and his two assistants, Mr Thomas (Francis Matthews) and Mr Reed (Terence Alexander), is how to replace their recently deceased double-agent, the redoubtable Major Cavendish, whom SCHLECT agents are waiting to make contact with in London. Sage, who has overheard Grant's discussions, ponders the problem while he takes a 'hot, frothy coffee' break in Morecambe's bar. When a SCHLECT agent mistakes Morecambe's impromptu rendition of 'It's a Long Way to Tipperary' for a snatch of *Swan Lake*, Sage gets the idea of passing Morecambe off as Major Cavendish. The pair blunder consequently through a series of adventures – which Sage half understands and Morecambe misconstrues entirely – until the climax is reached with a frenzied *Night at the Opera*-style chase backstage at Covent Garden.

*The Intelligence Men* is not so much a coherent movie as a number of discrete television sketches stitched awkwardly together. Anyone familiar with *The Morecambe and Wise Show* would have felt instantly at home: all of the catchphrases were there ('Geddoff!', 'He knows nothing!', 'I'll smash your face in!', 'Get out of that!'), several of the old routines were there, and there was even a cameo appearance by Hills and Green (playing, as far as one could tell, two writers waiting eagerly for their lines to arrive). As a big-screen showcase for a small-screen show, it worked quite well, and as an attempt at luring a large television audience back into the cinema, it made sound commercial sense. It was certainly not, as far as début movies are concerned, a poor effort. There are some decent set-pieces (notably Eric's inept demonstration of a variety of self-defence techniques in the presence of a puzzled-looking Francis Matthews), a few Bob Hope-style comic lines (ERIC: 'Look, there's only one thing I want to do before I die.' ERNIE: 'What's that?' ERIC: 'Live a long time.'), and two surprisingly assured performances by the stars themselves (Wise, apart from seeming a little subdued at times, is always competent, while Morecambe, in particular, has some excellent moments). 'They adapted with such ease,' observed William Franklyn:

> You didn't feel, 'Oh, we've got a lot to teach *these* two!' On the contrary, you thought, 'They've taken to this *so* easily!' It was very striking, because, you know, stage comedians can struggle when they first attempt to make a film, because it's a whole different technique, a different set of disciplines, but Eric and Ernie looked at home right from the start.
>
> Eric, I remember, was really quite exceptional. If we went one take, two takes, three, four, five, six, he managed to do it like *that* [clicks his fingers] – perfectly each time. It didn't get dissipated, it didn't fade away, it still had the same quality at take nine that it had at take one, two or three. That was the thing that impressed me more than anything else – watching someone new to film, doing comedy in front of an audience that doesn't laugh, and he was still managing to maintain that accuracy and freshness through every take.[21]

Francis Matthews was particularly struck by Eric Morecambe's gift for improvisation:

> He was inspired. I remember when we were rehearsing the martial arts scene – You know: 'Get out of that! Now try and get the briefcase off him. Go on!' – at one point Eric was speaking to Ernie and he said, 'I'll show you what I mean. Can I borrow your briefcase for a moment, Mr . . . er . . . ?', and I was supposed to say yes and give him the briefcase. Well, instead of that I said, 'Do, do.' And he said, 'Mr Do-Do, thank you very much!' And that was one of his improvisations that they kept in. And in all of the other scenes we had he'd say, 'Hello, Mr Do-Do!', or 'Can Mr Do-Do come, too?' That was totally Eric's. That's what he did.[22]

The performances were good, but they were let down by the

production. Whatever subtlety and wit Morecambe, Wise, Franklyn and Matthews brought to a scene was vitiated by the combination of Philip Green's cliché-ridden musical interjections (the aural equivalent of an unwelcome dig in the ribs) and Robert Asher's flat and feckless direction. Whereas a great director of comedy – a Leo McCarey, a Preston Sturges or a Howard Hawks – would shoot and edit a scene in such a way as to allow the audience to see the humour emerge from within a given situation, a director such as Asher had neither the patience nor the courage to consider anything other than to make the camera dart nervously and artificially from one supposedly comic point to the next. Far from having anything of the storyteller about him, Asher appeared content to film whatever the script told him to film and leave it to the audience to make sense of the resultant mess. 'You're not trying to photograph a budget or a cost sheet,' Howard Hawks once advised other directors of comedy. 'You're trying to make a scene that's going to be good, the best you know how. If you don't it's your own damn fault.'[23]

It was a pity that such good advice, in the case of *The Intelligence Men*, was allowed to go unheeded. Asher, to be fair, was only doing what Rank expected of any of its directors – shooting a movie as quickly and as economically as was practicable – but there can be little doubt that the comic potential of the screenplay suffered as a consequence both of his narrowmindedness and haste. It was sometimes, according to Franklyn, a singularly frustrating experience for the character actors:

I remember Fran, Terry and myself feeling terribly restricted. Whenever we tried to get some of the irony and some of the other elements that were there, Bob [Asher] would say: 'No, no, fellers, don't – *Eric* is here to get the laughs!' We weren't trying to get *laughs* – we were trying to add little things to *support* the comedy, but Bob, I'm afraid, was used to a very *broad* type of comedy style.[24]

Francis Matthews was similarly unimpressed:

Bob Asher was a journeyman director. I don't mean anything disrespectful by that, but I think he was more or less a staff director at Rank, and he was pretty well the one they used to direct a lot of their comedy films. They all had a certain style; he followed it. He *was* restrictive, but I didn't mind that quite as much as Bill [Franklyn] probably did, because I'd worked with Bob before on a Norman Wisdom film, *A Stitch in Time*, only a year or so before, so I'd sort of resigned myself to it. You know, we'd do something very, very, understated, and then Bob would just put it on the cutting-room floor and that would be the end of that. He would always do the covering shots of us listening, or talking to each other, but if it was at all subtle, if it was at all interesting in character terms, Bob would just cut it – he'd stay on Eric and Ernie and you'd just hear our voices. But I was ready for that; if you're working with stars like Eric and Ernie you do expect that.

What I *really* disliked, however, was his undercranking [operating the camera at a slower than normal speed so that the action appears accelerated when projected on the screen]. It was none of my business, but I never agreed with Bob on that. You know, he used to undercrank a lot in his films – he used to think it was *terribly* funny. Even Norman Wisdom used to say to him, 'Don't undercrank it, Bob. Bob – you're not going to undercrank this, are you, Bob, promise?' Norman hated it. And I wish they hadn't used it in *The Intelligence Men*, because as soon as a chase starts or something, and they undercrank it, I just think, 'Oh, sorry, you've lost me', because there's no tension, there's nothing real, and it stops being funny.[25]

The shooting schedule, at least as far as Morecambe and Wise were concerned,[26] grew increasingly 'frantic' as each day went by.[27] They were due to arrive at the Palace Theatre in Manchester on 12 December to begin their usual two weeks of rehearsal for their forthcoming pantomime season, but shooting shut down at Pinewood only on 22 December, leaving them just one day to travel up to Manchester and one day to rehearse before opening on Boxing Day for what was set to be a sixteen-week run. There was no time for reflection; no time for either man to sit back and evaluate the experiences of the past few weeks. The movie was over; they would not see the finished article for another two months.

The premiere of *The Intelligence Men* was held at the Odeon in Manchester at the end of March 1965.[28] Several members of the cast – including Terence Alexander, William Franklyn and Francis Matthews – travelled up to accompany Morecambe and Wise to the first screening. 'It was a good occasion,' Matthews remembered. 'There was a big crowd outside – Eric and Ernie were a bit taken aback by the warm reception they got – and the film seemed to go down very well with the audience.'[29] Eric Morecambe, according to Matthews, seemed particularly relieved by such a positive response:

We could see that he wanted to celebrate but wasn't sure what to do, so I said to him: 'Come out to dinner with us, Eric.' His eyes lit up and he said: 'I'd *love* that!' So we all went off to this late-night restaurant, where they had dancing as well, and we celebrated. I'll always remember one thing about that night: Angie, my wife, was very pregnant, and Eric, that darling man, got up at one point and said, 'Will you dance with me, Angie?' and she said, 'Of course, Eric.' And apparently, Angie tells me that when he was dancing with her she said: 'I'm sorry I'm so fat – you can't get near me!' And he said: 'Oh, there's nothing more beautiful in the world than a pregnant woman. I love to see it. It's *wonderful*.' He made her feel so special.[30]

The mood changed abruptly the following morning with the arrival of the first few reviews. *The Times* was hostile: 'An unspeakable British farce in which two funny stage and television comedians, Morecambe and Wise, are fed through the Norman Wisdom sausage machine (by the team responsible for the last Norman Wisdom film) and come out looking as though they could not make a hyena laugh. Which is a shame, and a waste for all concerned.'[31] The London *Evening Standard* limited itself to a single sentence: 'Norman Wisdom please come back.'[32] What was interesting, however, was the fact that very few of these reviews chose to hold Morecambe and Wise responsible for the movie's shortcomings; some of them criticised Rank for misusing its latest stars, while several others, such as the *Monthly Film Bulletin*, reserved their ire for Robert Asher's direction: 'This exceptionally unfunny comedy makes it very hard to understand what, on any level, has contributed to the popularity of Morecambe

'It's a foursome really: us, Johnny and Eddie. It's a team.'

The theatrical experience: in front of the tabs.

Ann Hamilton, the show's singular female presence.

The dance:
devised by
Groucho
Marx . . .

. . . adapted by
John
Ammonds . . .

. . . and perfected by Morecambe and Wise.

Braben put Eric and Ernie 'into an enclosed space, so they couldn't escape each other . . .'

Double acts share double beds: 'If it's good enough for Laurel and Hardy, it's good enough for you,' Braben told them.

Peter Cushing:
the first of many
star guests.

Mr Preview, Mr
Morecambe, and
a difference of
opinion over
Grieg. 'The
funniest thing we
ever did,' said
Eric.

'Elton? Sounds like an exit on the motorway!'

Diana Rigg (as Nell Gwynn) joins Eric and Ernie for a typical 'romp'.

David Dimbleby was made to dance . . .

. . . and Robin Day made to suffer.

'All men are fools, and what makes them so is having beauty like what I have got.'

and Wise. A formal dinner-party scene, not by any means devoid of farcical possibilities, is so appallingly mishandled by the director that it emerges as an almost classic example of how not to amuse while apparently trying.'[33]

When, in the seventies, Morecambe and Wise came to reflect on this period in their career, they would describe *The Intelligence Men* as 'a flop' and 'a critical disaster',[34] but in doing so they were guilty of exaggerating the extent of its rejection. Not all of the reviews, by any means, were negative. The *People*, for example, while noting that the movie was 'a good deal less funny than you'd think from two such masters of lunacy',[35] was generally encouraging; *Films & Filming* judged 'the whole experience mildly but definitely amusing';[36] and Cecil Wilson, the *Daily Mail*'s critic, recommended it enthusiastically as a movie that 'bristles with comic invention'[37] – and it certainly performed creditably at the domestic box-office.[38] Morecambe and Wise, however, were in no mood to take any comfort from such saving graces. The worst of the reviews, said Wise, had struck them 'like bolts from the thunder god'.[39] Next time, they both agreed, there would have to be some changes made; next time, they insisted, it would all be very different.

## CHAPTER XI

# That Riviera Touch

*As popular entertainment, movies need something of what the vulgarian moguls had – zest, a belief in their own instincts, a sentimental dedication to producing pictures that would make their country proud of their contribution, a respect for quality, and the biggest thing: a willingness to take chances.*
PAULINE KAEL

*What we've got to do is give the public what they want. Keep it sharp, a lot of speed, and try to keep it to a 'U' certificate.*
ERIC MORECAMBE

*That Riviera Touch* turned out to be a surprisingly artful exercise in commercial ingratiation. The title, for example, appealed both to those who hankered after the kind of 'sophisticated' screen comedy (*That Night with You, That Uncertain Feeling, That Touch of Mink*) that had fallen out of fashion, as well as to those who preferred the kind of self-consciously cosmopolitan 'caper' movies (*Arabesque, The Great Race, Topkapi*) that were currently in vogue. The title song – with its references to jet planes and aperitifs, 'swinging attention', *chercher la femme* and the promise of *amour* 'forever and evermore' – was equally pliant, somehow managing to sound both gauche and urbane simultaneously. Everything about the movie, in fact, exuded an almost overbearing eagerness to please.

One genuine advantage that it had over its predecessor was the presence of a considerably more accomplished production team. Robert Asher had been replaced as director by Cliff Owen – a far more versatile film-maker who had worked in the past with such diverse talents as Peter Sellers, Melina Mercouri, James Garner and

Stanley Baker. The cameraman Jack Asher – Robert's brother – had given way to the distinguished Czech cameraman Otto Heller, whose many screen credits included *De Mayerling à Sarajevo* (1940); *The Ladykillers* and *Richard III* (both 1955); and *The Ipcress File* (1965). Rank had also arranged for Peter Blackmore – who had again been the man responsible for coming up with the premise for the movie – to assist the relatively inexperienced Hills and Green in the writing of the screenplay. Finally – and much to everyone's excitement – the greater part of the movie was to be shot not in the studio at Pinewood but on location in the South of France.

There appeared to be a mass of major film units scattered all over that region during the summer of 1965. In addition, for example, to the crew of *That Riviera Touch* in Cannes, Audrey Hepburn, Peter O'Toole, Charles Boyer, George C. Scott and Eli Wallach were working with William Wyler in Paris and Cannes on *How to Steal a Million*; Marcello Mastroianni, Omar Sharif, Yul Brynner and Angie Dickinson were making *The Poppy is Also a Flower* in Monaco; and Tony Curtis was shooting *Arrivederci, Baby*[1] at a variety of locations along the French Riviera. 'We met all the stars,' Joan Morecambe recalled:

> It was a wonderful experience, it really was – probably the best time of my life, in fact. We stayed at a lovely hotel [the Negresco], we met all the big names – your Omar Sharifs and what have you – who were staying there, we went out to dinner to all of these lovely little French restaurants, which *they* [the other stars] knew but we had no idea about. We were so naïve – innocents abroad, really! – but we had a wonderful time.

Doreen and I were very well-treated. For us it was a holiday! The boys, poor devils, were working most of the time, whereas we could take in the sights, you know, soak up the atmosphere. Even location filming was great. We had to get up at about five o'clock in the morning, but the sun would be shining and we'd get into these vehicles and go off to the spot of the location, which would be some millionaire's residence on the South of France coast, you know, and the beach things were mostly shot at Juan-les-Pins. And the moment we'd arrive, there'd be this wonderful smell of hot French bread and coffee. Oh, it was an unforgettable time for the whole lot of us.[2]

They also had plenty of opportunities to socialise with old friends from home, such as the singer Edmund Hockridge: 'Jackie, my wife, and I were on holiday in the South of France at the time, so they got in touch with us, called us over, and we had a wonderful party with Lionel Jeffries, Warren Mitchell and all of these friends. We had a *lot* of fun.'[3]

Even the work itself – thanks in large part to Cliff Owen's far more assured style of direction – proved to be a relatively pleasurable experience. Francis Matthews – who returned, at the request of Morecambe and Wise, to make a cameo appearance in the movie – recalled the relaxed atmosphere on the set:

> Cliff Owen was an excellent director – and a lovely man – who had this kind of big, bubbling, Rabelaisian personality that would get everyone in the right sort of mood and generate a really up-beat atmosphere on the set. He certainly knew how to direct comedy, and I think Eric and Ernie felt as though they now had a kindred spirit to work with and bounce ideas off. Bob [Asher] had tended to keep pushing them on in order to keep to the schedule, but Cliff was more prepared to let them try a few things out, be more inventive, you know, which I imagine made the whole experience for them feel much more like the way they made their TV shows.[4]

A happy set does not always make for an effective movie,[5] but Owen was eager to capture on film something of the exuberance that informed Morecambe and Wise's television performances, and, on this occasion at least, his tactics looked like paying off.

Things started to happen: Eric Morecambe began to come up with a vast array of ideas for new visual gags and more incisive comic lines; Ernie Wise devised a number of novel little gestures and expressions to make his on-screen character seem at least a shade more believable; and, working in unison, they managed to weave some precious strands of wit into the patchwork quilt that passed for a script. Owen himself, as he had shown three years earlier when working with the mercurial Peter Sellers on the set of *The Wrong Arm of the Law*, was not averse to altering the pace or the shape of a scene if the quality of the performance seemed to warrant it, and he did so again in response to the best of Morecambe and Wise's improvised contributions. They continued to feel constrained by the old familiar formula, but at least they had found some space to play in.

The movie's plot was fashionably intricate: 'Eric' and 'Ernie', two errant traffic wardens, set off in their vintage car for a vacation on the French Riviera. They are directed to a deserted villa by a man whom they take to be a travel agent but who is in fact an employee of Le Pirate, the head of a ruthless gang of jewel thieves. Le Pirate plans to secrete a stolen diamond necklace in the petrol tank of Eric and Ernie's car in order to smuggle it through Customs; in further-ance of this scheme, another member of the gang, a sensual *femme fatale* called Claudette (Suzanne Lloyd), pretends to be attracted both to Eric and to Ernie. When Eric – quite by accident – wins a large sum of money at the casino, he announces, much to the distress of Claudette, that he intends to buy a new car; Claudette responds by plotting to have his winnings stolen, but Eric and Ernie, having grown increasingly suspicious of her motives, are by now on their guard. The remainder of the movie is devoted to wild and rapid chases by land, sea and air as the two anxious Englishmen do their best to elude their various pursuers.

Owen elicited some appealing performances from the supporting cast – such as Armand Mestral's world-weary police inspector – as well as ensuring that at least a fraction more of Morecambe and Wise's familiar humour made it up on to the screen, and – apart from the use of some patently unconvincing back-projection during a number of the action sequences – the movie certainly *looked* more stylish than it had any right to do on such a low budget. The screenplay, however, was, once again, a major disappointment: instead of having the courage to make the plot seem relatively inci-dental to the characters, it was content to make the characters seem relatively incidental to the plot, and thus make the two stars seem peripheral to their own starring vehicle.

The reviews, when they appeared, were mixed. Some were harshly negative: the somewhat austere *Monthly Film Bulletin*, for example, praised Otto Heller's 'diamond-sharp photography' but argued that, in most other respects, the movie was 'a dismal affair of antediluvian comic routines' that was 'strictly for hardened Morecambe and Wise fans'.[6] Others were merely ambivalent: the *Daily Mail* declared that Morecambe and Wise 'have it in them to be a side-splitting film comedy team, but they need funnier material than [this] to prove their mettle';[7] the *Sun* argued that Morecambe and Wise were 'deservedly popular television comedians' whose latest attempt at big-screen success had been undermined by a plot that was 'so contrived and convoluted that I found myself having difficulty in keeping up with it';[8] and the *Sunday Telegraph* judged the movie to be 'sharper than *The Intelligence Men*' but regretted the fact that the stars had been allowed to be somewhat overshadowed by the 'lovely, dotty' chase sequences.[9] A fair number of the reviews, however, were broadly enthusiastic: *The Times*, for example, acknowledged the appropriateness of Cliff Owen's style of direction, pronounced the plot to be 'serviceable enough' and concluded that the movie as a whole was 'a considerable improvement on their first';[10] and *Films & Filming*'s critic confessed that he had 'laughed more consistently at this film than at any [other] British comedy in the last year or so'.[11]

Although it failed to make much of an impression in America, where it suffered the inevitable consequences of scant promotion and limited distribution, it performed relatively creditably in Britain, and won over some doubters in the process. Kenneth Williams, for example, recorded the following entry in his diary upon returning home from seeing the movie at his local cinema: '[Morecambe and Wise] have always been my unfavourite comedians, but there were some v. funny & original things in this film, which was v. well done. These two came out of it v. well indeed – v. much innocents abroad and at times a real note of pathos established.'[12]

The general feeling was that a reasonable amount of progress had been made. *That Riviera Touch* was certainly no British comedy classic – indeed, its supposed superiority to *The Intelligence Men* had rather more to do with the packaging than it did with the product – but there was still an air of smart efficiency about it that encouraged one to believe that something rather better might be built on its foundations. The third movie in the series, it seemed, might just be the one to make the all-important breakthrough. As one of the critics had said: 'Better luck, perhaps, next time.'[13]

CHAPTER XII

# The Magnificent Two

*Films? Exactly the same as TV. Bigger, that's all.*
ERIC MORECAMBE

*Collectivism is indispensable in the film, but the collaborators must be
blended with one another to an exceptionally close degree.*
V. I. PUDOVKIN

It was probably the sight of the volcano that did it. Shortly after
Morecambe and Wise had arrived back at Pinewood to start work
on their third – and, they hoped, their best – movie, they discovered,
on a backlot, the craggy exterior of a massive volcano that was under
construction for use in the forthcoming James Bond project, *You
Only Live Twice*. This volcano, someone pointed out to them, was
probably going to cost somewhere in the region of £250,000 to
complete – rather more, in other words, than the entire budget
Rank had set aside for the next Morecambe and Wise movie. They
returned, somewhat crestfallen, to the empty place where their own
humble set was about to be built and did their best to come to terms
with the sad disparity that separated their dreams from their means.

They would have been forgiven had they felt that the British film
industry had abandoned them at the beginning of 1967. Every other
movie being made at a British studio at that time seemed to owe its
existence in part or in full to American money: John Schlesinger's
*Far from the Madding Crowd*, for example, was co-produced by Metro-
Goldwyn-Mayer; Albert Finney's *Charlie Bubbles* was produced by
Universal; Jack Clayton's *Our Mother's House* was financed largely by
Filmways; *Half a Sixpence* by Paramount; and the Bond movies by
United Artists. In its January preview of the year's home-based

projects, *Films & Filming* lamented: 'If one looks at the current productions here, there is in fact only one totally "British" film on the floor . . . and that's Morecambe and Wise.'[1]

The Morecambe and Wise production seemed to epitomise much that was wrong with the British film industry at that time. The stars wanted to make a high-quality, character-driven comedy; the writers (Hills and Green, assisted on this occasion both by Peter Blackmore and the more experienced Michael Pertwee) wanted to make a gently political satire; the director, Cliff Owen again, appears to have intended to make a big, brash action-adventure; and Hugh Stewart and Rank wanted merely to make something that was competent, cheap and delivered on time – and what they all ended up with was a great mess of a movie that failed to satisfy any one of these ambitions.

*The Magnificent Two* – far from being Morecambe and Wise's best movie – turned out to be their worst. Its plot (which was based loosely on an idea that had been used before – *The Great Dictator*, *To Be or Not to Be* – and would be used again – *Bananas*, *Moon over Parador*, *Dave*) concerns the plight of two travelling toy salesmen, Eric and Ernie, who become involved in a bloody revolution in the South American town of Parazuellia: Eric is persuaded to pose as Torres, the guerrilla movement's recently deceased figurehead, for whom he has already been mistaken. After the revolution, Eric not only becomes the new President but, spurred on by the advice of the visiting British Ambassador (played by Cecil Parker), also goes on to make all manner of rash promises to the people, which horrify his more cynical associates. While they plot to assassinate him and resume the pursuit of their original base objectives, a Women's Army – led by Carla (Margit Saad), the one member of the Revolutionary Committee who has a conscience – emerges as an alternative political force. It did not help matters that the movie's 'sun-drenched' South American countryside looked suspiciously like a cold and damp Denham in Buckinghamshire, or that the usually reliable Cliff Owen directed certain parts of the movie as if he was auditioning for Arthur Penn, or, indeed, that the denouement – which features a swarm of (visibly cold) bikini-clad women – appeared to have been the feverish handiwork of a fourteen-year-old boy.

The critics, understandably, were perplexed. Barry Norman, writing in the *Daily Mail*, captured the general mood:

The trouble with this film is that it stars Morecambe and Wise and has a U certificate, two things which are simply not compatible.

They are strictly A certificate comedians, this pair. Robbed, as they are here, of the deplorable and hilarious *double entendres* which spice their TV shows, they seem strangely uneasy and inhibited.[2]

It was not as though the movie was devoid of all humour – it contained, perversely, some above-average routines and a few reasonably amusing comic lines (e.g. CARLA: 'Always, wherever you go, I shall be the woman behind you.' ERIC: 'You'll come round the front now and again, won't you?'), as well as the odd affectionate nod in the direction of music-hall's ancient history (ERN: 'I'm going to siesta.' ERIC: 'Give her my regards.'). Nor was it as though Morecambe and Wise were shown to be out of their depth in this medium – both of their performances (and Wise's in particular) were, in technical terms at least, an improvement on their two previous efforts, but, crucially, there was no sense of cohesion: one moment there was a Laurel and Hardy-style piece of innocent comic playfulness (when Ern is knocked out one actually hears the sound of twittering birds), and the next there was a distinctly humourless shot of a character being killed (the 'body count' for this movie must have been some kind of record for a comedy.) More reviewers struggled, understandably, to make any sense of these awkward juxtapositions. *Films & Filming* complained that the movie was 'one of the most violent films I have seen for a long time and it's [only] in the brief lulls between the protracted and bloody street battles that one recalls with something of a shock that this is intended to be a comedy'.[3]

*You Only Live Twice*, meanwhile, was doing very well indeed. Everyone seemed to agree that the movie's spectacular centrepiece – the massive volcano that functioned as SPECTRE's secret headquarters, complete, at a final cost of $1 million, with fully working monorails, elevators and a helicopter launch pad – was worth the price of admission alone. The same could not be said, alas, for the rather more modest, and considerably less expensive, talking-points on offer in *The Magnificent Two*: 'A friend of ours saw the [movie] in a flea-pit of a cinema in Amman, Jordan, with Arabic sub-titles,'

Eric Morecambe recalled. 'There were eleven people in the audience despite a commando raid with sten guns by a platoon of girls in bikinis.'[4]

*Monthly Film Bulletin*'s reluctant conclusion – that 'a lot of energy [had been] expended to small purpose'[5] – was echoed by Morecambe and Wise themselves when they came to look back on their three disappointing movies for Rank. 'We were caught up in something that was bigger than us that wasn't under our control,'[6] said Wise. 'We know those films were too static for us,' said Morecambe. 'But let's face facts: they weren't that funny. We must take the blame as well.'[7] It was clear, however, that both of them felt ill-used by a Rank Organisation that had never seemed either willing or able to take their ambition seriously. While the 'penny-pinching budget', complained Wise, had been a constant irritation, the scripts – although formally the work of their regular writers – had, in reality, been 'based on a formula decided by a production committee'. This would not have proven to be quite so frustrating had the formula in question been something more coherent than 'a hotch-potch of what had been found successful for other funny men in films for the past forty years'.[8]

Rank, unsurprisingly, arrived at a different conclusion. According to producer Hugh Stewart, the movies 'were successful, but I think [Morecambe and Wise] are primarily television people ... They were sketch artistes and my job on the films was really to turn a series of sketches into a ninety-minute film.'[9] Although this sounded like a tacit admission that he had made a mistake in signing them up so eagerly in the first place, he remained unrepentant: 'I adored making [all three movies] and they've all done well, but they didn't get the critical acclaim we all hoped for.'[10]

Morecambe and Wise left Rank on relatively amicable terms. It seems unlikely that any further movies of a similar kind – had the original deal been extended – would have performed any better than the first three efforts, but Morecambe and Wise never abandoned their hope of making at least one movie that would compare favourably to the work of their childhood heroes. The enormity of their task, however, was greater than many people seemed to realise. No genuine double-act in the history of movies has ever started its screen career with a critically and commercially successful starring vehicle.

Laurel and Hardy, for example, only made their first feature-length movie – *Pardon Us* – in 1931, after appearing together in more than forty shorts over the previous four years, yet it still received a merely ambivalent critical response. Abbott and Costello had only secondary roles to play for their first movie appearance – *One Night in the Tropics* (1940) – and the subsequent plan to use them merely as comic relief in a series of B movies was revised only after the entirely unexpected box-office success of the two low-budget efforts *Buck Privates* and *In the Navy* (both 1941). Even Hope and Crosby's *Road to Singapore* (1940) – the first in a hugely popular but irregular series – owed much of its appeal to the established solo success of both of its stars. Morecambe and Wise, therefore, had only 'failed' in the very specific sense of having failed to surpass the early achievements of their predecessors, and yet their disappointment seemed profound.

During the next ten years or so the shortcomings of their three movies would be blown out of all proportion – not so much by the critics or the fans as by the stars themselves. Rather as Jack Benny had been notorious for doing with his final – and somewhat under-valued – movie, *The Horn Blows at Midnight* (1945), Morecambe and Wise seemed to take a strange kind of masochistic delight in exaggerating the inadequacies of their movies for Rank, ignoring all of the positive reviews but quoting from the worst ones in excruciating detail.[11] Their first attempt, they would always claim, had been 'a flop', and the other two had been 'panned even more mercilessly by the critics'[12] – none of which was true. It was as though they felt that anything other than a clear and unqualified admission of abject failure would weaken their resolve to try again and expunge from their memory any trace of these wretched imperfections.

Looking back on their abortive screen career from the vantage-point of the late seventies, they would again sound a note of deep regret at a rare opportunity that had been allowed to slip away: 'If we had gone on making films in the sixties we might [have become] very successful film comedians,' argued Ernie Wise. 'But we didn't know the medium then, and we never had a chance to get to know it.'[13] His partner went even further: 'If we had Neil Simon writing for us and Billy Wilder directing, I know we could be international stars.'[14] Whatever the truth of this observation, it did little to shake the belief that Morecambe and Wise had arrived at the wrong place at the wrong time as far as their movie career was concerned. The late sixties, as Billy Wilder himself had remarked, was a bleak period for screen comedy:

> Today we are dealing with an audience that is primarily under 25 and divorced from any literary tradition. They prefer mindless violence to solid plotting; four-letter words to intelligent dialogue; pectoral development to character development. Nobody *listens* anymore. They just sit there, y'know, waiting to be assaulted by a series of shocks and sensations . . . It is a difficult time. Ernst Lubitsch, who could do more with a closed door than most of today's directors can do with an open fly, would have had big problems in this market.[15]

It was probably for the best, in the circumstances, that Morecambe and Wise's movie career came to a halt when it did; had they continued, it would surely have been difficult for them to have navigated their way safely beyond the Scylla of spurious modernity (note Norman Wisdom's pathetic descent into the tepid salacity of 1969's *What's Good for the Goose*) and the Charydbis of craven commercialism (knee-jerk low-budget productions of current television ratings winners).

They had, after all, fulfilled at least one long-standing ambition by starring in a movie of their own, and, if it, and the other two that followed, had failed to live up to their high expectations, they should still have taken some consolation from the fact that all three compared favourably to the vast majority of the output of their early role models, Abbott and Costello. What *was* disappointing about each of their movies, however, was their failure to convey more than the merest hint of the very thing that had made Morecambe and Wise so special as a *double-act*. While the casual observer, unaware of their television record, would probably have seen enough in certain scenes to have been alerted to something of Eric Morecambe's comic brilliance, Ernie Wise, badly let down by a succession of underwritten roles, would have paled in comparison to, say, Jerry Desmonde's full-blooded screen performances, and the real point of their partnership remained difficult to discern.

'The critics can say what they like about them,' Eric Morecambe remarked, 'but the makers could give me a few quid.'[16] Although, according to Ernie Wise, they had been 'promised we would become millionaires out of the profits',[17] all that they claimed to have received for their labours was their basic fee; looking for a spread of earnings, they had signed a contract with Rank in 1964 which had promised them a series of deferred payments, including a percentage of the box-office takings, but they were surprised to be informed subsequently that – contrary to Hugh Stewart's remarks – no profits had been accrued. Even after the initial television rights to all three movies had been purchased by the BBC, Morecambe and Wise, much to their irritation, received nothing in the way of remuneration: 'Don't forget the BBC paid a lot to run them,' observed Ernie Wise. 'Money's changing hands, and it ain't coming our way.'[18] The money, however, had always mattered less than the glamour and the glory, but too little of those things had come their way either.

The hurt would never really fade away. They had experienced setbacks before – on stage, radio and television – and they had overcome every one of them, but, as far as the medium of movies was concerned, they would wait in vain for that one chance of redemption. 'Critics still say, "Morecambe and Wise are in this film – a shame that they never did make the transition from small screen to the big,"'[19] Eric Morecambe complained. 'People keep telling us you can't transform from very good television to very good films,' he went on. 'That's a load of rubbish – of course you can. The writing's got to be right; the production has to be right; the direction has to be right.'[20] Such perfectionism would continue to be frustrated by the vagaries of the movie business, but during the next decade it would at least find a television programme in which it could at last begin to flourish.

# A NATIONAL
# INSTITUTION

*Commercial broadcasting in whatever form exists to sell goods,
and public-service broadcasting to serve the public.*
HUGH CARLETON GREENE

ERNIE      *Wait a minute! Aren't you going to say 'good evening'
to the ladies and gentlemen in the audience?*
ERIC      *Sorry.*
ERNIE      *I mean, they are our bread and butter.*
ERIC      [squinting into the darkness] *There's one or two crusty
old cobs out there as well!*
     MORECAMBE AND WISE

## CHAPTER XIII

# The Show of the Week

*Creativity in television depends upon the building up of teams of individuals whose talents are complementary and who, in combination, are able to make programmes which are more original, more effective and more valuable than any of them can achieve alone. There is no simple recipe for the creation of such teams.*
GRACE WYNDHAM GOLDIE

*We never try to irritate our audiences. We're not trying to annoy them in any way or hurt them. We're simply trying to entertain them.*
ERIC MORECAMBE

Early in 1968, Morecambe and Wise elected to start the most auspicious period of their professional lives in the most unpromising of fashions: they picked a fight with the most formidable figure in British television. Their contract with ATV was up for renewal, and Lew Grade, puffing away contentedly on his trademark cigar, was confident he had made them an offer they could ill-afford to refuse: £39,000 for 39 25-minute shows spread over a period of three years. While Eric Morecambe was inclined to accept, Ernie Wise, the dominant partner when it came to business matters, remained unimpressed: in order for them to continue to improve the quality of their shows, he insisted, they would not only need more money than was currently being offered, but they would also need to make them in colour. Grade leaned forward, narrowed his eyes and said menacingly, 'You'll have colour when *I* say you have colour.'[1] It turned out to have been the worst thing he could possibly have said. According to Wise, a 'furious row' broke out, with him and his partner pointing out in no uncertain terms that they were not going to be 'bullied into a deal' by anyone, and Grade exclaiming several times over, 'Why do you boys want all this money?'[2]

In the absence of Billy Marsh – who was on vacation in the United States at the time – it was left, somewhat ironically, to his younger partner – Lew's beloved nephew, Michael – to step into the fray: 'Lew was being stubborn. He thought he had Hills and Green tied to ATV, and he probably felt that Morecambe and Wise would never leave when it came to the crunch, so he'd got a little complacent. I gave him one last chance and he again said no, so I went ahead and called Bill Cotton.'[3] Bill Cotton Junior was by this stage Head of Variety at BBC Television, but he had known and admired Morecambe and Wise since his days as a song plugger in the early fifties:

> When Michael 'phoned me up and said, 'I think Morecambe and Wise are available,' I said, 'Don't move!' To cut a long story short, we negotiated a three-year contract at a great deal more money than the BBC would have been prepared to pay if only they had known that it was only for the first year! I was working on the basis that, if I was right, the second year would be just about right and the third year would turn out to be a bargain. And, indeed, the third year turned out to be *such* a good bargain that we actually *volunteered* to give them a rise! Lew Grade very rarely made mistakes, but he certainly did make a big mistake when he fell out with those two.[4]

In addition to the financial inducements, Cotton promised them a colour series on BBC2 (neither BBC1 nor ITV was able to offer viewers a colour service until the end of 1969[5]) with the guarantee of repeats in black-and-white on BBC1. It had been this aspect of the deal, they would always insist, that had won them over: 'The money really wasn't such an important factor,' Eric Morecambe explained. 'What we wanted was backing and production facilities. In exchange for the right studio back-up I would have been quite willing to earn less cash.'[6] Ernie Wise, though doubtless relieved that such a noble sacrifice had proven to be unnecessary, was happy to agree: 'Bill Cotton came to us and said he would give us colour, and of course we would be backed up by the BBC's prestige.'[7]

In Bill Cotton they had a warm and wise protector. 'I was always somebody who the BBC realised had one foot in the entertainment world and one foot in the BBC,' he reflected:

> And I tried to be very even-handed. I tried to teach the BBC that the people who performed, wrote and directed were the important people, they were the *real* BBC – not the administrators. On the other hand, I appreciated that the BBC was not only very powerful but, in those days, very dedicated to excellence, and that therefore I could concentrate on entertainment shows and I only had to achieve excellence in the *programmes*. I didn't have to achieve it anywhere else – and that suited me just fine.[8]

According to Frank Muir, who in the mid-sixties had been Assistant Head (Comedy) when Cotton was Assistant Head (Variety), it was this kind of attitude that enabled Morecambe and Wise to feel so quickly at home at the BBC:

> They were the good days, the good years, the sixties at the BBC, and what we had at that time was really a cottage industry. Neither Bill nor I were *administrators*, you know, we were both just *pros* who happened to be on the other side of the desk for a while. The job – which Bill in particular did so well with Morecambe and Wise – was all about understanding the performers' worries. You understood because you've been there, you *know* – and you can't do that if you're a professional administrator. I'm sure that Morecambe and Wise chatted away to Bill and thought to themselves: 'He's one of us.'[9]

Cotton's first task, as far as Morecambe and Wise were concerned, was to assemble a new production team for their forthcoming series. He already had the writers in place – Morecambe and Wise had insisted on having Hills' and Green's involvement written into their contract – but he still needed to find a producer/director (it was customary in those days at the BBC for the two roles to be combined). The man whom he chose – John Ammonds – was not only one of the most experienced and well-regarded producers in British broadcasting (his time at the BBC stretched all the way back to

1941, when as a young trainee he provided sound effects for *ITMA*, and he had been responsible subsequently for cultivating the careers of such performers as Harry Worth, Ken Platt, Dave Allen and Dave Morris), but he was also (as the former producer of *You're Only Young Once*) someone whom Cotton knew would command the respect of Morecambe and Wise. 'I really didn't hesitate,' Cotton recalled. 'I knew that Johnny would be perfect for them.'[10] At the start of 1968 Ammonds was producer/director of BBC1's ratings winner *The Val Doonican Show*, and he was due for a vacation when the call came from Cotton:

I was in the bar at the BBC Club, as a matter of fact, when Bill Cotton came in and asked me if I would like to direct Morecambe and Wise. I said, 'Well, can a duck swim? Of course I would, but you won't get them – they're with Lew Grade and ATV.' 'No,' he said, 'I've managed to get them, and we haven't got much time before their first series is due to be recorded.' So I postponed my holiday – apologised profusely to my poor wife! – and got straight down to work.[11]

With Ammonds in charge of production duties, Bill Cotton – who had regarded the BBC's contractual obligation to hire Hills and Green as 'perfectly understandable' but none the less 'a bit of an imposition from our point of view'[12] – doubtless felt reassured that the series would now turn out to be the kind of highly polished piece of programme-making that he had envisaged originally. Ammonds enjoyed a reputation among comedy writers for being one of the shrewdest and most exacting script editors in the business. Barry Cryer, for example, had been known to joke that Ammonds' favourite piece of music was Stravinsky's *Rewrite of Spring*, and Spike Mullins once complained to his colleagues that he had sent Ammonds a Christmas card only to have it returned by the next post with orders for a rewrite,[13] so it was inevitable that he would be less than impressed by the somewhat idiosyncratic approach to the craft of scriptwriting exhibited by Hills and Green:

I *was* a bit taken aback by them, to be honest, because they'd turn up to rehearsals – not always on time, I might add – and they'd try to take over. Don't get me wrong – they wrote some good stuff, they were good writers, but I must admit I thought that they didn't always *help* with some of their critical interjections. In fact, I tackled Eric about this – privately – and said, 'Why on earth do you put up with it?', but he said, 'Don't worry. We've got our own way of dealing with them.' What he used to do was this: Sid and Dick would come in and Eric would sit back and say, 'Well, boys, I think that what you've written for us as an opening would be much better as a middle spot; it's not really right for an opening.' And, of course, you'd never see it again, because that's the way he had of dealing with them – tactful but sly. None the less, I can't pretend that things were ideal from *my* point of view, because they weren't.[14]

Ammonds, however, had other, more pressing things to worry about as he set about planning the show. As a director, his immediate concern was to find a way to accommodate Morecambe and Wise's request for a 'theatrical atmosphere' in the studio:

Eric and Ernie never, ever, got used to the idea of working on the studio floor with a television audience. They always had to work up on a specially built stage. I was rather horrified at the very beginning when they said, 'Oh, by the way, we like working on a two-foot-high stage,' because that meant that all of the cameras were going to have to crane up higher, and having that platform there was going to make it more difficult to set things and strike things [place and remove props]. But they wanted the studio to feel more like a theatre, you see, and I understood what they meant. I'm not sure they really saw *that* much more from the platform, because the cameras were still in the line of sight – they had to be, because otherwise they would have been shooting up Eric and Ernie's nostrils! – but it was all about trying to recapture that special kind of atmosphere that they'd had in their touring days.[15]

Not only did the use of this stage – together with the wings and the tabs – help to create the illusion that one was watching a theatrical performance from the front row of the stalls rather than from a seat in the living-room, but it also had the more subtle yet significant effect of bringing something of the *sound* of the old halls to the modern television studio: when Eric Morecambe bounded on to that platform it *sounded* like a proper wooden stage rather than a solid studio floor.

The next problem facing the director of a show like this was that of how to strike a happy medium between the spontaneity of a live theatrical production and the carefully choreographed nature of a recorded studio show. Ammonds had to work very hard – and very quickly – to find a suitable solution:

> As a director, Eric – at least to begin with – would be a bit of a problem, because he wouldn't be exactly in the same place twice running, and if you had the temerity to suggest to him that he *should* be in exactly the same place twice running you'd probably get a rude word back for your trouble! I do remember, in those early days, I'd press the talk-back key in the control gallery and ask the floor manager to get Eric to move a couple of feet to the left or something and I would hear him shouting, 'This bloke'll be having us on chalk marks next!' or 'Ye gods, he's after an *award* up there!' It was all good-humoured, of course, and I gradually got used to working in a certain way that enabled me to get a camera script out of it that was, shall we say, 'flexible'.[16]

According to Francis Matthews – a guest on the show several times – it was Ammonds, more than anyone else, who helped Morecambe and Wise to work with, rather than against, the technical side of television:

> It was John who really taught them to exploit the fact that they were on TV, you know, rather than on stage. I mean, as an example, the way in which he got them to make more use of the close-up: you know, that close-up of Eric grinning at the camera while Ernie was talking, or glancing into the camera and whispering, 'This boy's a *fool*' – that was John's innovation. He also brought in more close-up reaction shots. Eric took a bit of time to see the value of those and learn to perfect them.

I remember the first time I was on the show with them, Eric would be saying to John, 'Ah, no, come on Johnny, you want us in full-length! You don't see Fred Astaire dancing with only a close-up of his face, do you? Come on, show all the physical movements, all the hand gestures, it's important!' And John would say, 'Eric, we're on *television*, and it's like film – it's a close-up medium. Of course we want to have the long shots and medium shots and all of that, but some of the reactions can be very small and we have to get up closer to you.' Obviously, Eric – once he'd got used to it all – became just *brilliant* at it, but for a short while he was looking around at the cameras and going, 'What's he doing now? What's he up to? Where's he gone now?'[17]

Recording commenced on 3 August, with the first half-hour show in the series being transmitted on BBC2 at 8.10 p.m. on Monday, 2 September 1968. With Hills and Green making their usual appearances, and with the same tried-and-tested mixture of cross-talk, short sketches and musical interludes (and even a brief burst of the old 'Two of a Kind' theme tune) there was a general air of 'business as usual' about Morecambe and Wise's triumphant return to BBC TV. Bill Cotton was planning to give them a further twenty minutes per show – having concluded that they had outgrown the constraining rigidities of their ATV-style format – but he was prepared to wait until they felt entirely comfortable with the switch. 'That first series was all about getting them bedded in,' he recalled. 'Any innovations could wait a bit.'[18] Some of Morecambe and Wise's old audience had to wait a bit, too – only 32 per cent of the population were able to receive BBC2 at the time[19] – but those who did have access to the first run of the series were probably not disappointed; all of the old substance was there, but now with a little added sparkle.[20] After the last of the shows had gone out on 21 October,[21] the mood among the production team was one of quiet satisfaction: everything had gone more or less to plan, and, everyone agreed, the best was yet to come. 'I think Eric and Ernie must have been the only two artists to have had a flaming row with Lew Grade, walked out, and then got bigger and better after that!'[22] said John Ammonds. Ernie Wise, looking back on their career, would say of this moment: 'We seemed to have everything: financial and material success, popular and critical acclaim, and respect from within the profession itself.'[23]

Instead of slowing down and enjoying their success, however, Morecambe and Wise worked harder than ever. There were more club dates, more trips abroad, more recordings, more interviews, more public appearances. Commitments began to overlap with worrying regularity: they had to turn down an offer to star in their own West End show, and they also had to revise their schedule several times in order to fit in four spots in that autumn's Royal Command Performance, a further two spots at a New York night-club and an eight-week season in Glasgow for the end of the year. Both of them knew, deep down, that they were trying to push themselves on at, in Morecambe's words, 'a killing pace' – 'I was away all day and in the evening I was so exhausted all I wanted was to sit down with a drink and get off to bed'[24] – but then again, neither one of them could quite believe that it would not all end in just another few months or another few years, and so both of them kept on going, and neither one of them dared to stop.

Having determined that it was necessary to push themselves on until something happened, something, sure enough, duly happened: Eric Morecambe had a heart attack. It was 7 November 1968, and they were coming to the end of a lucrative but exhausting week of midnight performances at the Variety Club in Batley, West York-shire. Morecambe had been complaining for some days of a pain in his right arm, but, as a self-confessed hypochondriac,[25] he had struggled gamely on, causing his partner some concern but, to begin with at least, no real alarm. Driving back to his hotel after Thursday night's performance, however, he felt the pain spreading rapidly to his chest. Stranded inside his brand-new Jensen Interceptor on the outskirts of Leeds in the early hours of the morning, too ill to drive himself to the local Infirmary, he was rescued by a young man named Walter Butterworth.[26] 'Could you drive me there?' asked Morecambe of the stranger. 'Well,' replied a baffled-looking Butterworth, 'I'm in the Territorials. I've only ever driven a tank!'[27] Within minutes of their arrival, a heart attack had been diagnosed, and Morecambe – after Butterworth had inquired of the possibility of an autograph 'before you go'[28] – was rushed to intensive care. Although the media, on the advice of Billy Marsh, were informed that Morecambe had suffered a slight coronary thrombosis, he had in reality suffered a major attack. When Joan, his wife, set out from Harpenden, she was not at all sure if her husband would still be alive by the time she reached Leeds.

He survived, but for all the subsequent show of bravado – 'I can't recommend anyone to go in for what I have got,' he told reporters. 'Well, not regularly, anyway'[29] – the future of his (and, by implication, his partner's) performing career remained in doubt for some time to come. 'Nobody was really sure that he would ever work again,' recalled Joan.[30] After three weeks, he was allowed to go home to convalesce. The second television series was, inevitably, postponed indefinitely, but the BBC, Morecambe would note, 'were absolutely fantastic'[31] throughout this uncertain period. 'The first thing we tried to do', Bill Cotton recalled, 'was to reassure him that our primary concern was for him to get well again; the second thing was to reassure him – and Ernie – that we would honour their contract; and the third thing was to reassure him that we were prepared to do anything we could to accommodate how he wanted to work in the future.'[32]

While Morecambe convalesced, however, Ernie Wise did his best to keep their act firmly embedded in the public consciousness. He visited publishers, promoters, schools, luncheon clubs and fêtes, gave countless radio and newspaper interviews (never referring to himself as anything other than one half of a double-act), supervised the publication of *The Morecambe and Wise Joke Book* and promoted the first repeat on BBC1 of their opening series. Although he did receive a number of offers of solo work during this time – ranging from the prestigious (a Palladium appearance) to the bizarre (straight-man on *The Basil Brush Show*[33]) – he not only refused to consider anything other than 'Morecambe and Wise' engagements but he also took great care to ensure that half of whatever he earned, no matter how great or small the sum, was sent directly to his partner. 'It was quite touching to see him do all of this,' John Ammonds remarked. 'There were all kinds of rumours circulating, obviously, but he was absolutely devoted to Eric. He's a very nice man, Ernie, and I know that what he did meant an awful lot to Eric.'[34]

On the last day of May 1969, after six months' absence, Morecambe and Wise made their first highly publicised return visit to

Television Centre. In August, they performed together again on stage in Bournemouth – receiving a five-minute standing ovation from the audience. Bill Cotton, in a well-timed demonstration of his faith in them, not only extended their existing contract[35] but also arranged for each new show to be scheduled so as to relieve some of the pressure on Eric Morecambe. It was agreed that they would take four months to make the next four 45-minute shows,[36] have an extended break, and then record a series of thirteen more shows, limiting themselves to a schedule of one every three weeks, six months prior to the transmission date. It was an unheard-of luxury for a light entertainment show, and, as John Ammonds observed, it provided them, and him, with an extraordinary opportunity to go on to make something genuinely special: 'It allowed them to work on every little detail until they were completely happy with it; it obliged them to concentrate on studio work; and it let them experiment. Although it only really came about as a result of Eric's poor health, it turned out to have very, very beneficial consequences for the standard of their work.'[37]

Each morning at 10 a.m. precisely, Eric Morecambe, Ernie Wise and John Ammonds (sometimes accompanied by his production assistant and assistant floor manager) would arrive at the BBC's rehearsal room at the North Kensington Community Centre on Delgarno Way and begin work on the show. A cold, spartan, bare-bricked building at the back of Wormwood Scrubs, it provided, Ammonds recalled, a defiantly unglamorous working environment for the BBC's most popular entertainers:

We didn't mind it. The boys were very down-to-earth people – they were never remotely spoilt – and, in a way, they probably quite liked it. We'd have some tea, work until about one, have some sandwiches and Eric's famous pea-and-ham soup, then work again until about five. The only distraction happened on Thursday afternoons: we'd be upstairs rehearsing, and downstairs there'd be all these little old ladies taking part in community singing. We'd be trying to work on some line or other and there'd be this incessant 'Dai-*sy*, Dai-*sy*' coming up from below![38]

Their attitude, said Ammonds, was faultless: 'They were professional in the extreme. That's one of the reasons I so enjoyed working with them. If Eric, for example, was, say, five minutes late for rehearsal, he'd apologise to me. Sincerely. He'd be genuinely concerned.'[39]

Before they could begin work on the first of their new shows, however, they had another serious problem to resolve: they needed someone to write the scripts. During Eric Morecambe's convalescence, Ernie Wise had taken his wife, Doreen, to New York, where he had an appointment arranged with Ed Sullivan to discuss the possibility of selling him a package of their old ATV shows. Instead of returning home immediately after the meeting, they decided to fly down to Barbados for a brief holiday. As they were relaxing on the plane, Wise had been startled to hear from the chief steward that it had just been reported in the British press that Hills and Green had left Morecambe and Wise and signed an exclusive contract with ATV. Neither he nor his partner had known anything about it. 'Eric was particularly hurt,' recalled Joan:

> In fact, I was surprised just how hurt he was, and I believe that was because of the manner in which it was done. I know Sid and Dick didn't mean any harm: they didn't see it as being underhand in any way. But after all those years of working together, Eric and Ernie heard about it third hand. That hurt. And Eric, I know, thought that Sid and Dick didn't think he could ever return to full strength after his heart attack and were writing him off.[40]

Roger Hancock, Hills' and Green's agent, had been to see Bill Cotton a few days previously. It was at this meeting, according to Cotton, that the problem first arose:

> Roger turned up. We went to have some lunch, and before we'd done the avocado and prawn he'd informed me that unless Hills and Green could be the executive producers on the show they wouldn't write the second series. They'd had a counter-offer – to do their own show – from ATV, so they felt as though they were in a good position to make that kind of demand. Well, we'd *never* consider that sort of thing, and I told

Roger it wasn't worth discussing. It was a fairly good-natured meeting, but after it was over I went back to my office and sat down and thought to myself, '*Now* what have you done?'[41]

Morecambe and Wise, once the news had reached them, were understandably anxious: 'I thought that was the end of Morecambe and Wise, to be honest,'[42] said Wise.

It turned out, in fact, to be a new beginning. One week after his meeting with Roger Hancock, Cotton received a call from a colleague – the producer Michael Hurll – who alerted him to the fact that Ken Dodd had recently parted company with his writer of thirteen years standing, Eddie Braben. Braben – a tall, sensitive, gentle man with thick black hair and deep, merry, blue eyes – had grown up in the Dingle in Liverpool, and had started writing jokes while he was working on a fruit and veg stall in St John's Market. 'I didn't like it one little bit,' he said of his first job, 'and I was desperate for a way out.'[43] After an unsuccessful trial for his beloved Liverpool FC – 'I was aiming to deprive Billy Liddell of his place in the team'[44] – he started sending out gags to professional comics: 'I used to write about five hundred jokes a week. Now, anyone can write five hundred very poor, very bad jokes, but you've got to do that to learn. And I did that for many years, and, eventually, I began to get the idea of what a joke was and how it was constructed.'[45] Soon after selling his first joke to Charlie Chester – 'Hopalong Cassidy always knew he was going to be a cowboy, because when he was a baby he wore a ten-gallon nappy' – he sold his fruit and veg stall for £100 and became a full-time writer. During his time with Ken Dodd he enjoyed a sustained period of success on stage, radio and television that culminated in a record-breaking run at the London Palladium. When Bill Cotton heard that he was available, he called him immediately.

'It's funny,' said Braben, 'but I can remember that particular day very, very clearly':

For some reason, offers seemed to be coming in from all over the place, which rather surprised me, and I'd just had one from an ITV company to write for Mike and Bernie Winters. Obviously, I was never a great admirer, but at the same time I knew

I had to earn a living, so I said, '*Well* . . . call me back in two hours.' In the interim, Bill Cotton rang from the BBC and said, 'Would you like to write for Morecambe and Wise?' I'd known Bill for a length of time, and I thought – I still do think – a great deal of him, but I said: 'No.' And he said, 'Why not?' And I said, 'To be honest, I don't think I'm good enough.' And that's the way the conversation went. But he said, 'Well, *I* think you are.'[46]

'I'd worked with Ken Dodd,' Cotton recalled, 'and I realised that Eddie wasn't a *conventional* gag writer. What Eddie wrote was something very unusual, not stand-up – *Ken* used it for stand-up, but if you really *listened* to it, you could make *pictures* out of it.'[47] It was true: not only did Braben love humour, but he also loved language, too. Like S. J. Perelman, he cherished obscure, eccentric and anti-quated words and phrases ('I have a long-felt want'; 'It's common knowledge that your wife has another.' 'Now there's a novelty!'; 'I've come to arrange your knick-knacks – I take it you've brought them with you?'), comical – and, invariably, vaguely unsettling – homonyms ('Nurtured? Isn't that what they do to tom-cats?'; 'He has a tryst? Then you've nothing to worry about!') and surreal (mis-) associations ('Are you prepared to ratify my proposals?' 'Certainly. Put them on the table and pass me that mallet'; 'I think I curried her favours.' 'You very nearly casseroled her dumplings!'; 'Have you got the scrolls?' 'No, I always walk like this'; 'I've got the capabilities.' 'Try lying on your left-hand side – that usually stops it.'). Whereas Hills and Green concentrated on comic situations, Braben thrived on comic communication. 'What Eddie Braben excelled at', said Frank Muir, 'was his own unique kind of comic *riff*. He'd give performers strange, funny riffs to work through until they'd done enough with them. They weren't *sketches*, as such, but they were more like jazz pieces, "word riffs" – not conventional at all but very well done.'[48] His greatest influence had probably been Dave Morris – the straw-hatted and bespectacled star of the fifties radio series *Club Night*:[49]

He was very, very underrated, Dave Morris. Talk about being surreal – this man was surreal before most people knew what surreal was. *Club Night* used to be set in this working man's club in the North, and Dave was always the loud mouth who knew it all. Each week, before he arrived at the club, they would have a topic of conversation, and one week, I remember, they were talking about court cases and great barristers. Dave came in and said, 'If you're talking about great barristers, there was only one – the greatest barrister who ever lived,' and somebody would say, 'Who was that?' and he'd say, 'You're looking at him!' He was a terrible liar. They'd say, 'What did *you* ever do?' and he'd say, 'I defended Crippen! I got him off the murder charge, but they hung him for having his chimney on fire.' They said, 'Hung 'im?' and Dave said, 'Yes, but I *did* appeal, but I lost the appeal – and, just for spite, they hung him again the following Friday!' I mean, that, to me, is brilliant. I *loved* that. I'd place him at least level with Jimmy James, because his humour was quite incredible. He was long, long before his time, because most people didn't know what he was talking about![50]

Braben's own lunatic fantasies would often contain implicit, heartfelt homages to Morris – an example being his 'Mutiny on the Bonty' sketch:

ARTHUR
| | |
|---|---|
| LOWE | I think there's been a typing error in the title. |
| ERNIE | Typing error in the title? That's *Mutiny on the Bounty*. |
| LOWE | Oh. But you've got *Mutiny on the Bonty*. |
| ERIC | Ah, no, that's not Ern's fault. That's a typing error, you see, because his typewriter is made out of his old bike. |
| LOWE | (*incredulous*) Made a typewriter out of his old bike? |
| ERIC | That's true. And every time now he cocks his leg over the ribbon he knocks the keys with his saddlebag. |
| LOWE | (*bemused*) Saddlebag? |
| ERIC | Yes. |
| ERNIE | But I'm going to have it fixed. |

| ERIC | Don't worry. It *has* been fixed. A man called not more than half an hour ago. |
|---|---|
| ERNIE | Oh, yes? |
| ERIC | You've had it pumped up. |
| LOWE | Pumped up a typewriter? |
| ERIC | Of course. |
| LOWE | Oh! That makes it all quite clear, then! |

When Bill Cotton first suggested Braben to Morecambe and Wise, they were unsure of how suited his material might be to their style: 'Our immediate thought', said Morecambe, 'was: if he writes as well for us as he does for Ken Dodd, then the answer must be "yes",'[51] but Cotton recalled that 'they were still a *bit* sceptical about him, because they sort of said, "We don't work like Ken Dodd, we've got different approaches," but I said, "Well, let's just give him a try and you can see what you think." '[52] A meeting was duly arranged, with Braben travelling down from his West Derby home to London to join Morecambe and Wise and Bill Cotton at Television Centre. Although Braben had watched them perform on several occasions – the first time being at the Liverpool Empire in 1952, 'when they were so far down the bill that their names were smaller than the printer's'[53] – he had never actually met them in person before. It was, therefore, with a palpable sense of relief that he found their company to be so congenial:

> The wonderful thing was that within *minutes* we all knew that we were right for each other. Before we did any comedy. Because we were all from the North of England, we were all from working-class backgrounds and we all laughed at the same people. We all had that love of music-hall, and the same favourites – Jimmy James, you know, Dave Morris, all the same heroes. It was wonderful. Very nice, very *comfortable*, right from the very beginning.[54]

After a couple of hours of increasingly relaxed and good-humoured conversation, Cotton suggested that Braben go off and write a sample piece of material for Morecambe and Wise to look at. 'I said, "Well, I've got to make this clear at the start," ' recalled Braben. 'I said, "It won't be anything like the way you were before," which rather surprised Eric and Ernie. I said, "I can't write like Hills and Green, I can only write the way *I* see you and the way *I* think you will be funny.'[55] Both parties departed – each, in their own way, and for their own reasons, a little anxious about what might materialise – after agreeing to return in a week's time for another, more serious, discussion. According to Braben:

> I went back the next week, and I had a flat sketch with me. They'd never seen anything like it before. I remember both of them were astonished. Eric actually said to me: 'But you've got, "*ERIC*: a line, *ERNIE*: a line, *ERIC*: a line, *ERNIE*: . . .".' And I said, 'Yes, I know.' He said, 'Right through to the end.' I said, 'Yes, I know.' He said, 'We've never worked like that before. We used to just come in and Sid and Dick would have an idea on a piece of paper or something and we'd all work on it.' He was quite surprised that the whole thing was written down for them. But the thing was that they *laughed*. They really did laugh – loud and long – and then they put the papers down and said they couldn't do it! Because they'd never done anything like that before, and because it was against everything they'd ever done. And it was Bill Cotton who clinched it. He said, 'Well, look, the best thing to do is for Eddie to go off and write a whole show, and then we'll just put it out on BBC2 and, with a bit of luck, nobody will ever see it, and your careers won't be in shreds.' So they agreed to do that, and I went off and wrote a whole show, and that was it, really. It took off from there.[56]

Braben delivered his script for the first 45-minute show, and, for the next three weeks, Morecambe and Wise and John Ammonds sat around the table in their room at Delgarno Way and subjected each routine to their usual rigorous analysis – debating the inclusion or exclusion of certain words, altering the pace or the length of particular sketches, exploring possible alternative bits of business, incorporating ad-libs and new visual ideas. Anxious to make sure that their first 'extended' show lasted the distance without any discernible sign of strain, they added an additional sketch by the Yorkshire-based writing team of Mike Craig and Lawrie Kinsley, and then, at last, they felt satisfied. 'The one other thing that they did', said Bill Cotton, 'was to take the opportunity to ensure that they always had a writing credit from that point on – because in the past they'd found that they were contributing so much only to find, after they'd worked on the material and got it round right and taken it on stage, that they had to pay for it all over again, and they weren't prepared to tolerate that any longer, so in future they always got a credit for it: "Additional material by Morecambe and Wise".'[57]

The show – scheduled, along with the other three, to fill BBC2's Sunday night 'Show of the Week' slot – was recorded on 1 June 1969 and transmitted on 27 July.[58] It opened with Eric Morecambe walking briskly towards centre-stage, pausing to look inside his jacket, pat his chest and say, 'Keep going, you fool!' The next forty-odd minutes flew by, with a succession of short, spirited sketches, two guest vocalists, some flawless cross-talk and a longer, more elaborate, finale that the production team had come to refer to as 'the romp'. The tumultuous applause at the end meant a great deal: 'Once you've done the first show after you've been ill', Eric Morecambe would say, 'you're all right,'[59] and the sight of his smile as the credits rolled by sent out the only message that really mattered.

It had been, Joan Morecambe recalled, a triumphant return to television: 'They'd had a pretty good career up until Eric's first attack . . . and I think everyone at the time [had] thought that was the end of it. That's what so amazed the profession: they didn't just bounce back, they bounced back bigger and better than ever. What Eric had done, you see, was to use the enforced break to make himself really well so that when they returned to TV their shows were not just as good, but further improved.'[60] The BBC's own Audience Research Report certainly made encouraging reading: whereas their first BBC2 series had achieved an average Reaction Index of 69 – itself a perfectly respectable figure – the first of the new shows received an exceptional 83. The report noted that the 'extremely enthusiastic sample audience' had found the show 'hilariously funny' and well balanced, with Morecambe and Wise's 'very individualistic and fantastically funny comedy style' being well served by 'sparkling and inventive' material by Eddie Braben that had provided them with 'every opportunity to exploit their talent for comedy to maximum effect'. The conclusion was that 'there can be no doubt that for the majority of the sample audience this was indeed a quite outstandingly entertaining and highly enjoyable show'.[61]

The beneficial effect of reports such as these on the confidence of Morecambe and Wise should not be underestimated. John Ammonds had discovered early on that their 'authoritative' nature could usually quell the more niggling anxieties of his two notoriously self-critical stars. 'If I'm worrying about a write-up,' Eric Morecambe once confirmed to an interviewer, 'I show it to [Ammonds] and say, "Johnny, were we that bad?" and he just gets out these graphs [and reports] he's got. "*Morecambe and Wise Show*, August 1969: 15.5 million viewers; *Morecambe and Wise Show*, August 1970: 17.5 million viewers. There's your proof." '[62] Indeed, when Morecambe had been recovering in hospital, he had written to Ammonds, joking that 'while I have been here I have had over one thousand letters and one hundred telegrams which, if you work it out, gives me a RI of 84'.[63] The significance of an actual RI of 83 for that first show back would not have been lost on anyone involved in its production: not only did it underline the growing popularity of Morecambe and Wise with the viewing public, but it also suggested that in Eddie Braben they had found a writer who had the potential to match – and, perhaps, even eclipse – the not inconsiderable achievements of Hills and Green.

'Teaming Eric and Ernie up with Eddie was a masterstroke by Bill Cotton,' Michael Grade remarked. 'A brilliant, *brilliant* idea which actually represented another huge leap forward for them.'[64] It was not just Braben's humour that Morecambe and Wise admired, but his professionalism, too. Having worked for Ken Dodd – a performer so assiduous in his approach to his work that he would record, after every single appearance, such details as the date, venue, season of year, weather conditions, size of audience, pace of performance and how well or poorly each joke (in a show that usually lasted some four or more hours) had been received – Braben was an extremely disciplined writer: 'When I was working with Ken, we used to aim for at least four gags a minute – always – and that was the ratio I aimed for with Eric and Ernie. I never wanted to let them go more than two lines without a laugh.'[65] He was also an accomplished observer and an appreciative listener: within weeks of meeting Morecambe and Wise, he seemed to know them – *understand* them – far better than Hills and Green had ever done during the previous seven years.

Having observed both of them at close quarters – hearing how each of them spoke, watching how each of them moved, noting how both of them responded to other people – Braben developed a remarkably sure sense of what kinds of material and situations, even what kinds of words and sounds, would probably suit their respective personalities. 'What I set out to do', he said, 'was to take what was already *there* – what already existed within their relationship – and then place it under a microscope. What I tried to do was to exaggerate the main traits. I didn't want to create anything that didn't "fit" them. So the Morecambe and Wise on the screen were, as far as I was concerned, just a highly exaggerated version of the off-screen Eric and Ernie.'[66] Braben proceeded to conjure up a whole world for these characters, tracing their development – or lack of it – right back to their shared Northern working-class childhood, and insinuating so many biographical references into their on-screen conversations that it would eventually be possible to compile their own special *Who's Who* entries:

**Eric**, Educated at Milverton Street School – mainly by next-door neighbour Ada Bailey. Obtained twelve 'A' levels in absenteeism. Had his first break – just above the ankle – at the Central Pier, Birmingham after telling the gag about the three Irishmen who wanted to start a one-man band. Favourite food: chips from Lee Wong Fu's on the corner of Tarryassan Street. Favourite wine: Fleur de Vie Birkenhead from the House of Tucker, 37 Tarryassan Street. Retains a love of the open air – particularly when Ada Bailey is hanging her knickers out on the line. Reads the *Dandy*. Hobbies: Luton FC or football.

**Ernie**, educated at Milverton Street School. Learned to read French and many other words besides. It was at school that he first started to show his propensity, and, as a consequence, was ordered to stand behind the blackboard as punishment. Obtained twenty-three 'A' levels (seventeen in Mathematics and two in Sums) and one 'O' level (you could tell from the shape of his legs). Worked in a circus as 'Ernesto and His Vanishing Ferret'. Only one woman ever came up to his expectations, and even then he had to stand on a box. The many plays what he has wrote have earned him the sobriquet 'the Yehudi Menuhin of the nib', as well as his own unstinting affection. His fan – Vernon from the wig boutique – comes to each show on a hand-cart from Carlisle and never forgets to send him a bag of mint humbugs every Christmas. Reads the *Financial Times*. Hobbies: accountancy and authoring.

Although Braben would always claim that he had 'not touched Eric's character at all'[67] and concentrated instead on Ernie's, both of them, in fact, bear Braben's fingerprints. Braben's 'Eric' is the fast-talker, the free-thinker, the face-slapper, sharp-witted but unfocused, naughty and saucy, an irresistible misfit – an altogether more devious and dangerous creature than the earlier, somewhat fatuous, incarnation from the ATV days.[68] Braben's 'Ernie', on the other hand, now became an even smaller man bewitched by even bigger dreams, a simpleton posing as a sophisticate ('A man of great education like what no other man had got'), the supposed worldliness of his gestures forever belied by the homeliness of his vocabulary. 'One of the ways I liked to point up Ernie's character', said Braben, 'was by giving him these old-fashioned words to say':

> Ernie, for example, would say 'sums' – not 'maths' or 'arithmetic', but '*sums*'. That brought his pompous character back down to earth. He'd always let it slip that he was really quite an ordinary, humble, working-class man. Another example: he'd never say, 'That's a nice dress.' The line *he'd* say was, 'I like your frock!' 'Frock' is very old-fashioned, very Ernie. When he said 'frock' instead of 'dress', he was revealing himself to be very ordinary. His ego was deflated by him, not by anyone else. He did it himself.[69]

'What Eddie Braben did for Ernie', commented an appreciative Eric Morecambe, 'was to make him into a *person*. Before, anybody could have played his part. Not now, Ernie is his own man . . . He's part of an act called Morecambe and Wise and not Eric Morecambe and

That Feller He Works With.'[70] Braben did something else, too: he helped create a comic yet compelling portrait of a friendship, injecting an element of real feeling into the relationship between Eric and Ernie. There was always something slightly cold, slightly cruel, about the way in which the 'Eric' of Hills and Green was continually being hectored at and outwitted by their 'Ern', but Braben's Eric, in contrast, often betrayed a subtle kind of compassion in the face of Ernie's more gauche remarks. Take, for example, the occasion when a guest appearance by Cliff Richard prompts Ernie to reconsider his self-appointed status as the unrivalled 'great little mover':

| | |
|---|---|
| ERNIE | Cliff surprised me in that play. |
| ERIC | I told him to be careful with that umbrella. |
| ERNIE | I meant he could really act. Just a little more style, a little more sophistication, and he could well be another me. |
| ERIC | (*indignant*) Never! |
| ERNIE | No, I suppose you're right. |

Or the scene in which Eric wanders into the room just as Ernie decides to read aloud from the opening paragraph of his latest 'masterpiece': 'Rocky felt a tingle of excitement as his executive jet touched down in Amsterdam. It was his first visit to Italy . . .'. Instead of mocking his companion, Eric averts his head discreetly, limits himself to a swift, pitying grimace, and then turns back to say encouragingly: 'That's knockout, that, Ern.' As Morecambe observed: '[Eddie Braben] has made me a lot sharper and a lot more protective towards Ernie. *I* can knock him – like in a Northern family – but I wouldn't let somebody else do it.'[71] Teasing him was one thing – Eric would never let a chance go by to remind his partner of the short, fat, hairy nature of his legs or the admirable condition of his unique, whirlpool-styled 'wig', nor, in private, would he ever fail to offer him such helpful 'advice' as that there is only one 'f' in 'Pharaoh' – but he would always spring unhesitatingly to his friend's defence if anyone else dared to treat him disrespectfully. It was all very reminiscent of the unspoken affection that had tied Laurel to Hardy: at the end of their *A Chump at Oxford* (1940), for example, Hardy is just about to leave for good when Laurel – whose temporary amnesia had caused his partner all manner of humiliations – suddenly regains his memory; 'Hey, Ollie!' he shouts out. 'Aren't you going to take me with you?' Hardy rushes back and hugs him: 'Stan! You *know* me!'

Braben made the connection even stronger by placing Morecambe and Wise in the classic Laurel and Hardy contexts of the single apartment and the double-bed:

> That idea came very early on. You see, one of the first things that struck me about their relationship was its *closeness*. Like I said: there shouldn't have been an 'and' in 'Morecambe and Wise', it should've been 'Morecambewise', because they were *so* close. So my idea was to put these two people into an enclosed space – the equivalent of being inside a music-hall horse-skin – so that they couldn't escape each other, they were closeted together, and that way I could develop the characters and the dialogue the way I wanted them to go. That was how the 'in-bed' and 'at-home' situations came about. I think, at the start, they weren't too sure about this idea of two men being in bed together, and they were quite wary, but they also agreed that the situation was too good to lose. They feared that people might read something into it that wasn't there. I remember that I said to them, 'Well, if it's good enough for Laurel and Hardy, it's good enough for you!' That did it. Eric said, 'Sod 'em! We'll do it!' And they did.[72]

Although Eric Morecambe – employing a beguiling logic all of his own – elected to keep his pipe with him at all times in the bedroom 'for the masculinity',[73] these bed sketches still played on the sense of this partnership as, in Ernie Wise's words, 'a marriage without the fun'.[74]

Tony Hancock used to reject any scripts for *Hancock's Half-Hour* that featured him and Sid James doing housework together because, he claimed, the audience might find overtones of homosexuality in the situation.[75] It appears that some BBC executives, when they first heard of Morecambe and Wise's bedroom scenes, attempted to replace the intimate double-bed with two chaste singles,[76] but it was surprising how often, and to what extent, their sketches played on the implicit masculine/feminine axis of their on-screen relationship ('Had some great times with Ern,' said Eric in one of them. 'I liked him – we were like brother and sister').

The Hollywood screenwriter Garson Kanin once remarked that 'all teams of two are Male and Female. Boldly male and coyly female. Passively female and actively male. Coquettishly female and desiring male. Definitely He and oh boy She.'[77] It is the kind of theory that mistakes a stereotype for an archetype, but, in the case of the Eric and Ernie of the Braben era, there was certainly something rather *epicene* about Ernie's screen persona. It had more to do with sensibility than it did with sex (which, in any case, neither character seemed to understand entirely): although Eric called most attractive young women 'sir',[78] he still felt strangely drawn to them, whereas Ernie – whom Braben once referred to as 'vaguely Victorian'[79] – became tongue-tied and bashful in their presence; Eric was physically demonstrative (it was usually a case of 'goose or be goosed' with him around), while Ernie, usually, was very prim and proper; and while Eric's hobbies conformed to a certain, somewhat boyish, masculine stereotype (football, Airfix kits, looking out for Ada Bailey's knickers), one felt that Ernie, had it not been for those plays he was always writing, might well have taken up knitting.[80]

It was by no means an easy effect to imitate. When, for example, the perfectly competent writing team of Craig and Kinsley contributed sketches to that first 1969 show (Eric and Ernie as, respectively, male and female tortoises: ERIC: 'Who won the cup?' ERNIE: 'Manchester City.' ERIC: 'I fancied them from the start.' ERNIE: 'I fancied *you* from the start.' ERIC: 'Oh, don't start *that* again!') and the 1972 Christmas special (Eric and Ernie as two of Santa's reindeer: ERIC: 'What's a girl doing on a job like this?' ERNIE: 'I wanted to be near you. I fancy you!' ERIC: 'Hey! You dirty little devil!'),[81] the original innocence was missing, but when Braben employed it, it worked extraordinarily well. 'It made their relationship seem more intimate,' Frank Muir observed, 'and it made the viewer feel a little more privileged for being made privy to it. The plot was always irrelevant – as it was always irrelevant with Laurel and Hardy – because *they* had become their own self-contained sit-com; the "situation" was their own relationship.'[82] Braben's great achievement had been to write comic material for two *characters*, rather than one character and a feed. The transformation, as Kenneth Tynan pointed out at the time, represented something far more interesting and original than that of a simple reversal of roles: 'Ernie today is the comic *who is not funny*. And Eric . . . is the straight man *who is funny*.'[83]

All of this was made to seem so natural, so *right*, that audiences would have been forgiven for believing that those two men on the television screen were simply improvising their way from show to show: 'I suppose basically that there is a script,' went a typical response, 'but Morecambe and Wise take such liberties with it that it can only be an outline.'[84] One viewer, in fact, was so convinced that this was indeed the case that he sent in a sample script, in all seriousness, that read: 'Eric slaps Ernie on the face, puts his arm around him and says "My little fat friend." Then Ernie says "There's no answer to that." Eric then says "You can't see the join", and Ernie replies "What do you think of it so far?"' Morecambe and Wise's would-be scriptwriter then added the telling postscript: 'You can put the rest in yourselves.'[85] The reality of the situation was, of course, rather different: every single show was actually the result of an intensive and exhausting period of creative interaction between the stars, the producer and the writer.

The process would begin with Eddie Braben retiring to his small, exotically wallpapered study on the outskirts of Liverpool and not emerging again until he had typed out a first draft of the script. This would then be posted straight to London, where it would arrive early on a Monday morning at the seventh floor of Television Centre for delivery to Room 7019 – the office occupied by John Ammonds – and from there on to Delgarno Way and the expectant eyes of Morecambe and Wise. Everyone involved appreciated the need for a full and frank exchange of views – 'They are perfectionists and expect everyone working with them to put everything into the show' (Braben),[86] 'It's no criticism of the writer, but we feel we can improve [any script] in places' (Morecambe and Wise),[87] 'Arguments were inevitable' (Ammonds)[88] – but none of them ever pretended that such an exchange was always easy. 'We were sweet and nice to each other *most* of the time,' said Ammonds, 'but by no means *all* of the time':

If I didn't think an idea was good I'd say so, and, if I needed to, I'd jolly well keep *on* saying so! Eric wouldn't have wanted or expected anything other than that, and nor would Ernie. When we read through the script together, and also when we rehearsed, they needed me to be entirely honest with them, and I always was. Of course, you know, they didn't always *like* what I had to say, but they never, ever, resented my saying it. After I'd shut up they knew that they were going to have to face the audience, so they wanted me to be tough.[89]

When it came to Eddie Braben's role in these proceedings, how-ever, things were more problematic. Unlike Hills and Green, who liked to be present throughout the rehearsal period, Eddie Braben preferred, whenever possible, to stay at home in Liverpool:

It wasn't London that I disliked; it was what happened there. And what happened was three men sitting at a table, passing judgements, who'd eventually reach a verdict on something I'd sweated blood over for over three weeks. You know: fourteen hours a day – which isn't an exaggeration – and all I could do was just sit and wait. It was horrible. It really was *horrible*. And, eventually, there'd be the initial laugh that would break the silence – what a *relief*!

It wasn't London I disliked; it was just going down to be judged. I was going down to be judged, and, deep down – I suppose every writer feels this – the fear was that someone was going to say, 'This isn't even *remotely* funny! *You're* not a comedy writer – go home and take this rubbish with you!' You know. Or you'd pick up the phone and some distant voice would say, 'You're no good. Bye-bye – you're finished!'[90]

What made matters even worse for Braben, according to John Ammonds, was the fact that Morecambe and Wise's first impressions of a script could not always be relied on to match their subsequent impressions:

The thing that I got stuck with – and Eddie knows it – was this. He'd come down to London with all his stuff for a read-through with the boys, and Eric, usually, would kill himself laughing at anything and everything Eddie came up with. So Eddie would rush straight back on the first available train to Liverpool from Euston, feeling – understandably – very pleased. The next morning, however, we'd reassemble – without Eddie – and we'd read it through again, and Eric would say, 'It's not quite right, this opening . . .' He'd killed himself laughing at it the day before! And I used to say, 'Well, Eric, you seemed to like it well enough yesterday . . .' It tended to follow that routine.

I don't know if it was because Eric felt a bit embarrassed with Eddie being there, and wanted to look appreciative, but I remember sitting there so many times as he was laughing his head off and thinking to myself, 'We're going to have trouble with this.'[91]

With Braben now back in Liverpool, however, it was left to Ammonds to alert him to any sudden changes of mind. 'Johnny Ammonds acts for us as a kind of buffer,' Ernie Wise admitted. 'If we don't think a gag is going quite right, we ask Johnny to give Eddie a ring and ask him if he can change it – and he does. We don't do that ourselves,' he added, 'because we don't want to get involved.'[92] It was fortunate for all concerned that Ammonds – having had years of experience of working closely with talented but harassed comedy writers – was able to fulfil this role so well, but, he reflected, it was never a role that he relished:

Of course, I knew that it was better that they left it to me to talk to Eddie, because performers aren't always as tactful with their writers as they probably ought to be, whereas I'd learned over the years that you needed to be *very* tactful: for example, you'd never say to a comedy writer, 'No, that's no good.' You'd always say, 'Why not do it *this* way?' None the less, I used to dread it sometimes, having to keep calling poor old Eddie, not least because the boys preferred to make it seem as though *I* was always the one complaining, whereas they were perfectly contented. They used to get a bit shy like that! So it was a bit awkward sometimes, and I'd have to use every last ounce of tact to sort it all out.

After that second day, for example, when Eric had suddenly realised that something wasn't perfect after all, they'd wait for me to say, 'Look, I'll ring Eddie up tonight.' And they'd say, 'Oh, yes! That's right! Ring him up tonight!' So I used to be on that telephone for an hour, an hour and a half, you know – it used to get red-hot sometimes! I'd say to Eddie, 'Look, the boys would like you to have another go at this.' And he'd say – quite understandably, you know – 'Well, Eric seemed to be laughing his socks off yesterday!' And I'd have to say, 'Well, you should know what Eric's like by now. That's what he always does, regardless of what he thinks.' So Eddie would have another go at it, send it down from Liverpool, and we'd work on it, and then they might get a few *more* ideas for changes, and so I'd have to spend the *next* evening on the telephone to Eddie![93]

Morecambe tended to laugh first and look for problems later, whereas Wise tended to look for problems first and then laugh (or not, as the case may be), but both, in their different ways, were perfectionists. 'It's a question of standards,' said Wise. 'Our ideas of perfection may not be somebody else's. We set our own standards. It doesn't mean we're right, but we think we are.'[94] Braben's professed ambition was to write a routine that was perfect at the first attempt – and Eric Morecambe felt that on at least two occasions he succeeded[95] – but he became used to the fact that they were very rarely *completely* satisfied with any material – even, it should be noted, when the material was their own: 'Ernie can come in one morning', said Morecambe, 'all bubbling, and say, "I've got a great idea," and we all look at him as if he's dropped dead. He expounds his theory and it is about as funny as a cry for help. When it doesn't work, we all get slightly depressed, mutter "bloody hell" a few times and then decide we all have to think harder.'[96] As far as their opinion of Braben was concerned, Morecambe and Wise acknowledged that he was 'the best writer in this country',[97] but they still made no apologies for pushing him hard: 'Sometimes we take stuff back to him. Like shopping at Marks and Spencer. Even Eddie can't give you twenty-four hours of brilliance.'[98]

The pressure that was placed on Braben, week after week, month after month, was immense. It was asking a great deal of any one scriptwriter, no matter how talented he or she might be, to keep coming up with first-rate material for thirteen forty-five-minute peak-time television shows and a high-profile seventy-minute Christmas special every year. In the US such a burden would have been shared by an entire team of talented writers. The great Jack Benny radio shows of the forties, for example, were the work of four brilliant comedy specialists (George Balzar, Sam Perrin, John Tackaberry and Milt Josefsberg), while Sid Caesar's much-admired *Your Show of Shows* in the fifties had a stable of writers that included Neil Simon, Danny Simon, Mel Brooks, Woody Allen, Larry Gelbart, Lucille Kallen, Mel Tolkin and Carl Reiner. Braben, in Britain, had sole responsibility for providing the country's leading light entertainment show with a seemingly endless supply of top-quality comic material.[99] He was well rewarded for his labours – and showered with awards (including several Writers' Guilds and a BAFTA) – but then those labours were prodigious. Even John Ammonds sometimes felt impelled to advise Morecambe and Wise to grant their beleaguered writer some respite:

We were all guilty at some time or other of pushing Eddie a bit too hard. *I* certainly wasn't ever *easy* on him. Eddie will vouch for that, I'm sure! But Eric and Ernie could really pile the pressure on to Eddie at times – when *they* were feeling the pressure, too – and I'd have to remind them: 'Look, it's not like a *tap*, you know. You don't just turn it on and get a load of great material and good sketches and good gags gushing out! It's a lot of hard work.' It takes a very rare talent, actually, to write comedy – top-class comedy – under that sort of pressure. It's rather like asking Beethoven, 'Can you knock off another nine symphonies in the next six months, because, you know, we *need* them?'[100]

There were – inevitably – periods in which the strain came close to being unbearable, and on at least two occasions, Braben acknowledged, he collapsed from complete exhaustion:

Twice it knocked me out. I mean literally. Sometimes my wife would come through and I would be asleep at my typewriter. There were many occasions when I've worked all day Saturday, through Saturday night, all day Sunday, right through Sunday night and finished mid-day on the Monday, and then just collapsed on the bed. But you can't do that too often, you know – which I did, and I was out for about a month, I think, as a result. It was just mental exhaustion. Which doesn't sound much, but it's not very nice.

I've never enjoyed writing. Never. I can't see how anybody can enjoy writing comedy at the sharp end. And writing for *The Morecambe & Wise Show* really *was* the sharp end. I enjoyed the end product. That was nice, to get the laughter. I enjoyed that. That was good. But the actual *process* of writing: no, no, it was like putting your brain through a mincing machine. I didn't enjoy that one little bit. I never have enjoyed it. Then again, what else could I have done? If I hadn't done that, I would probably have been on the buses and giving the wrong change.[101]

Only once, it appears, was this mild-mannered man moved to register any overt resentment at his treatment. After hearing of another set of requests for last-minute revisions to a script, he sent a package to Morecambe and Wise that comprised of forty sheets of blank paper stapled neatly together with a covering note that read: 'Fill these in – it's easy!'[102] Even this isolated outburst, however, was leavened with affectionate good humour.

One thing about which both Morecambe and Wise and Eddie Braben were agreed was the pivotal role played by John Ammonds. It was Ammonds, as Braben acknowledged, 'who mixed the ingredients together so successfully'.[103] A genial-looking man with a broad smile and a warm laugh, he enjoyed both the respect and the affection of everyone involved with the show. 'He really was one of the nicest of people to work with,' Mike Craig recalled. 'Men like him were rare then, and in today's television they don't exist at all.'[104] Morecambe and Wise might have delighted in teasing him whenever possible – Morecambe, in particular, appears to have taken great pains to ensure that at least some of his internal mail was addressed either to a 'Mr Salmon' or a 'Mr Hammond' – but there can be no doubt as to how greatly they valued his judgement: 'We want Johnny Ammonds to take the pictures for us as well as help us with the words and make other decisions,' commented Wise. 'We couldn't do it without him,' Morecambe agreed.[105] Whereas a less experienced producer/director might have hesitated to be critical of an idea or performance – it was, after all, *Morecambe and Wise* that one was dealing with – Ammonds experienced no such qualms. 'He is very honest,' Eddie Braben remarked; 'if he doesn't think a sketch works he will say so and we'll trust his judgement totally and abandon it. Or he can suggest the single gesture or line that could bring it to life.'[106]

One might, indeed, liken Ammonds' relationship with Morecambe and Wise to that of George Martin's with the Beatles: just as Martin possessed that rare combination of technical expertise and imaginative playfulness that enabled him to serve not just as a reassuringly authoritative advisor but also, occasionally, as a creative catalyst – suggesting, for example, the use of a string quartet on Paul McCartney's 'Yesterday', and remaining remarkably unfazed by John Lennon's urgent request for a vocal effect on 'Tomorrow Never Knows' that would sound 'like the Dalai Lama and thousands of Tibetan monks chanting on a mountain top'[107] – so too did Ammonds possess the right mixture of professional know-how and comic sensibility to enhance the content of the show as well as its form.[108] It was Ammonds, for example, who thought of rigging up Eric's stool during the 'Side by Side' routine with Ernie and Roy Castle so that he spent most of the song either high above the other two or way down beneath them; and it was Ammonds who devised – and, in some cases, wrote – the 'I worked with Morecambe and Wise – and look what happened to me!' running gags; and it was Ammonds who first thought of inviting Glenda Jackson and André Previn on to the show. One of his most eye-catching contributions – the curious skipping exit (likened by Kenneth Tynan to 'a sort of camp hornpipe'[109]) that ended each show from the early seventies[110] onwards – came about, he recalled, quite by chance:

I just happened to be watching this Marx Brothers film on television one night. *Horse Feathers*. Groucho had taken over a campus, I think, somewhere in America. Anyway, at one point he did a musical number or something, and he did this silly dance, you see, putting his hands behind his head and sort of hopping in the air. I found it amusing, and, the next morning, I came into rehearsal and I said to Eric – who was a big Groucho Marx fan – 'Did you see him last night?' He said, 'No?' So I said, 'Well, he did this funny dance at one point . . .' And I did it all the way around the room, you see, and both of them laughed like mad!

Well, we carried on rehearsing for the next show, which was due to be recorded in about a week's time, and then – I *think* it was on the dress run-through – after singing 'Bring Me Sunshine' they danced off with that funny dance! And they kept it in for the recording, and after that they did it every week. It became a trademark. And if I hadn't come across that film that night, and liked that little dance, it wouldn't have happened. So I can say: me and Groucho – we created it![111]

'The great unsung hero of *The Morecambe & Wise Show*,' Bill Cotton declared, 'the one who never got an award – *they* got awards for everything – was Johnny Ammonds. He had *enormous* expertise, and he had great experience, and his eye for details was just spot-on. He really deserved one of those BAFTAs – and a whole lot more – for everything that he brought to that show.'[112] Ann Hamilton – who appeared in very nearly all of the BBC shows – was similarly appreciative: '[Ammonds] was *so* underrated. He was *so* clever. The shows he directed got award after award and yet never anything for him. He should have had awards – not just one but many, because he was a very, very talented man as well as such a *nice* man, too. I refuse to believe that it would all have happened in the same way – and with the same kind of success – with Joe Bloggs at the helm. It wouldn't have done. The nice ones don't get the publicity, but John deserved it, he really did.'[113] It seems that Morecambe and Wise agreed, because, after collecting yet another one of their many BAFTA awards at a ceremony held in the Albert Hall, Eric Morecambe walked back from the stage and placed it on the table where Ammonds was sitting: 'Here,' he said, 'It's about time *you* had one of these.'[114]

'The important thing', Ernie Wise always insisted, 'is the team, the four of us: Eddie, the writer, Johnny Ammonds, the producer, and Eric and me.'[115] United by a common purpose and a shared sense of humour, these four men functioned together as the heartbeat of the great BBC *Morecambe & Wise Shows* of the late sixties and early seventies.

There were others, however, who made significant contributions on a regular basis. Peter Knight, for example, was, from the second series on, the brilliant musical director who could always be relied on to come up at short notice with a suitable pastiche to complement any situation. The multi-talented Ernest Maxin – who had last worked with Morecambe and Wise some ten years before in his capacity as producer of their Torquay summer season – was brought in by Ammonds in 1971 as dance director (but would also be responsible for devising such memorable musical comedy routines as 'Smoke Gets in Your Eyes', with Shirley Bassey, a bottle of champagne, an unsteady table and a hobnail boot). Peter Wesson, the lighting director, was ever-present from 1970 onwards, and had the opportunity to show his versatility as more and more 'Hollywood-style' musical numbers were introduced as the decade progressed. Bill King, who was responsible for all of the special effects on the show, had been working in television since the late forties, and was both conscientious (sometimes to a fault – he once inadvertently ruined a Bob Monkhouse routine on live television by installing shatter-proof glass in a prop door after seeing it smashed to pieces in rehearsal and thinking to himself, 'Now *that's* dangerous . . .'[116]) and ingenious (whatever was needed – be it a pair of alligator shoes with toe-caps that opened up like jaws, a set of maracas whose heads popped off in the presence of an attractive woman, a remote-controlled toaster, a pair of Turkish slippers that uncurled excitedly the moment their owner was kissed, or a replica of a street set from *Singin' in the Rain* that had the additional feature of strategically placed water pipes – he produced it).

On the other side of the camera, there were regular cameo appearances by the wizened Rex Rashley[117] (standing in for, among others, John Wayne, Bob Hope, Frankie Vaughan's son, one of Robin Hood's Merrie Men and the whole of the Harpenden Male Voice Choir), the crinkle-haired Arthur Tolcher (an old friend of Morecambe and Wise's from their *Youth Takes a Bow* days, he was the hyper-enthusiastic harmonica player who would always be stopped a few notes into the 'Spanish Gypsy Dance' with the cry of: 'Not *now*, Arthur!') and Janet Webb, the well-spoken woman with the generous (49-inch, in fact) embonpoint who would brush Eric and Ernie unceremoniously aside at the end of each show and launch into an emotional speech about how it had 'all been worthwhile' if the viewers had enjoyed watching 'me and my little show here tonight' ('We used to get letters from people saying: "How *dare* she say it's *her* show. She's nowhere *near* as good as Eric and Ernie!"' John Ammonds recalled[118]). The most enduring member of the supporting cast, however, was Ann Hamilton.

Hamilton appeared on the show whenever a sketch called for the presence of a female character: she played Eric's girlfriend, Eric's wife, Eric's mistress, the Queen of France, Maid Marion, Desdemona to Glenda Jackson's Cleopatra and innumerable shop assistants, au pairs, nurses, serving wenches, secretaries and sex objects. After she had joined the show, Eric Morecambe would often say to her, 'Stick with us: you'll be our Margaret Dumont'[119] – referring to the amorous, deluded, dignified woman of the classic Marx Brothers movies. The two women could hardly have been less alike in terms of physical appearance – Hamilton was young, slim and attractive, whereas Dumont was middle-aged, broad and, beneath her dark brown wig, as bald as a billiard ball – but Morecambe, having worked with her before on one of the last of their ATV shows,[120] felt that Hamilton could bring something of the same slightly shaky *sang-froid* to a wide range of comic situations. There was, nevertheless, a problem: unlike Dumont, who was notorious for never understanding what was supposed to be funny about any comic scene she was appearing in, Hamilton possessed a dangerously keen sense of humour:

It was so easy to laugh at them. That was the initial problem! I remember my first show with them over at ATV: it was a *Man from UNCLE* sketch, and I was supposed to be playing this very stern-looking female agent. Well, I had not stopped laughing all through rehearsal; I'd hardly been able to get my words out for laughing, laughing, laughing – because they were so funny. Eric, particularly, was *so* funny, and what made it worse was that he was always such a wicked little pixie: if he saw the twinkle – you know, the laughter welling up inside – he'd work on you to make you 'go'. So we did the show, and, sure enough, I started to *go*, because Eric just looked at me – you know, by this time all he had to do was catch my eye, and that was me finished – and I sort of went *uuggh*, and he said, 'Oh, no, don't *you* go, love – I've got enough trouble with *him*!' – pointing to Ernie.[121]

When she was invited to join them on the BBC shows, however, she was determined not to allow herself to go through the same comic ordeal again:

I really thought I'd blown it after that ATV show – I thought that was it, the end of my comedy career – but I said to myself at the time: if ever I'm in that position again where I have to work with them, or any other comic, I would *die* rather than laugh in front of the camera. And I never did – that was the first and last time I laughed. Never again. Never, *ever*, again. So what happened with Eric and Ernie over at the BBC was that I would go away after the final dress rehearsal and build up *hate*. Hate, hate, hate. I know that seems a great exaggeration, but I had to go off by myself and just really school the thoughts: 'Nothing is funny. From now on, *nothing* is funny.' If I hadn't done that I would never have got through the show – never – because Eric tried, he always *really* tried, the little devil. He was so *wicked*! And, of course, he did love it whenever anybody went, because he could always capitalise on it. His brain was quicksilver.[122]

Morecambe and Wise worked hard at making their shows look easy. The aim, they always said, was to come up with a performance that worked like 'a very carefully rehearsed ad-lib'.[123] Although it was never allowed to reach the kind of extremes that Neil Simon parodied so well in *The Sunshine Boys* (CLARK: 'Do you want to rehearse the sketch or what?' LEWIS: 'You're not against rehearsing?' CLARK: 'I'm against doing the show. Rehearsing is important.'), their preparation for each show was, none the less, painstakingly thorough: 'The secret of our success', revealed Wise, 'is practice, hard work and coming to rehearsal.'[124] If the frame was familiar, they reasoned, the work was free to be fresh: once every line, every word, every nuance, every pause, every last comical curlicue was fixed firmly in their minds, they felt able to go on to relax and even to enjoy themselves on stage in front of the television cameras. When, for example, Eric Morecambe delivered lines like, 'Lord Longford asked me what to do about the Pornography Bill. I told him straight. I said: "Pay it!"' he did so secure in the knowledge that every possible kind of rhythm and intonation had been tried and considered during the three-week-long rehearsal period. It was not that he lacked the ability to walk on and elicit the audience's laughter simply by reading the joke directly off the teleprompt – if any comedian could have done so, *he* could; it was rather that he knew that funny lines could always be made even funnier by the kind of clearly authoritative delivery that resulted only from the most meticulous form of preparation. 'That was one of the reasons why actors respected him so much,' said William Franklyn. 'He'd make a line that you'd seen him rehearse and rehearse and rehearse seem like an ab-lib when it came to the recording. That's brilliant technique. It's rather like a great cricketer who can play his shots very late. Eric could lean back and think to himself, "Right, I'll pick this off with my eyebrows and get a laugh," and he'd do it with such *grace*.'[125]

The proof was to be found in the performance: in one particularly elaborate sketch, for example, Morecambe repeated an entire speech three times, syllable for syllable: 'Another comedian', Kenneth Tynan observed at the time, 'would have made it louder every time, with diminishing comic returns; Eric [however] used the same even, rational tones throughout, and brought down the house.'[126] Such skill, when properly nourished by sustained periods of honest effort, could not just enhance the best material but also – and perhaps even more importantly – turn a clumsy line or a creaky sketch into a clever high-curvetting act. 'Eric and Ernie always give my scripts the final polish,' Eddie Braben acknowledged. 'Many writers wouldn't allow their scripts to be messed around with; to them every word is holy and unchangeable except by themselves. But it is different for us. I know that if I wrote a bad script they would make it acceptable; if I wrote a good one, they could make it brilliant.'[127]

Sometimes Morecambe and Wise would emerge at the end of a

long afternoon's rehearsal with little more than one brightly polished comic gem to show for their troubles, and sometimes they would set off for home with an entire, admirably refulgent routine securely in place, but, regardless of the special demands of any particular day, their commitment remained constant. 'I'd worked with many other entertainers,' John Ammonds recalled, 'but none of them came near to the professionalism of those two. They never let up. In fact, there'd be the odd time when I felt they'd done *so* much *so* well in rehearsals I'd say, "Take tomorrow off. You're well ahead of schedule – take a breather.' But they'd say, "No, no – *you* take the day off. We'll come in and work on it a bit more." That was what Eric and Ernie were like.'[128] Most of the lines in the shows that sounded spontaneous were actually, Ammonds confirmed, carefully rehearsed: 'The majority would've been added to the script during the first week of rehearsal, when Eric, Ernie and myself would go through Eddie's material line by line. Eric would sometimes do or say something and we'd say, "Keep it in."'[129] There might, of course, be the odd occasion during a show when one or the other of them would suffer from a momentary mental blank – if it happened to be Morecambe, he would probably slap his partner's cheeks to win a few precious seconds of 'thinking time',[130] and, if it happened to be Wise, then Morecambe would probably turn it into a joke ('I never give up. I wish *you* would sometimes!'), but such moments were few and far between. Ammonds recalled the recording of a particularly funny sketch – in which Ernie has a visit from the poet Adrian Fondle – which was almost ruined by a scene-hand who walked absent-mindedly past the window of the flat in full view of the audience: 'Eric saved the day by saying something like "He must have long legs – we're on the thirteenth floor!"'[131] Whenever possible, he observed, the inclination was to continue with the recording:

Once we'd started, they didn't like stopping. They didn't like stopping and admitting to an audience that they'd forgotten their lines – the shame of it, you know. It was their professionalism again; they didn't like to spoil it for the studio audience. The most difficult situation for me was when we were in the middle of one of those flat sketches and there might be, say, a boom shadow, and the sound man would say, 'Oh, God, can we do it again, John?' Because *they* were professional, too, you know. And I used to have to say to the floor manager, through his headphones, 'Look, I *know* this is going to be difficult, but I'd like to do that section again.' I knew exactly what Eric's reaction was going to be. He'd say, sarcastically, 'Well *done*, John! You're absolutely right, John! We'll get a *lot* of letters about that boom shadow!'

In fact, Eric used to tell me that when he was watching the show at home with his family, and he knew that there was a slight fluff coming up that we hadn't been able to edit out, he'd sit next to the ash can, and when the fluff was just about to happen he'd bash the ash can with his foot, or he'd cough or say something or other to distract them. Isn't that funny! He didn't want to admit to his family that he'd fluffed a line. Strange but understandable – he had his pride and he didn't want to admit that it was his mistake. He made sure his family didn't hear it even if the other eighteen million viewers did![132]

The execution had to be impeccable, and, just as important, the appeal had to be immense. The team would conduct a detailed post-mortem on each show, not just to assess how it might have been made funnier but also to consider how it might have been made more accommodating. Although their scripts were often stuffed with *double entendres* and Freudian slipperiness, they were careful to avoid anything that ventured beyond the freshly scrubbed, playful naughtiness of the old-fashioned seaside postcard:

| | |
|---|---|
| ERNIE | I've extended my repertoire. |
| ERIC | It didn't show from back there. |
| | |
| ERNIE | He wanted to expose her feminine folly. |
| ERIC | He can't do that – there's a frost about! |
| | |
| ERIC | A director rang from Hollywood. 'Alfred' some-body. |
| ERNIE | Hitchcock? |
| ERIC | He might have, I didn't ask. |

ERNIE    My auntie's got a Whistler.

ERIC     Now there's a novelty!

The sauciness lay inert like an unlit match: it was left to the viewer to strike it in order for it to ignite. 'We didn't do anything direct,' Eddie Braben insisted. '"Pardon?" was about as far as we got: "I'll go in the kitchen and have a look at it now." And we'd say, "Pardon?" That's all we needed. Out of the most innocent line we'd get a "Pardon?" and that would do it.'[133] *The Morecambe & Wise Show*, John Ammonds recalled, was made from the start with a mass audience firmly in mind:

> We weren't interested in going out of our way to offend people. That wasn't what the show was about at all. None of us believed that to be really good you needed to be offensive. We used to get terribly worried if we got any letters concerning matters of taste, because we were pretty careful about stopping the odd lapse of taste from slipping through.
>
> I remember we once did a sketch where, for some reason or another, a girl came to the door of the flat, and she was obviously pregnant, and Eric thought that Ernie was the father. Well, we received about a dozen letters about that, saying that this was a bit too much for Morecambe and Wise, you know. We'd get very upset about that, and we'd feel that we'd made a mistake – that we shouldn't have done it. Of course, you have to put it in proportion: we had twelve letters of complaint out of an average audience of a mere eighteen or nineteen million people! But I'm glad that it *did* worry us, because we didn't *need* to use any material that was remotely 'blue'. That was the thing: we didn't *have* to rely on vulgarity to make a genuinely funny show. We'd got Eric and Ernie, these two wonderful comic personalities, and, well, the world was our oyster.[134]

The show's burgeoning popularity would be their reward. The average audience, which had been growing steadily on BBC2,[135] increased dramatically once the show moved over to BBC1.[136] With its inspired and refreshingly unconventional use of its star guests – another innovation that had been prompted by the abrupt departure of Hills and Green[137] – the show soon became something of a national talking-point. There was something quintessentially British about the way in which even the grandest of guests was cut down to size: they might have been regarded as Very Important People by the rest of the world, but in the presence of Eric and Ernie they were made to seem very ordinary indeed – no less talented, and certainly no less admirable, but definitely more human. Once every week, the stars came down to earth on *The Morecambe & Wise Show*, and the viewing public savoured the sight of it.

By the end of 1971 the show had established itself as the pre-eminent light entertainment show on British television. 'I think the Christmas show of that year was probably the turning point,' Bill Cotton suggested. 'That was probably the biggest thing that had happened on British television up to that point – the one where you really had the whole country talking about, you know, who's going to be the big guest on *The Morecambe & Wise Show*. And to me, at the time, it felt like, you know, "Well, we've really got this *right*." '[138] It certainly was, by any standards, a memorable show: it featured Shirley Bassey in her size-ten boots; Glenda Jackson being serenaded by an odd assortment of BBC presenters; a Robin Hood 'romp' with Francis Matthews and Ann Hamilton; and – most impressively of all – André Previn, a thirty-five-piece orchestra, Eric Morecambe as soloist and a 'special – pre-decimal – arrangement' of Grieg's Piano Concerto.

In the Grieg routine, at least, one witnessed Morecambe and Wise producing a near-flawless comic performance. It began as usual in front of the tabs: André Previn, their special guest star, has just been informed by a sheepish-looking Ernie Wise that he will not now be conducting the Mendelssohn Violin Concerto with Yehudi Menuhin as soloist because, according to a suspicious-sounding telegram, Menuhin is opening in *Old King Cole* at the Argyll, Birkenhead. Previn goes on to discover that he will actually be conducting the Grieg Piano Concerto with Eric Morecambe as soloist:

PREVIN   Goodnight, gentlemen.

ERNIE    No, no! *Please* don't go, Mr Preview!

ERIC     Privit.

PREVIN   Previn.

ERNIE    I can assure you that Eric is more than capable.

PREVIN   *Well* . . . All right. I'll go get my baton.
ERNIE    Please do that.
PREVIN   It's in Chicago.

Eventually, but still very reluctantly, he relents, and they walk over to the orchestra area. 'Is this the band?' asks Eric. After offering Previn some invaluable last-minute advice – 'In the Second Movement, not too heavy on the banjos' – Eric prepares to make his way to the piano; such is his strangely circuitous route, however, that he fails to reach his seat in time for his cue. 'It's too short,' he complains of the introduction. 'If you could lengthen it by about a yard, we'll be in.' When Previn asks them what he could possibly be expected to do about that, Ernie, with the most wonderful of *naif* expressions, replies: 'Could we get in touch with Grieg?'

PREVIN   (*incredulous*) You mean . . . call him on the 'phone?
ERNIE    Why not?
PREVIN   (*sarcastic*) What a shame – I didn't bring his 'phone number!
ERIC     Well, er, it's 'NORWAY' something or other, isn't it?
ERNIE    What's the code?
ERIC     'Fingal's Cave', isn't it? Mind you, you might not get him – he might be out skiing.

They try again – this time with Eric already seated at the piano. Nothing happens: the lid of the piano, it seems, obscured Eric's view of Previn's cue. Previn, by this stage, is so desperate to end his ordeal and escape that he agrees to jump high up in the air in order to cue Eric in. This time it works, except for the fact that, as Previn exclaims, Eric is playing 'all the wrong notes'. Ernie, on hearing such a criticism, braces himself at a safe distance. Eric flinches slightly, gets up, grabs Previn by the lapels of his jacket, pulls him close, nose-to-nose, looks him straight in the eye and says menacingly: 'I'm playing all the *right* notes . . . but not necessarily in the right order!' Ernie does his best to act as peace-maker: 'That sounds quite reasonable to me.' Previn, however, is adamant. 'Don't forget', Eric points out, 'that for another four pounds we could've got Edward Heath!' Undeterred, Previn sits down and proceeds to play all the right notes in the right order. There is nothing but silence. Ernie glances down at his shoes. Eric puts his hands in his pockets, clenches his fists, hitches up his trousers, thinks of saying something, thinks better of it, pauses, then delivers his judgement: *'Rubbish!'* As the two of them walk off in disgust, Previn starts playing Eric's version. They rush back. 'That's it! That's *it*! You've got it!'

It was probably their finest moment: a moment in which talent, expertise and commitment came together to produce something unique, irresistible and wholly unforgettable. 'We all felt proud of that,' John Ammonds recalled. 'I know that Eric and Ernie did. It was about sixteen minutes of sheer entertainment from start to finish. Just two idiots and a super professional, and laughter – *real* laughter.'[139] As they danced beside Previn at the end of the sketch, they looked as though they were having the time of their lives. Television, far from ending up as their burial place, had become their home.

## CHAPTER XIV

# Mass Entertainment

*In the theatre or the cinema the revues, musical comedies, farces and so on
are written and produced to tickle the collective sense of humour of a mass
audience . . . What is the position for a television production? The
audience usually consists of two or three people in their own home; they
are surrounded by the everyday, mundane things of life; there is no 'electric
atmosphere' of laughter or excitement . . . Is there a solution?*
RONNIE WALDMAN

*Eric and Ernie were the best in their business. Johnny Ammonds was the
best in his business. Eddie Braben was the best in his business. No, there
wasn't much that was accidental about the success of* The Morecambe &
Wise Show. *Everyone knew what they were doing.*
BILL COTTON

'When a valued, cultured, and elegant friend sent me his new book
and I was about to open it,' the critic Walter Benjamin once confessed, 'I caught myself in the act of straightening my tie.'[1] It was
with a similar sense of keen and courteous anticipation that viewers
in the seventies settled down each week to watch *The Morecambe &
Wise Show.* No longer just a television programme, it had become
a cultural event: 'There comes a point', Kenneth Tynan observed,
'at which sheer professional skill, raised to the highest degree by
the refining drudgery of constant practice, evolves into something
different in kind, conferring on its possessors an assurance that enables
them to take off, to ignite, to achieve outrageous feats of timing and
audience control that would, even a few years before, have been
beyond them. Morecambe and Wise have now reached that point.'[2]

He was preaching largely to the converted. No other show could boast a range of devoted admirers that encompassed not only such pillars of the Establishment as the Royal Family,[3] the Prime Minister,[4] the Chancellor of the Exchequer[5] and some of Whitehall's grandest grandees,[6] but also at least two of the KGB's most distinguished British-based intelligence agents: the tall and balding Major-General Yuri Kobaladze (known to his colleagues as 'Morecambe') and his avuncular deputy, the short and stout Colonel Oleg Tsarev (also known as 'Wise').[7] Even a certain irascible, one-armed BBC commissionaire – notorious within the Corporation for his surly treatment of any stars or staff foolish enough to attempt to enter Television Centre – was unashamedly devoted to the show. Indeed, he once asked if he might be afforded the privilege of attending a recording, only for Eric Morecambe to inform him that his presence would not be welcome: 'Why?' begged the hurt commissionaire. 'I'm your biggest fan!' 'But you can't clap,' replied Morecambe.[8]

'The 1970s were, I guess you could say, something of a golden age for light entertainment at the BBC,' remarked Bill Cotton. 'We made some very good programmes *and* we got some very high ratings.'[9] Part of the reason for this, he suggested, was the fact that he and his colleagues – Paul Fox (Controller of BBC1 1967–73), David Attenborough (Controller of BBC2 1965–8 and Director of Programmes 1969–72) and Huw Wheldon (Managing Director of Television, 1968–76) – were united in their commitment to high-quality popular programme-making:

> They really understood what public service broadcasting was about ... The support and the enthusiasm that they showed towards producers was an inspiration. And in that they were following [in] the tradition that made the BBC such a formidable programme-maker. There was a clear way to the airwaves – a programme idea from the producer to the output head to the channel controller to the television set. It didn't always work perfectly, but the system was a good one, and it was backed up with effective financial and administrative controls.[10]

Bruce Forsyth – one of the stars of Cotton's hugely successful Saturday night schedule – was in no doubt as to the value of such a system:

The light entertainment at that time at the BBC was so *strong*: I mean, every Saturday, for example, you'd have *Dr Who*, followed by us [*The Generation Game*], then a popular drama – *The Duchess of Duke Street* or *All Creatures Great and Small* – then *The Morecambe & Wise Show*, then *Starsky and Hutch*, then *Match of the Day* and *Parkinson*. I mean it was a fantastic variety of entertainment, great viewing, and that is why the BBC – thanks in large part to Bill Cotton, by the way, who was brilliant – captured whole evenings in those days. You could start watching at about 5 o'clock, 5.30, and stay there until 11 o'clock at night. So it was about a six-hour bundle of very varied, very polished, entertainment – everything that the people wanted.[11]

The thing that the people wanted more than anything else, Cotton acknowledged, was *The Morecambe & Wise Show*: 'We had a vast repertory of very good comedy in those days: *Dad's Army*, for example, *Monty Python's Flying Circus*, *The Good Life*, *Not Only . . . But Also*, *The Two Ronnies* – that's a pretty good range. But there's no doubt about it: Morecambe and Wise were the jewel in the crown of the BBC as far as Variety programmes were concerned. I felt very proud of that show. In fact, I think everyone felt proud of that show.'[12]

Award followed award: five from BAFTA (in 1969, 1970, 1971, 1972 and 1973);[13] three from the Variety Club of Great Britain (1974, 1976 and 1978);[14] two from the Radio Industries Organisation (1971 and 1972); two from the Water Rats (1970 and 1974); and the Freedom of the City of London and an OBE each (both in 1976). They also enjoyed the traditional regalia of fame – a Rolls-Royce each, a luxury cabin cruiser (the *Lady Doreen*) for Wise, a villa in the Algarve for Morecambe and a villa in Malta for Wise. So great, in fact, was the scale of their off-screen success that – as Michael Aspel remembered – it rapidly became one of their on-screen running jokes: 'Eric, Ernie and I made several trailers together for the BBC which for some reason were never used. (We thought they were hilarious.) In one, I "interviewed" the boys beside a swimming-pool, ostensibly at their home. It ended with Eric asking me if I wanted my glass of champagne replenished. He snapped his fingers and a waiter (John Ammonds) dipped a ladle in the pool and filled our flutes.'[15] Similar jokes made it on to the show itself:

| | |
|---|---|
| ERIC | Dame Glenda. |
| GLENDA | *Dame* Glenda? I'm sorry, Eric – it's just plain |
| JACKSON | 'Glenda'. |
| ERIC | Oh dear. |
| ERNIE | Oh dear. |
| JACKSON | Is something wrong? |
| ERIC | Well, it's just that, you see, nowadays we only work with *titled* people. |

Such self-mockery was never misconstrued, however, because Morecambe and Wise remained so patently unspoilt by all of the bouquets that came their way. Even Kenneth Williams was moved to write after interviewing them: 'There is little doubt about the fundamental honesty & goodness of both of them. No wonder they're so universally popular.'[16] When John Mortimer wrote a profile on Eric Morecambe, he arrived at a similar conclusion: 'Eric is not only England's most popular comedian, he must be near to being our most popular person.'[17]

It was Kenneth Tynan, however, who, more than anyone else, heralded their elevation to the heady level of national institution. He saw them perform at the New Theatre in Oxford early in 1973, and, as Joan Morecambe recalled, he interviewed Eric over supper: 'He got Eric talking, and it just rolled out of him – he gave the most marvellous interview. But what fascinated me most was how Kenneth absorbed it all. He didn't tape a word of it, but he went away at the end of it and brought out this fabulous article.'[18] It was certainly one of Tynan's most enthusiastic pieces: he marvelled at Morecambe's comic timing (one of 'the wonders of the profession'), at Wise's skills as a straight-man ('dapper and aggressive, like a sawn-off Lew Hoad'), their unprecedented professional longevity ('a mobile repository of vaudeville lore, an encyclopaedia of English-speaking gags') and their unique appeal ('you cannot learn from films or TV the ability to control a thousand people by your physical presence').[19] It was a *tour de force* that left them feeling both flattered and vaguely uneasy. Eric Morecambe was, if anything, somewhat defensive when, at the end of the year, *The Listener* invited him to respond to this and other notable recent tributes: 'Whatever else 1973 has brought for Ernie Wise and me, it has been a year of analysis. Our psyches have been probed, our idiosyncrasies have withstood intense scrutiny, and the world has been exposed to our foibles.'[20] As far as Tynan's piece was concerned, he admitted that he was 'very impressed' by the 'brilliant writing' (as well as pleasantly surprised that the force behind *Oh! Calcutta!* had kept his clothes on throughout the meeting), but added sardonically that he had been relieved that what Tynan had referred to as his 'subliminal pause' had not gone unnoticed: 'In the old days of Variety, when we appeared way down the bill, my subliminal pauses came in very handy during our 12-minute spot, second turn on, first house Monday, at Aston Hippodrome.'[21] Addressing 'the great British public' directly, Morecambe argued: 'I don't think you want us turned inside out to find what makes us tick. You accept us for what we are: two ordinary middle-aged men who take a great amount of pride in making you laugh.'[22]

Keen as Morecambe was to play down the reverential remarks about his subliminal pauses – 'They worried me, those did. I thought I ought to go back to hospital'[23] – there was no doubting the high esteem in which he and his partner were now held. Even John Ammonds – who, having worked so closely with them for so long, could have been forgiven for sounding mildly iconoclastic about their increasingly lofty reputation – remained full of admiration: 'They were brilliant. Absolutely superb. And Eric: well, what *he* had was genius. That's not too high-flown a word for what it was. The way that he used to *create* comedy was amazing. In rehearsals, he'd work and work and work, find extra bits and pieces – visuals particularly – and it just needed one person in the room to laugh and he'd be *away*, pushing himself even harder. It really was a privilege to be there when he worked.'[24]

As far as Ammonds and the rest of the production team were concerned, the extraordinary popularity of the show – audiences by now were regularly topping the twenty million mark – helped concentrate the mind. Hearing of the extraordinary impact that it was having up and down the country, and learning of the warmth that audiences seemed to feel for its stars, there was a strong sense that they were all now involved in something very special, something wonderful, something genuinely worthwhile. Eddie Braben reflected:

> When I was living in my home in Liverpool, in the winter when the leaves had fallen, I could look out of my window and see a main road through the trees – I used to live round the back of a park – and I'd see buses and cars and bikes going past. And I used to start work very early in the morning, and I'd see all these people on buses going by, and I used to think to myself: there they go, off to the factory, shops, offices, wherever, and they might be saying, 'Oh, *great*! Eric and Ernie are on tonight!' Because, you see, when *I* was going to work, *I* used to say, 'Oh, good, so-and-so are on tonight!' And that was the way I felt. I felt I had to give this job everything I had for those people.[25]

It was an attitude that mirrored that of the stars themselves: 'I see myself as a paid entertainer who must fulfil a duty to the paying public,' said Morecambe. 'I'm not interested in doing my own funny thing. There's nothing smart or kinky about my jokes – they're meant for the masses to like. And you've got to work very hard to get people to like you.'[26] Wise agreed: 'Pleasing the public is the beginning and end of it.'[27]

Anxious not to lose touch with their audience, they darted around the provinces on what they jokingly referred to as 'bank raids': twice nightly, on irregular Fridays and Saturdays, they would appear at some of the biggest theatres outside London, offering fans of their television show a kind of potted history of post-war Variety. The first half of the programme was a straight Variety bill – a typical list of support acts from the early seventies would have included the Johnny Wiltshire Sound, Sheila Southern, Ray Alan and Lord Charles, and Mrs Mills.[28] The second half consisted of a selection of their old routines, including their excellent 'vent' act:

ERNIE    I can see your lips moving.
ERIC     Well, *of course* you flamin' can, you fool! *I'm* the
         one who's doing it for him! *He's* made of wood!
         His mother was a Pole, you know.

ERNIE     Has he got a good finish?

ERIC      He's french-polished – you can't get better than that!

ERNIE     Is he lacquered?

ERIC      He's *bound* to be! He's worked hard!

At the end of each performance they would preface a brief question-and-answer session with the audience by noting, 'You've just seen thirty years go by before your very eyes in one hour's performance,'[29] and it was, indeed, a remarkably effective way of reminding people of just how hard they had worked over so long a period to achieve their current level of success.

Back in the studio, they continued to behave with admirable humility. Although they were well aware that they were now making programmes that amounted to 'the best work of our lives',[30] they continued to think of themselves as ordinary members (more or less) of a very good production team. 'They were still working-class lads in many ways,' John Ammonds recalled. 'They'd turn up in their Rollers, of course, but that was always a bit of a joke as far as they were concerned. Once they got inside the rehearsal room they'd roll their sleeves up and get on with it.'[31] Ann Hamilton felt that they valued the routine behind-the-scenes stability that the rest of the team provided: 'They liked the family atmosphere, definitely. If you didn't fit in with the family, that whole atmosphere of everybody working with and for each other, then you wouldn't have stayed. It was never a case of "the stars and the rest", it was always a *team*: no side, no temperament – you just came in, did your work, you were friendly, warm, happy, and then you went home. That was what the show was all about.'[32]

Morecambe and Wise – to their credit – never took it for granted that the studio audience would like them. 'Sometimes', said More-cambe, 'we get the feeling that we inhibit them. So we have to work that bit harder.'[33] Before each show was recorded,[34] they would make sure that an unusually full and proper 'warm-up' session had been held. John Ammonds remembered: 'We'd start with a professional warm-up man. We used Barry Cryer for a bit, and then we had Felix Bowness, who was an amazing character. He'd sit as close as possible to the audience, talk absolute nonsense, and have them roaring with laughter. I don't quite know *how* he did it – some of his jokes were pretty ancient! – but he was the best in the business. Once he'd finished, or we'd dragged him off, I'd introduce the boys, who would chat to the audience and then do their vent act routine. After that, the mood was very warm and upbeat, and we were ready to start recording.'[35] Eric Morecambe, he noted, was particularly impatient to meet the audience on these occasions:

> In fact, you delayed Eric at your peril! In the early days I'd talk to the audience for a couple of minutes before I introduced Eric and Ernie. I'd just explain a bit about the recording, why we'd be stopping for this and that. I always kept this as short as possible, because I'd get insults otherwise. There was one time when I was explaining about video tape (this was before the days of home video), and Eric crept on and started shouting, 'They don't want to hear all that rubbish! *Gerroff!*' So after that I'd just say something like, 'Here they are: Morecambe and Wise!' and make a run for it![36]

The post-show rituals, Ann Hamilton remembered, were equally important:

> Everyone would gather in either Eric's or Ernie's dressing-room for one of their little champagne receptions, and, again, it mattered a great deal to them that everyone involved with the show – not just the guests – was included. I missed it once. I was delayed in the bathroom trying to scrub off this body make-up that the make-up department had smothered me with for a 'harem' sketch. By the time I got there they'd nearly all gone, and Eric was very concerned that I'd been delayed because of this make-up. Nothing more was said until the next time that we had to do a similar sketch. When the camera crew and the wardrobe and make-up people came in, Eric said, 'No body make-up for Ann.' And they said, 'Why?' And he said, 'No body make-up for Ann. It took her hours to take it off last time. I'm not having it!' And I said, 'Thank you, Eric.' All because I'd missed the party. We were family, you see. You felt appreciated.[37]

The most important show of the year was, without any doubt, the Christmas special – the show that the *Guardian* once described as 'the most compulsive curiosity shop of any Christmas'.[38] 'To many people they have become as important a part of the festive season as plum puddings and turkey,' said Ernie Wise of these shows. 'That gives us a certain sense of responsibility. Other programmes can flop – the Christmas ones must never be allowed to.'[39] Preparation for each one began, in effect, shortly after the last one: special sketches were planned, ideas for big budget musical routines debated, and, most important of all, possible special guest stars were considered and contracted. It had taken the enormous success of the 1971 Christmas special, and, in particular, the entirely unexpected but undeniably impressive guest appearance by André Previn, to make the production team sit up and realise just how much talent they now had, potentially, at their disposal. As John Ammonds recalled:

The Previn appearance represented our first big gamble. You see, first of all, we hadn't been sure that he'd even agree to come on. I mean, in those days, you just didn't have people like André – principal conductor with the LSO and all that – turning up on a *comedy* show. It just didn't happen. But I rang him up at his home in Surrey anyway. When he answered I said, 'I'm John Ammonds, I produce Morecambe and Wise –' And he said, 'Before you go any further, let me tell you: I think you've got a great show there.' I said, 'Well, I'm glad you said that, because I'm going to ask you to be on it.' I told him what we had in mind, and asked if I could ring his agent and say that he was interested. He said, 'You can do better than that – you can ring him and say I'll definitely do it.'[40]

There was still, however, the problem of rehearsal to contend with: Morecambe and Wise took even longer – five weeks – to prepare for their Christmas specials than they did for their other shows, and, as Ammonds noted, they expected their guests to organise their schedules accordingly:

I rang Previn's agent – who went under the rather Dickensian name of Jasper Parrott – and said, 'Could we have André for a week's rehearsal?' There was a very long pause – I think he'd collapsed from shock! – and then he said, 'Did I hear you correctly? Did you *actually* say you wanted him for *five whole days*? Because that is *ridiculous*. He's flying all around the world conducting orchestras and he can't *possibly* make *five* days.' Well, I explained that it wasn't for me, it was for Eric and Ernie: they loved rehearsing, and if anyone agreed to less than a week's rehearsal they'd get very worried. It always caused terrible problems with agents, but we had to sort it out. Anyway, *eventually*, I managed to get Previn's agent to agree to *three* days.

When I saw Eric and Ernie the next morning and told them that we'd got him, but that we could only work with him for three days, Eric said, 'That's ridiculous! How's he going to learn it?' So I said, 'Well, Eric, he's not *bad* at learning; he probably knows every note of Shostakovich's Fifth Symphony or something, so I doubt he'll have *that* much trouble with about twelve pages of dialogue.' Anyway, Eric rather reluctantly agreed that they'd go ahead, and I confirmed the dates. Previn duly turned up at Delgarno Way for the first day's rehearsal, and even at that first read-through it was obvious that he was first class. The next day, however, his agent – this Mr Parrott – phoned up and said that he was very sorry but André had had to fly to America because his mother was ill. I said, 'Well, when is he coming back?' And he said, 'The evening before the show.' I thought to myself, 'Oh dear!'

When I told Eric, his first response, predictably, was, 'Well, sod 'im then, we'll do without him. We'll use Ernie as the conductor instead.' It wasn't that he didn't think Previn was brilliant; it was just that Eric tended to panic in that kind of situation. So I said, 'Look, Eric, it's taken me a long time to get hold of this fellow, and I'm convinced it's going to be a very, very funny routine. I'll get a BBC car to meet him at the airport when it lands at 5 p.m. I'll get him to come straight to Television Centre, we'll have a room booked for us and we'll go through the script for about four hours.' Which is what we did. And every single time we did it he was word perfect – and *hysterically* funny. He'd actually learnt the whole thing in the back of the car, by torch-light, on the way from London Airport.[41]

Later that evening, after Previn had left, Morecambe still seemed apprehensive about the following day's recording session: 'John,' he said, 'this is not going to be as funny as you think it is.'[42] Twelve years later, Ammonds would ask him if he remembered making that remark. After a brief pause he smiled and then replied, 'John, I was absolutely wrong – it was the funniest thing we ever did.'[43] It was not, however, until the show itself was underway that Morecambe and Wise finally seemed able to relax. 'There's a moment, if you watch the sketch, when the nervousness disappears,'[44] observed Michael Grade. The moment in question occurs just after this exchange:

PREVIN   Well . . . all right. I'll go get my baton.
ERNIE    Please do that.
PREVIN   It's in Chicago.

Morecambe, upon hearing this exquisitely timed response, spins round, punches the air with his fist and cries out: 'Pow! He's in! I *like* him! I *like* him!' As Grade remarked:

You can see the tension evaporate in that moment. Eric's face lights up as if to say, 'Oh, *yes*! This is going to be *great*!' They'd both been pretty nervous, I think, because they knew that if Previn had lost his nerve, or fumbled his lines, the entire thing would've fallen flat on its face. But Previn was superb – rock-solid – and so you can see Eric mentally rubbing his hands together and thinking: 'Can't *wait* to get to the piano now. This is going to be a ride!' Wonderful, wonderful moment.[45]

After André Previn's guest appearance, the unexpected was expected on a regular basis, and Morecambe and Wise did their best to oblige: Yehudi Menuhin was instructed to turn up with his banjo; Rudolf Nureyev was informed that he owed his big chance to the sudden indisposition of Lionel Blair; Laurence Olivier 'evaded' an invitation by answering his telephone and saying, 'Velly solly. Long number. Chinese waundry 'ere!'; the famously disputatious Robin Day was beaten repeatedly about the head and neck with a wine bottle and a chair; and Angela Rippon revealed not only that she had legs but also that she could dance with them. 'It was a *huge* compliment to be asked,' Rippon recalled. 'There was this tradition of someone going on the show and letting their hair down and having a bit of fun – letting people see another side of them – and it was *so* much fun to do.'[46]

Celebrities were attracted to the show, it seems, for two principal reasons: first, as Barry Norman noted, 'because any invitation to work with the best is not to be turned down – and they *were* the best',[47] and second, as Robert Morley remarked, 'To be with them, you see, was to prove you were a *sport* – that's why the actors all did it.'[48] Glenda Jackson – who appeared on no fewer than five separate occasions, including two Christmas specials – agreed, but added that 'there was a particular national identification' with the show that served to further enhance its distinctive appeal:

The incredible thing about them . . . was not only that they were admired – I certainly admired them – but that they were loved by their audience. I don't think that's too extreme a word. And that's what made it so easy to say yes to their request to appear on the show . . . The response their audience had towards you was such that you, as a guest star, were enveloped in that love as well.[49]

The famous were never mocked by Morecambe and Wise, but they certainly were teased. When, for example, Edward Woodward suggested that he might dance, Eric replied, 'Good idea – you can't act!'; when the newsreader Richard Baker introduced himself brusquely as 'Baker', Eric merely said, 'A large sliced and two small browns'; and when Glenda Jackson walked on to the stage for the first time, Eric mumbled, 'Excuse me, Miss, or Madam, as the case may be, I'm afraid you can't stop up here. Only professional performers are allowed up here in front of the cameras. Go back to your seat. This isn't *The Generation Game*.' It was always the reputation that was ridiculed, never the person. 'We puncture them,' said Wise, 'but they are big enough stars to take it. Everyone knows it's a joke – and at our expense, not theirs.'[50] Morecambe agreed: 'Don't forget, we never get these big stars and push custard pies into their faces.

We either treat them rough verbally and have no respect for them, or we're over-respectful – which is worse.'[51]

There were certain stars for whom the experience, on the night, proved to be a little *too* unnerving: Frank Finlay, for one, so hated appearing as himself that he brought his opening scene to a premature end by muttering – through audience laughter – into Morecambe's ear, 'Get me off – get me out of this,'[52] but the vast majority, as Robert Morley confirmed, felt safe in the knowledge that they were appearing with two consummate professionals: 'You're never in trouble when you have an expert at your elbow.'[53] As long as a guest was willing, as almost all of them were, to fit in with the unpretentious ethos of the show – 'The "Big Star" bit', said John Ammonds, 'was really like a red rag to a bull with Eric'[54] – then their time with Morecambe and Wise was likely to be thoroughly enjoyable, although, as Ammonds recalled, the teasing was not always reserved for when the cameras were turned on:

Shirley Bassey, for example, got the full treatment from Eric. He was around when she was getting ready to record her solo spot on the show. She'd got her 'Diamonds are Forever' outfit on, you know, covered in all the sequins with the star filters on the camera to get all those sparkling effects, and Eric wandered over to her and said, 'Christ! You look like a bloody Brillo pad!' And Shirley laughed. Anybody else and she would probably have hit them, but not Eric!

They both wound Vanessa Redgrave up. She was excellent, but every tea break at rehearsal she'd be off outside selling this Workers' Revolutionary stuff – the *Morning Star* and all that. Well, we were with her in the BBC restaurant, and she tried to sell Eric and Ernie a copy of the paper. They just said, 'No thanks, love – we're capitalists.' Undeterred, she then said, 'But do you *own* the BBC?' And Ernie glanced around and said, 'No – but we're willing to make them an offer!'[55]

'We've always told our guest stars at the beginning what we want from them,' Eric Morecambe explained. 'Most comics give their guests nothing to do and make them look like idiots. We don't want that to happen to ours. If we can, we like to give them a lot of good lines. If they get a laugh, then it's in *The Morecambe & Wise Show* they're getting it.'[56] One consequence of this admirable policy, however, was that it became imperative for each guest star to concentrate fully for the entire duration of a sketch. As André Previn recalled:

They said to me two things which I'm very grateful for. First of all, Eric said, '*We* must never think this is funny, on camera. *Never think it's funny*: we're doing it for straight – if people laugh at it, that's fine – don't crack, don't laugh at the audience.' And he said, 'The other thing is: if something strikes us, and we want to improvise, *listen* to it.'[57]

Such attentiveness, as far as Morecambe and Wise were concerned, grew only out of hours of hard work, day after day, in the rehearsal room. Some guests found these intensive sessions to be somewhat excessive. Robert Morley, for example, was so disturbed on his first day at Delgarno Way by the meagre working lunch of pea-and-ham soup and sandwiches that on the following morning he insisted upon sending out for a Fortnum and Mason hamper, and Shirley Bassey, after her appearance was over, told Ammonds, 'John, I really enjoyed working with you and the boys, but could you manage with just a *little* less rehearsing next time?'[58] Others thrived on the thoroughness of it all. 'Oh, it was great fun,' William Franklyn recalled. 'I used to think to myself at the end of each day's rehearsal: "I've had a bloody good day today. *God* I enjoyed myself!" And they used to *pay* me for it! It felt like I'd just come down to meet some mates.'[59] It was a common response: 'What I thought was so terrific about their show', said Cliff Richard, 'was that they took two weeks to prepare it':

That was such a wonderful luxury. I've never done a show like that, before or since, and it was such a pleasure. You went in, read through the script, and then they said, 'We'll see you the day after tomorrow.' And I used to come back in and read through it again, then we'd kind of set it out and say, 'You stand here, I'll stand there.' You know, block everything out, get all the moves right. It was a fantastic thing to take part in and to have that much time to actually do a show. It was just wonderful. You ended up feeling proud of what you'd done. It was how shows ought to be.[60]

Angela Rippon agreed: 'They *did* take all that time, but the important thing is that they didn't waste a single second of it. They worked and worked damned hard until every single thing was as good as they could get it. And they never stopped: when I turned up for a rehearsal, someone else – another guest – was just leaving, and when *I* left, someone else would just be arriving.'[61]

The increasingly imaginative use – and choice – of guests was one of two significant trends that characterised the seventies shows; the other, largely complementary trend concerned the gradual shift in emphasis from the word to the image, from intimate sketch-comedy to spectacular musical-comedy. The man who, more than anyone else, was responsible for affecting this change was John Ammonds' successor as producer/director, Ernest Maxin. 'The ideal situation', Eddie Braben remarked, 'was when we had both John and Ernest on the show, because with the two of them we had the best of both worlds. They were the best in the business at what they did. John was the best comedy man you could get, and Ernest was the best song and dance man.'[62] Ammonds, however, left the show at the start of 1974:

There wasn't any row – it was all quite amicable. I just felt that our 1973 series had been slightly disappointing by the high standards we'd set ourselves, and we'd gone through some real heartaches at rehearsal trying to get it right. I also felt that the strain of writing all of the scripts all on his own was taking its toll on Eddie – his health was suffering – and I'd suggested to Eric that we might try to lighten the load for the next series by bringing in one or two other writers on the odd occasion to reinforce what Eddie had started. Well, Eric said yes, and then he said no, so eventually I said to Bill Cotton, 'I'm afraid I'm going to have to opt out.' So Ernie [Maxin] took over *The Morecambe & Wise Show* and I went off to do *The Mike Yarwood Show*. In retrospect, I suppose, I should just have kept my mouth shut, because later on they *did* bring in other writers and it just didn't work – it just wasn't 'Eric and Ernie'. The problem was that Eddie was simply *too* good at writing for Morecambe and Wise. He'd made himself indispensable. That, of course, was a great achievement, but I didn't care to see him ruin his health in order to go on being indispensable. So I left. Sadly. But I'd had five or six very successful years with them, we were still friends, and, of course, I was leaving them in very capable hands.[63]

Ammonds' departure was, without doubt, a serious blow, but, by 'promoting from within', Bill Cotton saw to it that a sense of continuity was maintained. As Edward Woodward – who had worked with both of them on the show – observed: 'Eric and Ernie with John Ammonds, and Eric and Ernie with Ernest Maxin were centred on one great truth – respect for each other's work and understanding for each other's point of view. Actors would drop everything to work with Eric and Ernie, and a great deal of that anticipation and enjoyment was because of John and Ernest.'[64] Francis Matthews agreed: 'They were both brilliant people. John was, I think it's fair to say, the one who was more of an "actor's director", while Ernest had this *extraordinary* gift for creating spectacular images and effects, but both of them were devoted to Eric and Ernie and both had the complete respect of everyone who worked with them.'[65] There was, however, a significant difference between them in terms of attitude: whereas Ammonds had been inclined to agree with Eric Morecambe's opinion that, 'Life isn't Hollywood, it's Cricklewood',[66] Maxin was much more in sympathy with Ernie Wise's insistence that he was, and always would be, still on his way to the magical land of Mickey Rooney, Judy Garland and Fred Astaire.

Maxin was, without any doubt, an extraordinary character. He had been a child star (touring with *The Black and White Minstrel Show*), a boxer, a jazz pianist, an actor, a singer, dancer and orchestral conductor and arranger, as well as the producer/director of several popular BBC television shows and a winner of the prestigious Charlie Chaplin International Award for Comedy. 'There was more than a touch of Hollywood about him,' Michael Aspel remarked. 'He was a virile performer who always reminded me of Gene Kelly mixed with Brian Donlevy.'[67] If anyone epitomised the old 'let's do the show right here' spirit, it was this talented, emotional and relentlessly enthusiastic man. Morecambe and Wise may not have made it to Hollywood, but Hollywood, thanks to the indefatigable Ernest Maxin, finally made it to them:

> From a kid I've always been a Hollywood man. I *loved* it. *Loved* it. Gene Kelly was my idol. So was Fred Astaire. Frank Sinatra. All of those wonderful dancers and singers. I *loved* that era – the *glamour* of it all. When I did a show with Petula Clark, for example, I drove everybody *mad* by putting varnish all over the stage floor because I really wanted everything to look *glossy*. I've always felt like that. When I came to work with Eric and Ernie, you see, I wanted to bring that Hollywood kind of glamour, that *gloss*, to the show – not instead of the comedy, but in addition to it, as another dimension. I suppose that, deep down, I'm still a ham, but I wanted to create a *style* – I've always done my best to *create* a style rather than follow an existing one – and I wanted the show to *look* like no other television show there'd been.
>
> I *like* to think that I brought a touch of MGM to *The More-cambe & Wise Show*. That's how I'd put it. A touch of make-believe, if you like. Oh, it was exciting – building from nothing! Eric and Ernie were big-screen movie-mad, like me. Maybe Eric wasn't obsessed like Ernie was, but he loved the old movies, the old musicals. They both had that interest. What I did was to try and open up the shell as much as I possibly could.[68]

Maxin carried his own private archive of classic images around with him inside his own head: the bright yellow hat that illuminates the gloomy bookshop in *Funny Face*; the dustbin lids that double as dance shoes in *It's Always Fair Weather*; Rita Hayworth's slow, soft, sensual motion in *You Were Never Lovelier*; the lean, taut, almost military precision of *Top Hat*'s smart setpieces; the free and easy energy of *On the Town*; the absurd invention of *Singin' in the Rain* and *Royal Wedding*; and the extravagant moodiness of *An American in Paris* – there was nothing that Maxin did not know about Hollywood musicals, and little that he did not love. He was more than capable of devising the slyest, smallest and most sensitive of routines – the charming little sequence that featured Eric and Ernie in white tie and tails dancing drunkenly to the tune of 'Show Me the Way to Go Home', and ended with Ernie carrying Eric off over his shoulder, was one of the most simple yet affecting things they ever did. It was, however, the lavish, MGM-style productions for which Maxin reserved a special relish:

> You have to have a talking-point in a show. That's important. Something visual – people don't remember dialogue, they remember images. We had the boys in the kitchen – *The Stripper* routine – the Angela Rippon dance routine, the *Singin' in the Rain* number, the *South Pacific* number with all the newsreaders. Strong visuals. Say 'Shirley Bassey and those boots' and everyone knows what you're talking about – the whole routine comes back to them in their mind. *Those* are the things that people remember, because they're not words, they're *images*. Of course, any great show needs a variety of things – the front-cloth routine, some sketches, some music – you need to use warmth, subtlety, you need changes of pace, but you also need *something* in the show that has everybody saying to each other the following day, 'Did you see *that*?'[69]

It was not, as a general theory, entirely convincing – after all, at one point in the seventies it seemed as though every student, estate agent and insurance salesman in the country was able to recite, unbidden but word for word, *Monty Python*'s 'Dead Parrot' sketch – nor was it what one might be inclined to describe as politic: Eddie Braben, understandably, was of a different mind on this matter. As a strategy, however, it was not just self-fulfilling but also, in Maxin's hands, exceptionally effective.

An account of the manner in which *The Stripper* breakfast routine was produced, for example, offers one a revealing insight into both the nature and extent of Maxin's inimitable contribution to the success of *The Morecambe & Wise Show*. The basic idea, in fact, originated twelve years before when Ernie Wise had scribbled into one of his 'ideas' notebooks the suggestion, 'Why don't we do "Making breakfast in the flat to *The Stripper*"?'[70] but, as was so often the case with their most memorable routines,[71] it had undergone a long and sometimes tortuous gestation period before the team finally deemed it to be ready for production. According to Maxin, it only really came to life several hours after he and Morecambe and Wise had discussed it, not for the first time, at rehearsal:

I couldn't get the idea out of my head, and yet, during the rest of that day, I couldn't quite work out what to *do* with it, where to take it. I'd promised them I'd have something for them the next day, but all through the evening I sat at home and I just couldn't think of anything. One of those days, you know. Nothing. But I *had* to come up with *something*, though, even if it took me all night.

What happened next was this. My wife said, 'Go to bed. Get some rest. Get up early and do it then. You'll think more clearly.' And I said, 'No. I've got to do it now.' So she said, 'Well, OK, in that case, what do you want for breakfast? Do you want toast? Grapefruit? Coffee?' She gave me this list, you know, and – this is absolutely true – *that* started me off.

Suddenly, I could visualise the whole routine in my mind. The toast popping up: *boing!* The grapefruit being cut: *bam! bam! bam!* Everything. I said, 'That's it! *That's it!*' And I stayed up through the night in our kitchen, writing the top line of music down and where all the gags came in – like the toast would come up on the third beat of the fourth bar, or whatever it was, you know. Then I put in the musical punches – like when the toast comes up the music would go *du-dum-phweep-doing*, you know, as they caught it. Chopping the grapefruit: *pum*-bah-*pum*-bah-*pum*-bah. Squeezing it: *diddly-diddly-diddly*. And in the middle phrase, where Ernie's catching and smashing the eggs, you get *rom-ching-crash-bang! rom-ching-crash-bang!* from the orchestra. Mixing the omelette: *brrruuummm-da-da-da-dum*. I had to write the top line in, all the little musical accentuations to synchronise with each visual gag.

Then I put in things like the one pancake going up and then four coming down, you know, all of those things. This went on and on. The next morning, my wife came down and saw me – and the mess all over the kitchen! – and thought I'd gone completely *mad*! But I'd *got* it. I'd got it down. I went to work that morning, explained the routine to them, and they said,

'OK.' We worked on it some more, and, of course, they used their skills to make it even funnier, and it was there. We shot it in just fifteen minutes – the whole thing. And we'd got our talking-point.[72]

Eddie Braben's pet-name for Ernest Maxin was 'Ernest Maximum',[73] and there was indeed something inspired – perhaps even a little manic – about his passionate pursuit of the most polished of visions. Star guests simply *had* to have the most beautifully designed[74] and most expertly cut costumes (see, for example, the blood-red creation that Vanessa Redgrave wore in Ernie's 'Latin-American Extravaganza', or Michele Dotrice's purple chemise in the 'Nobody Does It Like Me' routine); period pieces simply *had* to look convincing (part of the Diana Rigg/Nell Gwynne 'romp' was shot on location at Banbury Castle); 'Fred and Ginger'-style sequences simply *had* to resemble the real thing (steps that Hermes Pan would have been pleased with, diamantine chandeliers and ivory-white Tuscan columns at which not even Edward Everett Horton would have turned his nose up); and, yes, the floors simply *had* to look glossy. 'He was of the old school,' remarked Diana Rigg appreciatively, 'and he believed in upholding production values, i.e., don't skimp on sets, costumes and so on.'[75]

It was this devotion to detail that made Morecambe and Wise's *Singin' in the Rain* routine such an exceptional piece of work. The original idea, once again, had been gathering dust for several years prior to its happy re-invention. 'That was one of the proposals that we discussed quite a few times over the years,' John Ammonds recalled. 'It never got very far, though, because I used to say, "Look, we can't have water all over the studio, you know, everything will fuse!" So when they finally got round to doing it with Ernest, they went and made a virtue out of necessity and didn't use any water!'[76] It was the sight of the hyperactive Maxin essaying yet another one of his many dance moves that had reminded them of the neglected routine. 'Ah, sit down, Gene Kelly!'[77] said Morecambe, but the nostalgic conversation that ensued ended up with them coming to the realisation that a *Singin' in the Rain* routine in which there happened to be a conspicuous absence of any rain (except on Morecambe's head) was the perfect comic touch.

What happened next, however, epitomised the spirit of perfectionism for which the show was famous. Maxin – assisted by Victor Meredith, his set designer, and Bill King, his brilliant props and special effects specialist – went ahead and constructed a replica of the famous New York street scene that was as near to the original as the combined constraints of studio space and budget allowed. Ernie Wise wore the same grey, three-button suit that Kelly had worn, with the same turned-up collar, greyish-brown hat and reddish-brown leather shoes; Eric Morecambe wore a midnight-blue NYPD outfit identical to that of Brick Sullivan's in the original; and, as the camera began to track along the street, one could see the same 1920s-style spherical street lamps, the same music store façade, the same 'La Valle Millinery Shop' front, the same water pipe, the same 'Mount Hollywood Art School' sign, and the same high kerb. It was, clearly, a labour of love, as well as a remarkable technical feat.[78] 'That's the kind of thing that I worked for – that *all* of us worked for,' said Maxin. 'All of us wanted the very best. I can't tell you what a difference it makes when you've got other people like that with you. I could've done those routines with somebody else and they wouldn't have been the same. The thing that was *great* about them was Morecambe and Wise. Make no mistake about that. Being around them *inspired* you, made you more creative.'[79]

It certainly seemed as though Morecambe and Wise appreciated Maxin's Hollywood homages – particularly Ernie Wise, who, for a moment, looked to be in a state of sheer bliss during the *Singing' in the Rain* routine. 'Oh, they loved it,' said Maxin. 'Whenever we'd sit down to discuss a new musical number, they'd ask, "Are we going to have the full Hollywood go, Ernest?" And I'd say, "Yes, yes. The works – the moving cameras, the orchestral movement to match the actions, the sets, the costumes – everything." They adored all of that.'[80] For all the American gloss, however, there remained a grain of English grit: true, there seemed to be a vast, glittering, MGM-style staircase in every Christmas show, but it was never a *complete* staircase – Glenda Jackson climbed to the top of hers only to fall off into nothingness, while Penelope Keith came to the bottom of hers and found that it stopped a good seven feet from the floor.

There is a moment in Vincente Minnelli's musical *The Pirate* when one of the characters says, 'I realise there's a practical world and a dream world. I won't mix them.' Maxin's routines, on the contrary, derived much of their comedy from the way in which the former contrived to impinge on the latter. A slick, *Top Hat*-style, tap-dance soon disintegrates into an unseemly punch-up; the moody, beautifully lit 'Slaughter on Western Avenue'[81] is rendered absurd by the somewhat porcine appearance of Ernie's *femme fatale*; Ernie's stylish 'Latin-American Extravaganza' comes to an abrupt halt when the band get up halfway through and go off for a tea break; and the cheapness of Eric and Ernie's custom-built set is cruelly exposed when the heel of one of Shirley Bassey's sling-backs goes straight through a styrofoam step.

The change in emphasis from the word to the image may not have altered the dynamics of the relationship between Eric and Ernie – the former continued, much as before, to deflate the latter's pomposity – but it did draw attention to the fact that it was Morecambe the comic, not Wise the song-and-dance man, who was the more graceful of the two. Ernie Wise always insisted that 'I was the better dancer',[82] and, in terms of range and technique, he probably was right, but it was Morecambe – as Maxin's increasingly expansive routines revealed – who was actually the more stylish performer. 'Eric moved surprisingly well,' said John Ammonds. 'Ernie danced well enough, but I hope he'll forgive me for saying that you tended to watch Eric because he moved so well. There was more *character* in his movement.'[83] Mike Craig agreed: 'Eric was always a wonderful mover. He was less *predictable* than Ernie – that was the thing. Eric's movements were unpredictable – he'd *surprise* you. He also had that graceful style that so many great comics had – when he walked on to the stage you could see that immediately.'[84]

'Both of them took the dancing *very* seriously,' Maxin confirmed:

The laughter came later – when we knew we had it right – but when I started teaching them a routine they'd be deadly serious. They were pros. They made it look easy on the screen because they'd worked like mad in rehearsal. Ernie, I must say, was usually the one who'd pick it up first, but both of them were very conscientious about getting it right. You see, I never gave them things to do that they didn't want to do. They were very experienced people, and – this is very important – they knew what they *shouldn't* do just as well as they knew what they *should* do. If they didn't think they could do something very, very well, or if they thought that something just didn't suit their style, then they wouldn't do it. That's a major reason why they were as successful as they were. They knew what would be right for them.[85]

Maxin took particular pleasure in devising special routines for the show's star guests, although, as he acknowledged, he was not always able to realise the most intriguingly ambitious of his ideas:

There were certain ones that, unfortunately, didn't happen. There were certain people I wanted to get – and I think I could have got them – but the BBC didn't think it would be right. *I* think it would have brought the house down. I wanted to get [Harold] Wilson – the Prime Minister of the time – Jeremy Thorpe and Edward Heath. The three party leaders. I wanted to get them to come and do a routine together, you know – 'I promise you that, *da-da-da-dum*, and I promise you . . .' – a real kind of razzmatazz number. We were going to have Edward Heath on the piano, doing Eric's sort of Jimmy Durante bit, 'Sittin' at my piaana, de udder day', and the other two would've had a trombone and a banjo or something or other, and they would all have danced off at the end like Gene Kelly. It would have brought the house down. But the BBC were a bit cautious about that sort of thing, and they said it was wrong to go for that. They regretted it later, of course, and it would've endeared all three of those politicians to the public. A great talking-point, you know, but it didn't happen.[86]

One 'surprise' guest whom Maxin *did* succeed, famously, in luring on to the show was BBC TV's first female newsreader, Angela Rippon:

We were doing one of the weekly shows – this was early in 1976 – and during the lunch-break I came down the stairs from the control room and Angela was standing there at the bottom. She had, I think, one of her aunts and another friend with her, and she said, 'Can I show them around? They'd like to see the

Morecambe and Wise studio – they're up from Devon.' So I said, 'Yes, by all means.' I looked at her and – do you know? – it was the first time I'd seen her standing up! I'd seen her many times in the canteen, but I'm one of these people that go in quickly for lunch and I'm back out in fifteen, twenty, minutes, so I'd only seen Angela sitting down in the canteen or, of course, on the news.

So this was the first time I'd seen her standing up, and I noticed these gorgeous legs, and this wonderful figure, and she had this tight skirt on, and I thought to myself, 'There's something there . . .' So I said, 'Angela, do you dance at all?' She said, 'Yes, I can dance.' So I said, 'How would you like to come on to a show?' She said, 'Oh, I doubt my boss would let me do something like that, but, you know, I'd love to.' Well, I went into rehearsal and said to Eric and Ernie, 'Why don't we have Angela Rippon on the show? We can get her to dance.' And they looked at me and said, 'Well, you know, we need a big, *big* star', but I was determined that, some way or other, she was going to go on the show.

As it happened, they were invited to lunch at Lord's cricket ground – a Lord's and Lady Taverners Luncheon – and Angela Rippon was there. I knew about that, but I didn't tell them. Well, they came back from the lunch and said, 'Um, what about Angela Rippon?' I don't know what she was wearing, but she must have impressed them!

I rehearsed her, to make sure she'd be able to do the kind of routine I had in mind, but she just lifted her leg up and it went right round the other side and I knew there and then we'd be able to do something great. A talking-point, you see. So I got my way in the end.[87]

It did not take long, Rippon recalled, for her to overcome her initial feelings of anxiety:

I was *slightly* worried, to begin with, because I hadn't actually danced properly for about seventeen years, so I knew I'd have to go back to ballet school for a month or so just to get reasonably fit again. And I was also aware that these two men were the most famous men on television, and that their Christmas show was the top-rated show of the year. But they were so lovely about it. They kept saying to me, 'We want you to feel good and look good.' And, you know, they meant it. So that relaxed me.

The other thing was that they were such professionals that you got an awful lot done in an hour-long rehearsal. It was a lovely working atmosphere. Ernest was a hoot – he reminded me of Gene Kelly, the way he'd seem to make everything he did into a kind of dance movement. And Eric and Ernie took the mickey out of him something terrible all the time, but there was a wonderful feeling of camaraderie because they worked so well as a team.

When we started, they knew that they wanted to open with me sitting behind a desk, and they knew that they wanted a dress designed for me in such a way that it would look, to begin with, as if I was wearing a shirt or something fairly innocuous, and they also knew that they wanted to start with 'Let's Face the Music and Dance', but as for the routine itself we just put it together on the hoof, as it were. Ernest choreographed it, and, as he didn't know what I could do, he'd try things out and say, 'Can you do *this* step? Can you do *that* step?' And that was how we put it together. In actual fact, if memory serves me correctly, we put the whole of my routine together in just three hour-long rehearsals. Then we recorded it.[88]

'The reaction was unbelievable,' Maxin recalled. 'It made her into the biggest switch-on star overnight.'[89]

The critics were duly impressed: 'a game girl' (*Guardian*); 'the funniest thing that had happened all year (*Sun*); 'a latter-day Betty Grable . . . splendid' (*The Listener*).[90] So, too, was the massive audience: the 'Rippon sequence', according to the BBC's research report, was judged the 'definite highlight' of a 'brilliant' show.[91] Morecambe and Wise, however, were more ambivalent: happy though they were with the success of the show, they also realised that they would now have to start thinking seriously of how they might surpass it for the following Christmas. 'I think that *must* have taken some of the enjoyment out of it for them', John Ammonds suggested:

'It started out as a bit of fun: "I wonder if André Previn would come on to the show?" And we were pretty relaxed about it. Eric might come across a name in the *Radio Times*, or I might see an article about someone or other in the paper, and we'd say, "Well, what have we got to lose? Let's try them." I actually won a bet with Eric when Glenda Jackson agreed to come on the show for the first time. That was how we were. Once it got to be *expected*, however, then the pressure got worse and worse. They *had* to find a guest who'd be unusual, brilliant and funny. Every time. That's when it became just another worry.'[92]

Each December the media speculation grew increasingly intense: false information had to be 'leaked' to protect the surprise elements of the forthcoming show,[93] but by the mid-seventies, when the Maxin-produced specials were growing ever more spectacular, money was being offered surreptitiously by the tabloids for 'inside information'. Shortly before the 1976 show was due to be broadcast, a BBC TV duty editor succumbed to temptation and released a scanned image of the Rippon routine to the *Daily Mirror*.[94] On 21 December, the top right-hand corner of the *Mirror*'s front page bore the invitation: 'PSST! WANNA SEE ANGELA RIPPON'S LEGS? THEN TURN TO PAGE THREE.' The 'Mirror Exclusive' on page three, headed, 'GOOD EVENING, NOW HERE IS THE KNEES', heralded the appearance of the fugitive image with the announcement: 'It can now be disclosed . . . Angela Rippon's legs are long and shapely, and she is a lovely mover.'[95]

'This Christmas show is getting out of all proportions,' complained Eric Morecambe during the lead-up to the next show. 'It's becoming too important.'[96] So great, in fact, was the pressure to come up with an even more spectacular 1977 Christmas ratings-winner that Morecambe and Wise sacrificed an entire series in order to concentrate on their solitary 'special'.

Morecambe, it seems, was particularly affected by these increasingly high expectations. 'Eric did worry more than Ernie did,' said Ammonds. 'Eric was the worry-guts type. I'm sure Eric would go home and would still be thinking to himself, "Well, I hope that sketch is all right." I mean, he'd start asking me as early as *June* to start booking names for the Christmas show, even though it was obvious that none of them were likely to commit themselves that far in advance.'[97] Morecambe was well aware of the problem – 'I'm one of those people who feel tense all the time. It's hard to relax'[98] – but lacked a solution. His son, Gary, who attended many of the recordings during this period, recalled that his father could, on a few – admittedly infrequent – occasions, 'blow a fuse, and my mother would have to smile and cover up his outburst with gentle conversation'.[99] The first ten minutes of the journey home resembled 'Twenty Questions', with Eric quizzing his family as to how they thought various aspects of the show had gone, and then, suddenly, he would fall silent – 'as if someone had sneaked up from behind and coshed him' – and he would finally give in to exhaustion.[100] Although Eric relied on Joan for an honest evaluation of a performance – 'my wife is one of the best critics around. She has never once said to me: "You're the funniest man in the world." The greatest praise she gives me is to tell me I was "good" – and the rest is constructive criticism'[101] – it was not, she recalled, the easiest of tasks:

I had to be very careful. I used to go to all the recordings, and, when they were finished and they met in the dressing-room for the party, the difference in Eric and Ernie was that Ernie would take off his make-up straightaway and go off early with Doreen, whereas Eric just couldn't get changed and go home. He could never say, 'Well, good night, folks, I'm going home now.' So sometimes I was just drained. We were always the last to leave, you know. And back home, whereas I'm sure Ernie would go straight to bed and sleep quite happily, Eric would watch television, or play a tape or something, and he'd go on and on until he'd just go out like a light. So he was always on this very high adrenalin plateau, and he could be touchy sometimes if you were *too* critical, so you'd have to make sure that you told him all the good things before mentioning any of the negatives. He didn't want you *not* to tell him if you didn't think something had gone as well as usual, it was just that he was still quite 'up', so that was my problem. I had to pick the right moment.[102]

Ernie Wise understood (probably better than anyone else did) her predicament:

> All that Eric wants from Joan is praise, because underneath it all he is really working only for her . . .
>
> But Joan is no fool and Eric knows it. He knows that she knows she's got to be strictly honest. She can't wriggle out of it. She's got to say something like, 'Fine, but . . .' and that's when Eric blows up. Joan is Eric's safety valve and it's an important function because once he has got his irritation off his chest he is released from it.[103]

'I've got to be nice to people all of the time, all day long,' Eric said – by way of explanation – to the long-suffering Joan. 'You're the only one I can shout at!'[104]

Ernest Maxin had a novel way of assuaging Morecambe's anxieties: 'We'd stop for ten minutes or so and play a little game of cricket in the rehearsal room. That lightened the mood. Whenever Eric seemed to be getting a bit tense we'd say, "Right: let's break off for a quick game."'[105] Sometimes, however, nothing seemed to help. In the case of the preparations for the all-important 1977 Christmas show, for example, the problem centred on Maxin's pet project: a clever but technically complicated routine based on the 'There is Nothing Like a Dame' number from *South Pacific*. 'I'd explained it to Eric and Ernie,' said Maxin. 'I'd explained how I was going to get these newscasters to do all these acrobatic things. And I'd explained how I would do it technically – using acrobats and trick photography and how then I'd edit it all together – and they'd agreed to that.'[106] Then, however, Eric Morecambe began to have second thoughts: 'He started worrying about how we'd rehearse it, because we were going to have all these BBC people' – Michael Aspel, Richard Baker, Barry Norman, Richard Whitmore, Eddie Waring, Frank Bough, Philip Jenkinson and Peter Woods – 'but we couldn't get them all to rehearse at the same time because they were all on different shifts, reading the news, doing current affairs programmes and other things. So I could only rehearse two or three of them at any one time.'[107] The only ever-present member of this motley troupe was the endearingly sad-faced Peter Woods: 'He had the least to do of all of them – he just had the last "there's absolutely nothing like a dame" to sing in that deep baritone voice of his – but he'd come to everything and sit through it all because he loved it so much.'[108]

Eric Morecambe monitored all of these irregular comings and goings with a mounting sense of unease: 'Ernie wasn't bothered,' recalled Maxin, 'but Eric was. We were about two or three days away from going into the studio to record it, when Eric came to me and said, "This is never going to work. It's never going to happen." I said, "Trust me, Eric, I promise you it *will* work. We'll shoot it in bits and pieces on the Saturday night, I'll edit it and we'll show it to the audience on the Sunday night." But he said, "No, no, it won't work. I just can't see it happening." '[109] It was Ernie Wise who managed to persuade him to change his mind and persevere with the routine. 'Ernie, bless him, said, "Listen to the two Ernests on this one, Eric. You've got to give it a go. If you don't like it once it's been edited then we'll drop it, but give it a go." And Eric came round and said he'd do it.'[110] What followed, however, was – according to Maxin – an emotionally exhausting roller-coaster of uncharacteristic mood swings.

Recording of the 1977 Christmas special commenced in Studio 8 of Television Centre at 8 p.m. on Saturday, 10 December. The atmosphere, Barry Norman recalled, was pleasant but businesslike: 'Although it was a sort of jokey item, Eric and Ernie – like Ernest – wanted it to be as good as it possibly could be, so there was no larking about.'[111] Neither Morecambe nor Wise, in fact, had much to do in the routine, so most of the attention was focused upon the special contributions of their various guests: 'Ernest inspired us amateurs to give energetic performances,' Michael Aspel remarked self-effacingly, 'but in spite of my private conviction that I was born to be a movie star, I started off on the wrong foot and never quite caught up with the others'.[112] The acrobats, doubling for the guests, were called into action: a swift, disciplined, cartwheel for 'Bough', a thrusting somersault for 'Whitmore', an even more athletic-looking somersault for 'Aspel', two brisk handsprings each for 'Jenkinson' and 'Norman' and, most spectacularly of all, a spring-heeled forward somersault followed by a triple-backward somersault for a surprisingly spry 'Richard Baker'. The show, once again, had received its touch of make-believe. Only the visibly thrilled but somewhat over-rehearsed

Peter Woods looked in any danger of forgetting what it was that he was supposed to be doing. 'It all went very smoothly,' said Maxin. 'We shot the whole thing in about fifteen to twenty minutes. The whole of that sequence. And I could see that Eric, once he'd got going, had felt good about it.'[113]

At 10 p.m., the recording over, Morecambe and Wise hosted their customary party for all of their guests. As far as any of the other performers could tell, neither Morecambe nor Wise had any reservations about the success of the completed routine. 'Both of them seemed in very good spirits,' Barry Norman recalled. 'Eric was a man whom I didn't know all that well, but for whom I had enormous affection, and he was great beforehand and he was great afterwards. There was good chat and laughs aplenty afterwards.'[114]

At about 10.45 p.m. Morecambe sought out Maxin just as the latter was preparing to sit at the editing screen and start working on the footage that had been shot earlier in the evening. Morecambe, according to Maxin, again expressed his doubts as to the viability of the routine: 'I told him again that it would work, and he looked at me with this doubtful expression, so I said, "Look, Eric, I'll tell you what I'll do: it will take me an hour to put this all together, so why don't you come back in an hour's time and I'll show it to you then?" And he agreed to do that.'[115] While Eric Morecambe remained inside Television Centre Ernie Wise had set off home, perfectly content, it seemed, with how things had gone.

Maxin recalled Morecambe's return visit to the editing suite:

He'd been waiting in the canteen, I think, but he was still anxious – much more anxious than the Eric of old. He seemed very down, and he looked pale. He came in, sat down, started tapping away on the arms of the chair, and said, 'How is it? How is it?' I said, 'It's going to be great!' And the engineer who was doing the editing with me said, 'Oh, it's *wonderful*, Eric, you're going to love it!' He was still sceptical: 'I can't see it working.' So I said, 'Please, Eric, just wait five more minutes until we've finished it.' Once we'd finished, I said, 'OK, run the reel back. Now let's show it to him.' And I watched Eric, and he was concentrating *so* hard, looking so serious, puffing away at his pipe and staring at the screen. And then, suddenly, he smiled, and he nudged me and said: 'Bloody hellfire! It *works!*' And then, at the end of the thing, he put his arms round me and gave me a big kiss and a hug and the tears rolled down his cheeks. That started me off, too, and so we both ended up in tears.[116]

The recording of the Christmas show recommenced at 8 p.m. the following evening. At 8.45 p.m. the studio audience looked up at the monitors and prepared themselves to watch the start of the *South Pacific* routine. Normally, Maxin recalled, such a moment would have been the cue for Morecambe and Wise to go backstage and get changed for the next 'live' segment of the show, but on this particular occasion Morecambe insisted on staying behind so that he might see how the audience would react:

It meant cutting things really fine, because we were recording a show that lasted an hour and ten minutes and we only had from 8 o'clock to 10 o'clock, so we couldn't afford any delays. Ernie was saying to Eric, 'Come on, let's get going,' but Eric said, 'No, let's stay and watch this.' Well, thank goodness, it brought the house down! The audience was laughing, applaud- ing, cheering all the way through. Wonderful! The boys were absolutely thrilled. Eric was relieved and thrilled. I don't think his health had been too good, and he'd really been pushing himself hard, but, oh, the look of happiness on his face when he realised how much the audience was loving it![117]

As a talking-point the routine could hardly have been bettered. Shortly after the show had been broadcast, Maxin received a call from an agitated Richard Baker – a man who normally exuded an air of post-prandial contentment – explaining that he had been inundated with requests for further demonstrations of his remarkable and unexpectedly lissom acrobatic skills at various garden fêtes up and down the country. 'Just tell them you're on duty,'[118] Maxin advised. Barry Norman encountered a similar reaction:

I was amazed for some weeks after by the number of people who'd seen me in that show. They hadn't seen me in *my* programme, they'd seen me in *The Morecambe & Wise Show*. And they'd always say, 'How did you *do* that?' And I used to say, 'Well, the thing is, you have a springboard, you see, that you couldn't see on the screen, and you jump on that – because the important thing is to get the height. If you can leap up high enough, then you can twist around and do all those things.' And they'd *believe* it! I'd go away and think, 'Christ! What have I done? This idiot might go and get a springboard and break his back trying it.' But that was the impact that it had. Everybody came up and said, 'I didn't know you could do that!'[119]

Such experiences had long been a by-product of appearing on *The Morecambe & Wise Show* – André Previn, more than a quarter of a century after participating in that one routine, was amused to find that London taxi drivers continued to address him as 'Mr Preview';[120] Angela Rippon, more than twenty years after that dance routine, expressed her surprise at the fact that 'rarely does a week go by when someone doesn't mention it to me';[121] and Cliff Richard regarded each of these unanticipated responses as 'yet another sign that I'd been part of something really special'[122] – but the unprecedented ratings success of the 1977 Christmas special served to make these experiences more likely than ever before.

An estimated 28,835,000 viewers[123] had tuned in to watch that show – over 6½ million more than had tuned in earlier in the day for the Queen's Speech,[124] over 18½ million more than had watched ITV's most popular show of the same evening,[125] and over 22½ million more than had seen Morecambe and Wise's inauspicious television debut twenty-three years before.[126] It was quite an achievement, but then again, it was quite a show. The record audience, surely, was a testament not so much to what people thought of that particular Christmas special as it was to what they thought of a show that, from 1968 to 1977, had fulfilled – gloriously – Ronnie Waldman's old ambition 'to give viewers what they want – but better than they expect it'.[127] Thanks to Eric Morecambe and Ernie Wise, and thanks, too, to John Ammonds, Eddie Braben, Ernest Maxin and Bill Cotton, *The Morecambe & Wise Show* had become a television show not just to watch and enjoy but also to admire and cherish.

CHAPTER XV

# Get Out of That

*I am a pro and always will be until my face hits the soup.*
ERNIE WISE

*Sidle off – dignity at all times.*
ERIC MORECAMBE

The London *Evening Standard* broke the news early in 1978: 'Morecambe and Wise quitting BBC for ITV,'[1] read its front-page headline. It was hard to take in: Morecambe and Wise – whose show had for the past ten years been the jewel in the crown of the BBC's light entertainment output, and whose body of work over the same period of time had epitomised all that popular entertainment can achieve when envisioned as something to savour rather than something to sell – had left the BBC for ITV. It did not seem to make much sense. 'Morecambe and Wise quitting' – yes, perhaps, because they had worked so hard for so long and had achieved so much, but 'Morecambe and Wise quitting BBC for ITV' – no, surely not, because it sounded like a betrayal, not just of the BBC but also, and more importantly, of Morecambe and Wise themselves, a betrayal of everything that they had come to stand for.

The news hit Bill Cotton particularly hard:

Two things happened: I went from being Head of Light Entertainment to become Controller of BBC1, and Morecambe and Wise moved from the BBC to Thames the following day. I was in the States when the news reached me. I'll never forget it: I was ill with Asian flu, and I was in Los Angeles in a hotel called the Bel-Air – a beautiful place, but the kind that needs

269

sunshine, and on this occasion it was pouring with rain. And all of a sudden I got a phone call from my secretary in London, who said: 'I know you're ill, but Eric and Ernie have gone.' I tried to call Billy Marsh, and, eventually, I got through to the agency and said: 'Have they gone? Have they signed?' And they said: 'Yes, they've gone.' It was like a divorce. I just felt completely and utterly empty.[2]

The timing, he recalled, seemed almost unbearably cruel:

You see, for the previous ten years I had been in the position of supplying the Controller of BBC1 with all of those great shows, and then, one day after *I* became Controller, one day after it became *my* turn to run BBC1, they pushed off. It *did* hurt, I can't deny it, because I thought what we had there was something very special, and I thought that they knew that I would have moved heaven and earth to keep them at the BBC, but I think they'd just taken the line: 'Well, Bill Cotton has looked after himself, he's gone to be Controller of BBC1, and so we'll look after *our* selves.' You must, you know, decently look after yourself, and especially when you're in our business, but, yes, it made me very sad.[3]

How did it ever happen? 'We serenaded them,'[4] Philip Jones, Head of Light Entertainment at Thames Television at the time, admitted. Jones – a long-time friend of Ernie Wise's – and Bryan Cowgill, late of the BBC, now the new managing director of programmes at Thames, had actually been serenading them fairly strenuously for much of the previous year. 'They'd mentioned something about it while we were working on the [1977] Christmas show,' Ernest Maxin recalled. 'We were filming the "Starkers and Crutch" – the *Starsky and Hutch* – thing out over in South London somewhere, and during the lunch-break they called me over and Eric said: 'What do you think we should do, Ernest? We've had a marvellous offer. Five times as much.' And they were already getting a lot of pay from us, they were the highest paid performers on television. And I said: 'Well, you know, *you* have to decide.'[5] Jones and Cowgill persisted, and, soon after the Christmas show had been broadcast, Morecambe and Wise accepted their offer.

Why did it ever happen? Money, claimed Ernie Wise: 'The reason we left the BBC was very simple: we had a better offer from Thames Television and they paid us more money.'[6] This was not, in fact, entirely true: 'What didn't really come out at the time', said Joan Morecambe, 'was that the BBC *did*, at the eleventh hour, match the Thames offer.'[7] Bill Cotton confirmed this: 'Eric had come up to me at the [1977] Light Entertainment Christmas Party and said, "We've got this offer," and I'd asked, "How much are they paying you?" and he told me. And I'd said, "Please: don't go. I'll match the offer, but, *please*, don't go." I thought he'd talk to Ernie and win him over, but I had to go straight off to the States to buy programmes, and the next thing I knew I'd had that 'phone call and they'd gone.'[8]

Ernie Wise would always encourage the myth that he and his partner had acted out of a shrewd and sensibly unsentimental consideration of cold commercial logic: 'To be leaving Bill Cotton was a matter of personal regret,' he confessed, 'but to be leaving the Corporation as such was a simple professional decision. Thames was offering a better deal so we accepted it.'[9] The more closely, however, that one scrutinises this supposed 'better deal', the less one finds in it to satisfy Ernie Wise the hard-headed businessman, and the more one finds in it to seduce Ernie Wise the incorrigible Hollywood romantic. Thames was not offering Morecambe and Wise more money than the BBC; Thames was not offering Morecambe and Wise greater expertise than the BBC; Thames was not offering Morecambe and Wise better technical facilities than the BBC; and Thames was not offering Morecambe and Wise more security than the BBC.[10] The only thing, in fact, that Thames *was* in a position to offer Morecambe and Wise that the BBC, in those days, could not was the chance – via its subsidiary, Euston Films – to make another movie. 'That, in the end, was the only difference,' Joan Morecambe recalled. 'Thames offered them the film, and the BBC couldn't match *that*, so Thames dangled it on a line and reeled them in.'[11]

The desire to revive their dormant movie career had been evident throughout the seventies: in 1970, for example, they had made a cameo appearance in the Graham Stark short, *Simon, Simon*;[12] in 1971, Eric Morecambe had declared that 'what I'd really like to do is a Hollywood film', while Ernie Wise announced – presumptuously, as it turned out – that they would be 'making a film next year';[13] in 1973, Morecambe revealed that they had received a new offer – 'Money is no object, apparently' – but admitted that 'finding a story suitable for us to film' remained a problem;[14] and Gary Morecambe recalled his father rejecting a screenplay some time after this on the grounds that it 'was not quite right' for Morecambe and Wise.[15] Their many allusions in interviews to other movies, such as *Some Like It Hot, The Odd Couple* and *The Sunshine Boys*,[16] and directors, such as Billy Wilder,[17] suggested that they were thinking increasingly in terms of a major international production, as far away as possible from the low-budget and parochial Rank efforts of the mid-sixties. It is not difficult, therefore, to understand the significance to Morecambe and Wise of a movie deal, but that does not, however, explain why, at the end of 1977, they had found the Thames package irresistible.

What one needs to remember is that Morecambe and Wise, in order to arrive at their 'simple professional decision', had at least four, not two, options to contemplate: the first was to stay at the BBC and concentrate exclusively on television; the second was to leave the BBC and concentrate exclusively on movies; the third was to move to Thames and make both television shows and a movie via Euston Films; and the fourth involved staying at the BBC but also striking a separate deal with an independent production company in order to make another movie. The fact that Morecambe and Wise settled on the third, rather than the fourth, of those options suggests that their reasoning was by no means as clear or as rigorous as they would have had other people – and even, perhaps, themselves – believe. As far as their television career was concerned, Morecambe and Wise would have been better off staying where they were: not only would they have retained the invaluable assistance of an exceptional production team but they would also have won both the not inconsiderable gratitude of the increasingly powerful Bill Cotton as well as an unprecedented pay-rise. As far as their movie career was concerned, they would surely have been better off with a production company that could boast of a vastly more impressive track record, and superior international reputation, to that of Euston Films.

Euston Films had been set up in 1971,[18] and specialised in the production of prime-time adult drama for Thames, including *Special Branch*, *The Sweeney*, *Danger UXB*, and *Out* (and in the early eighties the list would go on to include *Minder*, *The Flame Trees of Thika*, *Widows* and *Reilly – Ace of Spies*).[19] As far as its movie-making ventures were concerned, however, it never appeared to have a sure sense of its proper purpose:[20] its first two projects – *Sweeney!* (1976) and *Sweeney II* (1978) – could hardly be described as adventurous, although they did, as co-productions with EMI, obtain a theatrical release (via the EMI-owned ABC cinema chain), while the next three[21] – *Charlie Muffin*, *The Knowledge* (both 1979) and *The Sailor's Return* (1980) – went straight to television. By forming an alliance with Euston Films, therefore, Morecambe and Wise had chosen, to put it mildly, a peculiarly circuitous route to Hollywood.

When the news of their departure from the BBC was first announced, it was reported that 'the film and the contract with Thames Television [would give] them a chance to build a reputation in America',[22] but ironically it would prove to be the BBC, and not Thames, that would do most to further this particular cause. In 1980, following the cult success of both *The Benny Hill Show* and *Monty Python's Flying Circus* on US local television, BBC Enterprises (with the energetic assistance of Ernie Wise) agreed a deal with Time-Life whereby fifty editions of *The Morecambe & Wise Show* were to be repackaged into seventy half-hour shows and syndicated five nights a week on local networks all over America.[23] Time-Life took the project very seriously indeed: several months before the shows were scheduled to be shown, franchised 'Morecambe and Wise Appreciation Study Groups' were set up in various parts of the country, enabling viewers, for a fee of $100, to be initiated into the arcane intricacies of Northern English humour. Lecturer Herb J. Finkelheim, positioning himself by the side of his television monitor, showed his class brief excerpts from classic flat and bedroom sketches, explaining in painstaking detail the meaning and significance of each joke ('When Eric says his father's task was to weld the crust to pork-pies, it is a joke about the unsavoury nature of the pies sold by British Rail'), and then he would play back each excerpt for a second, more considered appraisal. There was even an imaginary 'guided tour', via elaborate diagrams, of Milverton Street School ('I draw your attention to the minimal rest room facilities'): 'Such High Schools would not be tolerated in our community,' Finkelheim reassured his students, before adding gravely, 'but they are in Britain'.[24] The shows, when they were screened, fared fairly well, although, as Ernie Wise acknowledged at the time, 'It's the bottom rung of the ladder; we aren't yet on the major networks.'[25]

At the start of 1978, however, Morecambe and Wise's immediate priority was their first Thames Christmas special. Philip Jones had announced that the old familiar format 'wasn't going to change one bit',[26] but that, in practice, proved to be an unexpectedly difficult promise to keep. Morecambe and Wise – much, it seems, to their surprise – found themselves stranded without a production team. Ernest Maxin, who had just been awarded a BAFTA in recognition of his work on the 1977 show, had declined an offer to follow them over to Thames: 'I told them, "No, I don't think so." I said that the atmosphere [at the BBC] was so good, and the shows were going so well, a change didn't seem wise. So, you know, I wished them luck, and I prayed that they would do OK, but we'd reached such heights at the BBC – because of that special teamwork between us – and where else were you going to get 28 million viewers?'[27] Eddie Braben stayed behind, too – not, as has sometimes been suggested,[28] because the BBC moved in quickly to sign him to an exclusive contract, but for more personal reasons:

I didn't want to go. Nobody's ever asked me the question, so I've never been able to say it before. I didn't want to go. To be quite honest, it didn't appeal to me; the move to Thames didn't appeal to me one little bit. I've always disliked change, and, the other thing was, I felt comfortable with the BBC, I was *cosy* at the BBC. It was a bit like a favourite cardigan. I was at home at the BBC. More importantly still, I was treated with great *respect*. I didn't want adulation, I wasn't a celebrity, I wasn't a star, I was a comedy writer, and I got respect for that. Which pleased me greatly. And I only ever wanted to work for those three initials. Those three initials – BBC – filled me with awe. They really did. As a child I used to stare, almost in disbelief, at that music and those voices coming out of a box called a 'wireless'. I just didn't understand it. It was *amazing*. And, years later, the disbelief was still there, you know. Is that really *me* walking into BBC Television Centre? Is that really *my* name on the credits in the *Radio Times*? Had they really given *me* a star's dressing-room here at the BBC? And they *had*, they really had, and that, to me, was all part of the magic. I just didn't want to go. I was very upset even by the *thought* of going. So I didn't.[29]

Without Braben, however, Morecambe and Wise, whether they realised it immediately or not, were in serious trouble. After a proposal to bring back Hills and Green was rejected,[30] Philip Jones was obliged to find an alternative source of comic material.[31] 'When Eddie didn't follow Eric and Ernie over to Thames,' John Ammonds observed, 'Philip Jones was landed with a real headache':

> The problem was that Eric and Ernie were comic personalities, not comic actors – which meant that the material had to be made to fit them rather than them being made to fit the material. You see, you could have written a sketch about an Irish barman and a Welsh customer for Ronnie Barker and Ronnie Corbett, and it would have worked very well on *The Two Ronnies*, because both of them were comic actors. You couldn't do that with Eric and Ernie. If you wrote a bar sketch for *them* it would be Eric being Eric and Ernie being Ernie. So while a show like *The Two Ronnies* could draw on any number of writers, *The Morecambe & Wise Show* would only work with writers who really understood Eric and Ernie inside out.[32]

Deprived of the one writer who really *did* understand Eric and Ernie inside out – Eddie Braben – Morecambe and Wise recruited the next best thing: Eddie Braben's old material. Although two veteran and highly versatile comedy writers, Barry Cryer and John Junkin, were drafted in by Thames, there would not, in truth, be much that was strikingly new in the first few shows, but there was much that would seem strangely familiar.[33] Both Junkin and Cryer had worked as warm-up men for Morecambe and Wise, and Cryer had substituted for Braben before – on the 1976 Christmas special – and therefore both could be relied on to preserve the basic style and shape of the Braben-scripted shows.

What followed, however, seemed more like an exercise in damage limitation than a bold new start. Not for the first or the last time, more thought and effort seemed to have been expended on the question of how a ready-made big-name BBC act might be lured over to commercial television than on the question of how that act might best be presented once it had actually arrived. The opening special, broadcast on 18 October 1978, had some very familiar guests (Peter Cushing, Ann Hamilton), some fairly familiar sketches (a post-*Python* pet-shop routine, several Braben-esque situations) and a Maxin-style moment of musical comedy (a Busby Berkeley send-up). The subsequent 75-minute Christmas special was, as one critic put it, 'a somewhat grey-haired show',[34] poorly paced, over-produced, but, like the curate's egg, good in parts. Keith Beckett, the show's new producer/director,[35] declared himself satisfied with the start they had made: 'We lived on nervous tension for months, but it has worked out.'[36] The general feeling, however, was that *The Morecambe and Wise Show* that Thames had produced was an uninspired and, arguably, vaguely cynical imitation of *The Morecambe & Wise Show* that the BBC used to produce.

The Christmas special, for example, continued the tradition of featuring 'surprise' star guests – in this case, a rather sleepy-looking Harold Wilson – but, as far as some reviewers were concerned, they 'hardly lived up to expectations'.[37] Philip Jones appreciated the problem. 'The BBC had had the tremendous advantage of having used up all the spectacular guests,' he would later point out. 'And we found it very difficult to top what had gone before.'[38] What was less easily excusable, however, was the febrile style of direction, which seemed intent on distracting the viewer from the pedestrian nature of much of the material, but which also managed in the process to miss some of Eric Morecambe's most telling expressions and gestures. As if all this was not enough to worry about, the audience figures for the 1978 Christmas special were some 9½ million viewers short of the previous year's record-breaking total,[39] and shortly after this the BBC started to run a series of cleverly made compilation shows under the unoriginal but knowingly significant title, *Morecambe & Wise at the BBC*. 'It wasn't an easy move for us,'[40] a somewhat crestfallen Ernie Wise admitted.

The following March Eric Morecambe's second heart attack made it immeasurably worse. Joan was ill in bed, suffering from gastro-enteritis, when Gary heard his father fall down in the kitchen. 'I think I'll be all right in a minute,' he said, the cold sweat creeping down his chalk-white face. 'Don't tell your mother.'[41] He was rushed to St Albans Hospital, where he recovered, but the doctors were sufficiently concerned about his condition to send him on for further tests, including an angiogram and a scan. In May, Magdi Yacoub, the distinguished heart surgeon, concluded that a triple by-pass oper-ation was inevitable.[42] It took place over seven hours at Harefield Hospital. 'I'm not afraid to die,' Morecambe had told his wife. 'If I go, then I shan't know anything about it. I'll have the injection and the happy pills, and that will be that. It's you and the family who will suffer, because you will have to carry on without me. I know you will grieve for me, and I want to be missed and remembered, but I don't want there to be any long faces. If I don't get through this operation, I don't want you to spoil your life because of me.'[43]

In the event the operation was judged to have been a complete success, although it left him in considerable pain for some time after. His leaving hospital made every televised news bulletin, not least because it was, considering the circumstances, so remarkably funny ('Yes, Ernie came visiting. He was in there making a nuisance of himself, walking under the beds.'), but, as he later confessed, 'It was [a performance] based on fear. If I'd come out looking the way I felt people would have said, "Not got much time left." After the cameras had gone, I sank back into the car. "Didn't do too bad, did I, love?" '[44]

In the mid-seventies, thinking back to the time of his first heart attack, Morecambe had observed: 'Getting over it was in its way harder than the initial pain. What worried me most was not that I wouldn't get out of the oxygen tent alive, but that I'd end up a chronic invalid, perhaps in a wheelchair, waited on hand and foot. It got to the point where I'd be frightened to face people on my left side – because I thought that if anyone touched me there, I'd have another attack.'[45] He also acknowledged that 'there isn't a day goes by when I don't think about that attack and what I can do to avoid another one'.[46] In the summer of 1979, as he recuperated from both that dreaded second coronary and the life-saving operation that followed it, he seemed on this occasion disinclined to think of his recovery exclusively in terms of the future of Morecambe and Wise.

This time, it became clear, he was determined to be a little more selfish. He wanted, for example, to spend more time with his children. All those years of touring, rehearsing and performing had robbed him – and them – of innumerable moments of intimacy. Fatherly advice had tended to be dispensed more swiftly and clumsily than ideally he would have liked. Gary Morecambe remembered his father attempting to explain to him the facts of life by going into the bedroom, pulling out his penis and announcing, 'These can be dangerous things, son. Be careful what you do with them!'[47] The countless unavoidable absences affected him profoundly. When in the sixties he arrived back one day from New York to find that his daughter, Gail, had been hurt in a riding accident, he was, she recalled, deeply distressed: 'Dad came in and sat on my bed in the darkness and said he would stay there until I was asleep ... After a few moments I became aware of a sound in the room. Then I realised it was Dad crying. Another few moments elapsed when he squeezed my hand, kissed my battered face and quietly left the room closing the door behind him. In those few moments he had communicated all his unconditional love and support – nothing was spoken yet everything was said.'[48]

By the early eighties, only Eric and Joan's youngest son, Steven – whom they had adopted in the mid-seventies – was still living at home with them, but, as Gail noted, Eric was now determined to make the most of what visits she and Gary might make: 'He was always pleased to see me, in fact I sometimes felt he had just been waiting for me to arrive. Then he would follow me around the house, up to my bedroom, back to the kitchen, asking questions like, 'How's things, then?' Having failed to get my undivided attention, he would disappear, leaving me to talk to Mum. But after a few minutes a voice from somewhere would call, "Gail ... Gail ... Come and have a look at this."'[49]

He was also keen, of course, to share more of the remainder of his life with his wife – the woman on whom, as all of his colleagues appreciated, he relied for so much. 'It can't have been easy living with Eric when he was carrying the worries of his work', commented Eddie Braben, 'but she never let it show. She's a remarkable lady; a lady of great charm, dignity and elegance which never left her, even when the going was severe. I honestly believe that because of this wonderful lady, we got a few extra years of Eric Morecambe's magic which we weren't really entitled to.'[50] They travelled and relaxed together more often than before – at their villa in Portugal, at their new apartment in Palm Beach – and, as Joan observed, their relationship grew more balanced, and mutually fulfilling, than perhaps it had been in earlier, more hectic times: 'With all the pressures of work in the fifties, sixties and seventies, we would all try to pamper him and make sure that he was happy, often agreeing with what he said even if we knew he was in the wrong. Basically it was a desire to make life as easy as possible, so he could relax and concentrate on his profession. He deserved all the help we could give him. But now, I don't always give in to him, and I stand up for my convictions more. He is far better since I *have* begun to dig my heels in.'[51]

Even when Eric Morecambe was meant to be relaxing, however, he somehow contrived to make relaxation sound suspiciously like hard work. 'My hobby', he took to saying, 'is . . . hobbies,'[52] and he was true to his word: he renewed an earlier interest in photography; he took up bird-watching; he painted; he indulged his passion for all kinds of electrical goods and gadgets (Scalextric cars, pebble-polishing kits, telescopes, archery sets, state-of-the-art video equipment, and so on); attended, as Vice President, Luton Town FC home games; played (as his house happened to be next door to Harpenden Golf Club) the odd round of golf; and, sometimes in the company of either John Ammonds or Philip Jones, went trout fishing on the River Test in Hampshire or the River Kennet at Newbury. His most significant new activity, however, was writing. Shortly before his operation, he had started work on a novel – *Mr Lonely* – and, during his convalescence, he completed it. Published by Eyre Methuen in 1981, *Mr Lonely* focused on the tragi-comic fate of Sid Lewis, an ex-club comic who dies, with heavy symbolism, by accidentally stabbing himself with his star-shaped showbusiness award. Morecambe appeared undecided as to the extent to which the narrative should confound or conform to fans' expectations. Playful autobiographical references to his mother,[53] John Ammonds,[54] Luton

Town and 'an unknown singer called Mr Desmond O'Connor'[55] rubbed shoulders with uncharacteristically adult-oriented gags (a prostitute's gravestone bears the inscription 'Together at last' in memory of her legs, and a small boy in a pirate costume who, when asked where his buccaneers are, replies, 'Under my buccanhat')[56] and some knowingly evocative descriptions of clubland ('Dancing was thrown in, rowdies were thrown out, and, now and again, dinner was thrown up'[57]), but it was generally well received, and he declared that, 'I've got much more of a thrill out of the book than I ever had from a television show.'[58] More books would follow[59] – he planned to write at least one a year.

In the short term, however, Eric Morecambe remained committed to Morecambe and Wise – which was extremely welcome news, of course, to Ernie Wise. For much of 1979, Wise had found himself, eleven years on from his partner's first attack, once again waiting anxiously in the wings, with the same old uneasy mixture of personal and professional fears for company. Wherever he went, it seemed, everyone wanted to ask him the same solitary question: 'How's Eric?' Once he felt sure that his partner's health was improving, he took to wearing a home-made badge that read: 'Eric's much better, thank you, but I'm not feeling too good.'[60]

When, at the start of February 1980, Eric Morecambe felt fit enough to return to work, there was a reassuringly familiar team waiting there to greet him. In addition to Bill King and Peter Knight – both of whom had worked on the earlier specials – John Ammonds was back as producer/director. Ammonds had been at Thames for a little over a year working on *Bernie* (Bernie Winters' first solo series after he and his brother had finally broken up as a double-act)[61] when Philip Jones called him with the news that Eric Morecambe wanted him to take over the show.[62] As Morecambe was still convalescing at the time, Ammonds travelled to Harpenden to see him:

> I said: 'Eric, I'm delighted to hear that you want me to do these shows, but there's one thing I do want to make quite clear before we go any further, and that is: I haven't changed. It may occasionally happen, as it did before, that you say something and then I disagree with you: if that happens in the future then I will still go ahead and disagree with you, and *keep* disagreeing

with you if I feel I have to.' And Eric smiled and said: 'No, no, that's *good*, because you'll be able to check me.' Now, there really aren't many stars who would say that, but that was Eric for you.[63]

With Morecambe, Wise and Ammonds reunited in the familiar environment of the rehearsal room – now situated at Richmond Athletic Club – the new series started to assume a more promising shape, although, as all three appreciated, there was one important ingredient that was still missing: a bona fide Eddie Braben script. Braben had found it too painful to watch the first of the Thames shows, but when Ammonds contacted him he was genuinely gratified to hear just how much he had been missed. 'I'm afraid – in another way, of course, I'm very, very glad – that Eddie was unique,' said Ammonds. 'It meant that he had to do it all – he was the one who captured their personal style – and I knew that we'd have to get him over to join us as soon as we could.'[64] Braben had been writing material for a number of BBC shows – as well as for his own well-received radio series – *The Show With Ten Legs* – and his exclusive contract still had several months to run, but he agreed to join them as soon as it was practicable ('only for them – I wouldn't have left for anyone else'[65]).

The shows, which were broadcast during the autumn of 1980, were, in general, well received. They topped the ratings with an average weekly audience of around 18 million viewers,[66] and several of the critics applauded the return of both Ammonds ('the director who has always known how best to handle their special polish and timing'[67]) and Braben ('unbeatable'),[68] but in truth there was precious little here that had not been done better before at the BBC. It was not that the shows failed to be entertaining – most of the time most of them were – but, judged by Morecambe and Wise's unusually high standards, they seemed sluggish and, beneath the customary professional veneer, somewhat joyless. Ammonds, looking back on this period, felt that they had, if anything, *over*-prepared for each show:

I know it sounds odd, but, in a way, I suspect that we had *too much* time to rehearse, and sometimes – most people who work in television will just have to take my word on this! – that can actually be a disadvantage. Thames, you see, had bent over backwards to please Eric and Ernie when they came over. The last thing anyone wanted was for them to say, 'Oh, we had this or that at the BBC and this isn't as good.' So Thames, shall we say, 'pampered' them a little. When it came to preparing for each show, Thames gave them about the same length of time that they'd had at the BBC; now, that was fine, and, once Eric's health got worse, it was probably erring in the right direction, but it meant that we actually had almost twice as long as before, because the BBC shows were 45-minute shows, whereas these ones were – minus the commercials – about 24-minute shows – and that created a different set of problems. If you have *too* long to sit around analysing a script you can end up pulling it apart rather than polishing it up, and if you look at any funny joke for long enough it'll stop seeming funny.[69]

The constant struggle to come up with new ideas, new bits of business, new sketches and new musical routines took its toll on everyone involved in the show. One niggling problem, Ammonds recalled, concerned the need to find a distinctive way of ending each performance:

The 'Groucho' dance reminded people of the BBC shows, you see, so they wanted something different leading in to that. Eric suggested – I think it had been their publicity man [George Bartram] who'd mentioned it to him – that they could get this tenor who could hold that sustained note from 'The Donkey Serenade' for about a minute. And Eric said that we could have him come on each week at the end and he'd hold this note while something comic happens around him. Say, one week Eric and Ernie are in a coal mine, another week they're in a First World War biplane, and this chap turns up and sings. I've no idea why all of us thought that was worth doing – it doesn't sound very funny now – but it was one of those things you get carried away with. So we did it. And a cameraman came up to me and said, 'That's not funny, John', and I said, 'Well, I can see your point, because I'm not too convinced myself.' Anyway, we did it on show 2 and show 3 of the series, and it's getting to the point of no return – I could film another ending for those shows, before they were broadcast, but we'd be stuck with the final three in the series. Well, I had to go to some function or other with Ernie and Doreen, and while I was there I said to Ernie, 'You know, this finish we've got – it's not really working, is it?' And Ernie said, 'Well, no, it isn't really, but it's Eric's idea.' I said I'd tackle Eric about it when we got back.

So I steeled myself and said to Eric – Ernie didn't want to say it himself – 'This finishing routine – I mean, it's not that good, is it?' And he said, 'No, it isn't.' He was waiting for somebody to say it, because he hadn't the heart to come out and say it himself. So we said, OK, let's come up with something else. And what we finished up with was this: Eric walks on and Ernie says to him: 'I'll see you outside.' Eric says, 'You're not going to do "Bring Me Sunshine", are you?' 'No, no, of course not.' So Eric goes off in the background, wearing his cap and that raincoat and holding his carrier bag, and Ernie starts singing (often joined by the guest on the show). Eric, now in the far background, turns and sees what's going on, comes back downstage, and a fierce argument breaks out whilst they are all trying to sing 'Bring Me Sunshine'. Then they do the 'Groucho' dance off.

It worked very well – got plenty of laughs – but we only just made it in time. But like so many ideas, it happened almost by accident.[70]

A greater cause for concern was the backbone of the show: the opening cross-talk, the flat sketches and bed sketches and the costume 'romp'. Eddie Braben found himself burdened with a near-impossible task: he had to devise new material that seemed sufficiently familiar to reassure the fans and yet sufficiently fresh to satisfy the critics (not to mention the performers and himself). He felt, as a consequence, increasingly uncomfortable: 'I've been writing non-stop for twenty-seven years,' he protested to one interviewer. 'That's a long time now if you are expecting miracles.'[71] Harsher styles of comedy – more direct, less compassionate – were coming into fashion, heightening his sense of isolation ('I want to keep my head in the sand. I don't want to see all the monstrous things in the world. My comedy doesn't have to be topical'[72]), and the move from the freedom and fluidity of the extensive BBC shows to the rather brutal concision of the shorter Thames shows was something Braben found particularly hard to bear:

> It was like a sort of comedic claustrophobia. There was nothing I could do in twenty-five minutes. Everything was cut to the bone. It was so compressed – there was no room to do anything. It was just, sort of, 'Here it is: take it or leave it.' I couldn't write in the long pauses, I couldn't do the slow dialogue, I couldn't *dwell* on anything. At the BBC I'd always try to pace the programme: a standard opening – I'd try to clobber the people at home right between the eyes with one gag after another, *bang! bang! bang!* Then the next sketch would be easy-paced, then a woofer, and so on. At Thames, on the other hand, there was no room to do anything with the comedy at all, no time to *establish* anything, it was just in and out, double-quick, right the way through. So I was never happy there.[73]

An air of resignation started to descend upon the show. Old sketches were dusted down and redeployed with increasingly regularity. This would not, in itself, have been too much of a problem – after all, even the BBC shows drew from time to time on old ATV material[74] – but, as Ann Hamilton shrewdly observed, it was rarely a device that was used with the same degree of sensitivity as before:

> When they adapted those sketches for Thames, the mistake they made, in my opinion, is that they gave the part that I, or Rex Rashley, or Allan Cuthbertson, or someone else played in the original version to *stars*. All of them. So you had an obvious feed part played by a star. That didn't work. If you've got a star in a sketch, whenever they say a line the camera is going to have to come back to them – you have to see the *star* – but the lines they had were written originally for supporting players. When *I* played, say, a shop assistant, I could say a line and the camera would stay on Eric, but when they did the same sketch with a guest star playing the shop assistant the camera had to

keep going back to the star. And I think that detracted from the whole concept of the show.[75]

John Ammonds summed up what was wrong when he remarked: 'I don't think, to be honest, that Eric and Ernie really knew *why* they were doing it any more. The spark had gone. They were still as professional as ever, and I don't think the shows were – by anyone else's standards – that bad, but, looking back, I can't think of many high spots or talking-points.'[76]

'I'm bored,' Morecambe admitted. 'I'm bored with the slap on the cheeks, the "What do you think of it so far?" But we never try to force anything new. I don't think it will change now.'[77] Coming back after his illness had been different. Coming back had been a challenge: 'Every time I change clothes,' he said, '[I see] the four and a half miles of bad road up and down my body. The doctors say, "Forget it." Well, they may, but I can't.'[78] For some time following the operation he found that he could not pick up his legs to dance, and it hurt if he attempted to stamp his foot. 'Frankly,' he would confess, 'I just didn't know whether I could still do anything properly or if the people were going to turn round and say, "Oh dear, how sad."'[79] It was important, therefore, that he should have come back to prove people wrong, as he had done before in 1969 after his first attack, and, when he did so – triumphantly – it was, for him, and for his public, symbolic confirmation of the fact that he still had a future, that he still had a life. Coming back, therefore, had been an absorbing, and ultimately a rewarding, test. Staying there, however, proved to be more of a chore than a challenge.

'Once you get to the top', he often used to say, 'there's only one way to go, and I assure you it ain't up.'[80] After he had satisfied himself that he could still perform, and still get laughs, and still charm the critics, he was forced to contemplate the immediate future: more rehearsal, more shows, and more and more recycled material – more borrowings from a brilliant past in order to lend lustre to a leaden-looking present. 'That brought him down,' said Joan. 'It bothered him. All that rehashing of the BBC stuff. The physical aspect wasn't really a problem – he became very active – but it was more a case of whether he should have accepted the physical and emotional commitment of doing the show at all. *That* was the question.'[81] His

mood was not improved by the realisation that, as far as the media
– and, he assumed, the public – were concerned, he was still, one
energy-sapping series on from his successful operation, 'the man who
had the heart attack': 'I shall never forget it but I want the public
to forget it. The trouble is they watch you in a show and instead of
laughing they are thinking, "Cor . . . he shouldn't be doing that
jumping." '[82] It was far from easy, however, for audiences to forget.
The list of comedy stars who had died from heart disease was a long
one – Sid Field, Arthur Haynes, Freddie Frinton, Sid James, Ted
Ray, Richard Hearne, Peter Sellers, Harry H. Corbett – and every
week in the *TV Times*, on the same page as the programme details
for *The Morecambe and Wise Show*, there would be an advertisement
for the British Heart Foundation ('Seriously folks, heart disease is no
joke').[83] 'I still get letters saying, "You shouldn't have done that
jumping up and down", or "You shouldn't have sprung over the
settee as you did," '[84] Morecambe complained, but the anxious
reaction was perfectly understandable: no one wanted to see him
jeopardise his health for the sake of twenty-five more minutes of
laughter; he meant far too much to far too many people for the risk
to seem remotely worthwhile. As a proud performer, however, he
found the reaction hard to take.

Morecambe and Wise were still popular, still successful, still loved,
but, as they entered the fifth decade of their extraordinary partnership,
they were starting to look their age. Morecambe, inevitably, seemed
a fraction less sharp and sure than before and Wise was white-haired
and weary-looking. Whenever they paused to discuss the future they
sounded more and more like strangers. By 1981, for example, the
hushed, almost reverential cadences that accompanied Wise's age-old
homage to Hollywood were clearly becoming too much for his
long-suffering partner to bear.

MORECAMBE What you like is the idea of walking
 around a swimming-pool with a dry Mar-
 tini in your hand.

WISE That was what I was sold on in the first
 place, when I was a kid.

MORECAMBE But you've *been* there – you've done it
 two or three times.

| WISE | Yes, but I'm still on the way. |
| MORECAMBE | But doing what? |
| WISE | I don't know.[85] |

Away from work, Morecambe, increasingly, looked to shut showbusiness out, whereas Wise, perhaps even more than before, looked to welcome it in. Aside from the occasional memorable meeting with one of his old heroes, Cary Grant (who took to calling him 'Sir Eric'),[86] Morecambe favoured a private life well away from most other performers, writing, fishing and relaxing with a select group of family and friends. Wise, on the other hand, continued (with Doreen) to host regular dinner parties for his circle of showbusiness friends (Harry Worth, Billy Dainty, Norman Vaughan, Vince Powell, Philip Jones, Pearl Carr and Teddy Johnson), darting backwards and forwards across the Atlantic on Morecambe and Wise business, doing his best to dodge the English winter (in Antigua, or Barbados, or his new holiday home in Florida), sitting and 'scheming' in his riverside garden in Maidenhead and, several times a month, affecting a look of mild indignation when the pleasure boats cruised past and broadcast the news, 'Ernie Wise lives there.'[87]

It seemed, to some, as though the appeal of being one half of Britain's best-loved double-act was, at last, beginning to pall. Forty-odd years was, after all, an awfully long time to be tied professionally and, in a sense, emotionally to one another – far longer than the duration of most marriages, and certainly far longer than any other successful double-act: Jewel and Warriss – who were cousins – lasted for thirty-two years; Laurel and Hardy lasted for thirty-one years (ending only with the death of Hardy); Abbott and Costello – ignoring the occasional angry spat – lasted for twenty-six years; and Martin and Lewis – ignoring even angrier spats – for ten. Neither Morecambe nor Wise wanted to see their partnership – or, indeed, their friendship – end in the kind of bitter and public feuds that destroyed Abbott and Costello (when the latter died, the former was suing him for more than $222,000, and attended his funeral in a pathetically inebriated state) or Martin and Lewis (who were only reconciled, awkwardly and unconvincingly, on live television after refusing to speak to each other throughout the previous twenty years). The current state of the relationship between Morecambe and Wise was never easy for outsiders to fathom, but that did not stop some of them from spreading rumours about an imminent split. There had been a time over at the BBC in the mid-seventies when such rumours became so rife that even the normally unflappable Bill Cotton felt that there might really be some cause for concern:

There was so much talk – rumours – about them breaking up, and the rumours about it eventually got to me, so I started to think that I'd better give it some thought. At the next meeting we had with them, I said, 'I've got an idea about your next contract: we could do, obviously, the thirteen or whatever number of *Morecambe & Wise Shows*, and then I'd be quite happy, if you like, to do a talent show with you, Ernie, and a game show or something else with you, Eric.' And there was a strange kind of silence, and then they said, '*No, no!*' It turned out that, when they were confronted with it, they had absolutely no intention of doing anything of the sort! In fact, *I* was nearly blamed for trying to come between them![88]

Few relationships would have been strong enough – or healthy enough – to have withstood the long hours of hard work in the rehearsal room, day after day, month after month, year after year, that Morecambe and Wise never failed to put in, and yet a surprisingly high number of onlookers never failed to seem surprised that Morecambe and Wise, unlike 'Eric and Ernie', might actually feel the need to spend a fair proportion of their private lives in the company of other people. As Michael Grade observed: 'They didn't socialise together that much, but that wasn't because they didn't *like* each other. They both had good marriages, different hobbies, different outlooks on life, and, understandably, they simply didn't want to live in each other's pockets for forty odd years.'[89] Bill Cotton agreed:

There really wasn't anything remotely sinister about it. They'd simply found a way of operating that made sense, and they stuck to it. They lived their own lives. You know, often, after they'd been on holiday, they'd come back to a meeting in my office and it would be the first time they'd seen each other since they'd last been working. I mean, they really were very, very friendly, there's absolutely no doubt about it. There was something between Eric and Ernie which was very, very special, and when they were left alone they had a certain magic between them – but their private lives were separate.[90]

Ever since the teenage Ernie Wise had surprised Sadie Bartholomew by stoutly defending her son's right to criticise him whenever he saw fit – 'Don't you see? Eric is only trying to make me the best feed in the country'[91] – neither man had doubted the other's devotion. Even when Eric dispatched the sharpest of on-screen barbs in his partner's direction – ERIC (To a guest): All you actors are the same. ERNIE: You're no good without the script. ERIC: And *he's* no good *with* one! – Ernie's reaction (an affectionate pat on Eric's back and a look of genuine admiration) said more about their relationship than any interview could have done.

Both of them, since the early seventies, had been open about their interest in trying out a new format: 'There's nothing we'd like to do more than get away from the old routine and make a complete switch.' Their problem, they admitted, was that they were now 'too well known. Audiences will not accept us doing anything different.'[92] Each had opportunities to try something independently of the other – Morecambe, for example, was offered the role of Bottom in the BBC's 1971 production of *A Midsummer Night's Dream*,[93] and Wise (during his partner's convalescence) had been invited to co-star with Bill Maynard in a revival of *The Odd Couple*[94] – but what both of them really craved was a new challenge for Morecambe and Wise.[95] When, by the start of the eighties, such an opportunity had failed to materialise, Morecambe, in particular, began to feel trapped: 'Ernie is my friend and we have spent many marvellous years together. You won't get me to say anything uncomplimentary about him. But frankly I have become bored with Morecambe and Wise.'[96]

Eric would have known what to do – TV PRESENTER: And now, friends, it's 'Make Your Mind Up Time!' ERIC (switching off the set): I have – but Morecambe did not. He would sit with his family and proceed to think out loud: perhaps, he would say, it was time for him to retire from showbusiness altogether and write novels, and fish, and fulfil an ambition to drive the length of America's east coast;

or perhaps he should continue to appear on television, but not as one half of Morecambe and Wise but rather as a guest on a variety of undemanding but enjoyable panel games; or perhaps he should just concentrate on making one Morecambe and Wise show each Christmas; or perhaps he should do something else again. 'What', he then would turn to them and ask, 'do *you* reckon?'[97] He would be the same with his partner: one day, he wandered into Wise's dressing-room, sat himself down, sighed softly and said, 'I'm not enjoying this any more. I've had enough. I think I ought to stop it. What do you think I should do?'[98] Wise's answer, quite understandably, was identical to that of Morecambe's family: 'That . . . is something only you can decide.'[99] It was patently clear, however, that Morecambe could *not* decide. 'If he hated performing,' said Wise, 'he hated decisions even more.'[100] It was oddly reminiscent of one of their old routines: 'Get out of that!' Eric would say as he tucked his outstretched hand under Ern's chin. 'You can't, can you? You can't move now!' Just as Ern could have moved whenever he cared to, but chose instead to stand rooted to the spot, so Morecambe, who could have extricated himself from their partnership with relative ease, remained exactly where he was.

When Thames Television executives invited Morecambe and Wise to meet them at Teddington in order to discuss their next contract, it actually seemed that Morecambe had, in fact, made up his mind to cut right back on all his commitments. 'That's it,' he told his wife just before he set off. 'We're not going to sign another contract.'[101] He returned in the evening looking happy and contented. 'How did it go?' asked Joan. 'Great,' he replied. 'Great. We've signed another contract!'[102] Joan was incredulous:

It turned out they'd all had a good lunch, and a nice talk, you know, and they'd ended up signing for three more years – to do another series, another Christmas special, chat shows, you name it. I said to Eric, 'You do realise, don't you, that you've gone and *doubled* your responsibilities? I thought you told me this morning that you were going to march into there and tell them that you were going to cut right down. I thought you said that you were going to take a year off.' And he said, 'Oh, well, you know . . .' And the ball would start rolling all over again. Absolutely incredible! Really, in a way, he was his own worst enemy.[103]

The year 1983 would prove to be particularly gruelling. In addition to yet another series of *The Morecambe and Wise Show* – this time produced and directed by Mark Stuart, as John Ammonds had been forced to pull out in order to care for his wife, Wyn, who was suffering from multiple sclerosis[104] – there was also the unfinished business of a Morecambe and Wise movie to attend to. Morecambe's health problems had caused the project to be delayed, but now, at long last, the filming could commence. The result – *Night Train to Murder* – came as something of a surprise to those people who had been following the progress of the project over the previous five years. A 'cinema film' – provisionally titled *Do It Yourself* – had been due to be made early in 1980, but, for some undisclosed reason, shooting never started.[105] Two screenplays – one of them 'virtually written'[106] – had been mentioned in 1981: the first concerned the comic adventures of Eric and Ernie in the US, and was set to feature – it was hoped – two well-known American co-stars;[107] the second was said to be based on the more intimate situation–comedy of their flat sketches.[108] *Night Train to Murder*, however, turned out to be something else again: a piece of 'House of Terror' hokum set in Britain just after the Second World War, it resembled a low-budget imitation of the kind of Bob Hope-style Hollywood comedy-thrillers of the thirties and forties – such as *The Cat and the Canary* (1939) or *The Ghostbreakers* (1940) – that Morecambe and Wise had enjoyed watching in their youth. Badly lit, poorly paced and conspicuously unfunny, it compared unfavourably with the similarly themed 'romps' from their television shows of the seventies,[109] let alone with the three movies they had made for Rank in the sixties. Neither More-cambe nor Wise, understandably, was happy with the final product. John Ammonds encountered Morecambe soon after the latter had seen a rough cut:

He looked *terribly* depressed. I said, 'What's it like?' And Eric just said, 'It's my fault – I should never have gone through with it. It's not at all what we set out to do.' He said they [Thames Television/Euston Films] should either put it on television during the children's hour or else in the middle of the night. I said, 'They can't do that, Eric! They must have spent an awful lot of money on it. They won't just chuck it down the loo like that.' But he really meant it. He wanted Thames to shelve it. He really was bitterly disappointed.[110]

This, then, was what Morecambe and Wise had left the BBC for: a feature-length movie that was barely good enough to be shown on television.[111] While not an embarrassment on the scale of *Atoll K* (1951) – the desperately sad coda to the career of Laurel and Hardy[112] – *Night Train to Murder* was, none the less, the worst – as well as the last – piece of work with which Morecambe and Wise would be associated. It was an unfortunate – and, surely, an unnecessary – way in which to bring forty-two years of hard work and immense success to an ultimate conclusion.

Both men, however – in spite of this deep but isolated disappointment – had every reason to stand back and survey the span of their shared career with a genuine and undisguised sense of pride. 'We have become part of British showbusiness history,' Eric Morecambe reflected, 'and that is a wonderful feeling.'[113] Years before, when they were still working the halls, someone had told them that the only sure way to please an audience was 'to go out there, give them six pennyworth of your best wheezes, and get off'.[114] It was excellent advice, and they would never forget it. From that very first evening on the stage of the Liverpool Empire to that final day in the studio at Teddington, Morecambe and Wise had always tried their hardest to serve up six pennyworth of their best wheezes and then get off. By the end of 1983, however, the time seemed right for them to get off for the final time and go their separate ways.

## CHAPTER XVI

# Loose Ends

*Isn't it funny how all the people who say death is nothing to worry about are all very much alive?*
PETER COOK

It was just after 4 a.m. when the call came:[1] Eric Morecambe was dead. Ernie Wise put down the telephone and went back to bed. Unable to sleep, he lay there, motionless in the early morning light, and remembered 'that dear, dear man':[2] in 1939 in Manchester, auditioning for Jack Hylton; in 1941 in Liverpool, appearing for the first time as one half of Bartholomew and Wise; in 1949 in London, walking sadly off in silence from the stage of the Windmill; in 1954 on television, reeling from the barrage of hostile reviews; in the sixties, the seventies and the eighties, in show after show after show, when, peerlessly and irreplaceably, he entertained a nation; and then, after one last sudden readjustment of the glasses, and one last sly smile for the camera, and one last swift, crisp, slap on the cheeks, the reverie was abruptly interrupted by 'a terrifying and unworthy' thought: 'How could he do this to me?'[3]

The year 1984 had started off so well. As Joan Morecambe recalled, her husband had been looking forward to retirement: 'He wanted to spend more time fishing and to see much more of his grandchildren. He had an ambition to drive from Boston to Florida, taking in the beauty of Maine and Vermont in the "fall". He wanted to see Rome and Venice. We were ready to relax and enjoy our own company in a way that we had almost never done before.'[4]

There had been a health scare during the making of the 1983 Christmas special. During a Keystone Kops-style sequence, Eric and

Ernie had been required to run at a wall; Eric, typically, had put rather too much effort into the scene and had hit the wall with such force that the impact jolted his heart out of rhythm. Filming was brought to a halt and he was rushed to hospital by ambulance. He stayed there for two nights and, although no permanent damage had been done, the accident served none the less to undermine his confidence. 'He had felt so safe since the operation,' said Joan, 'but now we had an uneasy feeling that he was still vulnerable.'[5] The incident spelt the end of Morecambe and Wise: 'You know', he confided in Joan, 'if I have another heart attack, it'll kill me. And if I do another Morecambe and Wise series, I'll have a heart attack.'[6] He was determined, she recalled, that nothing should now be allowed to jeopardise his health:

> He gave up all those little extras that had helped to relax him in the past – the Scotch in the evening, the cigars – and he got to the stage where he was slimmer and fitter than he'd been in years. He was so active – he loved life and he wanted to make the most of it. He absolutely loved his trout fishing, and now he had the time to accept these invitations he'd been getting to go up to Scotland and do some salmon fishing. And he went on his walks in the country. And he had his bird-watching – he was into the RSPB. What else? Oh, he also said that he was going back to playing golf – which he hadn't done much of in donkey's years – and photography. And, of course, there was the writing: his children's books had sold really well, and they'd been translated into all these other languages – Spanish, Italian, German – he'd been so thrilled that people were interested. So he would have done much more of that. He wasn't at all bored. Quite the opposite, in fact.[7]

As winter gave way to spring, Eric Morecambe appeared more contented than many hardened professionals had thought possible. 'Many people have told me Eric couldn't have retired, couldn't have given up the business', Joan remarked. 'But that wasn't true in 1984. I knew him better than anyone else, and although he had loved showbusiness, he'd worked in it all his life . . . [In] 1984, he wanted to give it all up.'[8] The death on 15 April of his good friend Tommy Cooper – from a heart attack, and in front of millions of television viewers during a live broadcast from Her Majesty's Theatre – convinced him that he had made the right decision. 'He was very upset,' said Joan. 'He thought it was just so awful that Tommy should have died in that way – doing the jokes, you know, and then collapsing in full view of everyone. He told me he had absolutely no intention of taking the same sort of risk himself.'[9]

By the end of April, however, his health was again beginning to concern him. He started to suffer from a stomach and chest complaint that grew slowly but progressively worse. He tried, at first, to do his best to ignore it in the hope that, given time, it might start to right itself. He went with Joan on a sentimental journey back to Lancashire, stopping first in Lancaster. He attended a service to commemorate the opening of a home run by Methodist Homes for the Aged, then paused at the lively market to buy some black pudding and Lancashire cheese. Then they went on to his home town, where he spent some time visiting his parents' graves,[10] sought out some of his relatives and then, just as he had done many times before in the company of his father, bought some fresh Morecambe Bay shrimps from the Trawl Shop and ate them in the cool open air while gazing out to sea. Back in Harpenden, however, his condition grew increasingly serious, and, early in May, he had no choice but to pay a visit to his local doctor: 'Joan and I have come for some advice on family planning,'[11] he joked, but his doctor could see that he was experiencing some difficulty in breathing and was clearly in considerable discomfort. Suspecting a possible hiatus hernia, he saw to it that an X-ray was taken as soon as possible; an appointment was also arranged for a heart specialist to conduct an ECG examination. The X-ray results, when they arrived, were negative: there was no hiatus hernia. On the evening of 25 May, the heart specialist arrived: he prescribed some different pills, and, after taking his very first dose, Morecambe started to experience a 'dramatic improvement'.[12] It seemed as if the problem had been solved.

It was during this period, however, that Joan noticed her husband behaving in ways that she regarded as 'uncharacteristic'.[13] He had always, for example, been a great friend of the press, and had always been amused rather than angered by certain journalists' evident flair for provocative embellishment, and yet, after reading an article in one of the tabloids which had clearly fabricated some mildly upsetting remarks about him and attributed them to Ernie Wise, he became highly agitated and had to be restrained physically by Joan on the next occasion that he encountered a reporter from the paper in question.[14] Joan was also intrigued by the fact that he decided quite suddenly to tidy up some loose ends. He started sorting through all of the papers in his dressing-table drawers, and, when he came across the sealed envelope containing the letter he had written back in 1979 – which he had told her to open in the event of his operation not being a success – he tore it up. 'I have since wondered,' said Joan, 'if it wasn't almost an act of defiance – he wanted so much to feel confident about the future. And yet, why should he suddenly start tidying his drawers, and doing other things which could well be described as "putting his affairs in order"?'[15]

Worries about his health would not go away. The ECG examination had revealed a slight enlargement of the heart which, though not in itself a cause for urgent concern, prompted the specialist to suggest, as a precautionary measure, another visit to Harefield Hospital for further exploratory tests. Morecambe agreed, but first of all, he said, he wanted to honour a couple of prior commitments over the Spring Bank Holiday weekend. A friend of the family was getting married on the Saturday, and he (along with Joan, Gail, Gary and Steven) had promised to attend the ceremony, and on the Sunday he had agreed to make an appearance at a tiny provincial theatre (the Roses) in Tewkesbury as a favour to an old friend, the actor and comedian Stan Stennett. After that, he assured the specialist, he would contact Harefield and make all of the necessary arrangements. In a way, recalled Gary, his family was relieved to know that something was being done: although he was still very trim, 'he had developed a grey and drawn appearance as well as a hoarse voice, apparently brought about by the enlarged heart'.[16]

When, on the morning of 26 May – the day of the wedding – Eric's daughter, Gail, arrived at Harpenden, she was shaken by the sudden change in her father's appearance. 'Whatever has happened to Dad?' she asked her mother. 'Last week he looked marvellous and now he looks so drawn.'[17] Joan, who was struggling to keep her own anxieties in check, agreed, but noted that neither the doctor nor the specialist had said that they had found anything that warranted the taking of emergency measures, and he was clearly looking forward to what promised, in spite of the unseasonably cold weather, to be a 'very nice family occasion'.[18] Before anything else could be said, however, their conversation was cut short because, 'true to form', Eric had come looking for Gail.[19] As the two of them sat in the car and waited for Joan, as usual, to double-check that the house was locked up, Gail continued to worry about her father's condition: 'I was sitting immediately behind him studying the curls on the back of his head, when something he used to say if I was obviously exasperated with him came into my head. With a mischievous backward glance as he left the room, he would say, "You'll miss me when I'm gone." As I fondly studied his curls in the car, I said, "I'll miss you when you've gone." '[20] The remainder of the day proved to be relatively reassuring: 'Eric seemed fine,' said Joan; 'it was a lovely occasion and he thoroughly enjoyed himself.'[21] The two of them left the reception early, however, so that he might have an early night in preparation for the following day's exertions.

On 27 May he woke up and said to Joan: 'I feel great – I've had a marvellous night's sleep – why didn't they give me those pills before?'[22] He was in excellent spirits as they set off for Tewkesbury. Although Joan, when she first learned of the invitation, had expressed serious doubt as to the wisdom of the appearance, Eric had won her over: 'It's not like television,' he reassured her. 'There's no strain with this. You know me, love. I'll enjoy it.'[23] Stan Stennett, whom Morecambe had known and liked ever since they appeared in pantomime together in the early fifties, had organised the event in support of a local charity: the first half of the evening comprised a mini-Variety bill (which included Alan Randall, the musician best-known for his impression of George Formby). The second half was set to feature Morecambe – prompted occasionally by Stennett – reminiscing about his life and career.[24] It was, Joan admitted, in part 'an experiment': 'Eric wanted to see whether the audience would accept him doing this kind of show – basically an ad-lib conversation – as entertainment. If they did, he planned to do the same sort of thing in retirement.'[25] Stennett recalled that there was 'something special' about that evening:

[Eric] arrived at the theatre about four o'clock in the afternoon. We didn't start the show until seven o'clock. He came in, put his arms around me and said, 'How long do you want me to do, boss?' And we laughed about that, and he laughed with the cleaners, he laughed with the people getting the scenery ready, he spent half the evening in the dressing-room just talking to the rest of the other pros, just talking about the old days of Variety.[26]

Alan Randall was one of those people who spent some time with him before the show: 'He was in a very happy, relaxed mood. He said he had lost some weight and I told him he was looking great. We reminisced a lot about showbusiness and Eric was very, very funny. He was having a great time.'[27] 'It's super to be doing something like this again,' Morecambe told him. 'I've not done a theatre for years. It's not like TV because you can relax here.'[28]

Once he was in front of the audience, said Joan, he seemed 'on top form'.[29] He talked about his childhood; his first music and dance lessons; the influence of his mother, Sadie; his time down the mines as a Bevin Boy; his first meeting with Ernie Wise; their subsequent struggles and successes; and he even joked about his open-heart surgery. Apart from the fact that his voice, as the evening wore on, became increasingly hoarse – causing him to drink several glasses of water and keep clearing his throat – he showed no obvious signs of discomfort; indeed, the assistant manager of the theatre, who was watching from the wings, would say that Morecambe 'gave a glittering performance that had the audience in stitches throughout'.[30] When it was all over, Joan recalled, he said goodnight and left the stage: 'Then – the most natural thing in the world – the musicians came back on and picked up their instruments. Eric joined up with them, and in no time at all it developed into a hilarious bit of nonsense with Eric playing away at the vibraphone, with the sticks flying off into the audience. Then he sat down at the piano and did a spot of his unique "out of tune" playing. In a very short time the act had gone from a calm chat show to a slice of pure music-hall – wild, noisy, and energetic.'[31] Several times he would leave the stage only to rush straight back on again and try something else. 'He was obviously elated by the audience response,'[32] said one who witnessed the performance. 'He was absolutely tearing over the stage and having a fantastic time,' said another. 'It was in the real tradition of the Eric Morecambe one knows from the television.'[33] Only Joan wanted it to end; only she was willing him to rest. Eventually, after his sixth and final curtain-call, he said, 'That's your lot,' gave the audience one last wave and walked off the stage. Just as he stepped into the wings, however, he seemed to catch his breath and then, quite suddenly, he fell forward, hitting his head first on one of the iron stage weights and then on the floor. 'I saw him collapse,' said Alan Randall. 'He just fell down without any warning. I shouted to Stan Stennett, "Pull the curtains."'[34] A stunned stage-hand rushed out to the front and appealed for a doctor. Down in the hushed auditorium, three rows back, Joan Morecambe, fearing the worst, rose to her feet and hurried backstage. She was followed by the mayor of Tewkesbury, Andrew Crowther, who happened to be a doctor, and his wife, who was a nurse. They found Eric Morecambe laid out on the floor, his face deathly white. Joan knelt down beside him while the doctor gave him the kiss of life and succeeded in getting his heart beating again. One of the other performers went back out on to the stage and told the audience, 'I think you realise something has happened. Would you please leave quietly?'[35]

An ambulance took Morecambe to Cheltenham General Hospital twelve miles away, where, once he was established in Intensive Care, Joan was allowed to sit with him. Although he was still unconscious, she noted that he seemed to be struggling to wake up. A nurse said, 'Let's try and bring him out of it. Speak to him loudly, as sharp as you like.'[36] Suddenly, as Joan and the nurse called out, 'Eric! Eric! Can you hear us?', he clenched their hands. 'Afterwards', said Joan, 'I almost wished he hadn't. I'd like to think that he wasn't aware of all that had happened. He hadn't the strength to somehow heave himself out of the blackness and back to consciousness, but he squeezed our hands with real force.'[37] Just as she was beginning to think that he was going to pull through, something happened on the screen that prompted the nursing staff to push her abruptly out into a side room and shut the door. She waited there on her own for about fifteen minutes – although, inevitably, it seemed far longer than that – and then suddenly a doctor emerged. 'We're terribly sorry, Mrs Morecambe,' he said, 'we couldn't save your husband . . . His heart just couldn't take any more.'[38]

He had remained alive for more than five and a half hours since suffering the initial attack, but now, just before four o'clock on the morning of Monday 28 May 1984, Eric Morecambe, at the age of fifty-eight, was pronounced dead. Joan managed to call their children in order to break the news to them herself, and then she called the one person who had shared even more years of her husband's life than she had, Ernie Wise, but she, like them, remained in a state of shock. 'I couldn't think,' she said. 'I simply couldn't believe that it was all really happening.'[39] In time, as the reality of the situation began to sink in, there would be feelings of relief – 'that he just made it off the stage in time; he'd absolutely dreaded the thought that he might go in front of an audience'[40] – and anger – 'that he'd been cheated: cheated of the retirement he deserved'[41] – and regret – that he had delayed making that appointment at Harefield. The abiding feeling, however, would, of course, be one of loss: 'Does that mean there won't be any more magic?'[42] asked Morecambe's three-year-old grandson, Adam, when he was told what had happened. 'The remark brought tears to our eyes', recalled Joan, 'for although Adam meant it in a quite literal sense, referring to the magic tricks Eric would perform for [him and his older sister, Amelia], to us it had a much deeper meaning. The magic *was* gone and could never return – only in our thoughts and memories would he remain alive forever.'[43]

Ernie Wise coped in the only way that seemed to make any sense to him: he got on with his work. Only an hour or so after learning of his partner's death, he had put on a black tie and driven from his home in Berkshire to the London studios of TV-AM for an interview that had been arranged several weeks before. 'I thought twice about going,' he said, 'but in the end it seemed the right thing to do.'[44] The remainder of the day was spent, inevitably, talking about the other half of Morecambe and Wise. 'We have lost a great comedian,' he said. 'Everywhere I went people, from royalty to the poorest, always said they felt Eric was one of the family. He was a natural comedian, and I am very, very proud to have been his partner. Through the years people will realise how great he was.'[45] Back inside his home, surrounded by pictures of himself alongside the man whom he described as 'a brother', he confessed: 'It's the saddest day of my life . . . I feel like I've lost a limb.'[46] He was not all there; there was something missing.

The tributes flowed on for several more days. The *Daily Telegraph* mourned the passing of a 'master comic', bracketing him with Chaplin, Keaton and Laurel as a performer whose 'gift for laughter . . . transcended mere scripts or comedy routines', a performer who 'could be funny just by *being there*';[47] *The Times* eulogised a 'comedian of genius';[48] and the *Sun* remembered a gifted comedian who represented 'one of the good things of life', someone who, quite simply, 'made people happy'.[49] Of all the countless eulogies delivered by his fellow professionals, the most perceptive was probably Dickie Henderson's, which spoke of Morecambe as one of that very special set of stars whom the public care about 'above and beyond the performance': 'They think about what they're like *after* the show, when they're at *home* – "Are they nervous during the show? What is their family like? Where do they live?" There are only a select few that the public have cared about like this, and certainly Eric was a first class member.'[50]

It was decided to hold the funeral in Harpenden, where Morecambe had lived since 1961, at the Church of St Nicholas. 'Eric was loved by thousands of people who would have been most unhappy to let him go without saying goodbye properly,' observed Joan. 'Any thoughts I may have had of holding a quiet funeral, possibly followed some weeks later by a memorial service, had to be quickly set aside.'[51] On the day itself, Monday 4 June, more than a thousand people[52] gathered outside the church for the service, which was relayed to them through loudspeakers. The principal address was delivered by Dickie Henderson, whom Morecambe himself had 'booked' specifically for the task after hearing him speak the year before at a memorial service for Arthur Askey:

> Stalag 13,
> Harpenden,
> East Berlin
>
> Dear Dickie,
>
> I very rarely write to famous people . . . that's why I'm writing to you.

I would just like to say that I thought you were superb the other day and I am sure that Big Arthur would have been proud of you. You made us all realise what a great loss we have suffered and at the same time you made us all happy. I would like to book you for mine . . . work permitting.

I would like to be cremated and my favourite music is 'Smoke Gets in Your Eyes'.

Okay, that's fixed.

Love,

Eric.

P.S. I'll pay you when I see you down there. Nothing in this letter constitutes a contract.[53]

'Even though it was a funeral,' Ann Hamilton recalled, 'it turned out to be full of laughter – a celebration, in a way, of everything he had been. When the time came for Ernie to step forward, I think everyone wondered how he was going to follow all of these funny speeches, but he simply recited the words to "Bring Me Sunshine". We'd all been very brave until then, but the words moved us to tears.'[54] After the service was over, Joan and the rest of the family went on to a private cremation service at Garston (the ashes would later be returned to the church in Harpenden and buried in its Garden of Remembrance). Among the masses of floral tributes outside was one from Elton John – 'To one of the funniest and sweetest men in the world'[55] – and another from Ernie Wise – 'Goodbye Sunshine, Miss you, Your little fat friend'[56] – and a tiny posy of pansies wrapped up in tinfoil and bearing the unsigned message, 'Thank you for all the sunshine'.[57]

It was not easy, during the months that followed, for those who had known Eric Morecambe to come to terms with the fact that he was no longer alive. Gary, his son, recalled that for some time after the funeral 'those closest to him truly felt he might suddenly come lumbering along in cloth cap and raincoat, a carrier bag in one hand and a gormless expression on his face, and say, "Evenin' all . . ." and ask what was going on.'[58] Back in 1979, as he was leaving hospital after recovering from his triple by-pass operation, he had joked to reporters, 'I am not really here at the moment. I am a recording,'[59] but now, late in 1984, that was precisely what he had become:

repeated on television, released on video, his intangible presence remained firmly and tantalizingly in sight.

To begin with, said Gail, his daughter, this strange ubiquity seemed of little consequence – 'For me, there was a very clear distinction between Eric Morecambe and my father' – but in time, as that sharp distinction began at last to blur, she found herself turning to the television and 'really watching him, exclusively, taking in every mannerism, listening intently to his voice and feeling very empty when the closing credits moved in to replace him on the screen'.[60] The Morecambe family would at least be spared the kind of media-sponsored 'revelations' that had followed the death of Tommy Cooper (whose wife, Gwen, discovered that he had been conducting a clandestine affair for the last seventeen years of his life[61]): 'I think that Dad is a disappointing subject for an awful lot of the media,' remarked Gail, 'because they tend to want to find that one story that might annihilate him, and, really, I don't think it's possible to come up with. Dad was Dad – he was just what he seemed to be.'[62] It helped, Joan would add, that the public appeared to appreciate this fact: 'I was just so overwhelmed at the reaction from everybody, that they should feel so much grief for someone who wasn't really a member of their family – and yet they all felt that he was.'[63]

Ernie Wise certainly felt that he was – 'I have been robbed of a partner and a brother'[64] – but, amid all of the many 'appalling moments of grief and pain'[65] that he was experiencing, he was also pondering the question: what now for the 'and Wise' of 'Morecambe and Wise'? After forty-three years of sharing a career with the other half of a double-act – and not just any double-act, but for the last twenty years the most popular double-act in the country – he found himself stranded, famous but futureless, at the age of fifty-nine. It could, of course, have been far, far worse: Jerry Desmonde – that other great comic feed – spent the last few years of his life in impoverished obscurity, forgotten by many of his friends and struggling to survive as a mini-cab driver, whereas Ernie Wise, healthy and wealthy, could look forward to a rock-solid retirement in which he would be free to divide his time between his two sumptuous homes in Berkshire and Florida, basking in one long, endless summer. The problem, however, was that Ernie Wise had no desire to retire: 'I needed the fulfilment which work brings,' he said. 'I felt that my life was my work and my work my life. And there was still a lot of life in me.'[66]

Eric Morecambe once said that, in the event of him and his partner deciding to go their separate ways, he could imagine Ernie Wise starting a new career in 'the agency business'.[67] At the beginning of 1985, however, the only career that Ernie Wise was willing to contemplate was that of a solo song-and-dance man – a return, in other words, 'right back to my roots'.[68] It would not, he acknowledged, be easy: without Eric Morecambe by his side, he admitted, he felt that he 'had lost all clout in the profession', retaining 'the respect and reputation but not the power to call the tune', but, he insisted, he was ready to cope with life 'back among the hard realities of show*business*'.[69] He spent three months touring theatres, clubs and hotels in Australia with a nostalgic one-man show that he described as 'a gentle celebration of a life in showbusiness rather than a professional obituary: a mellow evening of song and dance and reminiscence'.[70] He also finally made it to Hollywood, or at least to Los Angeles: some friends at Thames Television arranged for him to make a guest appearance in a situation-comedy entitled *Too Close for Comfort*, which starred Ted Knight (best known for his role as anchor-man Ted Baxter in *The Mary Tyler Moore Show*). In 1987, forty-eight years after his début appearance there as a child star in *Band Waggon*, he returned to the West End stage – this time at the Savoy Theatre – to play the part of the chairman, William Cartwright, in the musical version of *The Mystery of Edwin Drood*. The show was not a success, and, after staggering on for ten weeks, it closed. Undeterred by that setback – 'I was getting a taste for this'[71] – Wise was soon back again: this time as Detective Sergeant Porterhouse in Ray Cooney's long-running farce, *Run For Your Wife*, at the newly restored Whitehall Theatre; this proved a happier engagement, lasting for several months. He also kept up his 'hobby' of appearing as a special guest on television game shows, such as *Countdown* and *What's My Line?*,[72] and he also continued his charity work (in 1989 he raised money for the heart charity Corda by flying around the world dressed as Phileas Fogg). In 1990 he published his autobiography, *Still on My Way to Hollywood* (dedicated to Eric, 'the best partner a man could have'), and the following year he agreed to appear as the subject of the show that Morecambe and Wise had always resisted: *This is Your*

The 'Stripper' routine: several eggs . . .

. . . four grapefruit . . .

. . . and two hams.

Angela Rippon's legs: 'Every show needs a talking point,' said Ernest Maxin, 'something that makes everyone talk about it the next day.'

The South Pacific routine from the last BBC show in 1977: watched by a record 28,835,000 people. Michael Aspel, Philip Jenkinson, Barry Norman, Frank Bough, Eddie Waring, Richard Baker, Richard Whitmore.

Former members of the Soviet KGB get back together to celebrate Eric and Ernie.

A national institution: Eric and Ernie collect their OBEs in 1976.

The 'Cleopatra' romp recycled at Thames with Susannah York replacing
Glenda Jackson.

Reunited with John Ammonds at Thames.

When Eric met Archie: Joan and Eric Morecambe and Barbara Harris and Cary Grant at London's Royal Lancaster Hotel in 1979.

Ernie Wise and his agent, Billy Marsh.

Joan Morecambe said of the public's reaction to Eric's death in 1984: 'I was just so overwhelmed . . . that they should feel so much grief for someone who wasn't really a member of their family - and yet they all felt that he was.'

Ernie Wise continued to perform following his partner's death: it was what he did.

Double act, single vision: 'It is your audience that counts, not you.'

*Life*. He simply refused to stop working. He was still fit, he said, still keen, still able, still hungry for more of the 'VIP treatment' rather than any of 'the RIP treatment',[73] and besides, he added, he had been performing in front of an audience of some kind or another ever since he was six years old: it was what he *did*.

There would always be some people, however, for whom the very idea of Wise without Morecambe made no sense at all. In April of 1993, for example, Ernie Wise was made the subject of a deeply patronising BBC *40 Minutes* documentary entitled *The Importance of Being Ernie*. The theme, as one reviewer would put it, was 'the infinite pathos of being an "and" ';[74] not only, the programme seemed to imply, had Wise been impudent enough to have gone on living after his partner had died, but he was also misguided enough to have failed to live the remainder of his life according to the wishes of persons other than himself. The cameras followed him backstage at the Theatre Royal, Windsor, where, at the age of sixty-seven, he was in rehearsal for his first pantomime without Eric Morecambe; he spoke of his past (he was born to perform, he said: 'I had them all crying in their beer'), his present (he was *not*, he insisted, making a comeback: 'I never left!') and his future (he was willing to produce, direct and/or perform, he said hopefully: 'I have to have some *purpose*'), but at no point did this relatively guileless and (outside of business matters) somewhat gullible man seem to realise that the programme-makers were laughing at him rather than with him. At one point, for example, the frame filled with a close-up of Wise's 'star portrait' on the front of the theatre before cutting to a shot of Wise telling the joke about the performer who replies to the question, 'You can't sing, you can't dance, you're not funny – as a matter of fact, you've got no talent at all. Why don't you give up showbusiness?', by answering, 'I can't – I'm a *star*!'

The reviews ranged from the pitying ('What was pathetic here was the spectacle of an old-age pensioner putting on the motley because he couldn't not put it on'[75]) to the sardonic ('there could be no doubt, watching this programme, that "and Wise" was just as dead as Morecambe'[76]). There were two admirable exceptions: Craig Brown argued that 'if Ernie Wise were indeed such a sorry figure, the director wouldn't have had to camp it all up with such stagey techniques',[77] and Lynne Truss exclaimed, 'What a rotten thing to do to someone . . . Ernie Wise does not deserve this; if he wants to pursue a solo career . . . then let him do it in peace. It doesn't make him John Osborne's Entertainer.'[78] One of the well-meaning contributors to the programme, Bill Cotton, felt similarly aggrieved by the impact of the finished product:

I just *hope* that Ernie took no notice of it, because it was terribly unfair. When I agreed to take part, the thing, really, that I'd wanted to say was this: 'What does it *matter*? What does it *matter* if Ernie Wise wants to appear on stage? Why is everybody making such a song and dance about "he's trying to be a star in his own right"? The man *is* a star in his own right! He was one of the best straight-men this country has ever seen in what was probably the greatest double-act this country has ever seen. *That's* a star! So now he wants to appear on his own on stage: fine, but why make a big fuss about it?' In a way, I suppose, I was trying to get a message across to Ernie, actually; I wanted him to stop talking about, you know, 'I'm going to make it on my own.' He's *made* it! I thought he was silly, but, then again, I understood why. It was something he felt he needed to do.[79]

No straight-man has ever been fully appreciated by his audience. A straight-man needs to be selfless; his role is to serve the comic, not himself. The better the straight-man is, therefore, the less he appears to be doing. Take, for example, Jerry Desmonde's contribution to 'Following Through', the famous golfing routine he performed with Sid Field:

| DESMONDE | Can't you understand? When I say, 'Let's go,' I don't mean 'Let's *go*'; I mean 'Stay here and *let's go.*' |
| --- | --- |
| FIELD | What a per-*form*-ance! I can't understand what's come over you, Humphrey. You're not like this when we're painting together . . . |
| DESMONDE | Skip it! What are you jumping over the ball for? |
| FIELD | Well, you said, 'Skip it.' |

| DESMONDE | No, no! Get behind the ball. |
| FIELD | But it's 'behind' the ball all round! What a performance! |
| DESMONDE | Come *on*! Square up to that ball. *No*! Not like *that*, silly! Keep your eye on the ball. Ah! Get up! Address the ball. |
| FIELD | Dear ball . . . |
| DESMONDE | Get up! |
| FIELD | No! You've smacked me![80] |

Desmonde had none of the funny lines, and none of the memorable gestures, but without his discipline, his seriousness and his superb timing his partner would not have seemed so believably silly. It was the same with Wise:

| ERIC | I thought I would do a party trick. |
| ERNIE | What sort of party trick? |
| ERIC | Sawing a woman in half. |
| ERNIE | That's a very good idea. |
| ERIC | It is, isn't it? Get in the box. |
| ERNIE | *I'm* not a woman! |
| ERIC | I haven't used the saw yet! |

On the odd occasion, admittedly, he could be less than flawless:

| ERNIE | To appear in an Ernies Why play . . . |
| ERIC | 'An Ernie's Why'? |
| ERNIE | An Ernie Wise play . . . |
| ERIC | How about: 'To appear in an *Ernie Wise* play?' |
| ERNIE | To appear in an Ernie Wise play – and it's not my night. |
| ERIC | No. But I know one thing. |
| ERNIE | What? |
| ERIC | It's your name. And you can't even say that properly! |

Usually, however, his contribution was discreetly proficient. 'Ernie

was a very unselfish man', Bill Cotton remarked, 'but he was clever
with it: he *used* his unselfishness to both their advantage. He knew
how to get the *very* best out of Eric. He'd wait for him, give him
time, feed him a line at just the right moment. The consequence of
that, of course, was that Eric's response would get a big laugh and
*that* would be the thing people remembered. Ernie played his part
so well that he appeared to be contributing next to nothing.'[81]

The *40 Minutes* documentary hurt Ernie Wise, but not half as
much, of course, as he had been hurt by the death of the one person
who had never under-estimated the value of his contribution: Eric
Morecambe. 'Someone said it was the way we looked at one another,'
said Wise, somewhat wistfully, when asked to explain the success of
their partnership. 'I think we had a touch of magic when we were
working together.'[82] Now, he reflected, 'I feel like there's a cold
draught down one side of me where Eric should be.'[83] In December
1993 he suffered a minor stroke that forced him to spend all of that
Christmas in hospital. 'I'd like to have gone on for ever,' he would
say, but after the stroke, which left him still fit but somewhat forget-
ful, 'I realised I was finished.'[84] A second stroke followed in August
1995, prompting Wise to announce, on 27 November, his seventieth
birthday, his formal retirement from showbusiness.

A comeback was out of the question, but then again a comeback
was never the answer. 'The death of a comic actor', wrote a critic,
'is felt more than that of a tragedian. He has sympathised more with
us in our every-day feelings, and has given us more amusement.
Death with a tragedian seems all in the way of business. Tragedians
have been dying all their lives . . . But it seems a hard thing upon
the comic actor to quench his airiness and vivacity – to stop him in
his happy career – to make us think of him, on the sudden, with
solemnity – and to miss him for ever.'[85] Ever since that fateful call
came, just after 4 a.m. on 28 May 1984, Ernie Wise, along with so
many others, would miss Eric Morecambe – not always, perhaps,
with solemnity, but certainly for ever.

# EPILOGUE

*If you're lucky, you get to stand on Everest, and you can see the world below you at your feet. That's what it was like when we had* The Morecambe & Wise Show *— it felt like we were standing on Everest.*
BILL COTTON

*Ah, that was good, that was.*
*Took you back, took you out of yourself,*
*took you somewhere, you didn't know where.*
*It deserves a clap.*
THE GOOD COMPANIONS

*When I'm gone, I'm gone. No point worrying about me, you know. But you will still watch the shows, won't you? If you don't, then it's all been for nothing.*

ERIC MORECAMBE

In the summer of 1994 – ten years after the premature death of Eric Morecambe – the BBC broadcast a short series of compilation programmes entitled *Bring Me Sunshine* in celebration of *The Morecambe & Wise Show*. Not only did these programmes attract audience figures second only to the popular soap opera *EastEnders* in BBC1's weekly ratings, but they also managed to command the attention of an entirely new generation of admirers.[1] Encouraged by this exceptionally enthusiastic response, the Controller of BBC1, Alan Yentob, scheduled a repeat of Morecambe and Wise's 1971 Christmas special for the night of 25 December 1994; once again, though the show was not just another repeat but in this case a *23-year-old* repeat, it attracted one of the highest audiences of the day and some of the warmest reviews of the week. It was happening all over again.

'We were powerful together,' reflected Ernie Wise, 'and some of our shows were so beautiful they still bring tears to my eyes. It's a wonderful legacy.'[2] Morecambe and Wise were indeed powerful together, and they certainly did leave behind them a wonderful legacy, but one doubts that they would have appreciated the manner in which this legacy has been exploited. It is hard to think of another recognised television 'classic' that has been subjected to quite the same degree of sustained disrespect as *The Morecambe & Wise Show*; time and again the original award-winning shows have been hurriedly and clumsily gutted, griddled and garnished in order to disguise the poverty of many a prime-time menu. 'I don't think it's right,' said Bill Cotton. 'I don't like to see those shows going out now with all of these cuts. You have to *live* with a television show. I really resent seeing Morecambe and Wise – of all people – cut down from forty-five minutes to half an hour, with three odd sketches bunged in and some new credits stuck on the end. I think it's disgraceful.'[3] One would have thought that the BBC would at least have had the good sense, if not the simple decency, to have invited back one or both of the show's distinguished producer/directors, John Ammonds and Ernest Maxin, to supervise the changes to the programmes whose original success they had played so large a part in making possible, but neither man was contacted. 'It was rather sad,' admitted Ammonds, 'because, obviously, those shows meant a lot to me, and I would have liked someone to have asked me back and said, "Why don't you edit these together for us, because, you know, they were your shows." '[4] Ernest Maxin agreed: 'I'd have gone in and done it for nothing, but I wasn't invited.'[5] Not even Ernie Wise was invited back for that series in 1994: 'I do find it odd,' he was quoted as saying at the time. 'You would think they'd ask for my memories.'[6]

The previous year, Bill Cotton (who had left the Corporation in 1988) had made a speech in which he had warned his former colleagues that 'the BBC is forgetting that it has always been the entertainer of the nation, that its core activity is to make programmes that people enjoy. America has Hollywood and Britain has the BBC.'[7] His warning went, as far as one could tell, unheeded. While the BBC was more than happy to remind its viewers of the days in which *The Morecambe & Wise Show* was such a highly prized fixture in its schedules, it was rather less keen, it seemed, to remind itself of the internal culture which had enabled such a remarkable show to flourish. 'That', observed Frank Muir, 'would have made for an uneasy sort of comparison':

You see, *The Morecambe & Wise Show* was a product of Bill Cotton's BBC, not John Birt's BBC – and those are two very different institutions. Nowadays you still get all the brain work, you still get the intelligence, but you don't get the imagination or the wit. All of this heavy industry simply doesn't encourage, or perhaps even allow for, *flair* in management. Nowadays the

BBC demands 'efficiency' above all else, and flair isn't efficiency – just as talent isn't professionalism: 'professionalism' is easy, you know, it's just turning up on time and knowing your lines, but talent is a bit different. And it's the same with management: proper, *fizzy* management involves dealing with *possibilities* – you deal with *hope*, because what you're dealing with is the immeasurable. Of course, today's 'management consultants' can't *bear* that which is immeasurable, because it makes them superfluous.[8]

Even in their brutally bowdlerised form, however, the repeats of *The Morecambe & Wise Show* still seem far fresher and funnier than most of the new shows in the schedules. 'I think part of the reason for that,' said Eddie Braben, 'is the fact that we never tried to be "fashionable". We just worked very, very hard to be funny':

It was timeless, their humour. In fact, I actually wrote a few lines about how they would be in the bed, if they were still working now, and I don't think it would seem out of place today. If you can imagine they're sitting up in the bed, and Ernie's writing in his notepad, Eric would turn to him and say:

ERIC       How many today?
ERNIE      How many what?
ERIC       How many epic plays have you written today?
ERNIE      Twenty-seven epic plays.
ERIC       And still only a quarter past ten! You could be
           another Brontë sister – you've got the legs for it.
ERNIE      Please! I am trying to create.

And there would be a long pause. I always used to write this in – 'A LONG PAUSE' – I was very fond of long pauses, because they built up the right atmosphere.

ERIC       Ern?
ERNIE      Yes?
ERIC       Good.

There'd be another pause.

ERIC      The Bard.

ERNIE     Who?

ERIC      William Shakespeare.

ERNIE     Oh, the Bard.

ERIC      Barred from every pub in Stratford-upon-Avon!

ERNIE     I am trying to finish a thriller.

ERIC      At your age that might take some time!

Another pause.

ERIC      I've never told this to another soul, Ern, but I'll tell you. I once appeared in *King Liar*.

ERNIE     *King Lear!*

ERIC      No – *King Liar*. I told them I could act!

Yet another LONG PAUSE. Ernie would still be trying to write.

ERIC      Do you remember when we were at Milverton Street School?

ERNIE     I'm *trying* to write ... How many 'f's are there in 'physicist'?

ERIC      The Chinese kids were very clever at school.

ERNIE     They were good at sums.

ERIC      Especially take-aways.

Then he'd do his laugh.

ERIC      That was a belter, that one! You walked right into that one! It was like reeling in a clapped-out salmon![9]

'It isn't a matter of being "old-fashioned",' John Ammonds agreed. 'Comedy – *good* comedy – doesn't really age that much, if it ages at all. Eric Morecambe is funny – whether you're watching a recording of him in 1980 or 2000 or 2020.'[10] Ernest Maxin added: 'It's the same with Morecambe and Wise as it is with Laurel and Hardy: just as long as there are movies, people will laugh at Laurel and Hardy, and just as long as there is television, people will laugh at Morecambe and Wise.'[11]

Morecambe and Wise certainly never allowed themselves to forget the axiom that Stan Laurel had once referred to as the first and most important thing that any entertainer ought to learn: 'It is your audience that counts, not you.'[12] There is no art to making people miserable – most of us, alas, are more than capable of achieving that condition without the assistance of any cultural stimulus – but there is an art to making people happy; we can struggle to make ends meet, we can come to see some of our dearest dreams dashed, we can lose those for whom our love was most deep, we can feel bitter and cheated and hurt, and yet there are still certain rare individuals who can, against all the odds, make us laugh, and make us feel, in spite of everything, that life is still worth living. Morecambe and Wise succeeded – where most had failed – in making such an art seem easy.

'A TV set is not a bad box to be buried in', wrote Nancy Banks-Smith, 'when you have been the best on the box.'[13] Morecambe and Wise, after years of hard work, ended up not just as the best entertainers on British television but also the best-loved, too. Their attitude can – and should – be copied, but their appeal will remain unique and unforgettable. As one elderly woman was heard to say on the day of Eric Morecambe's funeral: 'That thing about sunshine, laughter and love. That was ever so nice. We'll never forget that . . .'[14]

# List of Performances

Every effort has been made to assemble a list of recorded performances that is as comprehensive as possible; any unintentional omissions or inaccuracies will be corrected in a future edition.

## RADIO

LP = Light Programme; H = Home Service; FP = Forces Programme; MH = Midland Home Service; NH = Northern Home Service; R2 = Radio 2; R4 = Radio 4. An asterisk indicates that an acetate was made for broadcasting purposes overseas. A dagger indicates that a recording is preserved in the BBC Sound Archive.

**1943**
| | |
|---|---|
| 16 April | *Strike a New Note* (FP) |
| 4 May | *Youth Must Have Its Swing* (H) |
| 11 May | *Youth Must Have Its Swing* (H) |
| 18 May | *Youth Must Have Its Swing* (H) |
| 25 May | *Youth Must Have Its Swing* (H) |
| 8 June | *Youth Must Have Its Swing* (H) |
| 15 June | *Youth Must Have Its Swing* (H) |

**1947**
| | |
|---|---|
| 6 June | *Beginners, Please!* (LP) |

**1948**
| | |
|---|---|
| 20 March | *Beginners, Please!* (LP) |
| 19 August | *Show Time* (LP) |

**1952**
| | |
|---|---|
| 10 January | *Workers' Playtime* (H) |
| 13 March | *Variety Fanfare* (NH) |
| 4 May | *Variety Bandbox* (NH) |
| 15 May | *Variety Fanfare* (NH) |
| 12 June | *Variety Fanfare* (NH) |
| 1 July | *Variety Fanfare* (NH) |
| 22 July | *Variety Fanfare* (NH) |
| 27 July | *Variety Bandbox* (NH) |
| 19 August | *Variety Fanfare* (NH) |
| 2 September | *Variety Fanfare* (NH) |
| 16 September | *Variety Fanfare* (NH)★ |
| 10 October | *Variety Fanfare* (NH) |

| | |
|---|---|
| 31 October | *Variety Fanfare* (NH) |
| 21 November | *Variety Fanfare* (NH)★ |
| 12 December | *Variety Fanfare* (NH) |

**1953**
| | |
|---|---|
| 9 January | *Variety Fanfare* (NH★ |
| 10 January | *Variety Fanfare* (NH)★ |
| 13 February | *Variety Fanfare* (NH)★ |
| 19 February | *Workers' Playtime* NH) |
| 13 March | *Variety Fanfare* (NH)★ |
| 27 March | *Variety Fanfare* (NH) |
| 29 July | *Blackpool Night* (LP) |
| 23 September | *Blackpool Night* (LP) |
| 22 October | *Workers' Playtime* (H) |
| 25 October | *Variety Fanfare* (NH) |
| 9 November | *You're Only Young Once* (NH) |
| 16 November | *YoYo* (NH) |
| 23 November | *YoYo* (NH) |
| 1 December | *YoYo* (NH) |
| 7 December | *YoYo* (NH) |
| 14 December | *YoYo* (NH) |
| 19 December | *Variety Playhouse* (H) |
| 22 December | *YoYo* (NH) |
| 28 December | *YoYo* (NH) |

**1954**
| | |
|---|---|
| 4 January | *YoYo* (NH) |
| 14 January | *YoYo* (NH) |
| 19 January | *Variety Fanfare* (NH) |
| 9 February | *Variety Fanfare* (NH) |
| 28 February | *Variety Fanfare* (NH) |
| 18 March | *Workers' Playtime* (H) |
| 26 March | *Henry Hall's Guest Night* (H) |
| 15 April | *Variety Fanfare* (LP) |
| 29 April | *Workers' Playtime* (H) |
| 6 May | *YoYo* (NH) |
| 13 May | *YoYo* (NH) |
| 20 May | *YoYo* (NH) |
| 27 May | *YoYo* (NH) |
| 3 June | *YoYo* (NH) |
| 10 June | *YoYo* (NH) |
| 17 June | *YoYo* (NH) |
| 24 June | *YoYo* (NH) |
| 3 August | *Workers' Playtime* (H) |
| 5 August | *Workers' Playtime* (H) |
| 1 September | *Blackpool Night* (LP) |
| 5 September | *Having a Wonderful Time* (NH) |
| 1 October | *YoYo* (NH) |
| 8 October | *YoYo* (NH) |
| 14 October | *Workers' Playtime* (NH) |
| 15 October | *YoYo* (NH) |
| 22 October | *YoYo* (NH) |
| 29 October | *YoYo* (NH) |
| 5 November | *YoYo* (NH) |
| 12 November | *YoYo* (NH) |
| 19 November | *YoYo* (NH) |
| 26 November | *YoYo* (NH) |

| | |
|---|---|
| 3 December | *YoYo* (NH) |
| 9 December | *YoYo* (NH) |
| 17 December | *YoYo* (NH) |

**1955**

| | |
|---|---|
| 8 January | *Spotlight* (H) |
| 24 February | *Workers' Playtime* (H) |
| 21 March | *Spotlight* (LP) |
| 31 March | *The Show Goes On* (LP) |
| 7 April | *The Show Goes On* (LP) |
| 11 April | *Spotlight* (LP) |
| 14 April | *The Show Goes On* (LP) |
| 21 April | *The Show Goes On* (LP) |
| 28 April | *The Show Goes On* (LP) |
| 5 May | *The Show Goes On* (LP) |
| 12 May | *The Show Goes On* (LP) |
| 17 May | *Spotlight* (LP) |
| 19 May | *The Show Goes On* LP) |
| 24 May | *Spotlight* (LP) |
| 26 May | *The Show Goes On* (LP) |
| 31 May | *Spotlight* (LP) |
| 2 June | *The Show Goes On* (LP) |
| 9 June | *The Show Goes On* (LP) |
| 27 June | *Blackpool Night* (LP) |
| 10 August | *Blackpool Night* (LP) |
| 18 August | *Workers' Playtime* (H) |
| 7 September | *Blackpool Night* (LP) |
| 19 October | *The Morecambe and Wise Show* (NH) |
| 26 October | *The Morecambe and Wise Show* (NH) |
| 2 November | *The Morecambe and Wise Show* (NH) |

**1956**

| | |
|---|---|
| 30 May | *Call Boy* (LP) |
| 21 June | *Workers' Playtime* (H) |
| 24 June | *Variety Fanfare* (NH) |
| 18 July | *Blackpool Night* (LP) |
| 24 July | *Let's Make a Date* (NH) |
| 7 August | *Variety Fanfare* (NH) |
| 9 August | *Workers' Playtime* (H) |
| 24 August | *Morecambe Illuminations* (LP) |
| 23 October | *Call Boy* (NH) |
| 26 October | *Mid-day Music Hall* (LP) |
| 15 December | *Variety Playhouse* (LP) |

**1957**

| | |
|---|---|
| 3 January | *By the Fireside* (NH) |
| 18 March | *Mid-day Music Hall* (LP) |
| 26 March | *Workers' Playtime* (H) |
| 29 March | *Henry Hall's Guest Night* (LP) |
| 1 May | *Call Boy* (NH) |
| 2 May | *Worker's Playtime* (LP) |
| 3 May | *Blackpool Night* (LP) |
| 14 August | *Blackpool Night* (LP) |
| 31 October | *Workers' Playtime* (H) |
| 23 December | *Star Train* (LP) |

**1958**

| | |
|---|---|
| 17 February | *Call Boy* (LP) |
| 9 April | *Workers' Playtime* (H) |
| 23 April | *Workers' Playtime* (H) |
| 11 May | *Mid-day Music Hall* (LP) |
| 12 May | *Mid-day Music Hall from the North* (LP) |
| 17 July | *Workers' Playtime* (H) |
| 21 July | *Laughter Incorporated* (LP) |
| 22 July | *Blackpool Night* (LP) |
| 23 July | *Blackpool Night* (LP) |
| 28 July | *Laughter Incorporated* (LP) |
| 4 August | *Laughter Incorporated* (LP) |
| 10 August | *Mid-day Music Hall* (LP) |
| 11 August | *Laughter Incorporated* (LP) |
| 18 August | *Laughter Incorporated* (LP) |
| 25 August | *Laughter Incorporated* (LP) |
| 1 September | *Laughter Incorporated* (LP) |
| 2 September | *Blackpool Night* (LP) |
| 8 September | *Laughter Incorporated* (LP) |
| 15 September | *Laughter Incorporated* (LP) |
| 20 September | *Mid-day Music Hall* (LP) |
| 22 September | *Laughter Incorporated* (LP) |
| 22 October | *Workers' Playtime* (H) |
| 1 November | *Mid-day Music Hall* (LP) |
| 30 November | *Mid-day Music Hall* (LP) |
| 21 December | *Mid-day Music Hall* (LP) |

**1960**

| | |
|---|---|
| 28 January | *Workers' Playtime* (LP) |
| 7 April | *Workers' Playtime* (LP) |
| 21 April | *Workers' Playtime* (LP) |
| 2 May | *Mid-day Music Hall* (LP) |
| 11 May | *London Lights* (LP) |
| 24 July | *Holiday Music Hall* (LP) |
| 15 August | *Seaside Nights* (LP) |
| 6 October | *Workers' Playtime* (LP) |

**1961**

| | |
|---|---|
| 9 January | *From the Top* (MH) |
| 2 March | *Workers' Playtime* (LP) |
| 21 March | *Workers' Playtime* (LP) |
| 11 June | *Seaside Nights* (LP) |
| 18 September | *Flying High* (LP) |
| 9 December | *In Town Today* (H)★ |

**1963**

| | |
|---|---|
| 18 August | *Blackpool Night* (LP)† |

**1965**

| | |
|---|---|
| 23 October | *Blackpool Night* (LP) |

**1966**

| | |
|---|---|
| 24 July | *The Morecambe & Wise Show* (LP)† |
| 31 July | *The Morecambe & Wise Show* (LP) |
| 7 August | *The Morecambe & Wise Show* (LP) |
| 21 August | *The Morecambe & Wise Show* (LP) |
| 28 August | *The Morecambe & Wise Show* (LP) |

**1971**

25 December        *Morecambe and Wise Sing Flanagan and Allen* (R2)

**1975**

26 January        *The Eric Morecambe and Ernie Wise Show* (R2)†
2 February        *The Eric Morecambe and Ernie Wise Show* (R2)†
9 February        *The Eric Morecambe and Ernie Wise Show* (R2)†
16 February       *The Eric Morecambe and Ernie Wise Show* (R2)†
23 February       *The Eric Morecambe and Ernie Wise Show* (R2)†
2 March           *The Eric Morecambe and Ernie Wise Show* (R2)†
31 March          *Eric and Ernie's Hall of Fame* (R4)†
3 July            *The Eric Morecambe and Ernie Wise Show* (R2)†
26 December       *Eric and Ernie's Second Hall of Fame* (R4)†

**1976**

5 September       *The Eric Morecambe and Ernie Wise Show* (R2)†
12 September      *The Eric Morecambe and Ernie Wise Show* (R2)†
19 September      *The Eric Morecambe and Ernie Wise Show* (R2)†
26 September      *The Eric Morecambe and Ernie Wise Show* (R2)†
3 October         *The Eric Morecambe and Ernie Wise Show* (R2)†
10 October        *The Eric Morecambe and Ernie Wise Show* (R2)†

**1977**

4 December        *The Eric Morecambe and Ernie Wise Show* (R2)†
11 December       *The Eric Morecambe and Ernie Wise Show* (R2)†
18 December       *The Eric Morecambe and Ernie Wise Show* (R2)†
25 December       *The Eric Morecambe and Ernie Wise Christmas Show* (R2)†

**1978**

25 March          *The Eric Morecambe and Ernie Wise Show* (R2)†

## TELEVISION

This lists limits itself to Morecambe and Wise's own original shows – guest appearances, repeats and compilations are not included.

### Running Wild (BBC)

21 April 1954     Alma Cogan, The Four in a Crowd, Ray Buckingham, Marjorie Holmes, Hermione Harvey, Amanda Barrie
5 May 1954        Alma Cogan, The Four in a Crowd, Bernard Bresslaw, Ray Buckingham, Marjorie Holmes, Hermione Harvey, Amanda Barrie
19 May            Alma Cogan, The Four in a Crowd, Ray Buckingham, Hermione Harvey, Amanda Barrie
2 June 1954       Alma Cogan, The Four in a Crowd, Ray Buckingham, Hermione Harvey, Amanda Barrie
16 June 1954      Alma Cogan, The Four in a Crowd, Ray Buckingham, Hermione Harvey, Amanda Barrie
30 June 1954      Jill Day, The Four in a Crowd, Ray Buckingham, Hermione Harvey, Amanda Barrie

### The Morecambe and Wise Show (ATV)

*Series 1*

12 October 1961   Jack Parnell and His Orchestra
19 October 1961   The Confederates
26 October 1961   Acker Bilk
2 November 1961   The McGuire Sisters
9 November 1961   The Peters Sisters

| | |
|---|---|
| 16 November 1961 | Cleo Laine |
| 23 November 1961 | Gary Miller |
| 30 November 1961 | Mickie Ashmon's Ragtime Jazz Band, Valerie Masters |
| 7 December 1961 | The Kaye Sisters |

### Series 2

| | |
|---|---|
| 30 June 1962 | Terry Lightfoot's Jazzmen, The Kaye Sisters |
| 7 July 1962 | Kenny Ball's Jazzmen, The Beverley Sisters |
| 14 July 1962 | Alex Welsh and His Band, The Beverley Sisters |
| 21 July 1962 | Acker Bilk, The Beverley Sisters |
| 28 July 1962 | The Mike Cotton Jazzmen, Susan Maughan |
| 4 August 1962 | Chris Barber's Jazzband, Ottilie Patterson, The Beverley Sisters |
| 11 August 1962 | The Clyde Valley Stompers, The Beverley Sisters |
| 18 August 1962 | Eric Delaney and His Band, Teddy Johnson and Pearl Carr |
| 25 August 1962 | George Chisholm's Jazz Gang, Teddy Johnson and Pearl Carr |
| 1 September 1962 | Humphrey Lyttelton and his Band, Lita Roza |
| 8 September 1962 | Alex Welsh and his Band, Janice Marden |
| 15 September 1962 | The Mike Cotton Jazzmen, Teddy Johnson and Pearl Carr |
| 22 September 1962 | Jack Parnell and his Debonaires, Teddy Johnson and Pearl Carr |

### Series 3

| | |
|---|---|
| 15 June 1963 | Joe Brown and his Bruvvers, The Michael Sammes Singers |
| 22 June 1963 | Acker Bilk, The Michael Sammes Singers |
| 29 June 1963 | The King Brothers, Barbara Law, Murray Kash |
| 6 July 1963 | Sheila Buxton, The Michael Sammes Singers |
| 13 July 1963 | The King Brothers, Janice Marden |
| 20 July 1963 | The King Brothers, Susan Maughan |
| 27 July 1963 | The King Brothers, Sheila Southern |
| 3 August 1963 | Roy Castle |
| 10 August 1963 | Shani Wallis, The Michael Sammes Singers |
| 17 August 1963 | The King Brothers, Maureen Evans |
| 24 August 1963 | The King Brothers, Kathy Kirby |
| 31 August 1963 | Eric Delaney's Band, Lucille Gaye |
| 7 September 1963 | The King Brothers, Rosemary Squires |

### Series 4

| | |
|---|---|
| 4 April 1964 | Eddie Calvert and the 'C' Men, The Raindrops |
| 11 April 1964 | Janice Marden, Yvonne Antrobus, Kenny Ball |
| 18 April 1964 | The Beatles |
| 25 April 1964 | Chris Rayburn, The Viscounts, Pearl Lane, Janet Webb |
| 2 May 1964 | Jackie Trent, Penny Morrell, Yvonne Antrobus, Freddie Powell, Acker Bilk |
| 9 May 1964 | Pasty Ann Noble, The Fraser Hayes Four, Sally Williams, Janet Webb |
| 16 May 1964 | Sheila Buxton, Alan Curtis, Yvonne Antrobus, Edmund Hockridge |
| 23 May 1964 | The King Brothers, Freddie Powell, Kathy Kirby, Marilyn Gothard, Janet Webb |
| 30 May 1964 | Joe Brown and the Bruvvers, Joy Marshall, Pearl Lane, Jeannette Bradbury |
| 6 June 1964 | Four Macs, Jo Williamson, Dickie Valentine |
| 13 June 1964 | Valerie Masters, Gladys Whitehead, Alan Curtis, Jo Williamson, The Bachelors |
| 20 June 1964 | Ray Ellington, Barbara Law, Penny Morrell |
| 27 June 1964 | The Migil 5, Sandra Boize, Jo Williamson, Sally Douglas, Thelma Taylor, Valerie Van Ost, Christina Wass, Julie Devonshire, Susan Maughan |

### Series 5

| | |
|---|---|
| 22 January 1966 | Lulu, Paul and Barry Ryan |
| 29 January 1966 | Morgan James Duo |
| 5 February 1966 | Jackie Trent, The New Faces |
| 12 February 1966 | Millicent Martin |
| 19 February 1966 | Georgie Fame and the Blue Flames, Julie Rogers |
| 26 February 1966 | The Settlers, Barbara Law |
| 5 March 1966 | The King Brothers |
| 12 March 1966 | The Shadows, Janice Marden |
| 19 March 1966 | Herman's Hermits, Teddy Johnson and Pearl Carr |

### Series 6

| | |
|---|---|
| 1 October 1967 | Millicent Martin, Freddie & the Dreamers |
| 22 October 1967 | Millicent Martin, The Small Faces, Bobby Rydell |
| 12 November 1967 | Millicent Martin, The Hollies, Tom Jones |
| 10 December 1967 | Millicent Martin, Manfred Mann, George Maharis |
| 4 February 1968 | Millicent Martin, The Tremeloes, Peter Nero |
| 25 February 1968 | Millicent Martin, Eric Burdon and the Animals, Gene Pitney |
| 17 March 1968 | Millicent Martin, Georgie Fame, Bobby Vinton |
| 31 March 1968 | Millicent Martin, The Dave Clark Five, Cliff Richard |

## The Morecambe & Wise Show (BBC)

### Series 1 (BBC2)

| | |
|---|---|
| 2 September 1968 | Georgia Brown, Los Zafiros, Jenny Lee-Wright, Bettine Le Beau, Kenny Ball and His Jazzmen |
| 9 September 1968 | Acker Bilk, Jenny Lee-Wright, Sheila Bernette, Caron Gardner, Bettine Le Beau, Judy Robinson, Tina Martin, Jenny Russell |
| 16 September 1968 | Trio Athenee, The Paper Dolls, Jenny Lee-Wright, Jimmy Lee, Kenny Ball, Ann Hamilton |
| 23 September 1968 | Bruce Forsyth, Kenny Ball, Jenny Lee-Wright, Ann Hamilton |
| 30 September 1968 | Ronnie Carroll, Kenny Ball, Jenny Lee-Wright, Michele Barrie, Jane Bartlett, Wendy Hillhouse, Bebe Robson |
| 7 October 1968 | Edmund Hockridge, Kenny Ball, Ann Hamilton |
| 14 October 1968 | Michael Aspel, Chris Langford, Kenny Ball, Jimmy Berryman, Lesley Roach, Ann Hamilton, Jenny Lee-Wright |
| 21 October 1968 | Matt Monro, Kenny Ball, Ann Hamilton |

### Series 2 (BBC2)

| | |
|---|---|
| 27 July 1969 | Peter Cushing, Bobbie Gentry, Vince Hill, Kenny Ball, Ann Hamilton, Janet Webb, Constance Carling, Diana Powell |
| 10 August 1969 | Trio Athenee, Malcolm Roberts, Ann Hamilton, Janet Webb |
| 24 August 1969 | Juliet Mills, Moira Anderson, Ann Hamilton, The Pattersons, Kenny Ball, Janet Webb, Lynda Thomas |
| 7 September 1969 | Edward Woodward, Kenneth McKellar, Ann Hamilton, The Pattersons, Kenny Ball, Rex Rashley, Karen Birch, Richard Scott, Janet Webb |
| 25 December 1969 | Susan Hampshire, Frankie Vaughan, Nina, Ann Hamilton, Janet Webb |

### Series 3 (BBC2)

| | |
|---|---|
| 14 January 1970 | Herman's Hermits, Ann Hamilton, Janet Webb |
| 28 January 1970 | Ian Carmichael, Nina, Ann Hamilton, Janet Webb |
| 11 February 1970 | Fenella Fielding, Sacha Distel, Ann Hamilton, Janet Webb |
| 11 March 1990 | Diane Cilento, Vince Hill, Deryck Guyler, Ann Hamilton, Janet Webb |

| | |
|---|---|
| 25 March 1990 | Edward Chapman, Clodagh Rogers, Nanette, Ann Hamilton, Janet Webb |
| 8 April 1970 | Nina Golden, Ann Hamilton, Janet Webb |
| 22 April 1970 | Richard Greene, Nana Mouskouri, Ann Hamilton, Janet Webb |

### Series 4 (BBC2)

| | |
|---|---|
| 1 July 1970 | Eric Porter, Jan Daley, Trio Athenee, Ann Hamilton, Janet Webb |
| 15 July 1970 | Kenneth McKellar, George A. Cooper, Margery Mason, Samantha Jones, Ann Hamilton, Janet Webb |
| 29 July 1970 | Nina, Craig Douglas, Ann Hamilton, Jenny Lee-Wright, Janet Webb |
| 12 August 1970 | Fenella Fielding, Ray Stevens, Sylvia McNeill, Ann Hamilton, Janet Webb |
| 26 August 1970 | Barbara Murray, Dusty Springfield, Michael Redgrave, Robin Day, Ann Hamilton, Janet Webb |
| 25 December 1970 | Peter Cushing, William Franklyn, Nina, Eric Porter, Edward Woodward, Ann Hamilton, Alan Curtis, Rex Rashley, Janet Webb |

### Series 5 (BBC1)

| | |
|---|---|
| 8 April 1971 | Flora Robson, Esther Ofarim, Peter & Alex, Kenny Ball, Ann Hamilton, Alan Curtis, David March, Janet Webb |
| 22 April 1971 | Arthur Lowe, Robert Young, Susan Maughan, Dad's Army, Ann Hamilton, Janet Webb |
| 6 May 1971 | Frank Ifield, The Settlers, Ann Hamilton, Kenny Ball, Richard Caldicot, Michael Ward, Gordon Clyde, Grazina Frame, Brychan Powell, Janet Webb |
| 20 May 1971 | Jack Jones, Sheila Southern, Ann Hamilton, Kenny Ball, Gordon Clyde, Grazina Frame, Frank Tregear, Arthur Tolcher, Lillian Padmore, Michael Mulcaster, Stanley Mason, Janet Webb |
| 3 June 1971 | Glenda Jackson, Mary Hopkin, Ronnie Hilton, Ann Hamilton, Janet Webb |
| 17 June 1971 | Ian Carmichael, Matt Monro, Kiki Dee, Peter & Alex, Ann Hamilton, Janet Webb |
| 15 July 1971 | Trio Athenee, Kenny Ball, Ann Hamilton, Design, Rex Rashley, Gerald Case, Janet Webb |

### Series 6 (BBC1)

| | |
|---|---|
| 19 September 1971 | Francis Matthews, Anita Harris, Robert Young, Ann Hamilton, Janet Webb |
| 26 September 1971 | Keith Michell, Design, Ann Hamilton, Janet Webb |
| 3 October 1971 | Cilla Black, Connie Carroll, Percy Thrower, Ann Hamilton, Janet Webb |
| 10 October 1971 | John Mills, Mrs Mills, Trio Athenee, Ann Hamilton, Kenny Ball, Arnold Diamond, Tony Melody, Janet Webb |
| 17 October 1971 | Nina, The Pattersons, Kenny Ball, Ann Hamilton, Christine Shaw, Frank Tregear, Janet Webb |
| 31 October 1971 | Tom Jones, Design, Ann Hamilton, Kenny Ball, Gordon Clyde, Rex Rashley, Janet Webb |
| 25 December 1971 | Shirley Bassey, Glenda Jackson, Francis Matthews, André Previn, Ann Hamilton, Los Zafiros, Kenneth Hendel, Rex Rashley, Arthur Tolcher, Ken Alexis, Dick Emery, Frank Bough, Robert Dougall, Cliff Michelmore, Patrick Moore, Michael Parkinson, Eddie Waring, Janet Webb |
| 25 December 1972 | Glenda Jackson, Jack Jones, Vera Lynn, Pete Murray, Shirley Bassey, André Previn, Ann Hamilton, Kenny Ball, Ian |

Carmichael, Fenella Fielding, Eric Porter, Flora Robson, Janet Webb

## Series 7 (BBC1)

| | |
|---|---|
| 5 January 1973 | Cliff Richard, Vikki Carr, Ann Hamilton |
| 12 January 1973 | Robert Morley, Vicky Leandros, Ann Hamilton, New World |
| 19 January 1973 | Lulu, Rostal Schaefer, Henry Cooper, Ann Hamilton |
| 26 January 1973 | Susan Hampshire, Georgie Fame, Alan Price, Ann Hamilton, The Settlers |
| 2 February 1973 | Frank Finlay, Wilma Reading, Ann Hamilton, Design |
| 9 February 1973 | Helen Reddy, Alex Welsh and His Band |
| 16 February 1973 | Anita Harris, Reg Lye, Anthony Sharp, Ann Hamilton |
| 23 February 1973 | Wilma Reading, Ann Hamilton, Springfield Revival |
| 2 March 1973 | Hannah Gordon, Mary Travers, Christopher Neil, Ann Hamilton, Raymond Mason, Hatti Riemer, Anthony Sharp, Christine Shaw |
| 9 March 1973 | Roy Castle, Pete Murray, Anna Murphy, Ann Hamilton, The Pattersons |
| 16 March 1973 | Nana Mouskouri, The Black and White Minstrels, Harry Corbett and Sooty, George Hamilton IV, Ann Hamilton |
| 23 March 1973 | Peter Cushing, Wilma Reading, Alan Price, Ann Hamilton |
| 25 December 1973 | Vanessa Redgrave, Hannah Gordon, John Hanson, The New Seekers, Yehudi Menuhin, Rudolf Nureyev, Laurence Olivier, André Previn, Ann Hamilton |

## Series 8 (BBC1)

| | |
|---|---|
| 27 September 1974 | André Previn, Magnus Magnusson, Mrs Mills, Ann Hamilton, Wilma Reading, Arthur Tolcher |
| 4 October 1974 | Ludovic Kennedy, Wilma Reading, Ann Hamilton |
| 11 October 1974 | The Syd Lawrence Orchestra, Wilma Reading, Ann Hamilton |
| 18 October 1974 | Richard Baker, Wilma Reading, Ann Hamilton |
| 25 October 1974 | Hughie Green, David Dimbleby, Wilma Reading, Ann Hamilton |
| 1 November 1974 | June Whitfield, Wilma Reading, Ann Hamilton |
| 25 December 1975 | Diana Rigg, Des O'Connor, Gordon Jackson, Robin Day, Ann Hamilton |

## Series 9 (BBC1)

| | |
|---|---|
| 7 January 1976 | Peter O'Sullivan, Gilbert O'Sullivan, Dilys Watling, The Vernons, Arthur Tolcher |
| 14 January 1976 | Michele Dotrice, Frankie Vaughan, Patrick Moore |
| 11 February 1976 | Lena Zavaroni, The Spinners, Allan Cuthbertson, Ann Hamilton |
| 10 March 1976 | Jackie Damell, Allan Cuthbertson, Anthony Sharp, Ann Hamilton |
| 24 March 1976 | The Karlins, Vincent Zarra, Ann Hamilton |
| 19 April 1976 | Diane Solomon, Champagne, Maggie Fitzgibbon, Ann Hamilton |
| 25 December 1976 | Elton John, Angela Rippon, John Thaw, Dennis Waterman, Kate O'Mara, Marion Montgomery, The Nolans |
| 25 December 1977 | Penelope Keith, Elton John, Francis Matthews, Arthur Lowe, John Le Mesurier, John Laurie, Richard Briers, Paul Eddington, Angharad Rees, Stella Starr, Angela Rippon, Michael Aspel, Richard Baker, Frank Bough, Philip Jenkinson, Kenneth Kendall, Barry Norman, Eddie Waring, Richard Whitmore, Peter Woods, Sandra Dainty, Jenny Lee-Wright, Valerie Leon |

# List of Performances

**The Morecambe and Wise Show** (THAMES)

*Specials*

| | |
|---|---|
| 18 October 1978 | Donald Sinden, Judi Dench, Leonard Sachs, Peter Cushing, Derek Griffiths, Ann Hamilton, Kenneth Watson, The Syd Lawrence Orchestra |
| 25 December 1978 | Leonard Rossiter, Frank Finlay, Harold Wilson, Jenny Hanley, Anna Dawson, Frank Coda, Jan Hunt, Jilliane Foot |
| 25 December 1979 | David Frost, Glenda Jackson, Des O'Connor |

*Series 1*

| | |
|---|---|
| 3 September 1980 | Terry Wogan, Ann Hamilton |
| 10 September 1980 | Hannah Gordon, Hugh Paddick, Frank Coda |
| 17 September 1980 | Dave Prowse, Anthony Chinn, Raymond Mason, Fiesta Mei Ling |
| 24 September 1980 | Deryck Guyler, Gerald Case |
| 1 October 1980 | Suzanne Danielle, Valerie Minifie |
| 8 October 1980 | Gemma Craven |
| 25 December 1980 | Peter Barkworth, Peter Cushing, Jill Gascoigne, Alec Guinness, Peter Vaughan, Gemma Craven |

*Series 2*

| | |
|---|---|
| 1 September 1981 | Gemma Craven, Kate Lock, Kay Korda |
| 8 September 1981 | Richard Vernon |
| 15 September 1981 | Diane Keen |
| 22 September 1981 | George Chisholm |
| 29 September 1981 | Peter Bowles, Suzanne Danielle, Faith Brown, April Walker |
| 6 October 1981 | Robert Hardy, Ian Ogilvy, Kay Korda |
| 13 October 1981 | Joanna Lumley, Richard Vernon |
| 23 December 1981 | Ralph Richardson, Robert Hardy, Suzannah York |

*Series 3*

| | |
|---|---|
| 27 October 1982 | Richard Briers, Diana Dors, Bonnie Langford, Peter Salmon |
| 3 November 1982 | Trevor Eve, Wayne Sleep, Jimmy Young, Penny Meredith |
| 10 November 1982 | Roy Castle, Peter Salmon |
| 17 November 1982 | Colin Welland, Isla St Clair |
| 24 November 1982 | Patricia Brake, Royce Mills |
| 1 December 1982 | Alan Dobie, Marian Montgomery, Kay Korda |
| 8 December 1982 | Nigel Hawthorne, Patricia Brake |
| 27 December 1982 | Robert Hardy, Rula Lenska, Richard Vernon, Wall Street Crash, Diana Dors, Denis Healey, Glenda Jackson, André Previn, Jimmy Young |

*Series 4*

| | |
|---|---|
| 7 September 1983 | Margaret Courtenay, Anna Dawson, Maggie Moone |
| 14 September 1983 | David Keman, Jenny Lee-Wright |
| 21 September 1983 | Cherry Gillespie, Anita Graham, Penny Meredith |
| 28 September 1983 | Stutz Bear Cats, Denise Kelly |
| 5 October 1983 | Cherry Gillespie, Anita Graham, Penny Meredith |
| 12 October 1983 | Margaret Courtenay, Stutz Bear Cats, Peter & Jackie Fimani |
| 19 October 1983 | Harry Fowler, Peter Finn, Valerie Minifie |
| 26 December 1983 | Gemma Craven, Nigel Hawthorne, Derek Jacobi, Felicity Kendal, Burt Kwouk, Tony Monopoly, Fulton Mackay, Jennie Linden, Patrick Mower, Nanette Newman, Peter Skellern |

# List of Performances

## MOVIES

V signifies the existence of a copy of the movie on videocassette

### The Intelligence Men (US: Spylarks), Rank, 1965
| | |
|---|---|
| *Director* | Robert Asher |
| *Screenplay* | Sid Green and Dick Hills, based on a story by Peter Blackmore |
| *Cinematography* | Jack Asher |
| *Editor* | Gerry Hambling |
| *Cast* | Eric Morecambe, Ernie Wise, William Franklyn, Terence Alexander, Francis Matthews, April Olrich, Gloria Paul, Richard Vernon, David Lodge, Jacqueline Jones, Warren Mitchell, Brian Oulton, Michael Peake, Peter Bull, Tutte Lemkow, Rene Sartoris, Graham Smith, Dilys Rosser, Johnny Briggs, Elizabeth Counsell, Gerard Hely, Joe Melia, George Roderick |
| *Running Time* | 104 minutes. V. |

### That Riviera Touch, Rank, 1966
| | |
|---|---|
| *Director* | Cliff Owen |
| *Screenplay* | Sid Green, Dick Hills and Peter Blackmore, based on a story by Peter Blackmore |
| *Cinematography* | Otto Heller |
| *Editor* | Gerry Hambling |
| *Cast* | Eric Morecambe, Ernie Wise, Suzanne Lloyd, Paul Stassino, Armand Mestral, George Eugeniou, George Pastell, Peter Jeffrey, Gerald Lawson, Michael Forrest, Clive Cazes, Steven Scott, Paul Danquah, Francis Matthews, Alexandra Bastedo, Nicole Shelby |
| *Running Time* | 98 minutes. V. |

### The Magnificent Two (US: What Happened at Campo Grande), Rank, 1967
| | |
|---|---|
| *Director* | Cliff Owen |
| *Screenplay* | Sid Green, Dick Hills, Michael Pertwee and Peter Blackmore, based on a story by Michael Pertwee |
| *Cinematography* | Ernest Steward |
| *Editor* | Gerry Hambling |
| *Cast* | Eric Morecambe, Ernie Wise, Margit Saad, Virgilio Teixeira, Cecil Parker, Isobel Black, Martin Benson, Michael Godfrey, Sue Sylvaine, Henry Beltran, Tyler Butterworth, Sandor Eles, Andreas Malandrinos, Victor Maddern, Michael Gover, Charles Laurence, Larry Taylor, David Charlesworth, Hugo De Vernier, Sara Luzita, Bettine Le Beau, Aubrey Morris, Carlos Douglas, Anna Gilchrist, Catherine Griller |
| *Running Time* | 100 minutes. V. |

### Simon, Simon, Denouement Films/Shillingford Associates, 1970
| | |
|---|---|
| *Director* | Graham Stark |
| *Screenplay* | Graham Stark, based on an idea by Graham Stark |
| *Cinematographers* | Derek Vanlint, Harvey Harrison |
| *Editor* | Bunny Warren |
| *Cast* | Graham Stark, John Junkin, Julia Foster, Norman Rossington, Kenneth Earl, David Hemmings, Paul Whitsun-Jones, Peter Sellers, Michael Caine, Eric Morecambe, Ernie Wise, Bernie Winters, Bob Monkhouse, Pete Murray, Tony Blackburn, Tommy Godfrey |
| *Running Time* | 30 minutes |

**Night Train to Murder,** Euston Films, 1985

| | |
|---|---|
| *Director* | Joe McGrath |
| *Screenplay* | Morecambe and Wise and Joe McGrath, based on an idea by Morecambe and Wise |
| *Cinematography* | Adrian Fearnley |
| *Editor* | Dave Lewington |
| *Cast* | Eric Morecambe, Ernie Wise, Lysette Anthony, Fulton Mackay, Roger Brierly, Pamela Salem, Kenneth Haigh, Richard Vernon, Edward Judd, Ben Aris, Tony Boncza, Frank Coda, Robert Longden, Penny Meredith, Tim Stern, Zoe Nicholas, Michelle Tascher |
| *Running Time* | 79 minutes. V. |

## RECORDS

An asterisk denotes that the recording has been deleted.

### Singles

'We're The Guys'/'Me and My Shadow' (HMV POP 957), 1961★
'Boom Oo Yatta-Ta-Ta'/'Why Did I Let You Go?' (HMV POP 1240), 1963★
'A Wassailing'/'The Happiest Christmas Of All' (HMV POP 1373), 1964★
'That Riviera Touch'/'Now That You're Here' (HMV POP 1518), 1966★
'12 Days of Xmas'/'Bingle Jells' (Pye 7N 17436), 1967★
'Bring Me Sunshine'/'Just Around The Corner' (Columbia D B 8 646), 1969★
'(We Get Along So Easily) Don't You Agree?'/'Positive Thinking' (EMI 2475), 1976★

### LPs

*Mr Morecambe Meets Mr Wise* (HMV CLP 1682/EMI ECCS 46), 1964/1997
*An Evening With Ernie Wise at Eric Morecambe's Place* (Wing WL 1217), 1966★
*Get Out of That!* (Philips 6382 005/7176 024), 1966/1997
*Bring You Sunshine* (EMI SRS 5066), 1971★
*Morecambe and Wise Sing Flanagan and Allen* (Mercury 6308 059/6382 095) 1971★
*It's Morecambe and Wise* (BBC REB 128M), 1975★
*What Do You Think of the Show So Far?* (BBC REB 210), 1976
*Weekend Sounds* (BBC REC 258), 1982★
*Get Out of That* (EMI WORD 2022), 1993
*Bring Me Sunshine* (ZBBC 1611), 1994
*What Do You Think Of It So Far?*, vol. 2 (ZBBC 1734), 1997
*You Can't See the Join* (ZBBC 2134), 1998

# Notes

Opening epigraph: Penelope Gilliat, *To Wit: In Celebration of Comedy* (London: Weidenfeld, 1990), p.4.

## PROLOGUE

Eric and Ernie: *The Morecambe & Wise Show* (BBC), written by Eddie Braben.

David Thomson: 'Dennis Potter', *A Biographical Dictionary of Film*, revised edn. (London: Deutsch, 1994), p. 594.

W. H. Auden: *The Dyer's Hand and Other Essays* (London: Faber, 1963), p. 372.

1. Daily Viewing Barometer for 25 December 1977, BBC Written Archives Centre (WAC). This figure, as was so often the case during the period in question, was disputed by ITV.

2. The BBC began television experiments in 1932, and introduced the world's first regular high-definition television service on 2 November 1936.

3. BBC Audience Research Report (WAC: YR/77/701, 14 February 1978). For an account of how these reports were compiled, see chapter 6 and Roger Silvey, *Who's Listening: The Story of BBC Audience Research* (London: Allen & Unwin, 1974).

4. Prince Philip revealed this fact to both Morecambe (according to Joan Morecambe, in an interview with the author, 11 November 1997) and Wise (according to Wise's autobiography, *Still on My Way to Hollywood* [London: Duckworth, 1990], pp. 130–1) during a conversation in the late seventies.

5. J. W. W. Reith, *Broadcast over Britain* (London: Hodder, 1924), p. 34 (my italics). Cf. Frank Muir's spirited pamphlet, *Comedy in Television* (London: BBC, 1966).

6. As is, alas, so often the case today: consider, for example, some of the most popular entertainment shows broadcast by the BBC during the late nineties: *Men Behaving Badly* (made by Hartswood, and 'transferred' *in toto* to BBC1 after starting off on ITV); *Harry Enfield and Chums* (Tiger Aspect); and *Have I Got News for You* (Hat Trick). When, on 18 April 1998, BBC2 screened a special interview with Spike Milligan – one of the artists most closely associated with the BBC's past achievements in this area – it did so with a programme produced for it by Thames/Pearson Television.

7. Quoted by John Edwards, *Daily Mail*, 13 December 1984, p. 20.

8. Kenneth Tynan, 'The Top Joker', *Observer Magazine*, 9 September 1973, p. 20. By 'oeillade' Tynan was referring to Morecambe's sly wink to the camera.

9. Tynan, 'The Top Joker', p. 20.

10. They won the *Sun*'s 'most popular entertainers' award on more than one occasion.

11. The 'trick', resorted to by Eric Morecambe whenever he sensed a lull in the proceedings, involved him producing a carefully folded paper bag from the inside pocket of his jacket, unfolding it slowly, throwing an imaginary stone in the air and then 'catching' it in the bag (flicking the bag between forefinger and thumb to create the impression that something really had landed inside). According to Wise's autobiography (p. 131), the

Queen Mother asked for guidance on this subject, although, he added somewhat ruefully, she did not say if her intention was 'to pull this gag out of the hat on ceremonial occasions to break the ice'.

12.    Eric Morecambe died of a heart attack on 28 May 1984 (see Chapter 16). Ernie Wise fell ill during a Caribbean cruise at the end of November 1998. After suffering two strokes and a heart attack he was rushed to Northridge Medical Centre in Fort Lauderdale, Florida. Four days after admission he suffered a second attack. On 24 January 1999 he underwent a triple bypass operation and, early the following month, he was flown back to England by air ambulance to recuperate at the Nuffield Hospital in Wexham Park near Slough. However, after contracting pneumonia he died of heart failure at around 7 am on Sunday 21 March 1999 (see the *Finanacial Times*, 22 March 1999, p. 14 and the *Daily Telegraph*, 23 March 1999, p. 23).

### MUSIC-HALL

Ernie Wise: quoted by Byron Rogers, 'Morecambe and Wise', *Sunday Telegraph Magazine*, 14 September 1980, p. 37.

### Chapter 1

Eric Morecambe: *There's No Answer to That!*, p. 36.

Ernie Wise: Ibid., p. 34.

1.    Wherever possible, surnames will be used when referring specifically to the off-screen lives, and first names when discussing the on-screen personae. For further information on the lives and careers, see Gary Morecambe and Martin Sterling's *Morecambe and Wise: Behind the Sunshine* (London: Pan, 1995), Joan Morecambe's *Morecambe and Wife* (London: Pelham, 1985), Ernie Wise's *Still on My Way to Hollywood* (London: Duckworth, 1990) and Morecambe and Wise's two volumes of ghostwritten autobiography, *Eric & Ernie* (London: W. H. Allen, 1973) and *There's No Answer to That!* (London: Arthur Barker, 1981). For details relating specifically to the private lives, see Gary Morecambe's very engaging *Funny Man* (London: Methuen, 1982) and Gail Morecambe's brief but very appealing memoir in Gary Morecambe and Michael Sellers' *Hard Act to Follow* (London: Blake, 1997). Two articles among the secondary literature stand out as essential: Kenneth Tynan's typically insightful celebration of Eric Morecambe's comic talent, 'The Top Joker', in the *Observer Magazine*, 9 September 1973, pp. 20–23, and reprinted in the posthumous collection *Profiles* (London: Nick Hern, 1989), and Byron Rogers' perceptive feature article on Morecambe and Wise for the *Sunday Telegraph Magazine*, 14 September 1980, pp. 36–43.

The address of the Morecambe and Wise Fan Club is: c/o Dave Miles, 11 Victoria Parade, Morecambe, Lancashire, LA4 5NX.

2.    J. B. Priestley, *An English Journey* (London: Mandarin, 1994), p. 253.

3.    Ibid., p. 253.

4.    I am grateful to Mike Craig for reminding me of these particular phrases. His two volumes of profiles, *Look Back With Laughter* (Manchester: Mike Craig Enterprises, 1996), contain some interesting accounts of the traditional distinctiveness of Northern humour.

5.    Priestley, *An English Journey*, p. 253.

6.    Ibid., p. 254.

7.    It is surely not entirely coincidental that these particular performers enjoyed exceptional popularity in Lancashire. Harry Worth came to be thought of by television viewers as a Northerner rather than a Yorkshireman; Albert Modley settled in Morecambe and was known as 'Lancashire's Favourite Yorkshireman'; and Dave Morris lived for so long in Blackpool that many people believed he was a native of the place.

8.    It is beyond the scope of this book to discuss the intricacies of all the heated scholarly debates on this subject, save to note the irony of a cultural form as irreverent as music-hall attracting such an extraordinary number of humourless pedants. Nothing is uncontentious

(not even the lower-case 'm' and 'h' of music-hall, nor the hyphen), but the more thoughtful historians tend to put the beginning of music-hall at somewhere between 1830 and the early 1850s (Bolton's Star Music Hall opened in 1832, and Charles Morton opened London's first hall, the Canterbury Music Hall in Westminster Bridge Road, in 1852), and most put its eclipse by Variety at somewhere between 1900 and 1920. Music-hall was composed of up to twenty individual 'turns' introduced by a 'Chairman', who also controlled the boisterous working-class audience. Variety was composed of eight to ten individual 'acts', presented in rapid succession without the intervention of any compere, and it attracted a slightly broader audience in terms of social class. Valantyne Napier's eminently useful *Glossary of Terms Used in Variety, Vaudeville, Revue & Pantomime 1880–1960* (Westbury: The Badger Press, 1996) is a reliable source of information by a well-respected veteran Variety performer. Roger Wilmut's *Kindly Leave the Stage! The Story of Variety 1919–1960* (London: Methuen, 1985) and *Roy Hudd's Cavalcade of Variety Acts* (London: Robson, 1997) are two accessible accounts, while *Music Hall: Performance and Style*, edited by J. S. Bratton (Milton Keynes: Open University Press, 1986) and G. J. Mellor's much more readable *The Northern Music Hall* (Newcastle upon Tyne: Frank Graham, 1970) provide more specialised historical surveys and analyses; John Fisher's *Funny Way to be a Hero* (London: Frederick Muller, 1973) is a serious and entertaining history via a series of well-written profiles of the most distinctive performers.

9.  Quoted by Alix Coleman, 'They'll Always be Eric and Ernie', *TV Times*, 2 October 1980, pp. 16–17.

10.  Eric Morecambe and Ernie Wise, *Bring Me Sunshine: A Harvest of Morecambe & Wise* (London: William Kimber, 1978), p. 106.

11.  Quoted in the *TV Times*, 14–20 October 1978, p. 27.

12.  Robb Wilton: this version taken from the 78 r.p.m. recording (Sterno 851, 1931).

13.  Quoted by Wilmut, *Kindly Leave the Stage*, p. 31.

14.  Quoted by G. J. Mellor, *They Made Us Laugh* (Littleborough: George Kelsall, 1982), p. 24.

15.  Quoted by Fisher, *Funny Way to be a Hero*, p. 169.

16.  Quoted by Craig, *Look Back with Laughter*, vol. 2, p. 8.

17.  Transcribed from a recording of *The Al Read Show*, first broadcast by the BBC on 25 November 1954.

18.  Quoted by Wilmut, *Kindly Leave the Stage*, p. 169.

19.  Quoted by Wilmut, ibid., p. 207.

20.  Recalled by James's son, James Casey. Quoted by Stephen Dixon in the *Guardian*, 17 February 1975, p. 8.

21.  Quoted by Wilmut, *Kindly Leave the Stage*, p. 90.

22.  *Eric & Ernie*, p. 131.

## Chapter 2

Eric Morecambe: *There's No Answer to That!*, p. 67.

1.  See Eric Morecambe, 'My Happiest Days', published posthumously in the *Daily Mirror*, 29 May 1984, p. 9.

2.  He objected to Kenneth Tynan's description of Ernie Wise (in his 1973 'The Top Joker' profile) as having come from 'a lower social level' than himself. Writing in *The Listener* ('A Freudian Year for Ernie and Me', 20 December 1973, pp. 837–8), he insisted that, 'We both came from ordinary working-class families: that's why we keep our sense of values.'

3.  Eric Morecambe, *Eric and Ernie*, p. 6.

4.  The Bartholomews were staying temporarily at 42 Buxton Street – the home of Minnie Woodford and her family – while their own house underwent some alterations. Up until the late seventies, Eric Morecambe always referred to number 48 Buxton Street as his birthplace; from the late seventies onwards, however, he appeared, after a visit back

home to Morecambe, to have grown unsure of this fact, telling interviewers that he may have been born at number *45* Buxton Street. His birth certificate, however, confirms the place of birth as number 42.

On 7 August 1997 the Morecambe and Wise Fan Club unveiled a commemorative plaque on the front of number 42 Buxton Street to mark the 'official' birthplace of Eric Morecambe. Gary and Joan Morecambe, however, tell me that they remain unsure about the correct location. 'Let me just say', said Joan (interview with the author, 11 November 1997), 'that Eric always, *always*, was convinced that he'd been born at number 48 – that's the house he went back to and recognised as his home. I know the mind can play tricks, given the passage of time, but he *really* believed number 48 was the house.'

5. *Eric & Ernie*, p. 7.

6. In *Eric & Ernie* (p. 7) he says he 'could not have been more than nine or ten months old', while in 'Summer Place', *Sunday Times Magazine*, 11 July 1976, p. 46, he says he would have been 'eight months old'.

7. 'Summer Place', p. 46.

8. *Eric & Ernie*, p. 7.

9. Ibid.

10. Ibid., pp. 7–8.

11. Ibid., p. 8.

12. Ibid., p. 9.

13. *There's No Answer to That!*, p. 22.

14. Joan Morecambe (interview with author, 11 November 1997).

15. 'Summer Place', p. 46.

16. *Eric & Ernie*, pp. 6–7.

17. 'My Happiest Days', p. 9.

18. Ibid.

19. Nikolaus Pevsner, *The Buildings of England: North Lancashire* (London: Penguin, 1969), p. 27.

20. 'Summer Place', p. 46.

21. Ibid.

22. Ibid.

23. Ibid. Sydney Howard's other movies included *Splinters* (1929), *Once a Crook* (1941), *When We are Married* (1943) and, his one Hollywood appearance (alongside Jack Benny), *Transatlantic Merry-Go-Round* (1934). Born in Yorkshire in 1884, his career was relatively brief, but – during the 1930s at least – his box-office appeal as a somewhat mournful comic character was rather strong. He died, from a heart attack, in 1946.

24. 'Summer Place', p. 46.

25. Ibid.

26. *Eric & Ernie*, p. 10.

27. See the reports reproduced in Gary Morecambe's *The Illustrated Morecambe* (London: Macdonald, 1986) on page 26. Atrocious though they are, Eric's marks for Reading, at least, are perfectly respectable, and, as Gary points out, it was his failure to attend on a regular basis, rather than any serious intellectual shortcomings, that was the root of the problem.

28. 'Summer Place', p. 46.

29. Quoted by Gary Morecambe, *Morecambe and Wise*, p. 16.

30. See Gary Morecambe, *The Illustrated Morecambe*, p. 26.

31. Ibid.

32. *Eric & Ernie*, p. 10.

33. Interview with the author, 11 November 1997.

34. *Eric & Ernie*, p. 6.

35. *There's No Answer to That!*, p. 76.

36. Interview with the author, 11 November 1997.

37. Quoted by John Mortimer, 'Eric Morecambe, without a Peer', *Sunday Times*, 16 December 1979, p. 32.

38. There are innumerable sources for, and versions of, this story: one published version can be found in *Roy Hudd's Book of Music-Hall, Variety and Showbiz Anecdotes* (London: Robson, 1994), p. 154.

39. George Orwell, *The Road to Wigan Pier* (Harmondsworth: Penguin, 1989), p. 139.

40. See *Eric & Ernie*, p. 100.

41. Quoted by Anne Edwards in the *Sunday Express*, 6 June 1971, p. 6.

42. *Eric & Ernie*, p. 10.

43. Transcribed from Mike Craig's 1976 recorded interview with Eric Morecambe (the majority of which was broadcast on BBC Radio 2 on 26 July 1976 as part of the series *It's a Funny Business*).

44. See Mortimer, 'Eric Morecambe without a Peer', p. 32; Gary Morecambe, *Morecambe and Wise*, pp. 18–19; and *Eric & Ernie*, pp. 12–15.

45. See Mortimer, 'Eric Morecambe without a Peer', p. 32.

46. Transcribed from Mike Craig's 1976 interview with Eric Morecambe.

47. Ibid.

48. *Eric & Ernie*, p. 13.

49. Ibid.

50. Transcribed from Mike Craig's 1976 interview with Eric Morecambe.

51. Ibid.

52. Ibid.

53. *Eric & Ernie*, p. 10.

54. Quoted by Gary Morecambe, *Hard Act to Follow*, p. 138.

55. *Morecambe and Wise*, p. 18.

56. Interview with the author, 11 November 1997.

57. See *Eric & Ernie*, p. 6.

58. Gary Morecambe, *Morecambe and Wise*, p. 19.

59. Gary Morecambe, *The Illustrated Morecambe*, p. 19.

60. Transcribed from Mike Craig's 1976 interview.

61. Quoted by Gary Morecambe, *Morecambe and Wise*, p. 19.

**Chapter 3**

Ernie Wise: his standard phrase that opened every edition of *The Morecambe & Wise Show*.

1. Ernie Wise, *Eric & Ernie*, p. 19. Another invaluable source of information on his early years is his autobiography, *Still on My Way to Hollywood*, pp. 21–38.

2. *There's No Answer to That!*, p. 30.

3. This is certainly the impression given by the vast majority of Wise's recorded remarks about his mother, but one should note that in *Eric & Ernie*, (p. 20) he described her as 'a lovely little person, with a big smile, always brimming over with enthusiasm, and pure Yorkshire'.

4. *Still on My Way to Hollywood*, p. 21.

5. *Eric & Ernie*, p. 17.

6. Ibid.

7. *Bring Me Sunshine*, p. 118.

8. *Still on My Way to Hollywood*, p. 22.

9. Ibid.

10. Ibid., p. 24.

11. Ibid.

12. Ibid., p. 24. See also pp. 28, 36 and 37.

13. Recalled by Ernie Wise, *Eric & Ernie*, p. 20.

14. Ibid., pp. 20–21.

15. Ibid., p. 21.

16. *Still on My Way to Hollywood*, p. 30.

17. Ibid., pp. 28–9.

18. Ibid., p. 31.

19. *There's No Answer to That!*, p. 76.

20. *Still on My Way to Hollywood*, p. 28.

21. *There's No Answer to That!*, p. 119.

22. *Still on My Way to Hollywood*, p. 32.

23. Ibid., p. 36.

24. Ibid., pp. 36–7.

25. Ibid., p. 34.

26. Ibid., p. 35.

27. *Eric & Ernie*, p. 26.

28. *Still on My Way to Hollywood*, p. 39.

29. Ernie Wise, both in *Eric & Ernie* (p. 28) and *Still on My Way to Hollywood* (p. 39), says he arrived in London on Friday 7 January. The date that Friday was actually 6 January, and so the reviews the next morning actually appeared, of course, in papers dated 7 January.

30. *Still on My Way to Hollywood*, p. 39.

31. Report by the 'Theatre Reporter', 'Porter's Son in West End Show', *Daily Express*, 7 January 1939, p. 15.

32. Interviewed by Stewart Knowles for 'Eric and Ernie: Six of the Nicest Men You Could Wish to Meet', *TV Times*, 9–15 December 1978, p. 14. See also Arthur Askey's autobiography, *Before Your Very Eyes* (London: Woburn Press, 1975), pp. 103–4.

33. *Still on My Way to Hollywood*, p. 43.

34. Ibid., p. 41.

35. Ibid.

36. Quoted in the *Daily Express*, 7 January 1939, p. 15.

37. Quoted by Stewart Knowles, 'Eric and Ernie . . .'

38. *Still on My Way to Hollywood*, p. 45.

39. Ibid., p. 45.

40. Ibid., p. 47.

41. Ibid.

42. Ibid.

43. Ibid., p. 48.

44. Ibid., p. 49.

45. Ibid.

46. The Wisemans had moved from East Ardsley to 17 Oxley Street, Pontefract Lane, Leeds.

47. *Eric & Ernie*, p. 31.

48. *Still on My Way to Hollywood*, p. 50.

**Chapter 4**

Eric Morecambe: quoted by Lewis Chester, 'Wise, after the event', *Sunday Times*, 8 September 1985, p. 8.

Ernie Wise: quoted by Byron Rogers, 'Morecambe and Wise', p. 44.

1.  See Ernie Wise, *Still on My Way to Hollywood*, pp. 51–2.

2.  Eric Morecambe, *Eric & Ernie*, p. 15.

3.  Recounted by Eric Morecambe, ibid, p. 35. For Ernie Wise's (similar) version of that evening's occurrences, see *Still on My Way to Hollywood*, p. 52.

4.  *Eric & Ernie*, p. 36.

5.  *Still on My Way to Hollywood*, p. 52.

6.  Interview with the author, 11 November 1997.

7.  *Still on My Way to Hollywood*, p. 53.

8.  Ibid., pp. 52–3.

9.  *Eric & Ernie*, p. 39.

10. Ibid.

11. Ibid.

12. Ibid.

13. Ibid., p. 40.

14. It is not entirely certain what the song was that it replaced. Both *Eric & Ernie* (p. 39) and Gary Morecambe's *Morecambe and Wise* (p. 27) suggest that it was 'By the Light of the Silvery Moon', but Eric Morecambe, in his 1976 interview with Mike Craig (*It's a Funny Business*, BBC Radio 2, 26 July 1976), recalled them singing the lines, 'How's about a little ramble in the moonlight/How's about a little cuddle down the lane . . .'

15. This is the first time that the precise date of their début as a double-act has been recorded. Sadie Bartholomew (in *Eric & Ernie*, p. 40) said: 'None of us can remember the date except that it was a Friday night at the Liverpool Empire in 1941.' I consulted every issue of *The Stage* for that year, and the only time the 'Bryan Michie's *Youth Takes a Bow*' is listed as having been performed at the Liverpool Empire during 1941 is the week of Monday 25 August to Friday 29 August. The first half of the bill was entitled 'Jack Hylton presents *Secrets of the BBC*', and among those performers listed in the second half were Celia Lipton, Archie Glen, Alice and Rosie Lloyd, Nick Cardello, Jack Melville and Roy Verk.

16. *Eric & Ernie*, pp. 40–41.

17. According to Sadie Bartholomew's account (*Eric & Ernie*, p. 41), the tour went on from Liverpool to Glasgow. The relevant issue of *The Stage*, however, reveals that the Hylton/Michie production went from Liverpool to Edinburgh on 1 September 1941 (it had visited Glasgow during the last week of July).

18. *Eric & Ernie*, p. 41.

19. Ibid.

20. *Still on My Way to Hollywood*, p. 53.

21. *Eric & Ernie*, p. 41.

22. See *There's No Answer to That!*, p. viii.

23. The character's first appearance on Benny's radio show was as 'Rochester Van Jones'; later on he was just called 'Rochester'. The name was chosen in part because Jack Benny thought it sounded 'English', and, indeed, Benita Hume, the wife of Ronald Colman, always called Eddie Anderson 'Manchester' by mistake. See Jack and Joan Benny, *Sunday Nights at Seven* (New York: Warner, 1990), pp. 102–8, and Mary Livingstone Benny, *Jack Benny* (London: Robson, 1978, p. 76).

24. See the *Daily Mirror*, 29 May 1984, p. 4.

25. Even, surprisingly, by the BBC – see, for example, the on-screen introduction to the video *Morecambe & Wise's Musical Extravangazas* (1994).

26.   Recalled by Ernie Wise in *Bring Me Sunshine*, p. 151. It was a typical kind of question used by compères on these occasions, such as 'Who goes with Flanagan?' 'Allen.' 'Who goes with Abbott?' 'Costello.'

27.   Quoted in the *Radio Times*, 24 December–6 January 1977–8, p. 7.

28.   See the List of Performances on p. 328.

29.   Ernie Wise, quoted in the *Radio Times*, 24 December 1977, p. 7.

30.   It was called *Rookies* in the UK.

31.   Ernie Wise discusses the origins of the routine before the televised version is shown at approximately 38 minutes into the video *Classic Morecambe & Wise*, vol. 1 (Watershed Pictures, 1990).

32.   *Still on My Way to Hollywood*, pp. 18–19.

33.   Neither Eric Morecambe nor Ernie Wise remembered the name of this agent.

34.   The Hippodrome re-opened on 11 September 1985 as the restaurant-cabaret the Talk of the Town.

35.   Recounted by Ernie Wise, *Still on My Way to Hollywood*, p. 58.

36.   Ibid.

37.   *Eric & Ernie*, p. 48.

38.   Taken from the contemporary souvenir programme.

39.   Kenneth Tynan, 'Sid Field' (1950), in *Profiles* (London: Nick Hern Books, 1989), p. 12.

40.   Collie Knox, *People of Quality* (London: Macdonald, 1947), p. 165.

41.   *Eric & Ernie*, p. 49.

42.   Morecambe and Wise, when they came to discuss this show in *Eric & Ernie*, (pp. 51–2), misremembered several details: first, its title was *Youth Must Have Its Swing*, not *Youth Must Have Its Fling*; second, it was broadcast on the BBC's Home Service, not the Light Programme; third, Sid Field *did* take part in at least one of these shows (there were seven in all).

43.   Interview with the author, 20 May 1998.

44.   *Eric & Ernie*, p. 37.

45.   Ibid.

46.   Ernie Wise contributed to a 1980 Southern Television documentary on ENSA entitled *Every Night Something Atrocious*.

47.   Eric Morecambe recalled some of his experiences during this period in a BBC Radio 4 programme entitled *What Did You Do In The War, Daddy?* (first broadcast on 19 September 1969; a copy is preserved in the BBC's Sound Archive).

48.   See *Still on My Way to Hollywood*, p. 64.

49.   In *Eric & Ernie*, (p. 55), Eric Morecambe said that his mother took him to London *after* having seen the advertisement in *The Stage* for Lord John Sanger's circus. In later interviews, however, he said that the advertisement was noticed after they had settled in London.

50.   This is all rather puzzling. In *Eric & Ernie* – which, as it was Morecambe and Wise's first attempt at an autobiography, was based on the freshest memories – the sequence of events is as follows: Sadie and Eric go to London (p. 55); Eric joins *Lord John Sanger's Circus & Variety* tour (p. 55); he discovers Ernie is also in the show (p. 55); they work together in the show until it disbands in the autumn of 1947; Eric and Sadie next encounter Ernie in Regent Street (p. 62); they move in together with Sadie in Mrs Duer's rooms in Chiswick (p. 62); they begin their search for work in Variety (pp. 63ff).

In the 1976 interview that Eric Morecambe gave to Mike Craig, however, the sequence is different: Sadie and Eric go to London; they encounter Ernie in Regent Street, but go their separate ways; Eric joins Sanger's show, and discovers that Ernie is already in it; they tour together and then return to London and Ernie joins Eric at Mrs Duer's house.

In a third version, recounted in both *Still on My Way to Hollywood*, (pp. 66–73) and

Gary Morecambe's *Morecambe and Wise* (pp. 39–45), the sequence is as follows: Sadie and Eric go to London; they encounter Ernie in Regent Street and invite him to stay with them at Mrs Duer's; Sadie finds both of them work with Sanger; they tour together and then return again to Chiswick.

It is difficult to establish which of the above versions is the most accurate chronological account of these events. The earliest published reference to these events that I have been able to find is in an article by Eric Morecambe ('I only wear glasses 'cos I can't see without them!') in the *People's Journal*, Dundee, dated January 1964 (reproduced in *Bring Me Sunshine*, pp. 115–17); he notes that he did not meet Ernie Wise after the war 'until the day in 1947 when I saw his name on the same bill in Sanger's Circus show'. After considering each account carefully, however, I find the third version to be the most coherent, but I acknowledge that it is not without its own unexplained inconsistencies.

51.  *Eric & Ernie*, p. 62.

52.  The 'Lord' was a sarcatic resonse to Buffalo Bill being referred to as 'the Honourable William Cody' during a legal dispute between the two showmen. The press took up the nickname and Sanger chose to keep it for the rest of his career.

53.  Again, the accounts vary on this point. In both *Eric & Ernie*, and Eric Morecambe's 1976 interview with Mike Craig, both he and Sadie are surprised to learn that the comic's name is Ernie Wise. This suggests – if it is accurate – that Ernie could not yet have been living with them, although how he later came to do so is not made clear by either of these sources.

54.  Taken from the playbill for the 21 April 1947 performance at Byfleet Recreation Ground.

55.  Eric Morecambe, interviewed by Mike Craig.

56.  *Eric & Ernie*, p. 45.

57.  In both *Eric & Ernie* (pp. 64–5) and Gary Morecambe's *Morecambe and Wise* (p. 47), the other act is identified as Vic Wise and Nita Lane, but in Ernie Wise's autobiography (p. 75) it is identified as Campbell and Wise. Both acts featured Vic Wise, but the playbill for 8 March 1948 confirms that his partner, on this occasion, was Nita Lane.

58.  *Eric & Ernie*, p. 67.

59.  Interview with author, 9 December 1997. I am very grateful to Ann Hamilton for correcting several inaccuracies in an earlier version of this chapter.

60.  Ibid.

61.  See Sheila Van Damm, *We Never Closed: The Windmill Story* (London: Robert Hale, 1967), p. 111.

62.  See Harry Secombe, *Arias and Raspberries*, (London: Pan, 1997), p. 134.

63.  Peter Prichard, transcribed from the video entitled *The Golden Years of British Comedy: '40s* (Classic Pictures, 1993). Another common name for the 'Windmill Jump' was the 'Windmill Steeplechase'.

64.  Michael Bentine, ibid.

65.  £25 was hardly generous even by Van Damm's standards. Harry Secombe recalls being paid £20 per week for his solo act three years earlier, see *Arias and Raspberries*, p. 135. Hank and Scott, who were appearing there at the same time as Morecambe and Wise, were receiving £30 per week, see Freddie Hancock, *Hancock* (London: Ariel Books, 1986), p. 36.

66.  Quoted in *Eric & Ernie*, p. 72.

67.  *Still on My Way to Hollywood*, p. 79. See also Van Damm, p. 116.

68.  See *Eric & Ernie*, p. 72.

69.  They refused, however, to allow Van Damm to add their names to his Honours Board once they had become famous, because they objected to the implication that he had been in any way a benign influence on their development, let alone the man who had 'discovered' them.

70.  *Still on My Way to Hollywood*, p. 81.

71.   Performed on their ATV shows during the early sixties and on the 1964 album *Mr Morecambe Meets Mr Wise* (HMV CLP1682 CSD1522).

72.   See Mellor, *The Northern Music Hall*, particularly chapters 6 and 10, for background information on agents, managers and circuits from this period.

73.   The circuit included Bedford Royal County, Norwich Hippodrome, the Grand in Southampton, the Bristol Empire, Aston Hippodrome, Wolverhampton Hippodrome, Boscombe Hippodrome, Burnley Place, York Empire, St Helen's Royal and Grimsby Palace.

74.   Eric Morecambe, quoted by Rogers, 'Morecambe and Wise', p. 41.

75.   *Eric & Ernie*, p. 81.

76.   *Still on My Way to Hollywood*, p. 17.

77.   Ernie Wise, transcribed from the video *Classic Morecambe & Wise*, vol. 3.

78.   See *Radio Times*, 24 December 1977, p. 7.

79.   Harry Secombe, *The Golden Years of British Comedy: '40s*.

80.   Included by Roy Hudd in Roy Hudd's *Book of Music Hall, Variety and Showbiz Anecdotes*, p. 34.

81.   Recounted by Mike Craig, interview with the author, 6 May 1997.

82.   *There's No Answer to That!*, p. 31.

83.   *Eric & Ernie*, p. 82.

84.   Transcribed from Mike Craig's 1976 interview.

85.   *Still on My Way to Hollywood*, p. 9.

86.   *There's No Answer to That!*, p. 31.

87.   Interview with the author, 20 February 1997.

88.   Quoted by Gary Morecambe, *Morecambe and Wise*, p. 30.

89.   *Still on My Way to Hollywood*, p. 17.

90.   See the *Spectator*, 14 January 1949; Asa Briggs, *The History of Broadcasting in the United Kingdom*, 4 vols. (Oxford: Oxford University Press, 1961–1979), vol. 4, p. 712, note 5; and Derek Parker, *Radio: The Great Years* (London: David & Charles, 1977), p. 87.

91.   *There's No Answer to That!* p. 31.

92.   All of the quotations in this paragraph are taken from the BBC's *Green Book*. The complete text is reproduced in Barry Took's *Laughter in the Air: An Informal History of British Radio Comedy* (London: Robson, 1981), pp. 86–91.

93.   Interview with the author, 17 November 1997. See his *A Kentish Lad* (London: Bantam Press, 1997) for a detailed personal account of this period.

94.   Letter written by 'Morecambe and Wise' (but in Wise's handwriting) to Bowker Andrews on 1 July 1949 (BBC WAC, Morecambe and Wise Artists File 1: 1947–54). It was sent from Didsbury.

95.   Morecambe and Wise (*Eric & Ernie*, p. 128) said that they first appeared on both *Workers' Playtime* and *Variety Fanfare* in 1951. I found no record of this in the BBC archives. The date of the first appearance by them on *Workers' Playtime* was, according to the archives, 10 January 1952, and, on *Variety Fanfare*, 13 March 1952 (BBC WAC, Morecambe and Wise Artists File 1: 1947–54).

96.   From 1946 to 1967, BBC Radio offered three separate services nationwide: the Home Service (a broad-based programme designed to 'steadily but imperceptibly raise the standard of taste, entertainment, outlook and citizenship' throughout the United Kingdom); the Light Programme (a slightly more specialised programme that offered an undemanding mixture of popular music, plays and Variety); and the Third Programme (concentrating on 'serious' music and the spoken word). Although the BBC's Home Service provided a basic service of 'network variety' for the nation as a whole, each of the BBC's *regional* Home Services (the North of England, the Midlands, the West of England, Wales, Scotland and the North-East of England/Northern Ireland) had the right to opt out at any time (within reason) and broadcast its *own* shows to its own regional

audience. As far as the Northern Home Service was concerned, therefore, shows made in Manchester such as *Variety Fanfare* and *You're Only Young Once* were produced, in the first instance, exclusively for its own local audience; such shows would have needed to have been picked up by London and repeated on the nationwide Home Service in order to reach a larger audience. See *The History of Broadcasting in the United Kingdom*, vol. 4, Briggs, pp. 84–117.

97.  Morecambe and Wise (*Eric & Ernie*, p. 129) recalled making 45 editions of *Variety Fanfare*; I found evidence of 18 between 1952 and 1953, and several more between 1954 and 1956. Seven of these shows were recorded on disc (for exclusive use overseas): 16 September, 21 November 1952, 9 January, 30 January, 13 February, 13 March, 27 March 1953.

98.  Transcribed from 1976 Mike Craig interview.

99.  *Still on My Way to Hollywood*, p. 103.

100.  Transcribed from 1976 Mike Craig interview.

101.  See *Eric & Ernie*, pp. 128–9.

102.  'A Freudian Year for Ernie and Me', p. 838. They actually appeared on two editions of the show in 1952.

103.  *Eric & Ernie*, p. 129.

104.  Letter from Morecambe and Wise to Bryan Sears, 28 November 1950 (BBC WAC, Morecambe and Wise Artists File 1: 1947–54).

105.  The note is undated but appears – judging from its position in the file and also from Morecambe and Wise's itinerary – to have been written at some point between 17 and 22 July 1951. The author's identity is unclear: the scribbled note is signed 'HN' or possibly 'HM'. Pat Hillyard may not have known about this judgement, because he replied to Frank Pope on 23 July 1951 saying that he was not sure if any of his producers had seen Morecambe and Wise at the Finsbury Park Empire but that he would like a list of their next set of London engagements (BBC WAC, Morecambe and Wise Artists File 1: 1947–54).

106.  Their letter to Bill Worsley (another London-based BBC producer), dated 7 June 1952, requests a return booking on *Variety Bandbox*, which suggests that they remained committed to the idea of appearing on the show (BBC WAC, Morecambe and Wise Artists File 1: 1947–54).

107.  Andy Foster and Steve Furst, in their otherwise very helpful book *Radio Comedy 1938–1968* (London: Virgin, 1996), include some inaccurate information concerning *You're Only Young Once*: according to their account (pp. 185–6), the show ran for one series on the Northern Home Service between May and June 1954, with a repeat on the Light Programme during July and August. In fact, the show lasted for no fewer than three series: the first produced by Ronnie Taylor between November 1953 and January 1954; the second produced by John Ammonds between May and June 1954; and the third – also produced by Ammonds – between October and December 1954.

108.  Interview with the author, 16 April 1997.

109.  Ibid.

110.  Ibid.

111.  For biographical details, see Joan Morecambe, *Morecambe and Wife*, pp. 21–2.

112.  Interview with the author, 11 November 1997.

113.  Quoted by Gary Morecambe, *Morecambe and Wise*, p. 63.

114.  Interview with the author, 11 November 1997.

115.  Ibid.

116.  Ibid.

117.  *Still on My Way to Hollywood*, p. 108.

118.  Telegram dated 4 November 1953 (BBC WAC, Morecambe and Wise Artists File 1: 1947–54).

119.   George Campey, 'Would You Laugh at These? I Say Yes!', *Evening Standard*, 9 November 1953, p. 6.

120.   Ibid.

121.   Transcribed from 1976 Mike Craig interview.

### TELEVISION

Dennis Potter: 'The James McTaggart Memorial Lecture, 1993', *Seeing the Blossom* (London: Faber, 1994), p. 55.

*Third Rock from the Sun*: written by Michael Glouberman and Andrew Orenstein, YBL Productions, 1997.

### Chapter 5

Ronnie Waldman: 'The Toughest Job', *Radio Times*, 4 December 1953, p. 14.

Eric Maschwitz: quoted in Denis Norden *et al*, *Coming to You Live!* (London: Methuen, 1985), p. 7. (Maschwitz was Head of Light Entertainment at the BBC from 1958 to 1961.)

1.   *There's No Answer to That!*, p. 31.

2.   Ibid.

3.   See Asa Briggs, *The BBC: The First Fifty Years* (Oxford: Oxford University Press, 1985), p. 241.

4.   Roger Silvey, in his *Who's Listening?* (p. 164), notes that the 'Television Public' had risen to 14 per cent of the population of the United Kingdom by October–December 1952, 22 per cent by October–December 1953 and 31 per cent by October–December 1954 (the last period assessed before the end of the monopoly era).

5.   In 1947 the number of people who owned combined Radio & TV licences was 14,560; this had risen to 343,882 by 1950; 763,941 by 1951; 1,449,260 by 1952; 2,142,452 by 1953; 3,248,892 by 1954; and 4,503,766 by 1955 (source: Post Office/National Television Licence Records Office).

6.   Grace Wyndham Goldie, *Facing the Nation: Television & Politics 1936–76* (London: Bodley Head, 1977), p. 46.

7.   Quoted by Francis Wheen, *Television* (London: Century, 1985), p. 226.

8.   See Briggs, *The History of Broadcasting in the United Kingdom*, vol. 4, p. 429.

9.   The *Star*'s judgement appeared on 3 June 1953, and Hope-Wallace's on 6 June 1953 in *Time and Tide*; both are reproduced in Briggs, *The History of Broadcasting in the United Kingdom*, vol. 4, pp. 421 and 428.

10.   Ibid., p. 641.

11.   Sir Ian Jacob, 'The Tasks Before the BBC Today', *The BBC Quarterly*, vol. 9, no. 3 (1954), pp. 132–3.

12.   Quoted by Briggs, *The History of Broadcasting in the United Kingdom*, vol. 4, p. 641.

13.   Broadcast script: quoted at greater length by Briggs, ibid., p. 654.

14.   J. P. W. Mallalieu, 'Looking at Television', *Observer*, 23 May 1954, p. 10.

15.   See Burton Paulu, *British Broadcasting: Radio and Television in the United Kingdom* (Minneapolis: University of Minnesota Press, 1956), p. 284.

16.   Clifford Davis, *Daily Mirror*, 23 April 1954, p. 4.

17.   Quoted by Wilmut, *Kindly Leave the Stage*, p. 213.

18.   According to a memorandum (dated 15 December 1953) from Holland Bennett to Ronnie Waldman (BBC WAC: Morecambe and Wise TV Artists File 1, 1948–61), the highest paid Variety artistes on BBC Television at that time were as follows; Jewel and Warriss (200 guineas); Terry-Thomas (140 guineas); Jimmy James (140 guineas – including his two stooges); Arthur Askey (125 guineas); Eric Barker and Donald Peers (85 guineas each); Frankie Howerd (80 guineas); and Michael Howard (60 guineas).

19. See Briggs, *The History of Broadcasting in the United Kingdom* vol. 4, p. 654, note 114.

20. Waldman, 'Creating Light Entertainment in Television', *Radio Times*, 23 February 1951, p. 46.

21. Ibid.

22. Waldman, 'The Toughest Job', *Radio Times*, 4 December 1953, p. 5.

23. Ibid. George Campey's 'Mr Waldman Brings Home a Secret Report' (*Evening Standard*, 10 November 1953, p. 6) is a useful contemporary account of the kind and extent of interest in Waldman's American trip.

24. Waldman, 'The Variety of Television Variety', *Radio Times Annual 1954* (London: BBC, 1954), p. 56.

25. The earliest letter in the BBC's archives, requesting an audition, is dated 31 March 1948. It is signed 'Morecambe and Wise' but, as with nearly all of their subsequent correspondence, was composed almost certainly by Wise alone (BBC WAC, Morecambe and Wise TV Artists File 1: 1948–61).

26. BBC WAC, Morecambe and Wise TV Artists File 1: 1948–61. Tony Hancock, as one half of 'Hank and Scott', was auditioned five months later. He also scored an 8, and was engaged subsequently for an appearance on a television show called *New to You* on 1 November 1948: see Hancock, *Hancock*, pp. 194–5.

27. Letter to Morecambe and Wise from the BBC's Television Booking Manager, 27 April 1948 (BBC WAC, Morecambe and Wise TV Artists File 1: 1948–61). Although the letter concludes by noting, 'You will appreciate, however, that owing to prevailing conditions, we are unable at present to say exactly when this [audition] will be,' there is no record in the files that confirms that the eventual audition was actually attended by Morecambe and Wise.

28. *Youth Parade*, their television début, was broadcast on 28 September 1951. Other early appearances included *Stars at Blackpool*, 28 August 1953: *Variety*, 24 October 1953; *Face the Music*, 12 December 1953; and *Pantomime Party*, 23 December 1953.

29. Campey, 'Would You Laugh at These?', *Evening Standard*, 9 November 1953, p. 6. The article declared: 'Now I don't want to hear any moans from Mr Waldman and his henchmen about not being able to find [new] artists, because I have found them.' He goes on to say: 'Perhaps Mr Waldman is worried about money? I can report that Morecambe and Wise are making £150 a week. Television can run to that at least – if it sincerely wants new faces and new talent as much as the viewers do.'

30. BBC WAC, Morecambe and Wise TV Artists File 1: 1948–61.

31. *Still on My Way to Hollywood*, p. 112.

32. *Eric & Ernie*, p. 84.

33. Quoted by Rogers, 'Morecambe and Wise', pp. 41–2.

34. Although a (very young) trainee, Ernest Maxin, would be listed as the show's director, he has told me (interview with the author, 26 April 1998) that Sears, in practice, was responsible for both production and direction.

35. Quoted by Eric Morecambe, *Eric & Ernie*, p. 130.

36. BBC WAC, Morecambe and Wise TV Artists File 1: 1948–61.

37. Letter from Bryan Sears to Morecambe and Wise, 15 February 1954 (BBC WAC, Morecambe and Wise TV Artists File 1: 1948–61).

38. BBC WAC, Morecambe and Wise TV Artists File 1: 1948–61. Frank Pope (18 January 1954) informed Bryan Sears that Monkhouse and Goodwin *would* be contributing material to the series. Sears (15 February 1954) then wrote to Morecambe and Wise: 'I have spoken to the Bob Monkhouse "Organization", and apparently they tried to contact you when they were up in Manchester this last weekend [namely, the first weekend in February 1954]. However, I will send them a copy of the Running Order today which will give them some idea of the amount of script to be provided overall, and after that we will have to arrange some sort of meeting between you and them.' It is not clear why

the proposed association did not work out: Monkhouse was not able to clarify the matter, and Goodwin died in 1975.

39.   Ibid.

40.   Scriptwriters who contributed sketches and/or ideas to the series included: Len Fincham and Lawrie Wyman (best known for his later long-running BBC radio series *The Navy Lark*); Maurice Rodgers and Alan Blain; Denis Gifford and Tony Hawes; and Ronnie Hanbury (responsible for the popular Jewel and Warriss radio series *Up the Pole*).

41.   Around two years later the couple would move in briefly with Joan's family over the Torrington Arms, a large Victorian pub in North Finchley, before buying a house of their own near by in Torrington Park. A commemorative blue plaque was unveiled on the outside of the house in 1995 (see Dan Conaghan, 'Eric Earns His Plaque', *Daily Telegraph*, 15 May 1995, p. 7).

42.   Quoted by Gary Morecambe, *The Illustrated Morecambe*, p. 45.

## Chapter 6

Karl Kraus: *Half-Truths & One-and-a-Half Truths*, trans. Harry Zohn (Manchester: Carcanet, 1986), p. 47.

Eric Morecambe: *The Morecambe & Wise Show*, (BBC), 3 June 1971.

1.   The 1954 Television Act ended the BBC's monopoly on broadcasting in the United Kingdom, and allowed for a second, commercial, television channel to be set up. Independent Television was launched on 22 September 1955.

2.   Bryan Sears; quoted in 'Television Diary', *Radio Times*, 16 April 1954, p. 15.

3.   No official recordings of the show were preserved. I am grateful, therefore, to Joan Morecambe, Ernest Maxin, Bill Cotton, John Ammonds, William Franklyn and Francis Matthews for sharing with me some of their memories both of that first show and the series as a whole, and to the BBC's Written Archive Centre for allowing me to examine the surviving script material and internal correspondence.

4.   *Daily Mail*, 22 April 1954, p. 6.

5.   *Daily Sketch*, 22 April 1954, p. 5.

6.   *Daily Herald*, 22 April 1954, p. 3.

7.   *Daily Mirror*, 22 April 1954, p. 4. The pun makes more sense when one knows that a revival of Luigi Pirandello's 1921 play, *Six Characters in Search of an Author*, had been televised by the BBC two days before, on 20 April 1954.

8.   *Morecambe and Wife*, p. 42.

9.   *Eric & Ernie*, p. 31.

10.   Kenneth Bailey, *People*, 25 April 1954, p. 8.

11.   *Still on My Way to Hollywood*, p. 115.

12.   Quoted by Eric Morecambe, *Eric & Ernie*, p. 132.

13.   *Bring Me Sunshine*, p. 123.

14.   Memorandum (T12/334/1) from Huw Wheldon to Ronnie Waldman and Bryan Sears, 22 April 1954 (BBC WAC, Morecambe and Wise TV Artists File 1: 1948–61).

15.   See Roger Silvey, *Who's Listening?: The Story of BBC Audience Research* (London: Allen & Unwin, 1974), chapter 6, and Briggs, *The History of Broadcasting in the United Kingdom*, vol. 4, chapter 3, section 4, for detailed explanations of how all of these reports were researched.

16.   Each member of the viewing panel was required to sum up his or her reactions to the show by selecting from a five-point scale which went from A+ to C−. The results of these were then collated and an average score calculated (see Silvey, p. 163).

17.   Audience Research Report on 21 April 1954 edition of *Running Wild* (BBC WAC, VR/54/218, 5 May 1954). Such reports were not produced for every edition of any particular show: in the case of *Running Wild*, three were produced during the series.

18. Memorandum from Ronnie Waldman to Cecil McGivern, 23 April 1954 (BBC WAC, Morecambe and Wise TV Artists File 1: 1948–61).

19. Maurice Wiggin, *Sunday Times*, 25 April 1954, p. 11. Cecil McGivern appears to have arrived – rather gleefully by the sound of it – at a similar conclusion, writing to Waldman on 26 April: 'Dancing girls save no show, hardly succeed in helping even a good show, and are generally nowadays nearly as dead as mutton. Young producers, like ours, like chorus girls about – because they like girls about ... I agree personalities, comics, etc. are more necessary than ideas, but, the personalities and comics having been achieved, then new, bright and modern ideas are needed to back them up.' (BBC WAC, Morecambe and Wise TV Artists File 1: 1948–61.)

20. His assistant, Ernest Maxin, assumed sole responsibility for choreography from the third show onwards.

21. Quoted by Eric Morecambe, *Eric & Ernie*, p. 132.

22. Ibid.

23. Ibid.

24. Ibid.

25. Memorandum from Ronnie Waldman to Cecil McGivern, 23 April 1954 (BBC WAC, Morecambe and Wise TV Artists File 1: 1948–61).

26. Audience Research Report on 19 May 1954 edition of *Running Wild* (BBC WAC, VR/54/269, 2 June 1954).

27. Bob Kesten, *Evening Standard*, 20 May 1954, p. 6.

28. The estimated audience, for example, continued to decline from one show to the next: it started out at 48 per cent of the adult viewing public and ended up at 44 per cent – 17 per cent below the average (BBC WAC, Morecambe and Wise TV Artists File 1: 1948–61).

29. Letter from Frank Pope to Ronnie Waldman, 17 June 1954, ibid.

30. Letter from Ronnie Waldman to Frank Pope, 17 June 1954, ibid.

31. She had been replaced by another singer: Jill Day.

32. The sketch had been written in the expectation that Boris Karloff would be the show's star guest. Karloff, unsurprisingly, found that he had other things to do that day.

33. Audience Research Report on 30 June 1954 edition of *Running Wild* (BBC WAC, VR/54/358, dated 15 July 1954).

34. Memorandum from Bryan Sears to heads of departments, 1 July 1954 (BBC WAC, Morecambe and Wise TV Artists File 1: 1948–61).

35. Interview with the author, 16 April 1997.

36. Joan Morecambe, *Morecambe and Wife*, p. 43.

37. Ibid., pp. 42–3.

## Chapter 7

Woody Allen: *Crimes and Misdemeanours* (1989), screenplay by Woody Allen.

*You're Only Young Once* (1954): script by Frank Roscoe.

1. *Hancock's Half Hour* first appeared on BBC TV in 1956; *Life with the Lyons* in 1955.

2. *Still on My Way to Hollywood*, p. 15.

3. Ibid.

4. *Eric & Ernie*, pp. 131–2.

5. *Morecambe and Wife*, p. 20.

6. Quoted by Gary Morecambe, *Funny Man*, p. 20.

7. Interview with the author, 11 November 1997. Gail Morecambe was born on 13 September 1953.

8. Interview with the author, 16 April 1997.

9. The couple were staying at the time at Eric's parents' house in Torrisholme. Joan

told me that when, years later, they revisited the area they found that the concrete had been covered over.

10. *Morecambe and Wife*, p. 86.

11. *Still on My Way to Hollywood*, p. 109.

12. Quoted by Andrew Duncan, *Radio Times*, 24–30 April 1993, p. 22.

13. Quoted by Rogers, 'Morecambe and Wise', p. 44.

14. *Eric & Ernie*, p. 133.

15. Ibid., p. 134.

16. Quoted by Gary Morecambe, *Morecambe and Wise*, p. 84.

17. See *Eric & Ernie*, p. 135.

18. Quoted by Gary Morecambe, *Morecambe and Wise*, p. 82.

19. Ibid.

20. Quoted by Gay Search, 'They're Back!', *Radio Times*, 29 August 1968, p. 32.

21. Quoted by Gary Morecambe, *Morecambe and Wise*, p. 84.

22. *Still on My Way to Hollywood*, pp. 162–3.

23. Ibid., p. 163.

24. *There's No Answer to That!*, p. 44.

25. *Daily Sketch*, 9 January 1957, p. 3.

26. 'Mailbag', *Daily Mail*, 28 December 1960, p. 6.

27. 'Letters', *Daily Mail*, 14 December 1962, p. 8.

28. 'Letters', *Daily Mail*, 18 December 1962, p. 6.

29. See, for example, the London *Evening News*, 28 May 1960, p. 8: 'beer-mats', they explained, 'are reminders of many happy occasions'. With Bartram's assistance they became 'Honorary Joint Presidents' of the British Beer Mat Collectors' Society – a fact that Bartram's press packs rarely failed to point out.

30. Interview with the author, 11 November 1997.

31. Ibid.

32. Frank Pope wrote to Ernest Maxin on 12 July 1956 suggesting that he might consider Morecambe and Wise for a second BBC television series (BBC WAC, Morecambe and Wise TV Artists File 1: 1948–61). Maxin was not in a position to commission such a project.

33. Quoted by Jeremy Novick, *Morecambe & Wise: You Can't See the Join* (London: Chameleon, 1997), p. 113.

34. Quoted by Eric Morecambe, *Eric & Ernie*, p. 136.

35. Quoted by Novick, p. 113.

36. Letter (sent by Morecambe and Wise but written by Ernie Wise) to John Ammonds, 10 February 1959 (BBC WAC, Morecambe and Wise TV Artists File 1: 1949–65). The 'T.V.' they referred to may have been Winifred Atwell's new show, based in Sydney, entitled *The Amazing Miss A.*

37. Quoted by Roger Wilmut, *Tony Hancock: Artiste* (London: Methuen, 1978), p. 149.

38. Interview with the author, 20 February 1997.

39. Quoted by Eric Morecambe, *Eric & Ernie*, p. 149.

40. Ibid.

41. Ibid., p. 152.

## Chapter 8

*The Morecambe and Wise Show* (ATV): script by Dick Hills and Sid Green.

1. Six shows, written by *Beyond Our Ken*'s Eric Merriman, produced by *The Goon Show*'s John Browell and broadcast by the BBC during July and August 1966.

2. See the discography on p. 328.

3.   The strip appeared in the boys' weekly comic *Buster*. A similar strip appeared later in *Reveille*.

4.   See chapter 9.

5.   See chapters 10, 11 and 12.

6.   *Still on My Way to Hollywood*, p. 131.

7.   Marshall McLuhan's most significant book, in this sense at least, was *The Gutenburg Galaxy: The Making of Typographic Man* (London: Routledge, 1962). Jonathan Miller's *McLuhan* (London: Fontana, 1971) is still, by a long way, the clearest and best critical summary of his theories.

8.   Mary Whitehouse established her 'Clean-Up TV' campaign in 1964, and formalised it the following year as The National Viewers' and Listeners' Association. Her argument concerning the power of television to corrupt the mind of the average citizen by transmitting diverse images of moral turpitude directly into their home was undermined somewhat by the fact that she exposed her own average mind to far more of such images than she allowed the rest of the viewing public to partake of.

9.   Keith Waterhouse, 'Memoirs of a Televiewer', *Punch*, 20 July 1966; reproduced in Ray Connolly (ed.), *In the Sixties* (London: Pavilion, 1995), pp. 115–17.

10.   ITV was, in the early days, dominated by four companies: ATV, which ran Midlands schedules during the week and London's at the weekend; Rediffusion, which provided programmes for London during the week; Granada, which did the same for the North; and ABC, which had the Midlands and the North at weekends. In 1964 ATV took over the vast Stoll-Moss Empire, with Lew Grade later becoming Chairman of both of Stoll Theatres and of Moss Empires. He also owned ITC, which made TV movies for ATV. See Hunter Davies' *The Grades* (London: Weidenfeld, 1981) for background information on the Grade family.

11.   Recounted by Billy Marsh to Gary Morecambe, *Funny Man*, p. 85.

12.   The VAF was the principal union for Variety performers in Britain. Established in 1906, by 1914 it was affiliated with the White Rats Actors Union of America, the International Artists' Lodge of Germany, L'Union Syndicate des Artistes Lyriques of France and the Australian Vaudeville Artists' Association. The VAF merged with British Actors' Equity in May 1967, mainly as a result of the decline of Variety and the impact of television.

13.   Recounted by Billy Marsh to Gary Morecambe, *Funny Man*, p. 85.

14.   Morecambe and Wise had first written to Maschwitz on 25 November 1959 saying that they were 'very interested in doing more T.V. in the future'. Maschwitz gave a mildly encouraging reply on 3 December (BBC WAC, Morecambe and Wise TV Artists File 1: 1948–61).

15.   Early in 1960, Tom Sloan had invited Muir and Norden – arguably the most respected writing team in British comedy at that time – to join the BBC. They were given an office on the fourth floor of Television Centre, where they 'read every script submitted and reported on them'. See Muir, *A Kentish Lad*, pp. 217–41.

16.   The only writers referred to in the relevant section of the file in the BBC archives are Muir and Norden, but neither Muir (interview with the author, 17 November 1997) nor Norden (23 March 1998) had any recollection of the project, let alone of the precise nature of their involvement in it. 'It's like there's an enormous wall and anything may lie behind it,' said Norden. 'I rang my agent – the same one I had in those days – and it didn't raise the slightest tinkle with her, either. But if there are memos and letters about it then it must be so.' Maschwitz died in 1969, and Sloan in 1970; Bill Cotton, who was producing his father's BBC show at the time, said that he did 'not remember hearing anything about [*Four Aces and a King*]' (correspondence with the author, 7 March 1998). As Muir and Norden were already responsible for writing the Jimmy Edwards series *Whack-O!* (1956–60) and, presumably, were in the process of writing – or preparing to write – *The Seven Faces of Jim* (1961), it seems unlikely that they themselves had written the scripts for Morecambe and Wise: 'We only wrote one series, maybe two series, a year

while we were in the Department,' Norden explained, 'because all comedy scripts were funnelled through us in our "advisory capacity", and so we couldn't really function as writers.'

17. Muir and Norden, memorandum dated 6 October 1960 (BBC WAC, Morecambe and Wise TV Artists File 1: 1948–61).

18. No mention is made of *Four Aces and a King* in any of Morecambe and/or Wise's books, articles or interviews. I have not been able to find any recorded remark on the subject by Billy Marsh – save for his letter of 8 February 1961 contained in the BBC archive – and the Billy Marsh Agency was not able to shed any light on the matter. Morecambe and Wise's good friend Edmund Hockridge – who was appearing with them (higher up the bill) at Torquay during that summer of 1961 – recalled (interview with the author, 6 May 1998): 'I know that they were flummoxing around during the summer season, trying to make up their minds about various things and whether to take a risk on doing a totally new pattern of [television] programme, but whether there was any battle going on between ITV and the BBC, I don't know. I couldn't say – that would have been too personal.'

19. Letter from Tom Sloan to Billy Marsh, 23 January 1961 (BBC WAC, Morecambe and Wise TV Artists File 1: 1948–61).

20. Letter from Billy Marsh, 8 February 1961 (BBC WAC, Morecambe and Wise TV Artists File 1: 1948–61).

21. Correspondence with the author, 22 May 1998.

22. See *Eric & Ernie*, p. 152.

23. See, for example, his remarks in Gary Morecambe's *Funny Man*, p. 85.

24. See *Eric & Ernie*, p. 156.

25. Ibid., p. 157.

26. *Still on My Way to Hollywood*, p. 119. Wise was mistaken about Hills and Green being older: in fact they were slightly younger – Hills was born in 1926, and Green in 1928.

27. *Eric & Ernie*, p. 157.

28. Ibid.

29. Ibid.

30. J. B. Priestley, *English Humour* (London: Longmans and Co., 1933), p. 38.

31. *There's No Answer to That?*, p. 36.

32. Mortimer, 'Eric Morecambe, without a Peer', p. 32.

33. Their guest appearance was recorded at ATV Studios, Elstree, on 2 December 1963, and broadcast on 18 April 1964.

34. Correspondence with the author, 25 September 1997.

35. It has been said – see, for example, Jeremy Novick's *Morecambe & Wise: You Can't See the Join*, p. 36 – that Colin Clews, the show's producer, waited until the Beatles had finished their spot and then said to a colleague: 'I know we're doing six of these shows, but we'd better put out the one with the Beatles early in case they don't last.' The Beatles are also supposed to have overheard this remark. Paul McCartney, however, told me that he did not hear Clews, or anyone else in the studio, say anything derogatory about them, 'nor do I remember any of the other Beatles mentioning this' (correspondence with the author, 25 September 1997).

36. There are innumerable sources for this incident: see, for example, *Roy Hudd's Book of Music-Hall, Variety and Showbiz Anecdotes*, p. 82.

37. Michael Grade, who worked closely with both sets of performers (and was once asked by Mike and Bernie Winters to represent them), told me that 'there was no jealousy at all between them' (interview with the author, 20 February 1997), and Joan Morecambe (11 November 1997) agreed: 'Eric liked Bernie especially – they got on very well, and admired each other – but there was no rivalry at all between the two acts. It was all invented.' Bernie Winters' autobiography, *One Day at a Time: The Story of My Life* (London:

Ebury Press, 1991), contains several stories about his meetings with Eric Morecambe (see pp. 12–13, 108 and 126).

38.   Eric Morecambe, interviewed in the mid-1960s: excerpt included in the BBC2 documentary *The Importance of Being Ernie* (first broadcast on 27 April 1993).

39.   Interview with the author, 20 February 1997.

40.   See, for example, the *Daily Telegraph*, 6 May 1991, p. 19.

41.   Interview with the author, 20 February 1997.

42.   *Still on My Way to Hollywood*, p. 118. Eric Morecambe, in *Eric & Ernie*, was somewhat evasive about his true feelings concerning the collaboration with Hills and Green. On p. 165 he refers to them as 'very amiable characters', while on p. 157 he notes they clashed on occasion and on p. 178 he admits that their collaboration, though 'fruitful', was 'not the fun it had been with Frank Roscoe in *Variety Fanfare*'.

43.   Dick Hills and Sid Green, 'Sid and Dick', *TV Times*, 17 March 1966, p. 23.

44.   Dick Hills, 'Eric Morecambe', *The Dictionary of National Biography, 1981–1985* (Oxford: Oxford University Press, 1990), p. 287.

45.   Interview with the author, 11 November 1997.

46.   Ibid.

47.   *Eric & Ernie*, p. 156. See also *Still on My Way to Hollywood*, pp. 118–19.

48.   *Still on My Way to Hollywood*, p. 119.

49.   Interview with the author, 11 November 1997.

50.   *Still on My Way to Hollywood*, p. 119.

51.   See Bill Cotton's comments in chapter 13.

52.   Quoted by Gary Morecambe, *Morecambe and Wise*, p. 156.

53.   Interview with the author, 20 February 1997.

54.   Many people had started referring to the show by its sub-title – *Two of a Kind* – by this stage and, when six compilation videos of the ATV shows were released in 1994 by the ITC Entertainment Group, they were entitled *Two of a Kind*.

55.   Television Audience Measurement was the official television ratings contractor to the ITV system from 1956 to 1968. It used 'TAMmeters' in approximately 2,300 homes in the UK to measure audiences for each programme. The BBC had its own audience survey of daily viewing habits during this period. In 1968, the Joint Industry Committee for Television Advertising Research (JICTAR) awarded the contract to supply the official television ratings service for ITV to Audits of Great Britain (AGB). See Silvey, *Who's Listening?*, pp. 177–84 for a comparison between the BBC's and ITVs methods of audience measurement during this period.

56.   See *Eric & Ernie*, p. 176.

57.   Now known as BAFTA (British Academy of Film and Television Arts) awards, they began in 1947 as British Film Academy Awards, and from 1969 until 1975 they were called SFTA (Society of Film and Television Arts) awards.

58.   Confirmed by Edmund Hockridge, who was present at the meeting (interview with the author, 6 May 1998). Cary Grant became particularly friendly with Eric Morecambe from this point on, with the two of them corresponding and sometimes meeting for social events (see chapter 15).

59.   See the List of Performances at the end of this book for full details. The album was rereleased, with two additional tracks, as a single cassette (ECC5 46) in 1997.

60.   See chapter 10.

61.   See the report in the *Evening Standard*, 19 December 1964, p. 6.

62.   *Still on My Way to Hollywood*, p. 127.

63.   See the *Daily Sketch*, 3 June 1967, p. 3.

64.   Interview with the author, 1 May 1997.

65.   Quoted by David Hudson, *Daily Star*, 29 May 1984, p. 15.

66.  Eric Morecambe, *Eric & Ernie*, p. 174.

67.  Gary Morecambe, *Funny Man*, pp. 18–19.

68.  *Still on My Way to Hollywood*, p. 126.

69.  Joan Morecambe, *Morecambe and Wife*, p. 82.

70.  Eric Morecambe, 'I'm Not Joking', in the *Daily Sketch*, February 1971; reproduced in *Bring Me Sunshine*, p. 108.

71.  *Still on My Way to Hollywood*, p. 127.

72.  *There's No Answer to That!*, p. 93.

## MOVIES

*The Morecambe & Wise Show* (BBC, 1971): script by Eddie Braben.

### Chapter 9

Robert Hughes: *Culture of Complaint: The Fraying of America* (Oxford: Oxford University Press, 1993), p. 12.

Ralph Waldo Emerson: 'Experience' (1844), in *Essays and Poems* (London: Dent, 1995), p. 21.

1.  Morecambe and Wise, along with Joan and Doreen, made two brief visits to the United States on their way to and from their tour of Australia. They spent some time in New York, San Francisco, Los Angeles and Las Vegas before returning home to England.

2.  Ernie Wise, quoted in the *Radio Times*, 24 December–6 January 1977, p. 4.

3.  Ibid. Wise's fascination with Hollywood's America would never die. In 1993, for example, he submitted a list of his 'Top 10' movies to the *Modern Review* (February–March 1993, p. 9): *Singin' in the Rain*; *Seven Brides for Seven Brothers*; *Carousel*; *42nd Street*; *My Cousin Vinny*; *Home Alone*; *Mr Saturday Night*; *Raiders of the Lost Ark*; *Dances with Wolves*; and *Thelma and Louise*.

4.  Eric Morecambe, quoted in the *Sunday Express*, 6 June 1971, p. 8.

5.  Ernie Wise, *Eric & Ernie*, p. 49.

6.  Eric Morecambe, *Eric & Ernie*, p. 170.

7.  One should note, however, that Will Hay *did* enjoy some success in vaudeville (Jack Benny named him as an important influence), and his 1927 tour of the US proved particularly popular.

8.  Field arrived in the US on 3 March 1948. He spent the weekend at Bob Hope's ranch in Palm Springs, then was invited to dinner by Charlie Chaplin and, later that month, attended a testimonial dinner held in his honour at the Hollywood Masquers Club (the highlight of which was Cary Grant, billed as 'Archie Leach', performing an old vaudeville routine especially for Field).

9.  Norman Wisdom *did* appear in one Hollywood movie – *The Night They Raided Minsky's* (1968) – and received several favourable notices for his performance, but it was, none the less, an isolated success in an entirely untypical production. Tony Hancock's prospective US career did not really recover from the alienating effect that his first British movie – *The Rebel* (1961), clumsily retitled *Call Me Genius* for the American market – had on US critics.

10.  Quoted by Gary Morecambe, *Funny Man*, p. 154.

11.  Sources differ as to the year: Morecambe (in *Eric & Ernie*, p. 159) says, 'I remember the occasion well' – the year was 1964, when they were appearing in a summer season at the London Palladium with Bruce Forsyth at the top of the bill; Wise (in *Still on My Way to Hollywood*, p. 122) says the year was 1961, but also notes that they were appearing at the Palladium with Forsyth. Gary Morecambe's *Morecambe and Wise* (p. 147) also favours 1961.

I believe that 1964 is the correct year: in 1961, Morecambe and Wise had not even started their ATV series, and were hardly ready for a prestigious show like Sullivan's;

Morecambe (*Eric & Ernie*, p. 159) said that they performed 'Boom Oo Yatta-Ta-Ta' on their début, and this song was written in 1963.

12.  *Eric & Ernie*, p. 159.

13.  The only source that makes this clear is Ernie Wise's contribution to the video *Classic Morecambe & Wise*, vol. 3.

14.  Ibid.

15.  Sullivan hosted a televised Variety show called *Toast of the Town* from June 1948 until 1955, at which point it was renamed *The Ed Sullivan Show*.

16.  See Nick Tosches' excellent article, 'Mr Sunday Night', *Vanity Fair*, July 1997, pp. 130–45.

17.  It would continue to run until 1971.

18.  Quoted by Tosches, p. 132.

19.  Examples taken from Tosches, p. 132; Terry-Thomas, *Terry-Thomas Tells Tales* (London: Robson, 1990), p. 38; and the two laserdiscs, *The Very Best of the Ed Sullivan Show*, vol. 1 and 2 (Buena Vista, 1991; catalogue numbers 1345AS and 1351AS).

20.  Jack Carter, quoted by Tosches, p. 144.

21.  The A. C. Nielsen Company was at that time the largest audience research organisation in the world. It was responsible, since the early fifties, for the 'Nielsen Television Index'; it used a technical device known as an 'Audimeter', which was attached to television receivers, to measure the number of television sets tuned to certain programmes for periods of five minutes or more.

22.  See Tosches, p. 144 and also Lord Kilbracken's 'Beatles Smash US Viewing Record', *Evening Standard*, 17 February 1964, p. 11.

23.  *Still on My Way to Hollywood*, p. 122.

24.  Interview with the author, 20 February 1997.

25.  Jackie Mason, quoted by Tosches, p. 142.

26.  Ibid.

27.  See *Still on My Way to Hollywood*, p. 123.

28.  Ibid., pp. 122–3. Morecambe and Wise performed three separate spots in front of a studio audience but these were actually transmitted as insertions in the following week's show. This was – and, in some cases, remains – common practice in the US for this kind of television show.

29.  *Eric and Ernie*, p. 160.

30.  *Still on My Way to Hollywood*, p. 124.

31.  One should remember that many American performers of international standing have had no success at all in certain parts of the United States. Woody Allen, for example, has always been far more popular in Europe than he is in, say, the Midwest.

32.  Interview with the author, 20 February 1997.

33.  See the report in the *Daily Mirror*, 1 April 1968, p. 3. Pearl Carr and Teddy Johnson were also among the co-stars.

34.  Also on the bill were Pearl Carr and Teddy Johnson, the Schaller Brothers, Joe McBride, Ray Allen and Lord Charles and the London Palladium Boys and Girls.

35.  Interview with the author, 20 February 1997.

36.  The article, 'That's the Funny Thing about Humour', was part of the press pack that George Bartram sent to Jack Karr, the O'Keefe Centre's press officer. (I am indebted to Dave Miles of the Morecambe and Wise Fan Club for providing me with a copy of the pack.)

37.  *Piccadilly Palace* had been part of a package of colour shows that Lew Grade sold to the ABC network for $2 million.

38.  Ernie Wise's claim (*Eric and Ernie*, p. 187) that the shows had been 'smash hits' was, however, a slight exaggeration.

39.   Interview with the author, 20 February 1997. While they were in Toronto they also appeared on radio (*First Nighter* on 13 May and *The Russ Thompson Show* on 17 May), and television (*The Elwood Glover Show* and *Toronto Today*, both on 14 May).

40.   The New York *Daily News Record*, 6 May 1968; quoted by Ernie Wise, *Still on My Way to Hollywood*, p. 125. The majority of the reviews, however, made no mention of Morecambe and Wise's contribution to the show (see, for example, the *New York Times*, 6 May 1968, p. 8).

41.   Transcribed from *Classic Morecambe & Wise*, vol. 3.

42.   Lew Grade, *Still Dancing* (London: Collins, 1987), p. 223.

43.   Interview with the author, 5 February 1997.

44.   Between 1891 and 1900, the total number of immigrants entering the US was recorded as being 3,688,000; between 1901 and 1910, the number was 8,795,000; between 1911 and 1920, 5,736,000; between 1921 and 1930, 4,107,000. Source: Ben J. Wattenberg (ed.), *The Statistical History of the United States: From Colonial Times to the Present* (New York: Basic Books, 1976, p. 105). See also H. L. Mencken, *The American Language: An Inquiry into the Development of English in the United States*, abridged 4th edn (New York: Knopf, 1989) for an overview of the cultural initiatives during this period.

45.   The phrase – 'not merely a nation but a teeming of nations' – comes from the preface to Walt Whitman's *Leaves of Grass* (1855), included in *The Portable Walt Whitman*, ed. Mark Van Doren (Harmondsworth: Penguin, 1977), p. 5.

46.   *Still on My Way to Hollywood*, p. 124.

47.   *There's No Answer to That!*, p. 126.

48.   *Eric & Ernie*, p. 167.

49.   *Still on My Way to Hollywood*, p. 124.

50.   *There's No Answer to That!*, p. 124.

51.   *Still on My Way to Hollywood*, p. 122.

52.   *There's No Answer to That!*, p. 128.

53.   Interview with the author, 20 February 1997.

54.   Interview with the author, 11 November 1997.

55.   *Still on My Way to Hollywood*, p. 122.

56.   Ibid., p. 124.

57.   Ibid., p. 125.

58.   *Financial Times*, 19 February 1964, p. 6. Ernie Wise confirmed in an interview with John Coe of the *Bristol Evening Post* (18 February, p. 1) that the bid had definitely been sent to Edward Heath at the Board of Trade.

British Lion had been run by the British Government since 1955, but late in 1963 it was decided – partly, it seems, as a reaction to the increase in American money being invested in the British film industry – to privatise it. When, on 29 December, it was revealed that only one bid – from Sydney Box – had been received, Sir Michael Balcon and others urged the Government to put back its deadline and allow other bids to be mounted. Morecambe and Wise's was one of these late bids (others include Sir Michael Balcon's group, Leslie Grade's group, the washing-machine tycoon John Bloom's group and an eccentric right-wing body – led by Edward Martell – that called itself the Freedom Group).

59.   *Daily Telegraph*, 19 February 1964, p. 17.

60.   Ibid. Among the possible backers mentioned by Wise were Ken Dodd, Max Bygraves, Tommy Steele, Harry Secombe and Harry Worth. In an interview with the London *Evening News* (18 February 1964, p. 5) he added to this list the names of Sir Alec Guinness and Jack Hawkins; he also revealed that he had discussed the bid with Edmund Hockridge (who not only was appearing with them in Bristol but also was Wise's next-door neighbour in Peterborough). Ken Dodd, however, told me (24 February 1998) that he had no recollection of Wise contacting him at this time, and neither did Tommy Steele (12 April 1998) or Edmund Hockridge (6 May 1998), while Max Bygraves (9 February

1998) said that not only did he have 'no knowledge' of any bid for British Lion but also that 'in 1964, I think all [Morecambe and Wise] could afford was a coffee at British Lyons, Coventry Street, W1'.

61. Interview with the author, 11 November 1997.

62. By the middle of March the serious competitors had been reduced to two: the Balcon group and the Box group. Balcon's group won.

63. 'Oh We Do Love to be Beside the Seaside', *TV Life*, July–August 1975; reproduced in *Bring Me Sunshine*, p. 150.

## Chapter 10

Alberto Cavalcanti: 'Comedies and Cartoons', in Charles Davy (ed.), *Footnotes to the Film* (London: Reader's Union, 1938), p. 83.

Robert Asher: attributed to him by Eric Morecambe, *There's No Answer to That!*, p. 92.

1. Nikolaus Pevsner, *The Buildings of England: Buckinghamshire* (London: Penguin, 1979), p. 416.

2. *There's No Answer to That!*, p. 93.

3. Ibid., p. 124.

4. Ibid., p. 93.

5. Ibid.

6. Ibid., p. 94. The phrase, though used to capture the expectations of both men at this time, was actually Ernie Wise's.

7. Ibid., p. 94.

8. Quoted by Gary Morecambe, *Morecambe and Wise*, p. 119.

9. One ought to note that Norman Wisdom himself, far from encouraging such a formulaic approach to movie-making, felt somewhat frustrated by it. See, for example, Hugh Stewart's comments in Geoffrey Macnab's *J. Arthur Rank and the British Film Industry* (London: Routledge, 1993), p. 223. It was, ironically, due in part to a disagreement between Wisdom and Rank over the nature of his next project that led to Wisdom's usual production team being free in the autumn of 1964 to work on *The Intelligence Men* instead.

10. Cinema admissions in Britain for the year 1959 declined to below 600 million; in 1960, 520 million; in 1961, 449 million; in 1962, they declined by another 54 million, with 240 cinemas being closed; in 1963, admissions slumped by a further 37,800,000, and 240 more cinemas were shut. See Alexander Walker, *Hollywood, England* (London: Michael Joseph, 1974), pp. 469–72.

11. At one point in the sixties US companies, attracted by the prospect of lower production costs, were responsible for almost 90 per cent of the finance for movies made in Britain (see Walker, p. 16).

12. See Macnab, *J. Arthur Rank and the British Film Industry*; and Vincent Porter, 'Methodism versus the Market-place: The Rank Organisation and British Cinema', in Robert Murphy (ed.), *The British Cinema Book* (London: BFI, 1997), pp. 122–32.

13. The review, in the *Financial Times*, was of *On the Beat*; it is quoted in Richard Dacre's appealingly generous and informative book on Wisdom's career entitled *Trouble in Store* (Dundee: Farries, 1991), p. 117.

14. Wisdom was talking to the *Evening News* in 1964; quoted in Dacre, p. 47.

15. Among Franklyn's screen credits prior to *The Intelligence Men* were *The Secret People* (1951), *Above Us the Waves* (1956) and *Quatermass II* (1957), while his television credits included the starring role of undercover agent Peter Dallas in the series *Top Secret* (1961–2). He would go on to appear in countless other television shows, as well as such movies as Roman Polanski's *Cul de Sac* (1966) and Robert M. Young's *Splitting Heirs* (1993).

16. Among Matthew's screen credits prior to *The Intelligence Men* were George Cukor's *Bhowani Junction* (1956), *Nine Hours to Rama* (1962) and *Murder Ahoy* (1964), while his television credits included *Triton, Golden Girl, My Friend Charles* and *A Little Big Business*.

He would go on to enjoy considerable fame as the star of the popular BBC TV series *Paul Temple*, as well as appear in a wide range of roles on television and stage and in such movies as *The McGuffin* (1985).

17.   Interview with the author, 3 September 1997.

18.   Interview with the author, 11 September 1997.

19.   Ibid.

20.   Quoted by Brian McFarlane, *An Autobiography of British Cinema* (London: Methuen, 1997), p. 547.

21.   Interview with the author, 3 September 1997.

22.   Interview with the author, 11 September 1997.

23.   Quoted by Joseph McBride, *Hawks on Hawks* (London: Faber, 1996), p. 34.

24.   Interview with the author, 3 September 1997.

25.   Interview with the author, 11 September 1997.

26.   Both William Franklyn and Francis Matthews recall the schedule as being – by the standards of the time – relatively relaxed. Franklyn said (interview with the author, 3 September 1997): 'In those days schedules were far more relaxed than they are today. I mean, three minutes a day? Three-and-a-half minutes a day? I mean, come on, they really would be pushing it. No, no, there was no feeling of pressure at all. It was a very relaxed unit to be on.'

27.   Joan Morecambe (in *Morecambe and Wife*, p. 86) recalls that both Morecambe and Wise, during the final few weeks, found the schedule to be 'frantic'.

28.   Another 'premiere' was held in London at the Odeon, Leicester Square.

29.   Interview with the author, 11 September 1997.

30.   Ibid.

31.   *The Times*, 25 March 1965, p. 2.

32.   Alexander Walker, *Evening Standard*, 25 March 1965, p. 5.

33.   *Monthly Film Bulletin*, vol. 32, no. 376 (May 1965), p. 75.

34.   See *Eric & Ernie*, p. 179.

35.   *People*, 28 March 1965, p. 8.

36.   Allen Eyles, *Films & Filming*, vol. 11, no. 9 (June 1965), p. 34.

37.   *Daily Mail*, 23 March 1965, p. 14.

38.   See Hugh Stewart's interview with Brian McFarlane, *An Autobiography of British Cinema*, p. 547.

39.   *Eric & Ernie*, p. 180.

**Chapter 11**

Pauline Kael: *Taking It All In* (London: Arena, 1987), p. 17.

Eric Morecambe: *Bring Me Sunshine*, p. 34.

1.   The movie was retitled *Drop Dead, Darling* for its UK release in 1966.

2.   Interview with the author, 11 November 1997.

3.   Interview with the author, 6 May 1998.

4.   Interview with the author, 11 September 1997. William Franklyn, who also worked with Owen on a number of movies, was similarly positive (interview with the author, 3 September 1997): 'Cliff Owen was a smashing comedy director. He encouraged you to be inventive. Good directors of comedy don't try to restrict you; if you are imaginative they encourage that element, and Cliff was very good like that.'

5.   Take, for example, the 1964 slapstick comedy *Bedtime Story*, which Marlon Brando considered to be 'the only [movie] I ever made that made me happy to get up in the morning and go to work', but which failed to have a similar effect on its audience. See Marlon Brando, *Songs My Mother Taught Me* (London: Century, 1994), p. 305.

6. Anonymous reviewer, *Monthly Film Bulletin*, vol. 33, no. 388 (May 1966), p. 7.

7. Cecil Wilson, *Daily Mail*, 25 March 1966, p. 18.

8. Ann Pacey, *Sun*, 24 March 1966, p. 3.

9. Margaret Hinxman, *Sunday Telegraph*, 27 March 1966, p. 12.

10. Anonymous reviewer, *The Times*, 24 March 1966, p. 16.

11. David Rider, *Films & Filming*, June 1966, p. 57.

12. Kenneth Williams, diary entry for 4 April 1966, *The Kenneth Williams Diaries*, ed. Russell Davies (London: HarperCollins, 1993), p. 276.

13. Margaret Hinxan, *Sunday Telegraph*, 27 March 1966, p. 12.

### Chapter 12

Eric Morecambe, *Bring Me Sunshine*, p. 133.

V. I. Pudovkin: *Film Technique* (London: Vision Press, 1954), p. 103.

1. Robin Bean, 'Trapped in a Sandwich', *Films & Filming*, January 1967, p. 60.

2. *Daily Mail*, 6 July 1967, p. 10. Movies that the British Board of Film Censors judged to be suitable for universal viewing were awarded a U certificate; movies judged to be suitable for adults only were awarded A certificates. (A new system of certificates was introduced in 1982: U – universal; PG – parental guidance; 15 and 18, with a R18 rating for licensed sex cinemas only.)

3. Peter Davalle, *Films & Filming*, vol. 13, no. 11 (August 1967), p. 26.

4. *Eric & Ernie*, p. 171.

5. *Monthly Film Bulletin*, vol. 34, no. 403 (August 1967), p. 126.

6. *There's No Answer to That!*, p. 92.

7. Ibid.

8. *Eric and Ernie*, p. 186.

9. Quoted in McFarlane, p. 547.

10. Ibid.

11. See, for example, *Eric & Ernie*, pp. 171, 176, 179 and 186.

12. Ibid., p. 186.

13. *There's No Answer to That!*, p. 92.

14. Ibid.

15. Quoted by Maurice Zolotow, *Billy Wilder in Hollywood* (London: Pavilion, 1988), p. 327.

16. *There's No Answer to That!*, p. 92.

17. *Eric & Ernie*, p. 186.

18. *There's No Answer to That!* p. 92.

19. Ibid.

20. Ibid., p. 94.

### A NATIONAL INSTITUTION

Hugh Carleton Greene: *The BBC as a Public Service* (London: BBC, 1960), p. 4.

Morecambe and Wise: *The Morecambe & Wise Show* (BBC) written by Eddie Braben.

### Chapter 13

Grace Wyndham Goldie: *Facing the Nation* (London: Bodley Head, 1979), p. 155.

Eric Morecambe: *There's No Answer to That!*, p. 112.

1. Quoted by Ernie Wise, *There's No Answer to That!*, p. 4.

2. *Still on My Way to Hollywood*, p. 129.

3.   Interview with the author, 20 February 1997. After Bernard Delfont had been bought out in 1967, Marsh had formed his own theatrical agency, London Management, in partnership with Michael Grade.

4.   Interview with the author, 5 February 1997.

5.   On 1 December 1965 the Postmaster General announced that the Television Advisory Committee had concluded that the German PAL (Phase Alternation Line) colour television system – rather than either the American NTSC or the French SECAM systems – was preferable for United Kingdom viewers (the principal reason being a superior quality of picture: PAL, like SECAM, uses 625 lines [compared to the NTSC system's 525] and also has built-in colour correction). The first colour television service in the UK began on BBC2 on 1 July 1967; colour was extended to BBC1 and commercial television on 625-line UHF on 15 November 1969.

6.   *There's No Answer to That!*, p. 5.

7.   Ibid., p. 4.

8.   Interview with the author, 5 February 1997.

9.   Interview with the author, 17 November 1997.

10.   Interview with the author, 5 February 1997.

11.   Interview with the author, 16 April 1997.

12.   Interview with the author, 5 February 1997.

13.   Recalled by Frank Muir, interview with the author, 17 November 1997.

14.   Interview with the author, 16 April 1997.

15.   Ibid. Ammonds added: 'And, anyway, there was no point in arguing since this facility had been given them for all their ATV shows at Elstree.'

16.   Ibid.

17.   Interview with the author, 11 September 1997. As a review of the show in *The Listener* noted (10 June 1971, p. 762), all of the close-up asides to the television audience were 'all in the camera script'.

18.   Interview with the author, 5 February 1997.

19.   Silvey, p. 203, and BBC WAC, TV Viewing Barometer, 2 September 1968. See also Peter Black, *The Mirror in the Corner*, (London: Hutchinson, 1972), pp. 215–16, for a sense of a television critic's attitude to BBC2 at this time.

20.   According to the BBC's Audience Research Report (WAC, VR/68/534, 9 October 1968): 'There was a warm welcome for Morecambe and Wise on their return to BBC Television . . . It was, viewers said, delightful to see this great comedy team back in business again in a really hilarious show and they were looking forward to the rest of the series – "let's hope they can keep it up".' The estimated BBC2 audience was 1,717,000 (which was twice as large as the next biggest audience of the evening for the movie *The Playboy of the Western World*) and the Reaction Index was 70.

21.   The Audience Report for the last show in the series (WAC, VR/68/653, 13 November 1968) recorded the view that it had been 'an excellent climax to a series which had given great pleasure over the past few weeks'. A '(very) small minority' complained that 'the script was weak (and suggestive, too, in places) and the style altogether too predictable', but the vast majority responded 'with rare enthusiasm'. The report concluded that 'Monday night would not be the same without this inimitable pair and an early return would seem to be imperative'. The estimated BBC2 audience was 2,575,500 (second only to an edition of the Western series *Hondo*) and the Reaction Index was 77 (the series average was 69).

22.   Interview with the author, 16 April 1997.

23.   *Still on My Way to Hollywood*, p. 131.

24.   Quoted by John Kemp, 'Laughing Off a Heart Attack', *Pre-Retirement Choice*, February 1975, p. 24.

25.   Ibid.

26.   Just what Walter Butterworth actually did for a living is a little unclear. Newspaper reports of the time described him as 'a twenty-three-year-old tyre fitter'.

27. Quoted by Gary Morecambe, *Morecambe and Wise*, p. 138.

28. *Eric & Ernie*, p. 197.

29. Morecambe, 'The Unfunny Thing That Happened to Me', *News of the World*, November 1968; reproduced in *Bring Me Sunshine*, p. 120.

30. Interview with the author, 11 November 1997.

31. *There's No Answer to That!*, p. 4.

32. Interview with the author, 5 February 1997.

33. Reported in the London *Evening News*, 21 May 1969, p. 8.

34. Interview with the author, 16 April 1997.

35. Cotton began discussing this proposal with various heads of departments several months earlier – before Morecambe had returned to work. Robin Scott, then Controller of BBC2, expressed his full support for the renegotiated contract on 6 June 1969 (BBC WAC, Morecambe and Wise File 2: 1963–70). The new contract was agreed with Morecambe and Wise in July 1969.

36. These four additional shows were, in effect, the remaining shows on their old contract, although, as they were now made as 45-minute – rather than the original half-hour – shows, the BBC, strictly speaking, received one hour for free.

37. Interview with the author, 16 April 1997.

38. Ibid.

39. Ibid.

40. Quoted by Gary Morecambe, *Morecambe and Wise*, p. 154. Hills and Green were, bizarrely, to star in, as well as write, their own shows for ATV; they had, in fact, appeared in their own show on Southern TV – *That Show* – in 1965, and another – *Those Two Fellas* – for ABC in 1966. In 1970, anxious to assume greater control of their work, they moved to America, where they wrote *The Don Knotts Show*, as well as material for Flip Wilson and Bill Cosby. After four years, Hills returned to Britain for family reasons, but Green remained in America, working on *The Johnny Carson Show*. In later years, they would write – mainly independently of each other – for such performers as Tommy Cooper, Jasper Carrott and Russ Abbott. Hills died on 6 June 1996, and Green on 15 March 1999. See Sid Green, 'Leave 'em Laughing', *Guardian*, 11 July 1996, p. 17 and Denis Gifford, 'Sid Green', *The Independent* Review Section, 17 March 1999, p. 6.

41. Interview with the author, 5 February 1997. Cotton later added: (telephone conversation with the author, 3 April 1998): 'I can't be sure about this – it's a long time ago – but I *think* I called Eric soon after the meeting, so I think that's when he knew about Hills and Green leaving.'

42. *Classic Morecambe & Wise*, vol. 1.

43. Interview with the author, 30 October 1997.

44. Ibid. Billy Liddell played outside-left for Liverpool FC between 1939 and 1961, making 495 appearances and scoring 216 goals. During this period he had a similar stature within both the club and the city to that enjoyed by Kenny Dalglish in the 1980s, and it was not uncommon at this time for journalists to refer to the club as 'Liddellpool' in his honour.

45. Ibid.

46. Ibid.

47. Interview with the author, 5 February 1997.

48. Interview with the author, 17 November 1997.

49. Dave Morris (1896–1960) was best-known for *Club-Night*. John Ammonds – who produced the show and worked very closely with him for several years on both radio and television – recalled (interview with the author, 26 November 1997): 'He was wonderful. Very much a challenge to work with, though – his eyesight, for one thing, was awful; he had these thick glasses on, but I'd still have to teach him his scripts parrot-fashion . . . He was often in disagreement with the BBC hierarchy – usually when he was trying to

get his personal fee increased! On one celebrated occasion it was about advertising: he used to finish his stage act by playing a heckelphone – a baritone oboe – and he told his audience that "this instrument was made by Cammell-Laird, in a moment of weakness". When hauled over the coals by the Head of Programmes for slipping this into a live radio show, he said, "Oh yes, I can just see my cloth-capped listeners rushing out the following morning to buy battleships!" He had a Groucho Marx-style sense of humour, but he didn't realise he had it. People *idolised* him, because he was a one-off. A terribly funny man.'

50.  Interview with the author, 30 October 1997.

51.  *There's No Answer to That!*, p. 5.

52.  Interview with the author, 5 February 1997.

53.  Eddie Braben, 'Eric and Ernie's Public Secret', *TV Times*, 6–12 September 1980, p. 10.

54.  Interview with the author, 30 October 1997.

55.  Ibid.

56.  Ibid.

57.  Interview with the author, 5 February 1997.

58.  Apart from Braben replacing Hills and Green as writer, several other significant changes had been made: Peter Knight replaced Alan Ainsworth as the show's musical director; two new performers – Ann Hamilton and Janet Webb – became regulars; and the use of a guest star – Peter Cushing, in this instance – became an integral part of the show.

59.  *There's No Answer to That!*, p. 78.

60.  Quoted by Gary Morecambe, *Morecambe and Wise*, p. 140. See also Joan Morecambe, *Morecambe and Wife*, pp. 110–112.

61.  BBC Audience Research Report (WAC, VR/69/444, 12 September 1962).

62.  Eric Morecambe, 'Those Critics They Broke My Heart', *Slough Evening Mail*, June 1971; reproduced in *Bring Me Sunshine*, p. 124.

63.  Quoted by John Ammonds: interview with the author, 16 April 1997. In that same letter he also wrote: 'When I was brought into this hospital, the doctors gave me a 10% chance – which Billy Marsh immediately took.'

64.  Interview with the author, 20 February 1997.

65.  Interview with the author, 30 October 1997.

66.  Ibid.

67.  Ibid. See also Braben, 'Eric and Ernie's Public Secret', p. 12.

68.  Eric Morecambe said: 'Eddie made me tougher and less gormless': quoted by Gary Morecambe, *Morecambe and Wise*, p. 159.

69.  Interview with the author, 30 October 1997.

70.  *There's No Answer to That!*, (my italics), p. 36.

71.  Ibid.

72.  Interview with the author, 30 October 1997.

73.  *There's No Answer to That!*, p. 37.

74.  'Friendship', *Sunday Times*, November 1971; reproduced in *Bring Me Sunshine*, p. 98.

75.  See Wilmut, *Tony Hancock*, pp. 99–100.

76.  According to Eric Morecambe in *There's No Answer to That!* (p. 37): 'The hierarchy at the BBC once said, "You can't get into bed together. You have to have two separate beds." But we thought that would have made it worse.'

77.  Garson Kanin, *Together Again!* (Garden City, NY: Doubleday, 1981), p. 7.

78.  This was another Laurel and Hardy connection: Stan Laurel often used to confuse people's gender. In *Another Fine Mess*, for example, he responds to a burly policeman's

stern lecture by saying, 'Yes, ma'am!' – although when Morecambe did it, there was always something flirtatious about his manner, which was never the case with Laurel.

79.   Interview with the author, 30 October 1997.

80.   John Mortimer, however, chose to discuss the same kind of distinctions in a different way, saying Eric and Ernie's relationship was that of 'the anarchic housewife' (Eric) and 'the pushy little husband' (Ernie); see his 'Eric Morecambe, without Peer', p. 32.

81.   Craig and Kinsley, one should note, contributed more conventional sketches to other editions of *The Morecambe & Wise Show*, including, most significantly, the 1976 Christmas special.

82.   Interview with the author, 17 November 1997.

83.   Tynan, 'The Top Joker', p. 23.

84.   BBC Audience Report on the 21 October 1968 show (WAC, VR/68/653, 13 November 1968). A similar response recorded in an earlier Report (WAC, VR/68/534, 9 October 1968) was: 'With so much apparent ad-libbing, the script as such seemed hardly to matter.'

85.   Quoted by Ernie Wise, *Still on My Way to Hollywood*, p. 12.

86.   'Eric and Ernie's Public Secret', p. 12.

87.   *There's No Answer to That!*, p. 87.

88.   Interview with the author, 26 November 1997.

89.   Interview with the author, 16 April 1997.

90.   Interview with the author, 30 October 1997.

91.   Ibid.

92.   *There's No Answer to That!*, p. 87.

93.   Interview with the author, 16 April 1997.

94.   *There's No Answer to That!*, p. 120.

95.   Ibid.

96.   Ibid.

97.   Ibid., p. 119.

98.   Ibid., pp. 119–20.

99.   Braben also managed, somehow, to contribute material to other shows on an occasional basis (an example being the well-known 'mind-reader interview' for *The Two Ronnies*, the text of which was reproduced in *The Listener*, 20 December 1973, p. 838), as well as writing and performing in his own BBC Radio 2 series *The Worst Show on the Wireless* (which won him a Writer's Guild Award in 1973 for the Best British Radio Comedy Series of the year).

100.   Interview with the author, 16 April 1997.

101.   Interview with the author, 30 October 1997.

102.   Ibid.

103.   Ibid.

104.   Interview with the author, 6 May 1997.

105.   *There's No Answer to That!*, p. 87.

106.   Braben, 'Eric and Ernie's Public Secret', p. 12.

107.   See pp. 10, 18–19, 22, 35–6 and 41 of the accompanying booklet to The Beatles' *Anthology 2* (Apple 7243 8 34448 2 3; 1996), and also Barry Miles, *Paul McCartney*, pp. 205–7, 291–2, 330–31, 357 and 551–2; Ian MacDonald, *Revolution in the Head* (London: Fourth Estate, 1994), pp. 124–6, 148–53 and 188–9; and George Martin, *All You Need is Ears* (London: Macmillan, 1979), and *Summer of Love: The Making of Sgt. Pepper* (London: Macmillan, 1994).

108.   Ernie Wise acknowledged (*Eric & Ernie*, pp. 208–9) that 'a great deal of credit for ideas and gags and, most important of all, putting them across, is due to Johnny Ammonds'.

109.   Tynan, 'The Top Joker', p. 23.

110. Following the poor health of Janet Webb, who used to appear at the end of each show.

111. Interview with the author, 16 April 1997.

112. Interview with the author, 5 February 1997. The surprising failure – at least so far – of the BAFTA organisers to recognise Ammonds' achievements with an appropriate award was commented upon – independently of each other and without any prompting from me – by no fewer than five BBC insiders whom I spoke to in connection with this book.

113. Interview with the author, 9 December 1997.

114. Quoted by John Ammonds, interview with the author, 16 April 1997.

115. 'I'm a Song and Dance Man – Not a Comic', *Slough Evening Mail*, June 1971; reproduced in *Bring Me Sunshine*, p. 127.

116. Recounted by Bob Monkhouse in his *Crying with Laughter* (London: Arrow, 1993), pp. 119–20.

117. Rashley died not long after appearing in the 1971 Christmas Special. His finest moment was probably his appearance as a somewhat shrivelled John Wayne – a characterisation which, although his only lines consisted of the repetition of the word 'howdy', collapsed almost immediately in the face of Eric Morecambe's merciless ad-libs.

118. Interview with the author, 16 April 1997. Webb had appeared with Morecambe and Wise during their ATV days (the date of her first appearance was 25 April 1964), and it had been Eric Morecambe's idea to feature her in their BBC shows (from 27 July 1969 onwards) and in some of their theatre appearances. Ammonds recalls that 'she eventually started taking the publicity more seriously – I remember that she asked me if I'd give her a better dressing-room! She used to tour with Eric and Ernie, and she made quite a tidy sum from opening shops and fêtes and that sort of thing.' She died prematurely in the late 1970s.

119. Quoted by Ann Hamilton, interview with the author, 9 December 1997.

120. The sketch in question is featured on the video *Two of a Kind*, vol. 2 (ITC, 1992). Ann Hamilton had first encountered Morecambe and Wise in 1961 at a party in Torquay, where she was appearing at the Pavilion in *Laughing Room Only* and they were in *Show Time* at the Princess Theatre.

121. Interview with the author, 9 December 1997.

122. Ibid.

123. *Eric & Ernie*, p. 168.

124. *There's No Answer to That!*, p. 103.

125. Interview with the author, September 1997.

126. Tynan, 'The Top Joker', p. 23.

127. Braben, 'Eric and Ernie's Public Secret', p. 12.

128. Interview with the author, 16 April 1997.

129. Ibid.

130. Noted by Ernie Wise, *Radio Times*, 23 December 1976, p. 7.

131. Interview with the author, 16 April 1997.

132. Ibid. Neither Joan nor Gary Morecambe (interview with the author, 11 November 1997) recalled him doing this on any particular occasion, which, presumably, means either that he was very subtle or that he was not being serious.

133. Interview with the author, 30 October 1997.

134. Interview with the author, 16 April 1997.

135. The first BBC2 show of their second series in 1969 attracted 3.8 per cent of the UK population and 9.5 per cent of the BBC2 public; by 10 August these percentages had risen to 4.7 and 11.1 respectively; by 24 August, 5.9 and 14.4; and by 7 September 6.4 and 15.0 (BBC Daily Viewing Barometers, WAC, box R9/37/5).

136. The first Christmas special shown on BBC1 in 1969 attracted 35.5 per cent of the

UK population, and received an R1 of 81 (Daily Viewing Barometer for 25 December 1969 and Audience Research Report WAC, box R9/37/5).

137.   According to John Ammonds (interview with the author, 16 April 1997): 'We had to find people to play the parts that Hills and Green used to play. Stooges, really. So we used the special guests. Peter Cushing was the first. He was a bit bemused to begin with, but he got on with it and got us off to a great start. Then we got him back asking when he'd be paid, and we developed those running gags, and it started to take off.'

138.   Interview with the author, 5 February 1997. The BBC1 audience for the show was 19,392,000. Unfortunately, although the BBC's Viewing Barometer for 25 December 1971 indicates that an Audience Report was in the process of being prepared for *The Morecambe & Wise Show*, the Report is missing from the BBC's Written Archives.

139.   Interview with the author, 16 April 1997.

## Chapter 14

Ronnie Waldman: 'Creating Light Entertainment in Television', p. 46.

Bill Cotton: interview with the author, 5 February 1997.

1.   Walter Benjamin, 'One-Way Street' (1928), *Selected Writings*, eds. Marcus Bullock and Michael W. Jennings (Cambridge, Mass.: Harvard University Press, 1996), vol. 1, p. 463.

2.   Tynan, 'The Top Joker', p. 20.

3.   See *Eric & Ernie*, p. 184; *There's No Answer to That!*, p. 79; and the *Evening Standard*, 23 November 1976, p. 36. The Queen Mother, the Queen, the Duke of Edinburgh, Prince Charles and Princess Margaret were all known to be admirers of Morecambe and Wise. Prince Charles joined them on stage for a soft-shoe shuffle in 1976 at the Theatre Royal, Windsor.

4.   Harold Wilson was a particularly great admirer of them, inviting them to numerous functions at Number 10 both before 1970 and after 1974 (including his 1976 retirement party), and he appeared on their first Thames TV Christmas special in 1978 (see Roy Hattersley, 'Dining Street', *Sunday Times*, 5 December 1993, section 8, p. 16). They were also invited to Number 10 during Edward Heath's time as Prime Minister (see *Morecambe and Wife*, p. 119).

5.   Denis Healey met Morecambe and Wise for drinks at Television Centre after one of their shows (correspondence with the author, 13 March 1998). A picture of the occasion was included in his *The Time of My Life* (Harmondsworth: Penguin, 1990).

6.   See, for example, Douglas Hurd's reference to the show in *Letters from a Diplomat* (BBC Radio Collection, Z BBC 2001, 1997).

7.   They and their colleagues watched a great deal of television during their extended stay in this country, and *The Morecambe & Wise Show* was a particular favourite (hence the nicknames). Today, back in Russia, they meet at the so-called 'London Club' to reminisce about their days in Britain, and, as the illustration (kindly provided by Nicholas Bethell) included in this book makes clear, attempt some familiar gestures one associates with the show.

8.   This anecdote was recounted to me by several interviewees, but a published version of it has recently appeared in the second edition of Alan Bennett's *Writing Home* (London: Faber, 1997), p. 292. Bennett notes that one well-known BBC producer/director, Sydney Lotterby, became so infuriated by this commissionaire's obstructiveness that he wound down the window of his car and shouted: 'Let me in, you old bugger, or I'll tear your other arm off!'

9.   Interview with the author, 5 February 1997.

10.   Transcribed from *Bill Cotton's Double Bill*, part 4, first broadcast on BBC Radio 2, 11 March 1998.

11.   Interview with the author, 1 May 1997.

12.   Interview with the author, 5 February 1997. (Archive recordings of the shows exist

on the following formats: programmes dated 27 July–25 December 1969 on 1 in. PAL videotape, 14 January 1970–25 December 1977 mostly on D3 digital videotape.)

13.   They had previously received one in 1964, making six in all.

14.   They had previously received one in 1964, making four in all.

15.   Correspondence with the author, 8 September 1997.

16.   Kenneth Williams, *The Kenneth Williams Diaries*, p. 276.

17.   John Mortimer, 'Eric Morecambe, without a Peer', p. 32.

18.   Interview with the author, 11 November 1997.

19.   Tynan, 'The Top Joker', pp. 20–23.

20.   Eric Morecambe, 'A Freudian Year for Ernie and Me', p. 837.

21.   Ibid., pp. 837–8.

22.   Ibid., p. 837.

23.   *There's No Answer to That!*, p. 45.

24.   Interview with the author, 16 April 1997.

25.   Interview with the author, 30 October 1997.

26.   Morecambe, 'I'm Not Joking', *Daily Sketch*, February 1971; reproduced in *Bring Me Sunshine*, pp. 108–9.

27.   *Still on My Way to Hollywood*, p. 15.

28.   This was the line-up for their 1971 tour, at one date of which the author was present.

29.   A video recording of one of their final 'bank raids', *Eric & Ernie Live* (4 Front/ PolyGram), was released in 1987.

30.   *Still on My Way to Hollywood*, p. 141.

31.   Interview with the author, 16 April 1997.

32.   Interview with the author, 9 December 1997.

33.   *There's No Answer to That!*, p. 43.

34.   The musical numbers, dance routines and so-called 'quickie' sketches were recorded on Fridays and/or Saturdays, before the special stage was brought in. The remainder of the show – the opening cross-talk, the bed-sit scenes, the exchanges in front of the tabs, the costume 'romp' and the concluding song – were recorded live in front of a studio audience on a Sunday evening.

35.   Interview with the author, 26 November 1997.

36.   Ibid.

37.   Interview with the author, 9 December 1997.

38.   *Guardian*, 24 December 1976, p. 11.

39.   *There's No Answer to That!*, p. 106.

40.   Interview with the author, 16 April 1997.

41.   Ibid.

42.   Ibid.

43.   Ibid.

44.   Interview with the author, 20 February 1997.

45.   Ibid.

46.   Interview with the author, 20 January 1998.

47.   Interview with the author, 20 October 1997.

48.   Transcribed from the 26 July 1984 BBC Radio 2 tribute to Eric Morecambe, *One of a Kind*. Morley's explanation complements the typical audience response recorded in the BBC's Audience Research Reports (e.g. WAC, VR/70/642, 2 February 1971: 'I particularly like the idea of having well-known actors doing things "out of character" and being treated disrespectfully').

49.   Quoted by Gary Morecambe, *Morecambe and Wise*, p. 160. It was as a direct result of the producer/director Melvin Frank seeing Jackson's first appearance – in the 1971 'Cleopatra' sketch – that she was offered a starring role in *A Touch of Class* (1973), for which she won her second Academy Award.

50.   *There's No Answer to That!*, p. 12.

51.   Ibid.

52.   Ibid. (The request can be heard, very faintly, on the recording of the show – 2 February 1973.)

53.   Transcribed from *One of a Kind*.

54.   Interview with the author, 26 November 1997.

55.   Ibid.

56.   *There's No Answer to That!*, pp. 14–15. Stephen Lowe's biography of his father, *Arthur Lowe* (London: Virgin, 1997, p. 116), claims that Lowe, after getting a big laugh with an 'ab-lib' – ERIC: 'Do you think this is wise?' LOWE: 'No – *this* is Wise: the one with the short, fat, hairy legs' – was 'trapped' in the corridor by Eric Morecambe, who poked his finger into Lowe's chest and said, 'I do the laughs on this show, don't you forget it.' This seems entirely implausible. The so-called 'ad-lib' was, in fact, written by Eddie Braben and agreed on by Morecambe, Wise and Ammonds long before Lowe even turned up for his first rehearsal (and he was 'fed' not by Morecambe but by John Le Mesurier). Joan Morecambe, on hearing of the allegation, said (interview with the author, 11 November 1997): 'Load of rubbish! He was *thrilled* whenever *any* guest got a big laugh, and, anyway, he loved Arthur Lowe.'

57.   Transcribed from the BBC1 *Omnibus* documentary on André Previn (produced by Chris Hunt and directed by Robin Lough), first broadcast on 1 March 1998.

58.   Interview with the author, 16 April 1997.

59.   Interview with the author, 3 September 1997.

60.   Interview with the author, 10 October 1997.

61.   Interview with the author, 20 January 1998.

62.   Interview with the author, 30 October 1997.

63.   Interview with the author, 26 November 1997. I quote John Ammonds in some detail on this matter in order to correct the misleading impression given by Jeremy Novick's *Morecambe & Wise: You Can't See the Join* (pp. 54–8) that Morecambe and Wise decided in 1974 that 'it was time for a new dimension', and that this necessitated a change of producer/director. There was, in fact, a strong desire for Ammonds to stay: 'I'm positive they would have preferred to have stayed with Johnny,' said Joan Morecambe (interview with the author, 11 November 1997). 'Eric thought an awful lot of him, he always said that Johnny Ammonds was *the* one, and, of course, they asked him to come back when they were over at Thames. So there was never any question of them wanting to lose him.'

64.   Correspondence with the author, 19 September 1997.

65.   Interview with the author, 11 September 1997.

66.   Quoted by Joan Morecambe, *Morecambe and Wife*, p. 29.

67.   Correspondence with the author, 8 September 1997.

68.   Interview with the author, 27 March 1997.

69.   Ibid.

70.   Ernie Wise's own account of this, followed by the routine itself, can be found 43 minutes into the video *Classic Morecambe & Wise*, vol. 1 (Watershed, 1993).

71.   The Shirley Bassey routine with the army boots, for example, had been developed by Ernest Maxin from a similar routine he had devised years earlier for a show that featured the Australian baritone Ormond Douglas; the André Previn/Grieg routine drew on a similar – though considerably less effective – routine that Morecambe and Wise had performed back in 1964 over at ATV; and the 'Oggy' vent routine evolved out of a far

more basic routine that had first been performed at the ABC Theatre in Yarmouth in the mid-sixties.

72.  Interview with the author, 27 March 1997.

73.  Interview with the author, 30 October 1997. Jeremy Beadle, who worked with Maxin some years later, made a similar point (interview with the author, 9 June 1998): 'The maximum is exactly what Maxin always gives you. He's so well prepared, so disciplined, but he's also one of those rare people who can take something and, with just one brushstroke, one little tweak or twist, improve it immeasurably. He really is one of the greats – a genuine showbusiness genius.'

74.  Most costumes were designed by Paula Bruce.

75.  Correspondence with the author, 10 September 1997.

76.  Interview with the author, 26 November 1997.

77.  Recalled by Ernest Maxin, interview with the author, 27 March 1997.

78.  Gene Kelly greatly admired the 'revised' version of his routine. 'He went *mad* for it,' Ernest Maxin recalled (interview, 27 March 1997): 'We had to make a tape of it for him, and he showed it all over the place in the States.' Kelly made a speech at a Variety Club luncheon in the late seventies in which he said that 'I enjoyed it more than seeing my own version', and that it was, in his view, 'one of the funniest things I've ever seen'. The gesture was spoiled very slightly by him turning to look in the direction of a very proud Ernie Wise and saying, 'Thank you, Eric' (see *There's No Answer to That!*, pp. 48–9).

79.  Interview with the author, 27 March 1997.

80.  Ibid.

81.  A parody of 'Slaughter on Tenth Avenue' from the Gene Kelly movie *Words and Music* (1943).

82.  Transcribed from the BBC2 *Forty Minutes* documentary *The Importance of Being Ernie* (produced by Richard Curson Smith and directed by Russell England), first broadcast on 27 April 1993.

83.  Interview with the author, 16 April 1997.

84.  Interview with the author, 6 May 1997. The choreographer, actor, director and producer Wendy Toye remarked (interview with the author, 20 May 1998): 'Eric wasn't the dancer Ernie was, but he had a terrific *style* as a dancer, he really had. You could see it when they danced together.'

85.  Interview with the author, 27 March 1997.

86.  Ibid. There were other potential star guests who, for one reason or another, failed to materialise. Michael Caine thought that it would be 'dangerous for his career' (*There's No Answer to That!*, p. 53); Ernie Wise invited Gielgud on to the show when he came across him in the BBC canteen, but he 'continued eating his custard . . .' (*There's No Answer to That!*, p. 54); Albert Finney confessed that he found it 'difficult' to play himself (*There's No Answer to That!*, p. 14); Sarah Miles was booked but withdrew; and Sean Connery, Roger Moore and Paul McCartney were pencilled in for appearances but Morecambe and Wise could never decide what routine to write for any one of them.

87.  Ibid.

88.  Interview with the author, 20 January 1998.

89.  Interview with the author, 27 March 1997.

90.  Peter Fiddick, *Guardian*, 28 December 1976, p. 6; Margaret Forword, *Sun*, 30 December 1976, p. 13; and Joseph Hone, *The Listener*, 6 January 1977, p. 24.

91.  BBC Audience Research Report WAC, VR/76/760, 19 January 1977.

92.  Interview with the author, 26 November 1997.

93.  See *There's No Answer to That!*, p. 116.

94.  It was reported at the time that the individual in question had sold the image directly to the paper. However, when he appealed – unsuccessfully – against his subsequent

dismissal, he insisted that he had taken pictures from the videotape for a former colleague who was then working for Rippon's old paper, the *South Devon Times*. It was this friend, he claimed, who then sent the pictures on to the *Daily Mirror* (see *The Times*, 8 October 1977, p. 2; 16 February 1978, p. 2; 17 February 1978 p. 3).

95.   *Daily Mirror*, 21 December 1976, pp. 1 and 3. The paper had been thwarted in an earlier attempt to take a legitimate picture by Andrew Todd, Head of BBC TV News, who denied them access. See the *Daily Mirror*, 9 December, pp. 1 and 16–17.

96.   Quoted by Margaret Forwood, 'The Star Eric Can't Get', *Sun*, 24 December 1977, p. 17. Morecambe and Wise were not the only ones feeling the strain. When Eddie Braben missed the 1976 Christmas show because of ill-health, Maxin had to recruit Barry Cryer, Mike Craig, Lawrie Kinsley and Ron McDonnell to write the script. Even the normally mild-mannered Arthur Tolcher was finding the pressure increasingly hard to cope with: on 10 December 1974, the *Daily Mail* reported (p. 3) that Tolcher's long-cherished plan to bring out a Christmas novelty single entitled 'Not Now, Arthur!' had been ruined by cockney comedy star Arthur Mullard's decision to release his own Christmas novelty single entitled 'Not Now, Arthur!' Tolcher was reported to be feeling shattered: 'It's ruined everything for me.' Mullard, however, was unrepentant: 'All I know is my name is Arthur,' he boasted.

97.   Interview with the author, 16 April 1997.

98.   *There's No Answer to That!*, p. 67.

99.   Gary Morecambe, *Funny Man*, p. 77.

100.   Ibid., p. 78.

101.   'I'm Not Joking', *Daily Sketch*, February 1971; reproduced in *Bring Me Sunshine*, pp. 108–9, p. 109.

102.   Interview with the author, 11 November 1997.

103.   *Eric and Ernie*, p. 182.

104.   Quoted by Joan Morecambe, *Morecambe and Wife*, p. 86.

105.   Interview with the author, 27 March 1997.

106.   Ibid.

107.   Ibid.

108.   Ibid.

109.   Ibid.

110.   Ibid.

111.   Interview with the author, 20 October 1997.

112.   Correspondence with the author, 8 September 1997.

113.   Interview with the author, 27 March 1997.

114.   Interview with the author, 20 October 1997.

115.   Interview with the author, 27 March 1997.

116.   Ibid.

117.   Ibid., Joan Morecambe, it should be noted, does not recall her husband (interview with the author, 11 November 1997) expressing 'any *major* anxieties about [the *South Pacific* routine]. He had his cut-off point and he'd either stop or go ahead and be positive. He didn't muck around and be agonising about what to do.'

118.   Interview with the author, 27 March 1997.

119.   Interview with the author, 20 October 1997. The BBC's Audience Research Report on the show (WAC, VR/77/701, 14 February 1978) also acknowledged this response: 'A number of the sample commented on the agility and fitness of those taking part, whilst others praised the skill and precision of the editing that this number exhibited.'

120.   Previn *did* make it clear that such references amused him. He noted (correspondence with the author, 23 September 1997): 'I'm always happy to hear that the shows I did with Morecambe and Wise are still so kindly remembered. Of course I had the most wonderful time working with them.'

121. Interview with the author, 20 January 1998.

122. Interview with the author, 10 October 1997.

123. Estimated audience recorded in the BBC's Daily Viewing Barometer for 25 December 1977, WAC. ITV, however, claimed that another BBC programme – *The Mike Yarwood Christmas Show*, whose producer/director, ironically, was John Ammonds – was the most watched show of the Christmas period; this was rejected by the BBC's Audience Research Department. The reason for the dispute was that, until August 1981, television audience measurement was undertaken separately by the BBC's Audience Research Department and the Joint Industry Committee for Television Advertising Research (JICTAR). The Audience Research Department was interested in the number of people who had watched a programme, counting all of those who had seen more than half of it, whereas JICTAR, serving a commercial operation dependent on advertising revenue, sought out information regarding the specific audience available within a fifteen-minute segment for each advertising break. In response to such disputes the Annan Report of 1977 recommended that a common system be implemented, and BARB (Broadcasters' Audience Research Board), owned jointly by the BBC and the ITCA (Independent Televison Companies' Association), was set up in 1981.

124. According to the BBC's Daily Viewing Barometer for that day, the Queen's Speech was watched by 37.1 per cent of the UK population on BBC1 and, simultaneously, by 6.8 per cent on ITV, giving it a total audience of 22,169,500 – 6,665,500 fewer than that for *The Morecambe & Wise Show*.

125. According to the same source as above, ITV's most popular programme was *The Muppet Show*, which attracted an estimated audience of 10,756,500.

126. An estimated 6,278,125 people saw the first edition of *Running Wild* on 21 April 1954 (BBC Audience Research Report WAC, VR/54/218, 5 May 1954).

127. Waldman, 'The Toughest Job', p. 5.

## Chapter 15

Ernie Wise: *Still on My Way to Hollywood*, p. 14.

Eric Morecambe: *The Morecambe & Wise Show*, 25 December 1977.

1. Peter Atkinson, *Evening Standard*, 27 January 1978, p. 1.

2. Interview with the author, 5 February 1997.

3. Ibid.

4. Quoted by Gary Morecambe, *Morecambe and Wise*, p. 191.

5. Interview with the author, 27 March 1997. Ernie Wise (*Still on My Way to Hollywood*, p. 162) put the sum as 'something like three times what the BBC had been paying'.

6. Transcribed from *The Importance of Being Ernie*.

7. Interview with the author, 11 November 1997.

8. Interview with the author, 5 February 1997. Cotton also commented (correspondence with the author, 3 December 1997): 'I did in fact say [at the Christmas party] that the BBC would match the Thames offer for money, but quite honestly I think things had gone too far by then . . . [A]s Eric is reported as saying, "Bill looked after himself, we must look after us!" I think they really wanted a change.'

9. *Still on My Way to Hollywood*, p. 162.

10. Note, for example, the brisk, unsentimental manner in which Benny Hill – who had been at Thames Television for twenty years – was removed from the screen in 1989.

11. Interview with the author, 11 November 1997.

12. Graham Stark said of Morecambe and Wise's contribution (correspondence with the author, 8 April 1998): 'I had helped Eric and Ernie with one of their routines on an Alma Cogan show some years earlier and, being the gents they were, this was their way of repaying the debt. Like all the other guests, who included Peter Sellers, Michael Caine, Bob Monkhouse, Tony Blackburn, Pete Murray and Bernie Winters, they appeared free.'

13. 'When Eric and Ernie were Ivy Benson', *Southampton Evening Echo*, October 1971;

reproduced in *Bring Me Sunshine*, p. 134. Earlier that year, Ernie Wise said bizarrely (*Bring Me Sunshine*, p. 129) that he supposed that he would still like to make a Hollywood movie 'but I think that's a dream of Eric's, isn't it?'

14.   Quoted by Alan Day, 'We Want a Change, Say Eric and Ern', *Titbits*, 8–14 March 1973, p. 26.

15.   Interview with the author, 11 November 1997.

16.   See *There's No Answer to That!*, pp. 93 and 131.

17.   Ibid., p. 13.

18.   See the informative account by Michael Alvarado and John Stewart, *Made for Television: Euston Films Limited* (London: BFI/Thames, 1985).

19.   Overseas sales were impressive, too: e.g. *The Sweeney* was sold to 51 countries, *Special Branch* to 39 and *Minder* to 26 (*Made for Television*, p. 212).

20.   See *Made for Television*, pp. 30–114.

21.   Instigated by Verity Lambert.

22.   Peter Atkinson, *Evening Standard*, 27 January 1978, p. 48.

23.   This scheduling strategy is known as 'stripping' (meaning that the same series is played in the same slot five or six times each week to encourage channel loyalty at certain times of the day).

24.   See, for example, Stephen Danos, 'How Americans Get Wise to Eric and Ern', London *Evening News*, 13 October 1980, pp. 14–15.

25.   *There's No Answer to That!*, p. 124. The shows did, however, attract some notable admirers, including Cary Grant, Alan Alda, Harry Morgan (Colonel Sherman from *M*A*S*H*), Gene Kelly, Jay Leno and Shirley MacLaine.

26.   Jones was actually quoted in the *Evening Standard* on 27 January 1978 (p. 48) as saying that he intended to 'make the show as different as possible from the BBC's format', but he told Gary Morecambe (*Morecambe and Wise*, p. 196) that he had been misquoted and had, in fact, said the precise opposite ('when you buy a Rolls-Royce' he added, 'you don't try and convert it into an Austin Seven').

27.   Interview with the author, 27 March 1997.

28.   The BBC did indeed sign him up, but after he had turned down the invitation from Thames.

29.   Interview with the author, 30 October 1997. Braben also acknowledged that Morecambe and Wise's failure to inform him of their intentions, although it did not affect his subsequent decision, hurt him none the less. Bill Cotton observed (correspondence with the author, 3 December 1997): 'I think they made the mistake of taking him for granted. [Certain people] had done this to him before and I think he decided he was not going through it again.'

30.   John Ammonds recalls (interview with the author, 26 November 1997) Eric Morecambe mentioning this to him at some point during 1981–2 (when the proposal was discussed and rejected for a second time).

31.   Later on, at Ernie's request, Jones would commission pilot scripts from several of the most experienced comedy writers in the country, but none, it would turn out, were deemed suitable for Morecambe and Wise (interview with John Ammonds, 26 November 1997, and *Television Weekly*, 9–15 February 1983, p. 1).

32.   Interview with the author, 16 April 1997.

33.   One should note that none of *The Morecambe & Wise Shows* – prior to Eddie Braben's return – used any substantial material *verbatim* from the BBC years, although, as all those involved acknowledged subsequently, certain old ideas, formats and exchanges served, increasingly, as the basis for the new scripts.

34.   Sean Day-Lewis, *The Times*, 27 December 1978, p. 7.

35.   Among Beckett's directing credits was the 1966 ABC show *Those Two Fellas*, which starred Hills and Green.

36. Quoted by Celia Brayfield, *Glasgow Herald*, 23 October 1978, p. 8.

37. Sean Day-Lewis, *The Times*, 27 December 1978, p. 7.

38. Quoted by Gary Morecambe, *Morecambe and Wise*, pp. 197–8.

39. According to the figures produced by AGB (Audits of Great Britain) for JICTAR (the Joint Industry Committee for Television Advertising Research), the 25 December 1978 show attracted 19.15 million viewers. Although ITV had contested the BBC's record audience claim for the 1977 show, it had clearly reconciled itself to the figure when it was time to promote *its* first *Morecambe & Wise Christmas Show* the following year (see *TV Times*, 21 December 1978, p. 5).

40. *There's No Answer to That!*, p. 96.

41. Quoted by Gary Morecambe, *Funny Man*, p. 110.

42. See Joan Morecambe, *Morecambe and Wife*, pp. 149–54, for a detailed account of this period.

43. Quoted by Joan Morecambe, *Morecambe and Wife*, p. 152.

44. Quoted by Rogers, 'Morecambe and Wise', p. 42.

45. *There's No Answer to That!*, p. 4.

46. Quoted by Kemp, 'Laughing Off a Heart Attack', p. 24.

47. Quoted by Gary Morecambe, *Hard Act to Follow*, p. 127.

48. Gail Morecambe, ibid., p. 112.

49. Ibid., p. 117.

50. Quoted by Gary Morecambe, *Morecambe and Wise*, p. 178.

51. Quoted by Gary Morecambe, *Funny Man*, p. 47.

52. Quoted by Joan Morecambe, *Morecambe and Wife*, p. 99.

53. Sid's mother-in-law reacts to his disastrous televised show by saying (p. 120): 'I can't go out shopping here now' – which echoes Sadie's reaction to the reviews of *Running Wild*.

54. At BBC Television Centre, Sid overhears a messenger at Reception being told that Ammonds is no longer at the BBC (p. 141): 'I think he defected. I think he went to another company – you know, went to the other side.'

55. Ibid., p. 147.

56. Ibid., p. 31.

57. Ibid., p. 29.

58. *There's No Answer to That!*, p. 105.

59. Two children's books, *The Reluctant Vampire* (London: Methuen, 1982) and *The Vampire's Revenge* (London: Methuen, 1983); *Eric Morecambe on Fishing* (London: Pelham 1984); and the novel that he was working on at the time of his death, *Stella* (London: Severn House, 1986).

60. Quoted by Coleman, 'They'll Always be Eric and Ernie . . .', p. 16.

61. Ammonds, acting in response to a suggestion from Bernie, had come up with a popular replacement for Mike Winters – an eleven-stone St Bernard called Schnorbitz. Ammonds seemed to have a happy knack of suggesting such details; aside from the 'Groucho' dance at the end of *The Morecambe & Wise Show*, he had previously been responsible for having Val Doonican croon his Perry Como-style ballads from the comfort of what became his trademark rocking-chair.

62. This rather undermines the suggestion made by Philip Jones (quoted by Gary Morecambe, *Morecambe and Wise*, p. 198) that the producer/director's contribution to the show was relatively superficial and that all of 'the producers of the show were very lucky to be assigned to it'.

63. Interview with the author, 26 November 1997. This meeting is also referred to in Gary Morecambe's *Funny Man*, p. 81.

64. Interview with the author, 16 April 1997.

65. Interview with the author, 30 October 1997. (Junkin and Cryer had actually been signed – prior to Morecambe's heart attack – as writers of the series, but, following the subsequent change of plan, they were released to accept alternative offers.)

66. See the *Daily Express*, 24 September 1980, p. 27.

67. Elisabeth Cowley, *Daily Mail*, 27 October 1982, p. 31. Two years earlier (17 September 1980, p. 29), Cowley had written: 'No doubt about it – the pair are totally back on form now that their old producer, John Ammonds, is at the helm . . . and Eddie Braben is doing the scripts.'

68. Herbert Kretzner, *Daily Mail*, 4 September 1980, p. 23.

69. Interview with the author, 16 April 1997.

70. Ibid. The new ending was still not problem-free: 'Eric knew it was funnier if he came on from right at the back of this "infinity stage" [a brightly-lit cyclorama, combined with a lit floor painted the same colour, to produce the effect of an infinite horizon], rather than coming on from the side, but the insurance people would've gone mad if they'd known, because down below – they call it a "ground row" – you'd got all the lights and the electrical cables and it was pretty hazardous. The lighting director said, "You can't have him wandering about down there!" So Eric said, "I'll go on from the side, then you can tell me which is funnier." And he did, and the lighting director said, "Er, yes, I see what you mean . . ." So he went off and crossed his fingers. But it worked, and he kept on doing it.'

71. Quoted by Peter Sheridan, 'Too Late for New Jokes', *Daily Mail*, 30 December 1982, pp. 14–15.

72. Ibid.

73. Interview with the author, 30 October 1997.

74. For example, on more than one occasion, the quick sketch involving Eric and Ernie at the piano, with Ernie singing songs with a 'water' cue (such as 'April Showers', 'Singin' in the Rain') and Eric being drenched; the germ of the Grieg Piano Concerto routine; the 'Won't You Play a Simple Melody'/'Musical Demon' counter-melody routine revived in 1976 for Elton John; and several costume 'romps'.

75. Interview with the author, 11 December 1997.

76. Interview with the author, 16 April 1997.

77. Quoted by Rogers, 'Morecambe and Wise', p. 42.

78. *There's No Answer to That!*, p. 100.

79. Quoted by Gary Morecambe, *Morecambe and Wise*, p. 203.

80. Ibid., p. 122.

81. Interview with the author, 11 November 1997.

82. Quoted by Kemp, 'Laughing Off a Heart Attack', p. 25. Although this quotation dates from 1975, Gary Morecambe confirmed (interview with the author, 11 November 1997) that it reflected accurately his father's feelings in the early eighties: 'More so, if anything.'

83. Morecambe was an enthusiastic, and very active, supporter of the British Heart Foundation (see Joan Morecambe, *Morecambe and Wife*, pp. 119 and 122), and, it should be noted, his performances at this time also served to inspire many people who had undergone similar operations (see *There's No Answer to That!*, p. 123).

84. *There's No Answer to That!*, pp. 12–13.

85. *There's No Answer to That!*, p. 18.

86. Grant had first met Morecambe and Wise early in 1964, when he was in Bristol to see his mother and they were in pantomime at the Hippodrome. He saw them again several years later when they performed in Bournemouth. He became a great admirer of Morecambe, especially, and they used to write to each other using an old music-hall patois. In 1979, Eric and Joan joined Grant and his future wife, Barbara Harris, for lunch at a Fabergé Trade Fair at the Royal Lancaster Hotel in London. 'I will never forget that day,' Grant wrote to Gary Morecambe. 'We spent a wonderful lunchtime together,

especially Eric and I because we went down vaudeville memory lane, remembering names of past eras . . . I remember telling Eric that I had actually appeared on the same bill as George Formby, which rather puzzled him; but not as much as when I pointed out that I was referring to George Formby *Senior*, not his son.' He added, that, after lunch, 'While we were in the toilets, a man came in, recognized your father and asked whatever happened to Wilson, Kepple and Betty . . . Eric replied, "Not a lot. Two of them died." And that just finished me off. I fell about laughing. I'm sure that Eric's reply was well established with the British public, but I had not heard it used like that before, and I will never forget it.' See Gary Morecambe, *Funny Man*, p. 72; also Graham McCann, *Cary Grant: A Class Apart*, pp. 258 and 265–6.

87.   See Rogers, 'Morecambe and Wise', p. 44.

88.   Interview with the author, 5 February 1997.

89.   Interview with the author, 20 February 1997.

90.   Interview with the author, 20 February 1997.

91.   *Eric and Ernie*, p. 37.

92.   Quoted by Alan Day, 'We Want a Change, say Eric and Ern', *Titbits*, 8–14 March 1973.

93.   See Morecambe, 'Those Critics They Broke My Heart', *Slough Evening Mail*, June 1971; reproduced in *Bring Me Sunshine*, p. 124.

94.   See Coleman, 'They'll Always be Eric and Ernie . . .', p. 16.

95.   While still at the BBC Morecambe and Wise did host a series of six programmes entitled *Child's Play* (1976), featuring various guest actors appearing in brief playlets written by children, and, at Thames, they appeared in one of the last ever episodes of *The Sweeney* (1978). Morecambe alone, in 1979 and 1980, appeared in a couple of short films for Anglia Television based on poems by Sir John Betjemen. However, in spite of their efforts to find a new format, this was the sum of their experimentation.

96.   Quoted by Andrew Harvey, *Daily Express*, 29 May 1984, p. 43.

97.   Quoted by Gary Morecambe, *Morecambe and Wise*, p. 215.

98.   Quoted by Wise, *Still on My Way to Hollywood*, pp. 164–5.

99.   Ibid., p. 165.

100.   Ibid., p. 166.

101.   Recalled by Joan Morecambe, interview with the author, 11 November 1997.

102.   Ibid.

103.   Ibid.

104.   Wyn Ammonds had, in fact, been suffering from multiple sclerosis for many years, but in recent months her condition had worsened. 'She's a wonderful, beautiful lady,' said Joan Morecambe (interview with the author, 11 November 1997), 'and she never stopped smiling and was never, ever, heard to complain about that terrible disease. And Johnny retired to look after her, when she could no longer look after herself. What a man.'

105.   Eric Morecambe told reporters during his recuperation period that this movie 'would be the first thing we will do' once he and Wise returned to work the following year. See 'Eric and Ernie plan television comeback', *Daily Telegraph*, 6 August 1979, p. 11.

106.   See *There's No Answer to That!*, p. 125.

107.   Ibid., pp. 94–5. Vincent Price was one possible co-star mentioned.

108.   Ibid., p. 95.

109.   Such as the far funnier 'House of Terror' romp that featured Francis Matthews as Vyvyan Darling, private detective, and Ann Hamilton as Miss Kate (broadcast originally on 19 September 1971).

110.   Interview with the author, 16 April 1997.

111.  *Night Train to Murder* would eventually be shown on the afternoon of 3 January 1985 – six months after Eric Morecambe's death.

112.  *Atoll K* (also known as *Robinson Crusoe-Land* and *Utopia*) was Laurel and Hardy's final movie. A French-Italian co-production, it was made when Laurel, in particular, was in very poor health.

113.  Quoted by Gary Morecambe, *Funny Man*, p. 154.

114.  Charles Henry, responsible for comedy productions at the London Palladium during the fifties: quoted by Wise, *Still on My Way to Hollywood*, p. 178.

## Chapter 16

Peter Cook: quoted by Sarah Seymour, 'Peter, My Beautiful Brother', *Guardian*, 15 October 1996, G2T, p. 6.

1.  Joan Morecambe told me that she called Wise 'soon after' she had been told that her husband had died (interview with the author, 11 November 1997). Gary Morecambe agreed that she called Wise 'immediately' after receiving the news (see *Morecambe and Wise*, p. 227). Wise, however, recalled Joan ringing at 'two in the morning' (*Still on My Way to Hollywood*, p. 166); he told the *Daily Express* (29 May 1984, p. 2) that he had heard (from Billy Marsh) at 5.30 a.m.

2.  *Still on My Way to Hollywood*, p. 166.

3.  Ibid.

4.  *Morecambe and Wife*, p. 9.

5.  Ibid., p. 170.

6.  Ibid., p. 172.

7.  Interview with the author, 11 November 1997.

8.  Quoted by Gary Morecambe, *Morecambe and Wise*, p. 221. See also Joan Morecambe, *Morecambe and Wife*, pp. 172–3.

9.  Interview with the author, 11 November 1997.

10.  George Bartholomew died in 1976, and Sadie in 1977.

11.  *Morecambe and Wife*, p. 176.

12.  Ibid., p. 177.

13.  Ibid.

14.  Ibid., pp. 177–8.

15.  Ibid., p. 173.

16.  Gary Morecambe, *Morecambe and Wise*, p. 226.

17.  Quoted by Joan Morecambe, *Morecambe and Wife*, p. 178.

18.  Ibid.

19.  Gail Morecambe, *Hard Act to Follow*, p. 118.

20.  Ibid.

21.  *Morecambe and Wife*, p. 179.

22.  Ibid., p. 180.

23.  Ibid., p. 181.

24.  Ernie Wise had agreed to join Stennett for a similar appearance the following month (see *The Times*, 29 May 1984, p. 1).

25.  Joan Morecambe, *Morecambe and Wife*, p. 180.

26.  Transcribed from *One of a Kind*.

27.  Quoted by Ian Black and John Burns, *Daily Express*, 29 May 1984, p. 2.

28.  Ibid.

29.  *Morecambe and Wife*, p. 181.

30.  Quoted by Hugh Clayton, *The Times*, 29 May 1984, p. 1.

31.  *Morecambe and Wife*, p. 182.

32. Quoted in *The Times*, 29 May 1984, p. 1.
33. Ibid.
34. Quoted in the *Daily Express*, 29 May 1984, p. 3.
35. Ibid., p. 2.
36. Quoted by Joan Morecambe, *Morecambe and Wife*, p. 183.
37. Ibid.
38. Ibid.
39. Ibid., p. 184.
40. Interview with the author, 11 November 1997.
41. Ibid.
42. Quoted by Gail Morecambe, *Hard Act to Follow*, p. 109.
43. *Morecambe and Wife*, p. 193.
44. Quoted by *Daily Express*, 29 May 1984, p. 1.
45. Quoted in *The Times*, 29 May 1984, p. 1.
46. Quoted by Liz Phillips, *Daily Star*, 29 May 1984, p. 14.
47. Robin Stringer, *Daily Telegraph*, 29 May 1984, p. 3.
48. *The Times*, 29 May 1984, p. 32.
49. Leader in *Sun*, 29 May 1984, p. 6.
50. Transcribed from *One of a Kind*.
51. *Morecambe and Wife*, p. 186.
52. Estimated by *The Times*, 5 June 1984, p. 3, and *Guardian*, p. 4.
53. Quoted by Mike Craig, *Look Back with Laughter*, vol. 2, p. 176.
54. Interview with the author, 9 December 1997.
55. See *The Times*, 5 June, p. 3.
56. Ibid.
57. See *Sun*, 5 June 1984, p. 5.
58. Gary Morecambe, *Morecambe and Wise*, p. 230.
59. Transcribed from *Newsbeat*, BBC Radio 1, 28 March 1979.
60. *Hard Act to Follow*, p. 118.
61. See Mary Fieldhouse's *For the Love of Tommy* (London: Robson, 1986).
62. Telephone conversation with the author, 10 February 1998.
63. Transcribed from *One of a Kind*.
64. *Still on My Way to Hollywood*, p. 167.
65. Ibid. Apart from losing his partner, Wise also lost his mother, Connie, who died at the age of eighty-five just months after Morecambe.
66. Ibid., p. 169.
67. Quoted by Rogers, 'Morecambe and Wise', p. 42.
68. *Still on My Way to Hollywood*, p. 169.
69. Ibid., p. 168.
70. Ibid., p. 170.
71. Ibid., p. 173.
72. Terry Johnson's cruelly perceptive play *Dead Funny* (London: Methuen, 1994, p. 52) alludes to this: in Act 2, Scene 1, a psychic believes she has received a message for Ernie from Eric: 'Sorry about the early retirement. Don't let them get you on *Celebrity Squares*.'
73. *Still on My Way to Hollywood*, p. 175.
74. See A. N. Wilson, 'The Infinite Pathos of Being an "And"', *Sunday Telegraph*, 28 April 1993, p. 7.

75. Max Davidson, *Daily Telegraph*, 28 April 1993, p. 17.

76. A. N. Wilson, *Sunday Telegraph*, 2 May 1993, p. 7.

77. Craig Brown, *Sunday Times*, 2 May 1993, p. 9/11.

78. Lynne Truss, *The Times*, 28 April 1993, p. 31.

79. Interview with the author, 5 February 1997.

80. Transcribed and edited from the movie *London Town* (1945) and the video *The Golden Years of British Comedy: '40s* (Classic Pictures, 1993).

81. Interview with the author, 5 February 1997. Michael Grade made a similar point (interview with the author, 20 February 1997): 'Ernie was often underrated, but I've watched them over and over again, and there would be certain nights when Ernie was absolutely inspired, and it would just lift Eric, and on those nights when they weren't so good it was probably because Ernie wasn't feeling great or whatever. When Ernie had a good piece of material, he was sensational. Absolutely sensational.'

82. Quoted in *Daily Express*, 29 May 1984, p. 2.

83. Quoted in *Daily Star*, 29 May 1984, p. 15.

84. Quoted by Novick, p. 125.

85. Leigh Hunt, 'The Death of Elliston' (10 July 1831), *Dramatic Essays*, eds. William Archer and Robert W. Lowe (London: Walter Scott, 1894), pp. 214–18.

### Epilogue

Bill Cotton: interview with the author, 5 February 1997.

*The Good Companions*: J. B. Priestley (London: Heinemann, 1957), p. 521.

Eric Morecambe: quoted by Gail Morecambe, *Hard Act to Follow*, p. 118.

1. The first three shows were broadcast by BBC1 on 14, 21 and 28 May 1984; three more shows were hastily commissioned to exploit their success. See Gary Morecambe, *Morecambe and Wise*, pp. 242–4.

2. Quoted by Andrew Duncan in *Radio Times*, 24–30 April 1993, p. 22.

3. Interview with the author, 5 February 1997.

4. Interview with the author, 16 April 1997.

5. Interview with the author, 27 March 1997.

6. Quoted by Novick, p. 123.

7. Reported in *Independent on Sunday*, 11 July 1993, p. 3.

8. Interview with the author, 17 November 1997.

9. Interview with the author, 30 October, 1997.

10. Interview with the author, 16 April 1997.

11. Interview with the author, 27 April 1998.

12. Stan Laurel, quoted by Ronald L. Smith, *Who's Who in Comedy* (New York: Facts On File, 1992), p. 265.

13. Nancy Banks-Smith, *Guardian*, 29 May 1984, p. 9.

14. Quoted in *Daily Mirror*, 5 June 1984, p. 5.

# Bibliography

**Morecambe and Wise**

Braben, Eddie, *The Best of Morecambe and Wise* (London: Woburn Press, 1974)
  'Eric and Ernie's Public Secret', *TV Times*, 6–12 September 1980, pp. 10–12
Coleman, Alix, 'They'll Always be Eric and Ernie . . .', *TV Times*, 2 October 1980, pp. 16–17
Court, W. O., 'Swinging Doors on Their Minds', *TV Times*, 22 June 1962, p. 7
Craig, Mike, 'One of a Kind', *Look Back with Laughter*, vol. 2 (Manchester: Mike Craig Enterprises, 1996)
Day, Alan, 'We Want a Change, say Eric and Ern', *Titbits*, 8–14 March 1973, pp. 23 and 26
Edwards, John, 'Bring Me Sunshine', *Daily Mail*, 13 December 1984, p. 21
Fisher, John, 'Two of a Kind', *Funny Way to be a Hero* (London: Frederick Muller, 1973)
Goddard, Alan, 'There Were These Two Comedians . . .', *Weekend*, 8–14 July 1964, pp. 16–17
Hills, Dick, 'Eric Morecambe', *The Dictionary of National Biography, 1981–1985*, (Oxford: Oxford University Press, 1990), pp. 287–8
Hynd, Stewart, 'When Two Quarters Make a Whole', *TV Times*, 27 October 1961, p. 13
Kemp, John, 'Laughing Off a Heart Attack: The Secret Fear that Haunts Eric Morecambe', *Pre-Retirement Choice*, February 1975, pp. 24–5
Lewin, David, 'Eric . . . the Sunniest, Funniest Man of Them all', *Daily Mail*, 29 May 1984, pp. 6–7
Linden, Eric, 'Morecambe and Wisecracking', *TV Times*, 17 August 1962, p. 9
Midwinter, Eric, 'Morecambe & Wise: Twins of Mirth', in *Make 'Em Laugh*, (London: Allen & Unwin, 1979)
Morecambe, Eric, 'A Freudian Year for Ernie and Me', *The Listener*, 20 December 1973, pp. 837–8
  'Summer Place', *Sunday Times Magazine*, 11 July 1976, p. 46
  *Mr Lonely* (London: Eyre Methuen, 1981)
  *The Reluctant Vampire*, (London: Methuen, 1982)
  'My Happiest Days', *Daily Mirror*, 29 May 1984, p. 9
  *The Vampire's Revenge* (London: Methuen, 1983)
  *Eric Morecambe on Fishing* (London: Pelham, 1984)
  *Stella* (London: Severn House, 1986)
Morecambe, Eric and Ernie Wise, *The Morecambe and Wise Joke Book* (London: Wolfe, 1968)
  *The Morecambe & Wise Family Fun Book* (Ipswich: Premiums in Print, 1972)
  with Dennis Holman, *Eric & Ernie* (London: W. H. Allen, 1973)
  *Bring Me Sunshine: A Harvest of Morecambe and Wise* (London: William Kimber, 1978)
  *The Morecambe and Wise Special* (London: W. H. Allen, 1978)
  with Michael Freedland, *There's No Answer to That!* (London: Arthur Barker, 1981)
Morecambe, Gail, 'Eric Morecambe', in Gary Morecambe and Michael Sellers, *Hard Act to Follow* (London: Blake, 1997)

# Bibliography

Morecambe, Gary, *Funny Man* (London: Methuen, 1982)
    *The Illustrated Morecambe* (London: Macdonald, 1986)
Morecambe, Gary and Martin Sterling, *Morecambe and Wise: Behind the Sunshine* (London: Pan, 1995)
Morecambe, Gary and Michael Sellers, *Hard Act to Follow* (London: Blake, 1997)
Morecambe, Joan and Michael Leitch, *Morecambe and Wife* (London: Pelham, 1985)
Mortimer, John, 'Eric Morecambe, without a Peer', *Sunday Times*, 16 December 1979, p. 32
Novick, Jeremy, *Morecambe & Wise: You Can't See the Join* (London: Chameleon, 1997)
Pride, Margaret, 'Getting Wise Paid Off for Eric', *Reveille*, 18–14 April 1968, p. 8
Rogers, Byron, 'Morecambe and Wise', *Sunday Telegraph Magazine*, 14 September 1980, pp. 36–43
Tynan, Kenneth, 'The Top Joker', *Observer Magazine*, 9 September 1973, pp. 20–23
    'Eric Morecambe', in *Profiles* (London: Nick Hern, 1989)
Waterman, Jack, 'Double Vision', *The Listener*, 16 March 1978, pp. 346–8
Wise, Ernie, with Trevor Barnes, *Still on My Way to Hollywood* (London: Duckworth, 1990)

## General

Adorno, Theodor W., 'How to Look at Television', *Quarterly of Film, Radio and Television*, vol. 3, Spring 1954, pp. 213–35
Alvarado, Manuel and John Stewart, *Made for Television: Euston Films Limited* (London: BFI/Thames, 1985)
Askey, Arthur, *Before Your Very Eyes* (London: Woburn Press, 1975)
Auden, W. H., *The Dyer's Hand and Other Essays* (London: Faber, 1963)
Balcon, Michael, *Michael Balcon Presents . . . A Lifetime of Films* (London: Hutchinson, 1969)
Barker, Ernest (ed.), *The Character of England* (Oxford: Clarendon Press, 1947)
Barr, Charles (ed.), *All Our Yesterdays* (London: BFI, 1986)
Beloff, Max, 'Broadcasting and twentieth-century civilization', *The BBC Quarterly*, vol. 7, no. 1 (1952), pp. 18–24
Benjamin, Walter, *Selected Writings*, vol. 1 (1913–1926), eds. Marcus Bullock and Michael W. Jennings (Cambridge, Mass.: Harvard University Press, 1996)
Benny, Jack and Joan Benny, *Sunday Nights at Seven* (New York: Warner, 1990)
Benny, Mary Livingstone, *Jack Benny* (London: Robson, 1978)
Black, Peter, *The Mirror in the Corner* (London: Hutchinson, 1972)
Braben, Eddie, 'No Laughing Matter', *GQ* (UK edition), December 1996, p. 54
Briggs, Asa, *The BBC: The First Fifty Years* (Oxford: Oxford University Press, 1985)
    *The History of Broadcasting in the United Kingdom*, 4 vols. (Oxford: Oxford University Press, 1961–79)
Broadcasting Research Unit, *The Public Service Idea in British Broadcasting: Main Principles* (London: BRU, 1986)
Busby, Roy, *British Music Hall: An Illustrated Who's Who from 1850 to the Present Day* (London: Elek, 1976)
Cardiff, David, 'Mass Middlebrow Laughter: The Origins of BBC Comedy', *Media, Culture and Society*, vol. 10, no. 1 (1988), pp. 41–60
Caron, Sandra, *Alma Cogan: A Memoir* (London: Bloomsbury, 1991)
Connolly, Ray (ed.), *In the Sixties*, (London: Pavilion, 1995)
Craig, Mike, *Look Back with Laughter*, 2 vols. (Manchester: Mike Craig Enterprises, 1996)
Crowther, Bruce and Mike Pinfold, *Bring Me Laughter: Four Decades of TV Comedy* (London: Columbus, 1987)
Curran, Charles, *Broadcasting and Society* (London: BBC, 1971)
    *A Seamless Robe: Broadcasting – Philosophy and Practice* (London: Collins, 1979)
Curran, James and Vincent Porter, *British Cinema History* (London: Weidenfeld, 1978)
Dacre, Richard, *Trouble in Store* (Dundee: Farries, 1991)
Davies, Hunter, *The Grades* (London: Weidenfeld, 1981)
Davy, Charles (ed.), *Footnotes to the Film* (London: Readers' Union, 1938)

# Bibliography

Dunkley, Christopher, 'Funny icons of youth', *Financial Times*, 9 February 1994, p. 19

Emerson, Ralph Waldo, *Essays and Poems* (London: Dent, 1995)

Fisher, John, *Funny Way to be a Hero* (London: Frederick Muller, 1973)

Foster, Andy and Steve Furst, *Radio Comedy 1938–1968* (London: Virgin, 1996)

Fox, Paul, 'BBC1', *The Listener*, 7 January 1971, pp. 1–3

Frith, Simon, 'The Pleasures of the Hearth: the making of BBC Light Entertainment', in Tony Bennett *et al* (eds.), *Popular Culture and Social Relations* (Milton Keynes: Open University Press, 1983)

Gambaccini, Paul and Rod Taylor, *Television's Greatest Hits* (London: Network, 1993)

Gilliatt, Penelope, *To Wit: In Celebration of Comedy* (London: Weidenfeld, 1990)

Grade, Lew, *Still Dancing* (London: Collins, 1987)

Greene, Hugh Carleton, *The BBC as a Public Service* (London: BBC, 1960)

    *The Third Floor: A View of Broadcasting in the Sixties* (London: Bodley Head, 1969)

Hancock, Freddie and David Nathan, *Hancock* (London: Ariel, 1986)

Hewison, Robert, *Culture & Consensus: England, Art and Politics Since 1940* (London: Methuen, 1995)

Hoggart, Richard, *The Way We Live Now* (London: Chatto, 1995)

Honri, Peter, *Working the Halls* (London: Futura, 1974)

Horrie, Chris and Steve Clark, *Fuzzy Monsters: Fear and Loathing at the BBC* (London: Mandarin, 1994)

Hudd, Roy, *Roy Hudd's Book of Music-Hall, Variety and Showbiz Anecdotes* (London: Robson, 1993)

    *Roy Hudd's Cavalcade of Variety Acts: A Who Was Who of Light Entertainment 1945–60* (London: Robson, 1997)

Hughes, Robert, *Culture of Complaint: The Fraying of America* (Oxford: Oxford University Press, 1993)

Hunt, Leigh, *Dramatic Essays*, eds. William Archer and Robert W. Lowe (London: Walter Scott, 1894)

Jacob, Sir Ian, 'The Tasks Before the BBC Today', *The BBC Quarterly*, vol. 9, no. 3 (1954), pp. 132–3

    'Television in the Public Service', *Public Administration*, vol. 36, Winter 1958, pp. 311–18

James, Clive, *Clive James on Television* (London: Picador, 1991)

Johnson, Ian, '007 + 4', *Films & Filming*, vol. 12, no. 1 (October 1965), pp. 5–8

Kanin, Garson, *Together Again!* (Garden City, NY: Doubleday, 1981)

Knox, Collie, *People of Quality* (London: Macdonald, 1947)

Kracauer, Siegfried, *The Mass Ornament*, trans. Thomas Levin (Cambridge, Mass.: Harvard University Press, 1995)

Kraus Karl, *Half-Truths & One-and-a-Half-Truths*, trans. Harry Zohn (Manchester: Carcanet, 1986)

Lewis, C. A., *Broadcasting From Within* (London: Newnes, 1924)

Logan, Pamela W., *Jack Hylton Presents* (London: BFI, 1995)

McCann, Graham, *Cary Grant: A Class Apart* (London: Fourth Estate, 1996)

    'The Fawning That Shows Television Has Lost Its Nerve', *Evening Standard*, 20 November 1996, p. 9

    'Why the Best Sitcoms Must be a Class Act', *Evening Standard*, 21 May 1997, p. 9

McDonnell, James, *Public Service Broadcasting: A Reader* (London: Routledge, 1991)

McFarlane, Brian, *An Autobiography of British Cinema* (London: Methuen, 1997)

Macnab, Geoffrey, *J. Arthur Rank and the British Film Industry* (London: Routledge, 1993)

Mellor, G. J., *The Northern Music Hall* (Newcastle upon Tyne: Frank Graham, 1970)

    *They Made Us Laugh* (Littleborough: George Kelsall, 1982)

Miles, Barry, *Paul McCartney: Many Years From Now* (London: Secker, 1997)

Milne, Alasdair, *DG: The Memoirs of a British Broadcaster* (London: Hodder, 1988)

Monkhouse, Bob, *Crying with Laughter* (London: Arrow, 1994)

Muir, Frank, *Comedy in Television* (London: BBC, 1966)

    *A Kentish Lad* (London: Bantam, 1997)

Murphy, Robert (ed.), *The British Cinema Book* (London: BFI, 1997)

# Bibliography

Napier, Valantyne, *Glossary of Terms Used in Variety, Vaudeville, Revue & Pantomime* (Westbury: The Badger Press, 1996)

Nathan, David, *The Laughtermakers* (London: Peter Owen, 1971)

Norden, Denis, Sybil Harper and Norma Gilbert, *Coming to You Live!* (London: Methuen, 1985)

Parker, Derek, *Radio: The Great Years* (Newton Abbot: David & Charles, 1977)

Paulu, Burton, *British Broadcasting: Radio and Television in the United Kingdom* (Minneapolis: University of Minnesota Press, 1956)

Perry, George, *The Great British Picture Show* (London: Hart-Davis, MacGibbon, 1974)

Priestley, *English Humour* (London: Longmans and Co., 1933)

'English Films and English People', *World Film News*, vol. 1, no. 8 (1 November 1936), p. 3

*The Good Companions* (London: Heinemann, 1957)

*English Journey* (London: Mandarin, 1994)

Read, Al, *It's All in the Book* (London: W. H. Allen, 1985)

Reith, J. C. W., *Broadcast over Britain* (London: Hodder, 1924)

*Into the Wind* (London: Hodder, 1949)

Richards, Jeffrey, *Visions of Yesteryear* (London: Routledge, 1973)

Secombe, Harry, *Arias and Raspberries* (London: Pan, 1997)

Silvers, Phil, *The Man Who was Bilko* (London: W. H. Allen, 1974)

Silvey, Roger, *Who's Listening?: The Story of BBC Audience Research* (London: Allen & Unwin, 1974)

Smith, Anthony, *British Broadcasting* (Newton Abbot: David and Charles, 1974)

Smith, Ronald L., *Who's Who in Comedy* (New York: Facts On File, 1992)

Thomas, Terry, *Terry-Thomas Tells Tales* (London: Robson, 1990)

Thomson, David, *Movie Man* (New York: Stein & Day, 1967)

Took, Barry, *Laughter in the Air* (London: Robson/BBC, 1976)

'Whatever Happened to TV Comedy?', *The Listener*, 5 and 12 January 1984

Tosches, Nick, 'Mr Sunday Night', *Vanity Fair*, July 1997, pp. 130–45

Tracey, Michael, *A Variety of Lives* (London: Bodley Head, 1983)

Trethowan, Ian, *Split Screen* (London: Hamish Hamilton, 1984)

Tynan, Kenneth, *Show People: Profiles in Entertainment* (London: Weidenfield, 1980)

Van Damm, Sheila, *We Never Closed: The Windmill Story* (London: Hale, 1967)

Waldman, Ronnie, 'Creating Light Entertainment in Television', *Radio Times*, 23 March 1951, p. 46

'The Toughest Job', *Radio Times*, 4 December 1953, pp. 5 and 14

'The Variety of Television Variety', *Radio Times Annual 1954* (London: BBC, 1954), pp. 56–7

Walker, Alexander, *Hollywood, England: The British Film Industry in the 60s* (London: Michael Joseph, 1974)

Wheen, Francis, *Television* (London: Century, 1985)

Wheldon, Huw, *British Traditions in a World-Wide Medium* (London: BBC, 1973)

Whitley, Oliver, *Broadcasting and the National Culture* (London: BBC, 1965)

Wilde, Larry, *Great Comedians Talk about Comedy* (New York: Citadel, 1969)

Williams, Kenneth, *The Kenneth Wiliams Diaries*, ed., Russell Davies (London: Harper-Collins, 1993)

Wilmut, Roger, *Tony Hancock: Artiste* (London: Methuen, 1978)

*Kindly Leave the Stage: The Story of Variety, 1918–1960* (London: Methuen, 1985)

Winters, Bernie and Charmaine Carter, *One Day at a Time: The Story of My Life* (London: Ebury Press, 1991)

Wisdom, Norman and Bernard Bale, *'Cos I'm a Fool* (Derby: Breedon, 1996)

Wyndham Goldie, Grace, *Facing the Nation: Broadcasting and Politics 1936–1976* (London: Bodley Head, 1977)

# Index

'M&W' indicates Morecambe and Wise.

# Index

# Index

# Index